SOCIABILITY AND POWER IN

SOCIABILITY AND POWER IN LATE-STUART ENGLAND

THE CULTURAL WORLDS OF THE VERNEYS 1660–1720

Susan E. Whyman

OXFORD

UNIVERSITY PRESS

OXFORD
UNIVERSITY PRESS

Great Clarendon Street, Oxford OX2 6DP

Oxford University Press is a department of the University of Oxford.
It furthers the University's objective of excellence in research, scholarship,
and education by publishing worldwide in

Oxford New York

Athens Auckland Bangkok Bogotá Buenos Aires Cape Town
Chennai Dar es Salaam Delhi Florence Hong Kong Istanbul Karachi
Kolkata Kuala Lumpur Madrid Melbourne Mexico City Mumbai Nairobi
Paris São Paulo Shanghai Singapore Taipei Tokyo Toronto Warsaw

with associated companies in Berlin Ibadan

Oxford is a registered trade mark of Oxford University Press
in the UK and in certain other countries

Published in the United States
by Oxford University Press Inc., New York

First published 1999
First published in paperback 2002

British Library Cataloguing in Publication Data

Data available

Library of Congress Cataloging in Publication Data

Data available

ISBN 0-19-820719-0 (hbk)
ISBN 0-19-925023-5 (pbk)

1 3 5 7 9 10 8 6 4 2

Typeset in Baskerville
by J&L Composition Ltd, Filey, North Yorkshire
Printed in Great Britain
on acid-free paper by
Bookcraft Ltd, Midsomer Norton, Somerset

TO LAWRENCE STONE

PREFACE

I read my first letter in the Verney collection almost a decade ago. From that moment on, I was drawn into a world that combined great pastoral tranquility with the pulsing vitality of London. This book is an attempt to re-create those overlapping worlds in a way that remains faithful to hundreds of letter-writers. Fortunately, I have not been alone in my ten-year task. Over twenty generations of obsessive correspondents and collectors have been at my beck and call. I have created a computerized database to control their outpourings found in thousands of documents (see Appendix I), but I have told their tales in their own voices. I hope this book demonstrates that historians can manage and interpret large amounts of data without losing the anecdotal and human character which make it meaningful.

As I journeyed into the past, many present-day companions showed me the way. The journey itself would not have been possible without Lawrence Stone who prodded me to take the road less travelled. He helped me to see the splendours of a rigorously trained mind, a perfect sentence, and intellectual discovery. I will always be indebted to him and his wife Jeanne for innumerable acts of human kindness.

Lawrence Stone also introduced me to the Verney papers. I am deeply grateful to Sir Ralph Verney, Edmund Verney, and the Claydon House Trust for permitting me to use the Verney family papers at Claydon House and assisting me over a ten-year period. All documents remain the property of the Claydon House Trust in which copyright lies. I also thank archivist Susan Ranson for providing me with documents and sharing her knowledge of the collection. I owe a debt to John Broad's unpublished thesis 'Sir Ralph Verney and his Estates, 1630–1696' (Oxford, 1973) which gave me inspiration. I thank Dr Broad for generously sharing his notes, research, and insights over the years. Miriam Slater, whose *Family Life in the Seventeenth Century: The Verneys of Claydon House* was published in 1984, also gave me advice and encouragement.

In London, Sonia Anderson of the Royal Commission on Historical Manuscripts helped me to understand the world of the Levant merchant, took me to see seventeenth-century plays, and read the entire book. I thank her for her meticulous comments and references. Penny Corfield was perhaps the earliest British supporter of my work and influenced my thinking about history as did Tim Hitchcock, Julian Hoppit, Derek Keene, Arthur Burns, and Mary Clayton.

As a visiting scholar at Wadham College, Oxford, I received a warm welcome from C. S. L. Davies, J. P. Edwards, and John Fleming. I especially thank Joanna Innes for commenting on chapters in their early stages, as well as Clare Brant, Philip Carter, Elaine Chalus, Peter Dickson, Perry Gauci, Sir John Habakkuk,

Felicity Heal, Clive Holmes, Paul Langford, Vivienne Larminie, and my editors at Oxford University Press. I thank J. T. Cliffe for many helpful references. In England, David and Jose Patterson, Iris, John, and David Huckvale, and Harriet and Harold Montefiore offered friendship and hospitality.

I received expert assistance at British archives from William Hodges and the staff of Duke Humfrey's Library at the Bodleian Library, from Frances Harris at the British Library, from Vivienne Aldous at the Corporation of London Record Office, from Jeremy Smith at the Guildhall Library, and from Hugh Hanley, Roger Bettridge, Sue Hardy, and Janice Taylor of the Buckinghamshire Record office. I thank Eveline Cruickshanks and Stuart Handley of The History of Parliament Trust for permission to examine Buckinghamshire data.

In Princeton, the support of Moshe Sluhovsky, Betsy Brown, and Peter Brown was crucial to my intellectual development. I thank them for countless readings and for truly understanding my work and my goals. I also thank Alastair Bellany, Luis Corteguera, Natalie Davis, Kristin Gager, Phil Harling, William Jordan, Peter Lake, John Murrin, Simon Newman, Theodore Rabb, and Dror Wahrman. Mary George at the Princeton University Library gave help of the highest professional calibre in every way imaginable. Hannah Kaufman at the Computer Centre helped me to design my database and thus greatly enriched the scope of my work.

Outside Princeton, I thank Mary Robertson, George Clarke, and the Huntington Library for assistance and permission to use the Stowe and Ellesmere collections. Professors Linda Peck, Greg Dening, Gary De Krey, James Rosenheim, David Sachs, Paul Seaver and Rhys Isaac made helpful comments. I thank the *London Journal* for permission to include material published in 'Land and Trade Revisited: The Case of John Verney, London Merchant and Baronet, 1660–1720', 22 (1997), 16–32 and Ashgate Press for material published in '"Paper Visits"', *Epistolary Selves* (Aldershot, 1999).

Finally, my mother Carolyn Einhorn, my children Jennifer and David Greene, and Bill and Paula Whyman, all believed in my ability. My foremost advocate and husband Frank made constant sacrifices and shared every stage of the journey that produced this book. To all of the above, I offer my thanks.

S. E. W.

Princeton, New Jersey
November 1998

CONTENTS

x   *Contents*

LIST OF ILLUSTRATIONS

GENERAL ABBREVIATIONS

Berks CRO	Berkshire Record Office
Bodl	Bodleian Library
BL	British Library
Bucks CRO	Buckinghamshire Record Office
CH	Claydon House, Buckinghamshire
CLRO	Corporation of London Record Office
CSPD	*Calendar of State Papers Domestic*
EcHR	*Economic History Review*
EL	Ellesmere Collection, Huntington Library
GH	Guildhall Library, Corporation of London
HL	Huntington Library, San Marino, California
HLQ	*Huntington Library Quarterly*
HMSO	Her Majesty's Stationery Office
IO	India Office Library
Leics CRO	Leicestershire Record Office
LCC	London County Council
NRA	National Register of Archives
PRO	Public Record Office
PROB	Prerogative Court of Canterbury Records
RB	Rare Books
SP	State Papers
ST, STT	Temple Papers, Stowe Collection, Huntington Library
WM	Westminster Library

THE VERNEYS OF CLAYDON HOUSE

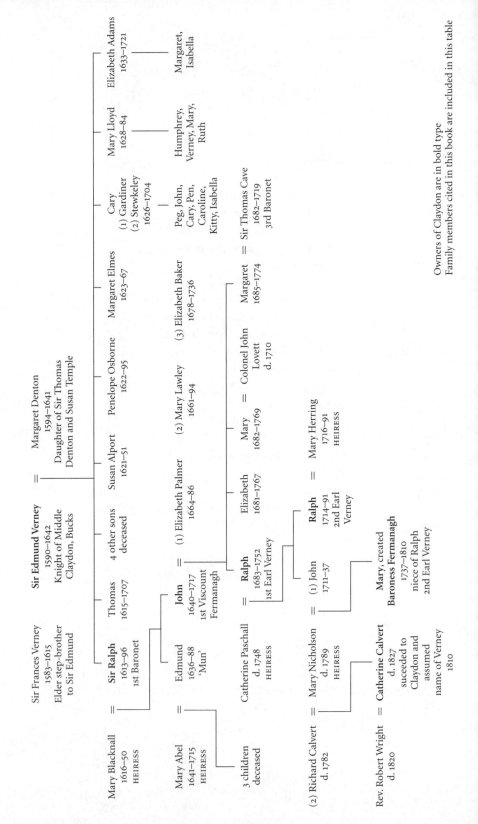

Owners of Claydon are in bold type
Family members cited in this book are included in this table

Part I

COUNTRY AND CITY NETWORKS

Introduction

On 25 September 1696, John Verney (1640–1717), a London merchant, received a letter from his cousin Peg Adams. It announced the death of his father, Sir Ralph Verney (1613–96), a Buckinghamshire baronet. Peg wrote easily and clearly on rough, untrimmed paper. She left one side blank according to social etiquette, but turned the page sideways and crammed farewells into the margin. Then she folded the paper to form an envelope, using a friend's Parliament frank to avoid postage.[1] During the summer, Peg had written daily to John, constructing a medical case history about Sir Ralph. By August, swelling of the legs and diarrhoea forced him to leave church 'nine or ten times a Sunday', as it 'ran down into his very shoes'. Soon he had watchers at night and was carried about by day, unable to swallow anything but his favourite mix of burnt wine and water.[2] With the help of Peg's narratives, John became a daily spectator in the invalid's sick chamber.

John also received 82 letters from anxious kin that summer. They jockeyed for favour with the future heir and reminded him of his duty to support poor relations. As John read their many versions of the same events, he was no doubt conscious of hidden rivalries and struggles for influence. Naturally, he considered each person's motives and probed beneath compliments of those who would become his dependants. Then he docketed each letter noting date, writer, and subject, as his father had taught him to do.

Because John's elder brother Edmund was dead, he would now inherit a baronetcy and the social and political networks of one of the most powerful men in Buckinghamshire. All the country gentry and Sir Ralph's city kin would expect to be present at the funeral, and John had to decide whom to invite. His city in-laws and aunts were well-versed in politeness and would advise him about important rites involving mourning coaches, servants' liveries, and gifts. He could not travel, however, until he obtained mourning clothes from his city tailor and cash from his bankers. The latter would manage his affairs at the Levant and Royal Africa Companies, the Royal Exchange, and the Exchequer. Ten days later, John Verney made his first symbolic journey from a booming, cosmopolitan London to the village of Middle Claydon. But he did not follow his kin's advice, and he alienated his neighbours by holding Sir Ralph's funeral privately. His financial skills and city contacts, however, greatly enlarged the family's fortunes. He would spend the rest of his life as a cultural intermediary journeying up and down the roads that linked his two overlapping worlds.

Peg's narrative allows the reader to enter Sir Ralph's sick chamber and react to a death in the family. It also illustrates the unique abilities of the Verney archive to evoke a dramatic moment, while addressing larger historical issues. Historians have no right to expect sources to provide uninterrupted dramas with vibrant plots and characters, not to mention beginnings and conclusions. But there they are in the Verney archive, in such abundance that readers wait to see the outcome of a conspiracy and mourn the death of a correspondent. Just as eighteenth-century families gathered to look through microscopes to discover complexities, we find clarity by observing variations and by focusing upon them 'up close'. Like Jane Austen, the Verney correspondents use their 'little bit (two inches wide) of ivory' with 'so fine a brush' that we are able to observe social mores and to interpret silences.[3]

The story of Sir Ralph's death warns us that we are entering a private world as voyeurs and eavesdroppers. We will listen in on the thoughts of an upper-gentry family and their friends as they struggled to adjust to change. Readers may be surprised at the tremendous impact of London upon individuals whom we think of as embodying the 'country'. In fact, this was a time when the values of London's polite, but competitive, culture were intruding upon those of landed families. Urban pressures on country custom had been increasing for centuries, but by the 1690s, many gentry were spending more than half the year in town.[4] There, they encountered a bewildering array of market forces that glorified self-interest, profit, and money. Many feared that the corrupting influence of commerce would erode ideals of civic virtue and gentility. But the Verneys understood that times of transition create opportunities as well as anxiety, and that families who accept change are most likely to succeed.

The Verney archive shows us how a broad range of people adapted to a commercial order and how mercantile interests were integrated into polite society. It demonstrates that sociability was a fundamental element of power in a society based upon personal connections. Gifts, letters, and patronage were forms of 'social commerce' that were critical to and inseparable from the political world. In London, however, the gentry learned new modes of socialization that took place in an urban public sphere.[5] Not surprisingly, the control of manners increasingly fell to women, as politeness became a mark of status. Merchants and the middling sort found social mobility in London's fluid, affluent environment. Attitudes to trade, money, and the professions were changing, offering advancement to entrepreneurial younger sons.

Of course, landed families wielded paramount influence,[6] but although agricultural productivity was rising, gentry rents and incomes had levelled off after a century of growth. More ominously, the numbers of elite offspring, and thus heirs, were declining. The archive suggests that neither the patriarchal family nor elite society were as stable as their polite façades indicated. Unresolved religious and political conflict still inflamed the usually dispassionate Verneys, who were ardent Protestants and would soon embrace Tory party politics. They feared popery but worried that landed incomes would be used to underwrite foreign wars. Despite their city/country rhetoric, however, most country folk had interests and kin in London and the capital depended upon its hinterland. The city and the country were never opposites, and with the coming of a commercial society their connections became more important.[7]

This book re-creates the overlapping city and country worlds of the Verneys, shows how they interacted, and explores the diverse networks of each. It analyses several generations of the Verneys and a broad range of their acquaintances from every walk of life. It finds changes in their personal attitudes, economic activities, political tactics, and modes of sociability. The importance of the archive of over 100,000 papers lies not merely in its bulk, but in its unusual continuity, literary quality, and capacity to describe fundamental, human concerns. As readers open the Verneys' mail and listen in on their secrets, they will enter an intimate world of the past.

The Verney Archive

The best way to describe the archive is to stand with Sir Harry Verney (1801–94) when he discovered it at Claydon House in 1826. We know he found 'a wainscoted gallery at the top of the house, forty feet long, full of boxes on tressels containing bundles of letters, acres of parchment . . . early editions of plays, account books, terriers and rent-rolls . . . .' They were stacked cheek by jowl with wills, marriage settlements, newsletters, broadsides, bills, recipes, and poems, and included papers of fourteen generations between 1495 and 1810.[8] Since that time, the collection has been catalogued and over 30,000 personal papers from 1643 to 1754 are available on microfilm. This number does not cover the legal and genealogical papers, estate correspondence, maps, and portraits held privately at Claydon House. The archive probably contains the largest unbroken collection of family letters for seventeenth and early eighteenth-century England. This book represents a ten-year study of over 12,000 papers from 1660 to 1720 as described in Appendix I.[9]

Sir Ralph amassed the bulk of the collection and saved copies of outgoing and incoming mail. Like the Pastons, he 'set more by his writings and evidences than he did by any of his moveable goods'. Rather than destroy a letter, he cut holes over confidential items. His son John reread and annotated the collection, identifying unnamed people and recording their fates in the margins.[10] In fact, the preservation of the archive was no accident. Each generation taught the next to protect the papers that recorded their family history.

The Verneys' correspondents were exceedingly diverse in terms of kinship, status, occupation, religion, political affiliation, and residence. Table 1 in Appendix II shows that the letter-writers came from every category mentioned in Gregory King's status and occupation table published in 1696: titled lords, esquires and gentlemen, officeholders, merchants, lawyers, clergymen, doctors, apothecaries, educators, farmers, shopkeepers, artisans, craftsmen, and even labourers. Thus, we can eavesdrop on the thoughts of people from every strata of life as they wrote to each other. Since John became a viscount after he inherited, we observe a rich mix of interactions—up, down, and across social hierarchies.

Table 2 shows that from 1692 to 1717, 2,185 letters (or 32% of 7,018 letters) were written to the nobility and gentry and 2,042 letters (or 29%) were received from these groups. Ninety nobility and gentry comprised 45% of the 202 most frequently mentioned people in John's networks. They included 33 women: 17 married to gentry; 16 with titled husbands. John's 57 male intimates included 2 earls, 1 marquess, 3 viscounts, 6 baronets, 8 knights, and 37 gentry.

On the other hand, there were 4,237 letters (or 60%) from people with occupations and 4,487 letters (or 64%) to them. 112 people (98 men/14 women) or 55% of John's inner circle had occupations or were married to those that had them. They included 6 officeholders; 14 merchants/2 wives; 15 lawyers/1 wife; 3 clergymen/3 wives; 10 farmers/1 wife; 4 doctors, 3 apothecaries, 3 educators, 8 shopkeepers, 4 artisans, 7 financiers, 6 military men/1 wife; 4 gentlewomen companions; 14 male/2 female servants; 1 workman. Appendix I explains how King's tables were adapted for this study, for his categories present problems. For example, some writers had more than one status or occupation and boundaries between them were extremely fluid. King's contemporary terms, however, fit this study's needs and show the archive's depth and breadth.[11]

Correspondents from all walks of life enjoyed composing letters. For example, John's nephew Ralph Palmer noted: 'When . . . writing, my pen is never weary'.[12] As the Verneys wrote, they created vast webs of personal networks which are described in Chapters 1 through 3. Seventy-seven kin and 125 non-kin inhabited the inner circle of John's networks including 33 female relations and 14 unrelated women. But relatives wrote prolifically in order to maintain family ties. Although they made up only 38% of John's intimates, they sent 3,474 letters (or about half of the letters) between 1692 and 1717. In return, they received 2,202 letters (or 31% of the total) which was 1,272 less than they wrote. This shows the assymetry of both their correspondence and status in relation to the head of the family.

Because the influence of the family head provides a foundation for the letters, a complex world of manly interactions may be observed. Research on masculinity and its tensions has revealed the centrality of this aspect of family and political life.[13] Letters permit us to analyse power relationships between patriarch and kin, father and sons, elder and younger brothers, gentry squires and the middling-sort, ne'er-do-well uncles and bachelor friends.

Fresh data is equally abundant over a long period for the interactions of different types of women, with men and with each other. We observe the strategies of wives and daughters, aunts and cousins, spinsters and widows— both poor and wealthy, gentlewomen companions and young girls without portions, as well as impoverished women who strive to retain gentility. The richness of the archive lets us see their roles, their motives, and their values which usually lie hidden.

Three basic types of letters are found in the archive: informal to intimates, sociable to friends and acquaintances, and contrived or artificial for patronage purposes. Specific types of papers found on the microfilm are itemized in Table 5 including begging, condolence, and congratulatory letters. The letters dealt with every aspect of daily life. For example writers gave sophisticated reports about financial and legal matters, religious and social trends, and domestic and foreign politics. They expressed fears about death (cited 247 times), illness (229 cites), and crime (114 cites). They were also concerned about their finances (684 cites), marriage (656 cites), patronage (330 cites), elections (570 cites), and their 'place' in society. Gossip was particularly useful, providing trenchant commentaries about social mores, while letter-writing itself was often discussed (236 cites). Subjects frequently mentioned in letters are listed in Table 6.[14]

The proper way to write was prescribed through education, example, and strict writing schedules. The exchange of letters was a serious affair, for the receiver paid the postage and failure to respond was a breach of conduct. Yet sometimes it was perilous to write. In 1686, Sir Ralph's nephew John Stewkeley warned him: 'Tis dangerous writing news . . . but . . . you shall certainly have all I may safely write'. Often it was suggested 'your name not be set to your letter'. Yet some things were easier to write than say. John's Aunt Gardiner hated to beg for money in person and would 'rather let my pen ask it'.[15]

The Verneys' letters were direct and to the point, for they wrote as worldly practitioners, not intellectuals or theologians. Even family retainers expressed themselves openly, reflecting a growing autonomy in social relations. Only men used Latin quotations, but John's London aunts were sometimes more informed about politics. Indeed, women regarded free articulation as a natural right. Sir Ralph's sisters begged for money and gave political advice in the same letter. Even the housekeeper lectured Sir Ralph and John about their duties to fulfil country customs. Yet earlier generations of women lacked epistolary training. Plagued by phonetic spelling, women of Sir Ralph's day referred to their efforts as 'imperfect', 'impertinent', or 'not worth paying for'.[16] Subsequent letters from John's daughters and servants stood in elegant contrast. In 1699, his black servant from Guinea wrote an elegant courtesy letter. Its nearest rival was a similar epistle from the Verneys' country cook.[17]

Method and Scope—Overhearing Secrets

The archive itself determined the methods used in this book and allows us to overhear private conversations. Readers listen to stories told in different voices, creating tragedies and comedies over time and through space. The family is treated in interconnected ways that link mainstream social history with 'ethnohistory' and the 'new cultural' studies. Thus, historical analysis is woven into narratives and an anthropological approach is adopted that employs Clifford Geertz's 'thick description'.[18] Often, multiple examples are used to take advantage of the depth of the material and to move from one person's actions to more general concepts. This technique helps us to recapture a sense of the dynamic process through which the archive was created. We see that family history is an evolutionary tale constructed as each letter is written. More chapters are appended to the story as letters are read and answered, as new characters cross the stage, and as treasured correspondence is annotated and reread. Not surprisingly, the letters reveal deep generational continuities as well as changing values.

At first the pace is slow, as we become familiar with the characters and their handwriting. Then patterns take shape as we read hundreds of little stories. Eventually, we grasp the rhythms of daily life and see how cognitive ideas and behaviour evolve. At the same time, we get to know the central characters, perhaps more intimately than present-day friends. 'Should you doubt that you exist, you have only to write a letter', notes Joyce Carol Oates. 'A personality will immediately define itself in the act of writing.' The Verneys' characters are revealed through their use of forms of address, spacing, style, and penmanship. Traits are further uncovered by decoding writers' anxieties and interests.[19] We see that Sir Ralph's god-daughter, Nancy Nicholas, invariably complains about court scandal and war, while his sister, Elizabeth Adams, worries about prices of Covent Garden luxuries. Sir Ralph's brother Thomas cannot write without asking for money, and his sister Cary Gardiner sends gossip gleaned over the gaming table.[20] Because of the archive's richness, we get to know individual personalities of people 'on the fringe' who are left out of other studies for lack of evidence.

Even the Verneys, however, omit important facts of life that are so basic that they are taken for granted. I try to tease out unexpressed thoughts by analysing repetitive symbols that are found in ordinary actions of daily living. With inspiration from Alan Macfarlane's *The Family Life of Ralph Josselin*, Emmanuel Leroy Ladurie's *Montaillou*, Rhys Isaac's *The Transformation of Virginia 1740–1790*, and Greg Dening's *Islands and Beaches*, I have searched the Verneys' texts for the rituals of everyday life. To this end, I compare traditional country gifts of venison with the 'modish' London fashion of visiting in a coach. These rites of sociability were both commonplace and significant. I use them to show personal networks and dynamic interactions. Both symbols appear and reappear throughout the book, as they did in the letters. Readers follow the paths of these deer and coaches as they move through society to and from the country and the city. In the process, we observe cultural values and historical change. This interdisciplinary approach has novel advantages. For when historical analysis is yoked to storytelling and ethnography, we see how ordinary experiences connect to larger issues.[21] Other sources would suggest different approaches, but this one capitalizes upon the archive's strengths, lets voices be heard, and seduces the reader with eloquent language.

The archive itself also determined the scope of this book. All historians have to make decisions about what voices to amplify, what material to exclude, and how to organize data. When one's source covers every aspect of life and each document addresses scores of topics, data control and selection pose major dilemmas. My solution has been influenced by three basic factors. First, the business records of John Verney do not survive. Perhaps they were lost in London or overlooked inadvertantly as the papers accumulated at Claydon House. Or there may have been a later reluctance by the family to acknowledge a background in trade. Secondly, financial and estate data for rents, income, expenses, and profits are not continuous or organized, but sporadic and mixed amongst the sources. Data that does exist has been ably analysed and empha- sized by Dr John Broad, who set high standards for utilizing the archive. I have used his work to reach my own conclusions, especially 'Gentry Finances and the Civil War: The Case of the Buckinghamshire Verneys' and his unpublished D.Phil. thesis 'Sir Ralph Verney and his Estates 1630–1696'.[22]

Thirdly, there are abstracts and collections of papers and histories written by family members, but with the exception of Miriam Slater's study of the Civil War period, there is no full-length book about the family.[23] With these factors in mind, I decided to work on the more private lives of the Verneys after the Restoration (1660–1720), outside the important but heavily mined subject of estate administration. Yet the personal papers alone contained such vast riches, that priorities still had to be set. The database was invaluable in making selection choices by ranking subjects and personal names cited in the papers. With the source material always guiding me, I chose to focus upon the Verneys' social lives, cultural values, and personal networks including their relations with each other, their families, and their wider communities. Like the Verneys, I was struck by the impact of London, and the ways that contemporaries bridged town and country. Of course, I am fully aware of the importance of economic factors and have incorporated them in non-statistical ways. But my primary goal has been to offer fresh insights on topics that are absent from more quantititative sources.

Even within this scope, readers will surely find topics of interest to them that are missing. For example, earlier drafts of this book contained additional material on the commercial revolution, conspicuous consumption, political attitudes, the performing arts, and how John enjoyed Bath. I can only promise readers that the material has been carefully selected to inform larger historical issues and illustrate the wider society in which the Verneys lived. I am confident that other historians will use the archive to write different types of books, and I look forward to their findings.

Letters as Historical Evidence

Although letters must be interpreted with care, it is hard to see why they have been considered a marginal form of evidence, especially in the seventeenth and eighteenth centuries when letter-writing became an art. No longer reserved for diplomatic, scholarly, and mercantile use, more people were just 'scribbling'. Letters permeated essays, periodicals, and romances long before Richardson's *Pamela*.[24] 'A letter to a friend' was a vehicle for anything in print, while the first newspapers were batches of letters. The Verneys owned many publications containing letters, including Roman classics, Voiture's works, and letter-writing manuals.[25]

The family's passion for letter-writing was stimulated by a convergence of factors including the rise of a literate culture that emphasized manners, the easing of laws limiting religion and speech, a hunger for information stimulated by a booming publishing industry, a nationwide growth of communications, especially postal services, and the spread of literacy. By 1720, the literacy rate was about 45% for men and 25% for women. For London women, however, it was nearer 48%.[26]

Letters were written by individuals, but they were also influenced by polite society and the corporate family. They strengthened social norms by teaching manners and providing vital proof of gentility (see plate 20). Letters also sustained social networks and eased fears about death, illness, and isolation. The family head used letters to maintain cohesion, for its members were often separated. John remarked that Sir John Busby and his lady were 'like buckets in a well; as one goes up the other goes down between town and country'.[27]

But letters not only promoted stability, they had liberating effects. Writing has been described as a psychological process which brings self-exploration and the means to relate oneself to society. Many factors encouraged writers to use letters in this way, including the Protestant focus on individual redemption and self-examination.[28] Writing gave individuals occasions to develop narrative skills, while its pauses, unlike speech, offered time for reflection. In the Verneys' patriarchal world, collective needs were paramount, leaving few private spaces for individual release. The outlets provided by letters were crucial for women, who had fewer alternative forms of self-expression than their male counterparts.

The archive is especially suited to address questions of authority and resistance, as well as recent issues of 'cultural politics'. Power and politics are defined here broadly, not only because they lie outside court and Parliament, but because they are perceived in the social, religious, and gendered aspects of life. This definition affirms Michel Foucault's argument that power is dispersed and interwoven with other relationships, such as family, kinship, and sexuality. Power is further defined as the ability generally to shape events, while authority is more formally recognized and legitimized power. While Verney elder sons had more authority than younger sons and daughters, younger brothers possessed more power to choose marriage partners. Moreover, Verney women held informal power to broker marriages and mould the social code.[29]

The Verney letters not only disclose this code, they show deference to norms, as well as when and where they were violated. Acts of defiance are normally seen through criminal justice records, but letters show more subtle forms of protest along with causes and outcomes. The Verney archive reveals cultural changes such as the decline of country hospitality, the precarious role of dependent kin, the growing desire for privacy, scepticism about ceremony, and the peace provided by religion. Because locations of writers are normally given, we can track geographic and spatial mobility. The mapping of social space may be a key to understanding questions about migration, urbanization, and the effects of neighbourhoods.

Clearly letters provide unique historical evidence, but they also present serious problems. Although many archives have been used, the dominance of one collection brings risks of exaggeration and distortion. Thus the Verney papers weight evidence in the direction of archival strengths. Moreover, even though the Verney letters have been called 'truly representative of their age',[30] we must consider whether they are typical.

Typicality is a helpful concept when one deals with statistical sources but it is less relevant for a rich trove of letters. This case study makes no claim that the Verneys were representative and its generalizations must undergo comparative testing. The book does maintain that the Verney experience is a documented cultural response in reaction to common elements that affected other gentry families. With this point in mind, the huge collection of the Temples of Stowe, the Verneys' kinsmen and rivals, was analysed for the period. The Wentworth, Hatton, Leeds and Godolphin, Egmont, Blenheim, Coke, Portland, Le Neve, and Trumbull papers were also compared for evidence about letter-writing practices.[31] Important references in the Verney papers were followed up, gaps were filled in, inconsistencies were tested, and the collection was enriched with other types of primary documents, especially those about London. In addition, a broad range of secondary material was used to situate the Verneys in the context of historical debates.

Readers will decide whether this approach is effective. In doing so, they may wish to consider new modes of historical analysis that warn against giving typicality undue weight. Natalie Davis urges us to search for cultural differences and complexities instead of stereotypes and absolute truths. James Goodman's *Stories of Scottsboro* illustrates her approach and reminds us of Japanese plays like *Rashomon* that tell a story from different points of view—all of which are true in the eye of the beholder.[32] Edoardo Grendi's concept of 'normal exceptions' focuses upon examples that may not fit predetermined norms, but are perfectly representative of their own milieu. Younger sons, like John, comprise a neglected category that aptly exemplifies Grendi's ideas.[33]

These problems of truth and doubt raise more subtle questions about all self-constructed forms of writing. Let no one who reads a memoir, diary, or letter naively conclude that there is a simple correlation between content and 'reality'. Letters always create tensions between art and artifice and are only partially transparent. The Verneys were aware that their letters might contain truth and hypocrisy, or as they put it, 'compliment and . . . lying'. Their comments show

how they resolved today's literary debates about naturalness and formality in texts.[34]

Finally, in considering the problems of reading letters, we must remember that the family head intended that they would be preserved. This fact may have affected the letters of those closest to Sir Ralph and John. Other less informed writers may have limited their speech for other reasons. Even when unrestricted, however, every author formulates a 'pose' and erects a screen in order to present 'the self' positively. At the same time, twentieth-century readers 'imaginatively duplicate the original relations letters evoke and . . . generate [their] own new relationship with the writer'.[35] These problems caution us to tread carefully as we read and interpret letters.

Themes and Chapters

As the book unfolds, the characters reveal themselves through their own voices. The first three chapters take the Verneys chronologically into the eighteenth century. The last three are thematic and address questions raised in current debates about cultural politics and power: Were women and younger brothers really as ineffectual as they have been portrayed? Was patriarchal authority absolute in the family? Does the Verneys' experience help us to understand the rise of politeness? What were the criteria for gentility and did they change over time? How did the gentry, merchants, and the middling sort interact? Can we observe their amalgamation into an expanded elite? Did London residence foster new modes of sociability and the absorption of market values? What effect did this have on marriage and party politics?

Chapter 1 opens with an analysis of Sir Ralph's Buckinghamshire networks and cultural values. His power relied upon face-to-face relationships cemented by sociability, favours, and carefully calibrated gifts of venison. Chapter 2 shows how and why his younger son John became a Levant Company merchant. It examines changing attitudes to trade after the Restoration and describes the life of an overseas English merchant. Chapter 3 reveals the importance of London to the Verneys and their friends, and compares John's city and country networks with those of Sir Ralph. It shows what it was like to live in London when society was becoming more commercial.

Long before John inherited, he learned the rules of London's polite society. It was symbolized by the urban visit and the conspicuous use of the coach. Chapter 4 illustrates the development of politeness by describing John's entry into society. It shows how a group of supposedly dependent women controlled daily rites of sociability. Unlike previous generations, John made use of the London marriage market. Chapter 5 shows continuities and changes in choosing spouses and makes distinctions about family power based upon gender, birth order, and marital status. John entered Buckinghamshire's Whig/Tory competition, with his third wife's help. Chapter 6 shows how John and his rivals, the Temples, took part in partisan politics which increasingly impinged upon family and community relationships. By integrating his city and country worlds, John brought new wealth and status to the family.

The life of John Verney, who was first a city merchant and later a landed viscount (see plates 1 and 2), is an ideal lens for observing a society as it adapted to change. His experience challenges the binary approach to historical and cultural studies. Although we must classify data to discuss it, in practice, there were few rigid spaces or categories for the Verneys. Family members shared social occasions with yeomen farmers, urban professionals, and titled friends. Cultural hybrids played multiple roles: gentry younger sons became professional men; middling sort shopkeepers and the Verneys' tenant farmers were also voters that had to be wooed; wives and husbands came from different social backgrounds. Not surprisingly, the most interesting arguments are found in the shaded spaces of overlap, like those in the middle of a Venn Diagram. Many books could have been written about the Verneys. It is hoped that this one will cause readers to question traditional categories and stereotypes such as family patriarchs and helpless women, independent heirs and dependent younger sons, land and trade, city and country, and sociability and power.

1

Sir Ralph Verney: Networks of a Country Gentleman—The Gifts of Venison

As Sir Ralph Verney lay dying in his country house at Middle Claydon, he appeared cheerful and comfortable. For the past four out of five years, he had spent eight or nine months in London. Yet he felt 'more natural' in the country, and he abhorred 'court compliment' and flattery. Still, he understood the importance of sociability and his hospitality was legendary. 'Tis a happiness to keep a fair correspondence with all your neighbours', he declared, and longed for peaceful relationships. In politics and religion, above all, he sought moderation and hated extremes. Unwilling to firmly back either king or Parliament during the Civil War, he avoided partisan politics. His greatest enemy called him 'a trimmer'.[1] Yet Sir Ralph's trimming grew out of constancy not change, strength not weakness, and he commanded immense respect in the county. (See plate 5)

Sir Ralph had deep feelings about his family's importance, and it was he who started saving every scrap of correspondence including the 638 letters he wrote and the 1,184 he received that have been used in this study. He also amassed a huge collection of books and pamphlets, especially religious tracts. His own Anglicanism was tinged with a Puritanical piety and was expressed in strict outward observance. He required the same high standards of worship, personal conduct, and cleanliness from those around him. Thus, he refused to hire a gardener until he discovered whether he was 'married or popish or phanatical or takes tobacco'.[2] Since he controlled the family purse, servants, family, and friends learned to conform to his expectations.

Sir Ralph had inherited an estate worth almost £2,000, but his debts and expenses were almost £10,000. Rebuilding the Verney estate became a life-long obsession, for he saw the family as 'an historical entity consisting of a long line of ancestors, as well as living members of the family and future descendants not yet born'.[3] Like other elite patriarchs who had survived the Civil War, he put his faith in dynastic continuity and male primogeniture. Sir Ralph was proud that his family had been in Buckinghamshire since the thirteenth century and had purchased Middle Claydon by the 1460s. He knew that his family also had ancient ties to the city. Sir Ralph Verney, a knight and mercer, had been alderman and Lord Mayor of London in the mid-1460s. The Lord Mayor's descendants later became courtiers through political and marital alliances. In keeping with this tradition, Sir Edmund Verney (1590–1642), John Verney's grandfather, was a member of Charles I's household and was knighted in 1611.[4] In 1620, he made Claydon House his seat. Seventeenth-century drawings show an H-shaped brick building that probably dated from Tudor times (see plate 7).[5] It was thirteen miles north-west of the country town of Aylesbury, but the London road passed close by the neighbouring parish of East Claydon.

Sir Edmund hoped to prosper by combining service to the king with a lucrative marriage. He wed his Buckinghamshire neighbour Margaret Denton (1594–1641) of Hillesden, who came from a socially prominent landed family. The couple and their ten surviving children spent part of each year in a large rented house in Covent Garden (see plate 16). But Sir Edmund's career at court did not produce the expected benefits. His expenses were far greater than the income paid to him by the king, and his attempts to make money from grants of offices, patents, and commodities ended in failure. He died on the battlefield of Edgehill while serving as the king's Knight-Marshal, and left his oldest son and heir, Ralph, with huge debts. The Civil War thus came at a time when the Verney estate was under strain. Moreover, Claydon House was located in the midst of Parliamentary military positions. Rising taxes, decreasing rents, and the disruption of war combined to make Sir Ralph's position extremely precarious.[6]

Fortunately, Sir Edmund had purchased from the Court of Wards the right to marry his son Ralph to an orphaned heiress, Mary Blacknall (1616–1650) for £1,000. He hoped that her lands in Buckinghamshire, Oxfordshire, and Berkshire would save the family from financial crisis. Sir Ralph had been educated at Puritan-dominated Magdalen College, Oxford, and he supported the Parliamentary cause, even though his father was a Royalist. But he soon became disenchanted with political and religious radicalism, and in 1643 he refused to sign a religious oath that made concessions to presbyterians. He withdrew from Parliamentary work that summer and fled to France in November after putting his property in trust. Due to a flaw in one of the trust deeds, however, his property underwent sequestration by the state. It was only lifted in 1649, when Sir Ralph's wife Mary courageously journeyed to England. She died after lobbying friends in Parliament on his behalf.[7]

In 1653, Sir Ralph returned to Claydon House. In order to obtain needed cash, he sold all but a tiny portion of his late wife's dower lands. But he doggedly kept his Claydon estate intact through frugal living and debt consolidation at low rates. He was not, however, able to give his seven sisters their promised £1,000 marriage portions or offer adequate annuities to his younger brothers. Without land for jointure, he had no way to remarry suitably unless he mortgaged Middle Claydon, so he remained a widower. The stressful circumstances of his inheritance had a profound effect upon the stern way that he functioned as family head.[8]

Sir Ralph had only two surviving children: Edmund ('Mun' 1636–1688) and John. Sir Ralph forced Mun to marry an heiress, Mary Abel, whose lands lay adjacent to Middle Claydon. But Mun was a feckless, undisciplined hunchback who was ill equipped for his role as heir. He sired many bastard children and ran up huge debts. Fate, however, intervened, and Mun and his two grown sons died from disease between 1686 and 1690. Thus, it was John who became his father's heir and received Peg Adams's letters about Sir Ralph's illness in 1696.

As Sir Ralph's condition worsened that summer, friends and kin not only sent letters, they exchanged gifts, performed favours, and visited the dying man. These rituals of sociability were particularly 'fit' for the season when a man lay dying. They allow us to reconstruct Sir Ralph's social networks by examining the events which occurred and the 130 gifts and favours that were exchanged during the four months before his death. Because Sir Ralph gave many gifts of venison during this time, they have been used, along with Sir Ralph's funeral rites, as a means to reveal cultural values. Like charity and hospitality, the giving and receiving of gifts and the pomp and ceremony of funeral rituals bore symbolic manifestations of power, status, and wealth. Thus, they provide us with a base-line for measuring cultural change.

Sir Ralph Verney and his Son John

Prior to the summer of 1696, Sir Ralph had spent almost eight months at his London lodgings in Lincoln's Inn Fields. His return to Claydon on 7 July 1696 roused the servants into a whirlwind of activity. The park-keeper, Ralph Pollard, the woodman, Thomas Roades, and the East Claydon steward, Anthony Dover, made sure that their accounts were in order. The cook bought beef, chicken, mutton, and bread from the market, as well as veal from the butcher. The steward William Coleman had two village men lie in and air Sir Ralph's bed on alternating nights, for there was great fear of sleeping on damp linen. 'When Hicks and Parrot lie in my bed give them strong beer', Sir Ralph instructed, 'and keep my coming as private as you can.' Elizabeth Lillie, the housekeeper, was sure to have her meals and her gossip ready, while Sir Ralph's secretary, Charles Hodges, would be eager to take dictation.[9]

Now letters would connect father and son, although they lived fifty miles apart. Sir Ralph sent his son at least twenty-three letters that July. If the message was important, he sent copies by two different methods using his carrier, John Innes, as well as a personal messenger. John, in turn, wrote sixteen letters to his father that month. John rarely visited Claydon House unless he was summoned, and then not more than once a year. In August 1693 he brought his wife for a visit and returned a year later with her body for burial. In 1695, only Aunt Pen's funeral drew him again to Claydon House. Nor was he involved in estate management. Each April, however, he visited his small Berkshire estate that his mother had left him. His only personal excursions were mid-summer trips to Tunbridge Wells or to see Essex kin. Nonetheless, he was the most important member of Sir Ralph's networks. Not only was he an obedient son, John was Sir

Ralph's London agent. He willingly responded to a steady stream of commands ranging from small domestic favours to important legal tasks. By 1696 this brokerage function was crucial to gentry families, for London affected every aspect of their affairs.[10]

Yet although John gladly served Sir Ralph from London, his business kept him in town. Since his return from Aleppo in 1672, he worked diligently as a merchant[11] and held office in the Levant and Royal Africa companies.[12] But he was never too busy to send the 'gift' of London's news, a favour that his father appreciated.[13] John's thoughts and actions between 1692 and 1717 are recorded in 1,450 letters, as well as 3,576 addressed to him. John's information was essential to Sir Ralph, for national events had local ramifications and often involved friends.

In 1696, for example, there were attempts to assassinate William III. Although Sir Ralph signed the Oath of Association and vowed to defend the King, some of the conspirators were Sir Ralph's allies. Edward Henry Lee, 1st Earl of Lichfield (1663–1716), was reported to be 'confined to his house or taken into custody' after the affair. Sir Ralph was a trustee of young Lichfield's estate, and the two families helped each other when in trouble.[14] The son of another Verney friend, Sir Miles Cooke was also implicated in the plot. Cooke's recent report as a master in Chancery had supported the Verneys' property claims in an East Claydon lawsuit. Now, Sir Miles needed assistance in obtaining a pardon for his son. To help matters along, Cooke asked Sir Ralph to send a side of venison to the Master of the Rolls.[15]

John not only served as Sir Ralph's information broker, he supervised the family's legal affairs. When the East Claydon lawsuit loomed, he spent days waiting in lawyers' offices and inserted detailed amendments on documents awaiting Sir Ralph's signature. John fought the Verneys' legal battles in London, so that his father could remain at home. John also kept Sir Ralph's London business accounts and helped him during economic crises. In 1696, when worthless clipped coins halted rent collection, John contacted his cousin Guy Palmes, an Exchequer teller. Palmes was able to exchange his old coins for new, heavier money. Yet such 'gifts' were risky for the teller, who almost lost his job by these actions.[16]

John described his efforts to tap London patronage networks in his letters. Sir Ralph, on his part, used their correspondence as a training programme for his heir. John planned no break in this routine. But when Sir Ralph's health declined in August, John rushed to Claydon for a month.[17] There, he became involved in his father's social networks.

Sir Ralph Verney's Social Networks

Sir Ralph Verney was connected to kin, in-laws, peers, gentry, clergymen, lawyers, shopkeepers, artisans, farmers, servants, and the poor by a series of overlapping linkages that operated in a fluid environment (see Table 2,

Appendix II). His networks, like those of his gentry neighbours—the Dentons, Temples, Tyrrells, Pigotts, Busbys, Dormers, Abels, and Duncombes—were marked by similar patterns. They radiated outward from the nuclear family, the country house, and the village in a series of expanding circles. During his life, Sir Ralph was constantly interacting with the networks of others, and his own bisected theirs. They formed moving chains of relationships that circulated through society like the goods, money, and gossip that people exchanged.

Diverse social groups were also clustered around Sir Ralph's gentry neighbours. Indeed, these landowners would not have recognized the bland, neutral, country community described by some English historians. Nor did their world manifest a simple dichotomy between rural and urban culture, but teemed with interconnections.[18] Furthermore, the social structure that underpinned their networks was flexible.[19] On the surface, society appeared stable, but networks were forever expanding and contracting in response to moral and practical considerations, which might unite or divide persons and groups.

Social rank was one variable. Status categories at either end of the social spectrum barred ordinary folk and the titled rich from participating in gentry social life. But in the middle, people mingled together on the basis of neighbourhood and shared interests, not just status or occupation.

Kinship provided another variable. Country networks were shot through with ties of cousinhood that were a product of years, or even centuries, of intermarriage. Sir Ralph received few letters from local gentry which were not signed by a 'faithful and obedient kinsman'. It was to everyone's advantage to interpret the word 'kin' in the widest possible sense.

A third nexus of common local interests clustered people at church or on court benches in shared instrumental networks. These groups often were disrupted by personal disputes that caused long-standing feuds cited in 135 letters. On the other hand, feuds within one parish halted when another parish threatened it with a lawsuit.[20]

Divisions within Buckinghamshire were greater than one might suppose. The county was divided into a northern, arable zone centred around the Vale of Aylesbury and a southern region of wooded Chiltern hills. The northern livestock/corn economy of the Claydons differed from the southern hilly wood/ pasture region. Moreover, enclosure followed northern geographic lines, and spilled over into other counties creating shared, land-use patterns.[21] Each geographical region put up its own Parliamentary candidates, and socialization often stopped at this natural geographical barrier.

Finally, religious and ideological considerations changed the political shape of gentry connections. In the summer of 1696 when John hurried to his father's deathbed, he observed all of these variables at work within Sir Ralph's social networks. John's son and heir, Ralph, was with him as their coach turned into the long drive that led to the house.

Claydon House could not be viewed by itself, for its impact depended upon its surroundings. Green fields embraced house, park, and gardens, and stretched as far as the eye could see. The village church sat so close to the mansion that it almost touched its back wall. From the public footpath used by the forty or fifty parish families,[22] it appeared that church and house were physically one. Thus, the dominance of the manor house over the village was visually proclaimed in stone.

The six-room almshouse still lay close by the house, although it would later be moved by the Verneys. Widow Hinton might complain it was haunted, but others sought its security of twelve pence a week and bread on Sundays and at Christmas.[23] William Butterfield's rectory was just a short walk past the stables, walled garden, and orchard. Near it lay a tiny cluster of cottages on the village's only street, where the Verneys allowed just one alehouse. Butterfield's rectory and two tenants' dwellings were probably the only other structures on the horizon.[24] But the dense web of hedges and ditches tended by day labourers would have marked a pattern on fields that had been enclosed since 1656.[25]

There were no 'middling-sort' people in the parish of Middle Claydon, which formed the first outward circle of Sir Ralph's networks. Tenant farmers, however, pursued local crafts and Tom Grimes worked potash deposits.[26] The heavy clay fields were leased to local dairy farmers, or increasingly to yeomen from other parishes. Rents were racked, leases were short, and turnover was rapid, for Sir Ralph openly sought the highest gain. In November 1696, skilled craftsmen earned a shilling per day, unskilled labourers received eight pence, and women were given four pence for field work. Many of the local people were literate, for the Verneys received at least 25 letters from artisans and craftsmen, 263 letters from freeholders and farmers, and 2 from workmen.[27] In 1684, a reduced staff of seven house servants cost Sir Ralph only £33. 10s., excluding the steward, William Coleman, and the secretary, Charles Hodges. They too were literate and sent reports on a regular basis. Indeed, servants wrote at least 579 letters and received 266 from 1692 to 1717.[28]

Rents might be high and discipline strict, but when a currency crisis caused hardships in 1696, Sir Ralph acted paternally. He worried about Goody Dixon's sickness and charged Coleman to 'tell me if she is in want, for I would not have her suffer much'. Coleman was 'to give her a half crown from me or more . . . a shilling at a time' and to advise him of her condition. When servant Nan Webb died, Sir Ralph told Coleman: 'I am contented to be at the charge of a coffin and winding sheet for her, and if they will bury her at Claydon, I will allow strong beer for the company . . . and also pay parish duties.' But if she was to be buried elsewhere, no duties were to be paid. Sir Ralph felt responsible for parishioners, but they had to obey his rules.[29]

As Justice of the Peace, Sir Ralph was also judge to the community. Questions of parish settlement were always a problem and villagers tried to ward off potentially expensive outsiders. Nothing was worse than an unknown loiterer. In March, parishioners became alarmed when they heard that 'Goody Matthews has a man that lies at her house'.[30] The tight-knit villagers disliked all intrusions and united to keep down the poor rates.

Not only was there little privacy in Middle Claydon, only the lord of the manor and his parson were able to vote. However, the poll books for East and Steeple Claydon showed a different situation. From 1700 to 1713, voters rose from nine to sixteen in tiny East Claydon, and from twenty-eight to forty-three in Steeple Claydon.[31] Although kinship linked the three parishes, social relations differed in East and Steeple Claydon, which lay in the next outer circle of Sir Ralph's networks. No landlord dominated either village of about eighty families each, and many properties were unenclosed. No doubt, Verney purchases of freeholds in both parishes created unease.[32]

Craftsmen, artisans, tenant farmers, and small freeholders rubbed shoulders with parish gentry. Some of the latter were newcomers, like the Abels. Others, like the declining Chaloners, had seen better days. As one Steeple Claydon observer put it, there was 'no person of quality or gentleman of estate'. Vexing lawsuits were continually filed against the Verneys and farmers jealously guarded customary rights. When Sir Ralph served as a trustee of the school at Steeple Claydon, villagers complained that the endowment had been mis-used. Rents were often in arrears, and in June 1696, an unknown person advised tenants not to take Sir Ralph's leases. Nor did the Church act as a restraining influence. Mr Green, the clergyman of East Claydon, rarely tended to minister-ial duties, while the Vicar Mr Fleetwood of Steeple Claydon was described as a 'lunatic' or at best 'distracted'. His patron Mr Chaloner, however, searched for a curate 'that would live on the spot, and bury, and christen, and do all those things'.[33] High standards were desired by both patron and parishioners.

Dairies dotted the landscape, and tenants increasingly found it more profit-able to stock cattle than to farm the heavy soil. Wealthy graziers had their own places in the Verneys' social networks, and their relations could be friendly or confrontational. A favoured group performed useful services for Sir Ralph and received benefits in return. When unclipped money was scarce, they brought John cash from Claydon rents on their way to Smithfield market. They were called 'Mister', and, if lucky, they dined with the gentry.[34]

One such middling-sort yeoman, Joseph Churchill, made himself indispen-sable to the Verneys and wrote at least 22 letters to the family. He served as the steward's estate adviser, proposed land purchases, appraised property, provided militia men, testified at lawsuits, and bought farm animals.[35] William Busby, another neighbour, was the Verneys' lawyer, as well as a Justice of the Peace and wrote 39 letters. Since lawsuits often severed country networks, his mediating skills were important. In the summer of 1696, he visited Sir Ralph regularly and few papers were signed without his approval. John saw Churchill and Busby often that summer, and it is likely that he noticed their usefulness.[36]

Neighbours of varied ranks dined together in the Claydons. The nearby Duncombes, Dormers, and Busbys were related to each other by marriage and served as magistrates, militia captains, and deputy lieutenants. Since Sir

Ralph was in London on New Year's Day 1696, his niece Cary Stewkeley entertained Mr Duncombe and his family, two clergymen and their wives, as well as Churchill and his daughter. At two in the morning several gentry younger sons joined them for cards. The group ate Sir Ralph's venison and, as usual, drank his health. In the last week of Sir Ralph's life, the same New Year's cluster dined at Claydon House,[37] where his game again graced the table. Neighbours of diverse ranks gathered from birth to burial in rituals of sociability. Beneath the civility, however, feuds simmered. They arose from competitive land purchases, unclear boundaries and taxes, rival appointments to office, or just plain personal dislike. Thus, at any point in time, the Verneys might provide hospitality to their neighbours and simultaneously face them in a lawsuit. What was more, everyone in the parish would know the minute details of both events.

The Claydon socialites were but one of many neighbourhood sub-groups clustered all over Buckinghamshire. Two equally diverse groups revolved around the nearby Dentons of Hillesden and the Temples of Stowe. Members of these clusters dined with Sir Ralph as late as a few days before he died. The Temples, Dentons, and Verneys had intermarried, stood for Parliament together, and served each other as trustees, godparents, weddingmen, and pall bearers. But although visits were maintained, relations with Sir Richard Temple and Sir Alexander Denton had cooled because of a political quarrel. In 1689, they had united to deny Sir Ralph his Buckingham borough seat, and in 1696 they still held it.[38]

The estates of these three kinsmen encircled the market borough of Buckingham, which lay in the third external ring of Sir Ralph's network (see plate 6). The Corporation's sixteen testy burgesses had been wooed, bribed, and dominated by the three families for as long as anyone could remember. Due to the growing political independence of the middling sort, however, freeholders' votes were becoming more difficult to secure. The burgesses' cat and mouse games affected daily life, for Sir Ralph's butcher, barber, and apothecary were not only burgesses, but his tenants.[39] In nearby Winchenden, a powerful Whig dissenter, Sir Thomas Wharton, was building a political base. Since the Exclusion Crisis, there had been stormy local elections marked by ideological divisions. As Wharton's ruthless tactics stimulated conflict, Whig/Tory party loyalties were hardening.

There also were well-established, dissenting communities including Quakers and Anabaptists, much to Sir Ralph's disgust. Although years ago he had ejected a dissenter, several Anabaptists still lurked in the neighbourhood.[40] Yet despite periodic popular outbursts against popery, Sir Ralph shared social occasions with the Catholic Dormers, Busbys, Atkinses, and Longvilles.

The county squirearchy formed a cohesive body of active 'natural rulers', of whom about half were long-time property holders. On the eve of the Civil War, about two hundred families had gentry status, forty of whom dominated the county. Thirty had estates worth over £1,000 per annum, while seventeen were assessed at over £2,000. The Temples' property valued at £3,000 in 1640 already dwarfed the Verneys at about £1,200 to £1,400 per year. But by 1688, East and Middle Claydon rents totalled over £2,000.[41] The gentry mixed with the middling sort on juries and vestries, and at assizes, elections, funerals, markets, fairs, and horse races. In this outer county circle of Sir Ralph's networks, he joined men from other hundreds in governing as magistrates, highway commissioners, militia leaders, tax assessors, and members of political caucuses. Social cohesion varied over time, but the county's gentry were generally a united group. Indeed, from 1692 to 1717, the Verneys received at least 667 letters from the gentry, 383 of which were from their wives and 44 from their daughters. The nobility normally appeared only at elections and sporting events but titled people, some of whom were kin, also wrote letters: 22 letters from marquesses, 22 from earls, 44 from viscounts and their wives, 773 from baronets and their wives, 634 from knights and their wives, and 43 from other titled women (see Table 2, Appendix II). In 1696 at Quainton, Cary Stewkeley did 'never see so many Lords at that race in my life'[42] (for a race at Windsor, see plate 9).

Buckinghamshire landowners did not confine themselves to their county networks. By 1696 Sir Ralph was spending up to nine months a year in London. He spent eight months there in 1692/3, nine months in 1693/4, five and a half months in 1694/5 when his sister's funeral drew the family home, and almost eight months in 1695/6. A database analysis of his journeys shows a pattern of spending November through July in London and the rest of the summer at Middle Claydon. He or his steward visited the Verneys' Wasing estate in Berkshire in April or October. During the summer, Sir Ralph might spend a week with his Denton/Nicholas kin in St Albans, Essex. He was no longer at home at Christmas to offer country hospitality. This pattern stands in contrast to John Broad's estimate of five months in London earlier in the century.

Naturally, this fact drastically affected Sir Ralph's social alliances.[43] He formed extra-county friendships in Parliament and developed ties with urban professionals, some of whom were friends of John. Indeed, from 1692 to 1717 the Verneys received 29 letters from officeholders, 437 letters from clergymen and their families, 534 from lawyers and their famililes, 27 from physicians and apothecaries, and 13 from educators. In addition, the networks of his Buckinghamshire friends and those of his son's London world constantly overlapped with each other. The Denton and Temple families had London residences near John's aunts in Covent Garden, and they all dined together in the capital.[44] Likewise, the Duncombes from East Claydon had kin on John's Hatton Garden street. In fact, most of Sir Ralph's upper gentry neighbours were shuttling in and out of town. Moreover, although many Claydon villagers had lived there for generations, some were moving to London.[45]

Finally, Sir Ralph was linked to people living 'beyond sea' in the outermost circle of his networks. He sent his cousin Lettice Porter money, textiles, and a bible so that she might survive on Virginia's Rappahannock River. Having lived in France during the Civil War, he still ordered wine from French merchants.

He and his son John also wrote letters to Ireland, Italy, Switzerland, and New York. Far from being a country bumpkin, books in many languages graced his shelves and newsletters linked him to Europe.[46] Sir Ralph's networks were rooted in local soil and still focused around the Claydons. Yet they were also widespread and they increasingly overlapped with their London counterparts.

John observed these networks during his August visit, but eventually he had to return to London. Now the responsibility for recording Sir Ralph's last days fell once again upon his cousin Peg Adams.[47] Sir Ralph was 83, and he knew that he was dying. His last acts portrayed his deepest concerns and sent a final message to those who knew him best. It is significant that they involved neither rents nor the coming elections: they were about his gifts of venison.

Sir Ralph Verney's Gifts of Venison

During the last months of Sir Ralph's life, presents of venison dominated his letters and were regularly received by members of his networks. Contemporaries viewed gifts, letters, visits, and other forms of exchange (see Table 4, Appendix II) as fundamental to the social order. Therefore, an analysis of Sir Ralph's gift-giving allows us to observe his networks in action and interpret their meaning. Sir Ralph's past relationship with the recipient, the nature of his present, his motivation in giving, and the response of the recipient were important aspects of that process.

But the most significant fact about Sir Ralph's gifts before death was that he only gave pieces of venison. This was in contrast with other times in his life when he gave different types of presents, as well as charity. Sir Ralph's deer were far more than simple tokens. They were embedded in medieval notions of status and evoked landed power. At the same time, their distribution revealed the intrusion of London's urban culture. Most of Sir Ralph's venison was sent to Londoners, not country friends, and was used for patronage purposes. Since Britain's bureaucracy was expanding and becoming more centred in the capital, this shift was understandable. Subtle changes were taking place in Sir Ralph's provincial networks,[48] and new patterns of social relationships were evolving beside older models.

Sir Ralph's carrier John Innes may have been sullen as he drove to London. Not only did he carry letters for the Verneys, he had to load their heavy, stinking, carcasses of deer onto his cart. If there had been a hole in the bottom of Innes's dirty wagon, an earthspun outline of the Verneys' networks would have been laid upon the landscape. It was reminiscent of the intricate patterns worked by Buckinghamshire lace makers, whose cottages he passed by.

Venison was privileged food that could only come from elite or royal deer parks. England's game laws were not to be taken lightly, and stealing venison would soon become a hanging offence.[49] Innes had to put up with demands from the Verneys' city kin, whose coachmen pocketed hefty tips at the venison's arrival. Recently, he had fallen asleep in his cart, and 'being wearied with his journey, so made all as wanted him wait until he waked'. Aunt Gardiner's maid stood two hours for her meat, and her mistress complained bitterly to Sir Ralph.[50]

During the summer of 1696, Sir Ralph, too, received gifts of deer from Woodstock Park, where Edward Henry Lee, 1st Earl of Lichfield was the ranger. Upon his marriage to Charles II's illegitimate daughter, Lichfield's father had transferred the office of ranger to his son. It gave him £3,000 a year and the right to dispense patronage and deer to others.[51] Lichfield's mother and the Verneys had been intimate friends for years, and she made Sir Ralph a trustee of her estate. Now, the young nobleman and the older gentry counsellor were linked together by a chain of gifts, favours, and letters, 20 written by Lichfield himself and 23 from his man of business, John Cary.[52]

Long before 1696, Verney had regularly received warrants for bucks from Cary. They were symbolic reminders of the two families' ties and were often preceded or followed by another favour. In September 1693, for example, Cary informed Sir Ralph that he had not used Lichfield's July warrant. But the letter's real purpose was to inform Verney that Lichfield needed cash: 'He . . . hath many creditors calling on him for debt', noted Cary, 'and presumes you will not deny him.' Although Sir Ralph was supposed to pay debts with Lichfield's money, he let him have a fine of £150 that had arisen from a change of tenure. A few months later, Cary sent another warrant for a brace of bucks. This time it followed a mortgage assignment by Sir Ralph that enabled Cary's son to receive '£2,000 in land of his wife's portion which lyeth in Lord Lichfield's estate'.[53] A good trustee like Verney found ways to help his patrons, and his acts generated further benefits to the network's humbler members.

In July 1696, Lichfield's present of deer accompanied the gift of a church living for the brother-in-law of the yeoman Joseph Churchill. Several peers had asked the Earl to give the benefice to their friends. But at Sir Ralph's request, Churchill's 'ancient and weary' in-law got the job. The Earl's buck was to be divided between John, his two aunts, and Sir Ralph's London landlord.[54] This task, however, was not so easy, for the deer's parts were valued as differently as the people who received them.

When Aunt Gardiner heard about the buck, she 'put it to the vote amongst her daughters, and they chose a haunch'. Her household of eight received a tiny annuity from Sir Ralph, but she could never live within her income. From May to September 1696, she wrote nineteen letters to Sir Ralph, eight to John, and was constantly begging from them both. She sent her maid for her venison because she had no coachman, and she gave no tip although it was expected. Her written thanks were accompanied by another request for money. In return, however, Aunt Gardiner provided valuable services. Her titled friends still visited her, and she recounted their racy gossip in her 518 letters from 1692 to 1717. She also obtained political secrets, which were crucial during an election. Matchmaking was her particular forte, and she helped many couples, including John.[55]

Sir Ralph's motive for the gift was charity, but he also appreciated his sister's concern. That summer, she made cloths to put on his aching legs and sent a recipe for his bath tub. When bathing made him ill, she prayed daily on her knees 'for the best of brothers'. She called him a 'father as well as a brother',[56] and his role was clearly paternal. His gift not only eased hunger, it confirmed her place in his network and his authority as a landed patriarch.

John's other aunt, Elizabeth Adams, existed on Sir Ralph's allowance of £50 a year. Because her family was small, her response to her gift was different from Aunt Gardiner's. She chose 'the side which was most to my liking . . . because I could make some friends with that, and yet save some for myself. I have lived upon venison ever since.' Her nephew Dr Blackmore of Cheapside was a Fellow of the College of Physicians. She loved to play his patron and sent a part of her piece to him. She proudly masked her begging, though she was always short of money, with resolves to 'trust in God he'll send me some in his due time'.[57]

Aunt Adams also did favours for Sir Ralph in return for her gifts. Because she lived in Covent Garden, she could offer him food and imported luxuries. Soon after receiving her venison, she sent a chocolate pot that cost 10d. and a 6d. coffee mill. Other summer purchases for Sir Ralph included a spitting pot, a urinal, a knit worsted waistcoat at 7s. 6d., a glass of lemon syrup, and forty-one yards of huckabuck for napkins. She sent only seven letters to Sir Ralph and three to John that summer. She was a more independent relation than Aunt Gardiner, but she still wrote 216 letters to Sir Ralph and John from 1692 to 1717.[58]

The other side of Lichfield's deer went to Captain and Rebecca Paulden. They were tenants of the house in Lincoln's Inn Fields, where Sir Ralph lodged in London. Although he paid £30 rent 'for his share and part of the house', he had little privacy. Lodgers crowded in clusters like extended families and performed favours for each other. Mrs Paulden, probably a relative of Grinling Gibbons, copied portraits for a living and acted as Sir Ralph's landlady. She ordered food and found someone to lie in his bed before each of his arrivals. He, in turn, helped the Paulden family. In April 1696, when they borrowed his coach, its brass toppings were stolen. Even so, Sir Ralph sent them venison that July, as he had done the previous year.[59] Just as London lodgings linked people of many ranks, so gifts of venison confirmed their ties when one of them left town.

The last section of Lichfield's deer was reserved for John, who served as broker for the other three pieces. John admitted to Sir Ralph: 'I have made a present of it to Miss Baker.' Daniel Baker, a haberdasher, was John's next door neighbour in Hatton Garden with whom he would soon negotiate a marriage settlement.[60] Although John was presently a merchant, the venison was sure to remind Baker of John's future landed position.

Sir Ralph's next gift of a buck that summer returned a favour from a powerful relative, instead of spreading good will among clients. This time it came from his own park. On 26 July, he wrote John: 'The best side send to my Cousin [Guy] Palmes the [Exchequer] teller, who . . . did me a kindness in helping me off with my bad money.' Cousin Mary Eure had married Guy's father William, a Whig Yorkshire politician with a 'linen manufacture'. Palmes had competed with the Duke of Leeds to obtain the teller's place that was valued at £2,000 to £2,600 per year. Fortunately, he had the Lord Keeper's support and 'could carry several counties for the king'. The office, which cost £800, 'had to go in the son's name because of William being a Parliament man'. By 1695, Guy also found a £400 place in his office for his brother Will and was set to marry a 'vast fortune'. Although the Verneys privately called Guy a 'knave', they were publicly attentive to their kinsman.[61]

Palmes was at the Duke of Gloucester's installation when Sir Ralph's 'fairest side' of venison arrived. Yet Guy would live to rue the act for which he received his deer. In 1697 he was suspended from the Exchequer for exchanging old clipped coins for heavy money before the old money ceased to circulate at par. Worse yet, he brazenly increased his debt after his acts were uncovered. Ultimately, the huge sum of £27,000 had to be repaid by Guy's father before his son could resume his place.[62]

Sir Ralph's god-daughter Nancy Nicholas received another section of Palmes's deer: the haunch 'which has had a shot'. Her husband was in Parliament and had a custom-house place. Nancy wrote 45 letters to John during nine months of 1696 and was a key family member writing 347 letters from 1692 to 1717. Unlike John's aunts with whom she competed, she saw the meat as a gift of status, not food. 'Dear parent is most extremely kind in remembering me', she wrote, after tipping a half crown. When she and John ate Sir Ralph's buck, they affirmed bonds uniting all three of them.[63]

Aunt Adams tipped only a shilling for her 'fairest haunch' that July. She sent it to Dr Blackmore, who had just given Sir Ralph free medical advice. But Blackmore's bills were often padded. In 1701 John would learn that 'for fees and physick, he has blown up a reckoning with a young heir to several hundred pound . . . and is looked on to be a sort of stock jobber, and that not fair'.[64] As in Guy Palmes's case, London's unregulated free enterprise led to dubious methods of profit. The Verneys showed disapproval by using metaphors about the market.

Sir Ralph sent John the 'fourth poor side' for 'Miss Baker either from me or yourself'. Since John was still negotiating his marriage settlement, he decided to send it in his father's name.[65] Sir Ralph's bounty again bore echoes of landed wealth that Mr Baker was bound to notice.

By September, Sir Ralph's life and the deer season were drawing to a close. Sir Ralph gave his last buck to his 'upper' servants, but, as always, one piece was reserved for John. Sir Ralph's employees held intimate places in his networks and kept him company as death approached. Peg wrote they were 'as diligent and careful of him as possible', and 'watched every night'. Sir Ralph's annuities would be much greater than those left by his son.[66] He called his servants 'my family' and when Coleman was ill, Sir Ralph wrote with concern: 'Pray be careful of a cold and advise the other servants to be so too. . . . I had much rather my business be undone, then you should receive any prejudice by doing it.'[67]

On 6 September, Sir Ralph told John to expect a Woodstock buck, 'a side of which, pray send Mr Horsenell from me, and a haunch from Lillie to him'. The housekeeper, Mrs Lillie, had a frank relationship with her master and chided him when she thought him wrong. She wrote at least 106 letters from 1692 to 1717.[68] Wealthy Mr Horsenell was Lillie's cousin, as well as John's neighbour in Hatton Garden.[69] Sir Ralph's gift acknowledged his own relationship with Horsenell, as well as Lillie's. As the venison reached Horsenell's door, both he and Lillie displayed their status.

Sir Ralph's secretary, Charles Hodges, received the third part of the deer. He occupied an upper level of the servant hierarchy, along with Lillie and Coleman. Because he wrote Sir Ralph's letters, he was privy to family secrets and he accompanied his master to London, while others stayed at home. He was entrusted with receiving money, examined family papers, and served as a witness in legal matters. Sometimes it was hard to know which identity he represented: his own, his master's, or a combination thereof.[70]

Sir Ralph left Hodges a £40 annuity and was constantly in his company, but he never guessed that Hodges had a wife and 'four or five brats'. John found him his next employer, who left him another £40 annuity. By 1702 he was carrying the Queen's robes for £103 a year.[71] His networks began with the Verneys, and he used them to further his career.

When Hodges was given his gift of venison, he begged 'it be sent to Mr Lovett, a linen draper at the White Bear in Cornhill'. Lovett was a prosperous London mercer and the 'eldest son of a gentleman'.[72] In 1700 he married a wealthy woman, but he was linked to the Verneys in his own right. The Lovetts of Lipscombe were an old Buckinghamshire family and Mr Butterfield, Sir Ralph's parson, was Lovett's brother-in-law. John's middle daughter Mary would marry a Lovett in 1703. In the 1690s, John and Lovett had their own intimate relationship. He trusted the draper with financial errands, and in 1697, Lovett loaned him £500.[73] Sir Ralph's gifts of venison let his upper servants act as patrons to a rising group of wealthy Londoners. They also confirmed his own personal connections with the middling sort.

Just before Sir Ralph stopped recognizing people, he wrote John: 'I have now sent you a side of venison. . . . Do not keep it long before you spend or dispose it'.[74] During the summer, Sir Ralph had carefully reserved a piece of each deer for his son. It was only fitting that his final death-bed gift of venison was sent solely to his heir.

Gift Systems and Social Networks

Sir Ralph's gifts of venison not only were linked to each other, they formed a symbolic gift system of great importance to all participants. This system was itself part of a larger network of social relationships that included alms, charity schools, and the poor laws, whose rules were well known to contemporaries.[75]

Each of Sir Ralph's gifts was bestowed according to the social code of his day. His careful planning about what piece individuals should receive, and whether it should come in his name or John's, was proof of a set of underlying principles. Lord Fitzwilliam of Milton showed the same 'obsessive concern with the disposal of venison, laboriously spelling out who should have a side, who a haunch, who a shoulder'.[76]

The shape of Sir Ralph's gift system was circular and expansive. It spread out from Sir Ralph at the centre and overlapped with similar systems. As it did so it drew outsiders into its vortex, creating a chain of new brokers and clients. A further ripple effect was created as his gifts were subdivided and additional persons joined in dining, toasting, transporting, and tipping. Sir Ralph's gift system moved with cumulative energy and persisted over time. This was so, because the social code mandated reciprocity and not to return a favour would be offensive. Society was based upon the exchange of mutual benefits and gift-giving bound subjects together. This amity was crucial to the restoration of both monarchy and family power after the Civil War. Classical works such as Seneca's *On Benefits* explained this concept. Courtesy manuals also encouraged recipro-cal bonds: 'Those who always receive or always give are not much esteemed in conversation', wrote Obadiah Walker in 1687.[77] As anthropologists have noted, reciprocal exchange fostered a stable social order.[78] This principle was evident in Sir Ralph's gift networks. Often, his presents were sent in gratitude for a favour or in expectation of a favour to come. Sir Ralph's venison met a variety of other needs for both donor and recipient. Some friends shared their presents and became patrons, while others satisfied their own desires for sustenance, good food, company, and friends. A side of venison became the centrepiece of a dinner party, where clients drank the donor's health as they ate his bounty.

Sir Ralph was also able to help friends and kin in the spirit of paternalism. As a recipient of Lichfield's deer, as well as disposer of his own, he could afford to be generous. His presents allowed him to express charity, largesse, friendship, kinship, love, gratitude, and generosity, as well as self-interest. Each recipient responded differently, but all returned the favour in an appropriate way.

Both kin and non-kin were part of Sir Ralph's gift system. But only a core group of relations received game regularly. They included John's immediate family, a few first cousins, and Sir Ralph's siblings. Relatives positioned on the outer rings of kinship received no gifts, unless, like Palmes, they did a favour or were influential. Non-kin like Cooke, Paulden, and Lichfield enjoyed long-standing relations and both helped and were helped by the Verneys. Thus, presents selectively reinforced family ties.

Sir Ralph understood the importance of gifts and tried to teach their value to his son. Gifts of venison, he told John, were not unusual, but 'such a small thing is oftener more kindly taken than a thing of great value.' In 1680, Sir Ralph acknowledged their significance when he asked John to 'let nobody know I send any venison to London, for I cannot send to others having lost half my stock last winter'.[79] Each piece of deer received placed the receiver in Sir Ralph's network. Since one's opportunities could be affected by this inclusion, much was at stake.[80]

Yet the venison affirmed rather than eliminated distinctions between Sir Ralph and the recipient. They emphasized his superior status and the assymetry of his relationships. His gifts of game usually flowed downward and attributed personal qualities such as impoverishment to people like Aunt Gardiner. The coachman knew she was needy too, for a tip established status and she gave not a six pence. The particular part of the deer bestowed also had meaning. As in wills, gifts were often matched with receivers according to status, and pieces of deer had their own hierarchy. Long ago Sir Ralph had asked John if he and his wife did 'love a side better than a haunch of venison. . . . I think you had best take the side', he wrote, 'for that is held the best'.[81] Power relations were most clearly viewed at the point of the deer's distribution.

Finally, Sir Ralph's suggestion that John send venison to a friend 'and give it him as from yourself'[82] recognized that gifts were active, not passive. They united, influenced, and interacted with others. In a final confusion between persons and objects, they took on new meanings at the time of death: farewell, love for a son, and dynastic continuity.

Gifts of Venison: Symbols of Cultural Values

Sir Ralph's venison possessed ethnographic significance over and above its importance as food. No other commodity would have had the same effect, for no other product was exclusively owned by the landed elite and the Crown. In fact, it was no accident that venison was his primary gift that summer. As today's controversies about hunting show, England's landowners always have had an obsessive relationship with their deer. Deer symbolized the hunt, and because hunters were qualified by their property, they also symbolized land. As Peter Beckford noted in his *Thoughts on Hunting*, the chase was 'the soul of country life'.[83]

Symbols of the hunt retained their power, in part, because they had evolved out of highly stylized ceremonies that gathered in local inhabitants and ordered them by rank.[84] The tale about English deer that Sir Ralph's contemporaries would have heard, included legends and myths. The retelling of this story adds an additional layer of meaning to the previous narratives of Sir Ralph's gifts of venison.

From the beginning, deer were regarded as miraculous creatures who had magical powers. Ancients said they lived 100 years, and this claim persisted in Sir Ralph's day.[85] Pliny and Ovid assigned medicinal value to their bones, marrow, and antlers,[86] while others cited their power over snakes[87] and their 'wit and cunning'.[88] Authors claimed that hunting was 'a sport to be followed only by a superior order of men'[89] and praised it in song, poem, painting, and essay.[90] Manuals described the noble qualities of the hunter[91] 'who made men as well as beasts yield to his strength'. Hunters were not only 'wise . . . and warlike',[92] they were virtuous and protected by God.[93] These notions had strong gender implications, for although women rode and took part socially, hunting was always described in masculine terms. Its focus on training warriors also excluded women.[94]

Thus, the hunt served as a metaphor for the patriarchal order and a locus for its values. King, nobles, neighbouring gentry, foresters, masters of the hounds, huntsmen, servants, dogs, deer, and the raven gathered together in a hierarchical display of the great chain of being. It would be difficult to create a more obvious setting for the clarification of relationships.[95]

The hunt culminated in the death of the deer, which included elements of a religious mass and a passionate climax for participants. The ceremony was marked by wine drinking and chants, as the deer's guts were dipped with bread into his blood. After four morts were blown, the animal was 'leisurely . . . and daintily . . . undone', and then 'broken up' for distribution[96] (see plate 8). This 'breaking up' of the deer was the focal point through which power relationships were revealed. Thus, body parts were distributed according to rank or roles in the hunt: the best morsels—tongue, ears, and testicles, for the chief personage; haunches, sides, and 'umbles' for the huntsmen; a shoulder each for harbourer and undoer; hides to the master of the hounds; and a gristle bit hung up on a tree for the raven.[97] This allocation of the kill defined personal identities, just as Sir Ralph's choice of deer parts demarcated his friends' status.

Sir Ralph's contemporaries knew this story of the hunt by heart and understood its affirmation of the social order. Indeed, the basic values of the landed elite were revealed during its rites: paternalism, hospitality, privilege, pride, glorification of private property, masculinity, and authority. Hunting rituals showed a delight in bloody domination. James I daubed men's faces in deer blood and refused to let them wash it off. Likewise, ladies of quality, who desired a white complexion, washed their hands and faces in the deer's blood after it was 'newly opened being hot'. Many squires insisted on being present at the execution. Thus, Sir Ralph's patron, the Earl of Lichfield, 'love[d] to be at the killing of all himself'.[98] The hunt was a passionate celebration of the land, its owner, and his power.

Gifts of Venison: Symbols of Gentry Power

By 1696 the gentry had increased their control over the land and its rights. Forest courts and the Crown no longer monopolized the taking of deer.[99] Now landowners in Parliament framed their own game laws with successively severer penalties that affirmed their privileges over other social groups. As Cox noted in 1697, the prerogative of hunting once monopolized by kings and nobles was now firmly in the hands of 'private gentlemen'. A seventeenth-century traveller believed that 'every gentleman of £500 or £1,000 rent . . . hath a parke', and in 1718 *The Complete Sportsman* boasted: 'There are more parks and forests in England than in all Europe besides.'[100]

Sir Ralph had enclosed Middle Claydon by the 1650s and he soon hired a gamekeeper. By at least 1672, his park was encircled with a wall, and by 1683, its fifty-five deer were providing many presents. Sir Ralph's neighbours also knew the importance of dispensing gifts of venison and received warrants from their friends. In 1682, Sir Richard Temple longed to buy more deer, so that he might feed his household and still give some away. By 1688 his overworked keeper complained he had 'employment for two men', what with 'hunting day and night' and carcasses 'being disperst so remote by coaches and carrier'.[101] Buckinghamshire's Lord Lieutenant, John Egerton, 3rd Earl of Bridgewater used his hunting rights in royal forests as a 'recreation' for his friends, while Sir Ralph's friend, William Cheyne, second Viscount Newhaven, had thirty warrants from Thoresby Park to add to his own.[102] Deer had become the private property of the landed elite and the government's role was to protect it. Since a gift was a mark of ownership, Sir Ralph and squires like him confirmed their privileges with each offering. Thus in 1683, Sir John Hotham 'set up venison feasts to all the tradesmen and companies' as he plotted against the government.[103] In the country and the city, gifts of venison were still an important element of patronage.

Indeed, four days before Sir Miles Cooke begged for his son's pardon, he requested a deer from Sir Ralph for his own superior.[104] And although Lichfield's politics caused problems, his deer-based patronage enhanced his authority. His gift-giving extended vertically, affecting people of varied social ranks from chapmen to peers. It also had a horizontal breadth, for he controlled offices, lodges, land mortgages, and religious benefices.

But while venison symbolized landed power, rising tensions about deer signified a countervailing trend. Thus, Sir Ralph's gifts also bore evidence of a booming, competitive society. Local disputes about Stowe's deer park had recently vexed the Temples and poaching appeared to be increasing. As the Verneys forced out tenants and erected fences, the deer within them assumed importance as inhabitants of liminal space. Harsh game laws were statements about needs to quell resistance as well as to affirm authority.[105]

Moreover, physical boundaries were not the only ones subjected to challenge. London's rising middling sort were starting to trespass upon social boundaries. As non-landed professionals accumulated wealth, they became disturbing wild cards in the social hierarchy. The ordered ranks, so clearly revealed in the hunt, were ambiguously blurred in town. Sir Ralph's gifts reflected London's fluid environment. They displayed his contacts with entrepreneurs, whose status was unclear. The breadth of occupations of those receiving venison was also significant. The list included drapers, merchants, doctors, lawyers, and office-holders. The neglected middling sort have recently been analysed by a variety of historians. The Verney letters document and confirm the growing penetration of this group into gentry networks.[106] Thus, Sir Ralph was willing to connect to various 'sorts' of people. He drew them into his own networks, and he was drawn into theirs as well.

Over time, Sir Ralph's networks became filled with various middling-sort agents.[107] Brokerage was increasingly at the heart of social relations, injecting complexity into patron/client alliances. John, Aunt Adams, and the servants inserted themselves into Sir Ralph's gift-giving and passed on their venison to the urban middling sort. The limited ways in which networks previously had developed were now open to a range of possibilities. As Sir Ralph's gifts flowed downward, he was drawn out of his landed confines into a potentially new, urban collective. Innovative patterns of social relations were becoming a cultural option and coexisted with traditional models.

Sir Ralph's gifts also bore signs of the competitive market place. Gift-giving had always changed with the times in response to shifts in power. As the Tudors centralized authority, court gift-giving overtook presents to wealthy magnates. After Elizabeth I's frugal reign, favours multiplied under James I, but charges of corruption led to late-Stuart reforms. By the eighteenth century, power politics were shifting again to London and to Parliament. Lords Lieutenant and party managers now dispensed favours along with sinecures, pensions, and places.[108]

Had Sir Ralph's gifts succumbed to the greater venality of a more competitive society? Because the line between gifts and bribery was always unclear, it is impossible to generalize. In every age, the English bemoaned corruption. Moreover, there was no uniformity across late seventeenth-century government, for each department operated in its own context. The bureaucracy was 'an extraordinary patchwork—of old and new, useless and efficient, corrupt and honest—mixed together'.[109]

What we can say is that what gifts were seen as acceptable changed over time. In Sir Ralph's day, rewarding friends and punishing enemies was a normal part of the political culture. On the other hand, bribery, cited 122 times, was a sensitive issue. Gifts such as venison appear to have been viewed as everyday tools of patronage, in contrast to more blatant forms of corruption. For years, Sir Ralph had refused to 'treat' freeholders, much to his fellow candidates' disgust.[110] But he felt comfortable giving and receiving gifts of venison.

Sir Ralph had stricter ideas than Guy Palmes about using place for profit. Yet he accepted a monetary favour and then rewarded Palmes with game. We cannot attribute his behaviour directly to the influence of London. Still, its commercial atmosphere nourished impersonal, instrumental approaches to achieving goals. Shady deals had always existed, but London's financial revolution was creating new ways to manipulate money, and Palmes was not removed because he used them.[111] His eventual dismissal was caused by party politics, not deceit or inefficiency. Prior to the 1660s, cash favours were probably seen as less than genteel. Palmes's case suggests that as people assigned money values to more aspects of their lives, the cash nexus was becoming more accepted.

Finally, Sir Ralph's deer were not just symbolic—they had economic value. In

1682 Sir Richard Temple hoped to get £4. 10s. for a buck. By the early 1700s, just its haunch fetched between £3 and £5, and its offal commanded up to 16s.[112] In years of scarcity, prices rose even more. Not surprisingly, this illegal market was centred, like the Exchange and marriage mart, in London.

Yet the deer's economic impact was far greater than the money it brought. When gifts were sent to London, they stimulated a stream of shillings to park officials, keepers, carriers, and coachmen. As the venison made its way from hand to hand, cash came to those who touched it. In 1694 Cary itemized a buck's delivery costs: 'The fee is to the keeper 10s., the underkeeper 2s. 6d . . . the shoulders and umbles 5s. . . . . The carriage of all will be 7s. at least, besides a shilling usually given the person that brings the venison.'[113] The rewards of a market economy extended deep into the social strata.

Some historians have contrasted gifts with markets, posing two mutually exclusive chronologies.[114] But presents of venison were never totally displaced. They were integrated into the Verneys' market and patronage systems. On the other hand, John did not bestow venison in the same liberal manner as his father. From 1692 to 1717 he mentioned gifts of venison only 13 times, 3 of which came from Lord Lichfield. And unlike Sir Ralph, he gave cash at the polls. He and his gentry neighbours would combine participation in competitive politics with the use of symbolic presents.

John arranged for each gift's delivery, but he was more than a coordinator. Each offering of venison to him was a symbolic passing of authority. By accepting a piece of his father's estate, John was preparing himself for inheritance. Sir Ralph, on his part, was blessing his heir. The venison also sent a message to John about his obligations as family head. Sir Ralph had devoted his life to rebuilding his estate after the Civil War. Now he was reminding John about patriarchy, duty, and obedience. It was no accident that this statement was made through gifts of deer, nor that it came precisely at the time of death. This was the proper time to proclaim the central importance of dynastic continuity and male primogeniture through John. The family would understand this declaration. They would also expect Sir Ralph's funeral to make the same statement.

The Death of Sir Ralph Verney

Cultural values were expressed in burials and wills, as they were in the hunt. Both the death of a deer and the death of a man were followed by communal rites that integrated varied ranks of people. In both cases, there was a division of property: the deer given in life; legacies announced after death.[115] What Sir Ralph included and excluded from his last testament tells us much about his beliefs. It is thus significant that his funeral and will altered custom and heralded change.

We can learn a great deal about John's values by seeing how he buried his father. Because he was sole executor of Sir Ralph's will, John's actions were read as texts by anxious members of his networks, for they indicated the priorities of the new family head. Since the 1620s, large ceremonial funerals had fallen out of favour. Now last rites often dispensed with heralds, embalming, sermons, feasting, and gifts.[116] John could choose from a range of old and new burial customs. But his decision to hold a private night burial with no reception upset family and friends. Close kin wished to attend his funeral in order to confirm status. Gentry neighbours also expected an invitation.[117]

John's action signified a scepticism about ceremony, a desire for privacy, a decline in country hospitality, and a reduced role for the clergy. The Verneys were closing themselves off from rural neighbours, as they had enclosed their land and their deer. This discarding of custom, however, entailed risk. If older notions of good lordship were to be jettisoned, new bonds would have to be substituted to maintain stability.

Sir Ralph died in the company of his servants. At the end, he was still optimistic, ordering 'twelve bottles of claret for . . . [his] own drinking'. His attitude towards death was calm and matter of fact: 'Old age is subject to many infirmities. May God fit us for heaven.' Soon he no longer left bed for 6 p.m. prayers, but although he did not take early communion, he prayed daily and was prayed for at church. Finally, on 24 September, the Parson was called 'to recommend his soul to God'. According to the standards of his age, he died a 'good death' for he was pious and prepared for 'eternal rest and happiness in the other world'. Sir Ralph believed that God was a 'divine guide and protector', who might 'dispose of us as he pleases'. If a person submitted to providence, accepted affliction, and tried to live a good life, he might 'attain a crown of glory hereafter'.[118] This unshakeable faith apparently sustained him at death, yet we know of no last statement.

Condolence letters urged John to enjoy his inheritance, but kin also voiced anxieties about their status. They prayed he would continue Sir Ralph's role of 'supporting those unfortunate relations he has left behind'. John was told to accept death, savour life, and remember dependent kin. He quickly sent two men to receive 'a treble coffin of wood, lead, and wood covered with cloth etc. all tacked up in black baize . . . and a hamper with . . . materials . . . to preserve the body'. The cart was covered with cloths 'that people along the way may not see what it is'. Three or four bushels of bran cushioned the body in the coffin, that it might hide the noise of a rattling corpse. Despite his frugality, John paid the special fine to bury in linen, not the traditional wool, for this proclaimed family status.[119]

The undertaker William Russell sent his son-in-law with a plumber to seal the lead. Russell had started his enterprise by concluding a deal with the College of Arms. But he soon took over the heralds' business and Sir Ralph believed he was 'worth £30,000'. Despite testimonials from a competitor, this middling-sort entrepreneur, not a herald, was chosen to conduct the funeral. Undertakers like Russell could provide 'all things proper for funerals . . . coffins, shrouds, palls, cloaks, caps, and gowns, mourning hangings, beds, black and white feathers, velvet hearse . . . and the figure in wax made to life'. His men 'measure[d] the hall all round and the best court porch . . . the entry . . . [and] the brick parlour'. The rooms and furniture were hung with heavy black baize, as were the church, chancel, and pulpit. Although John dispensed with most heraldic elements, he hired a painter to do a hatchment 'to be put up over the great fore door'. But he told the servants not to disclose the burial date: 'For if you should, one friend will tell another and so all the town and country will know.'[120]

In fact, questions about the funeral's privacy were of crucial concern. How was one to interpret Sir Ralph's last wish to be '*decently* buried . . . but as *privately* and with as little pomp as may be'? Sir Ralph had made several wills and codicils, including three in the 1650s, and none of them had mentioned the word 'private'. When he made his last will in 1695, his thinking had changed, and he coupled the term 'private' with 'decent'.[121]

For his family, however, the will was unclear, and John told Coleman of his problem: 'I had thought to invite the neighbouring gentry to the funeral, which I computed to be about forty or fifty. . . . But . . . not being able to find a medium (without giving offense) betwixt a private burial and inviting all the neighbouring gentry, makes me have thoughts of doing it as others of our family lately have done.' John was referring to his brother Mun's funeral in 1688. Sir Ralph had chosen to bury him 'privately in the night-time, without . . . inviting of neighbours to attend with their coaches', which is 'very troublesome and signifies nothing'. John apparently felt that his father would wish to have the same type of burial.[122]

Ageing kin and servants, however, longed to preserve tradition. Aunt Gardiner believed John had misinterpreted 'how to construe the meaning' between 'decent' and 'private' in the will. If Sir Ralph had wanted a funeral like Mun's, 'he would have named a private funeral'. She thought it was 'best to bury him publicly', but without 'streamers and those kind of fineries'.[123]

The housekeeper Mrs Lillie also believed that the community should be included. She dreaded a night funeral, which would 'not look well in the country, it not being used with anybody'. The feeding and entertainment of neighbours was a normal part of country hospitality. Just last February, the Verneys' funeral gifts of gloves, food, and money had been praised: 'It was like Sir Ralph', people declared. We 'go nowhere as they have so good vittles and drink . . . and all things for . . . horses'. Mrs Lillie thought that people not only liked the treats, they cared about ceremonial rites. Recently, she had warned Sir Ralph that if his coachman did not wear mourning 'there will be a great deal of notice . . . in the country'. Peg Adams brought up a more crucial point: 'A man so generally known and beloved in the country' required 'some of the neighbouring gentlemen [to] carry him to his grave'.[124]

The memory of Sir Fleetwood Dormer's funeral ten days before Sir Ralph's death might have been on her mind. He was buried with 'twenty gentleman and their coaches . . . to meet the body between one and two of the clock'. What is more, there was 'a noble treat of all sorts of cold things at Lee for the gentlemen after the burial'.[125] Gifts of food and drink placed guests under obligation and reinforced the Dormers' status. Moreover, as the gentry publicly shared their grief, they confirmed their ties with Dormer's heir.

But though John's printed public announcement stressed Sir Ralph's local position, the gentry were not invited to his funeral.[126] John arrived the day before the burial with only his son and daughters. The sole eyewitness to record the event was his cousin Cary Stewkeley. She came from East Claydon in the wind and rain, but no one invited her back for the customary reception or sent to see if she got home safely. Although 'a handsome and decent burial' was reported, no out-of-town guests were received. Aunt Gardiner told John of her sorrow not 'to attend your father to his grave . . . as I would most willingly have paid that last love and service, and I must say duty to him'.[127] Presumably, she was not invited. Sir Ralph's exit was witnessed by only the innermost core of his vast social network: John and his children, his servants, the minister, and some parishioners of Middle Claydon.

John did retain two symbols of respect for his father. The hatchment over the door and the escutcheons 'about the hall' stayed until late April, when John 'distribute[d] 'em among the tenants'. Hence, the villagers received a piece of Sir Ralph's dignity as a final, parting gift. John provided his servants with mourning dress, but he ended the costly practice of giving such clothes to kin. 'I have not given a shilling towards mourning to any one relation', he wrote, '(and many of 'em are in sufficient want)'.[128] This violation of custom threatened old kinship patterns, for mourning not only extolled the dead, it showed which of the living were important.

Although John easily dropped this tradition, Sir Richard Temple put 'a new black on' in honour of Sir Ralph.[129] Only the elder generation, it seems, kept this public display of remembrance. Gone were the days of hospitality, including food and drink for the parish. Pomp and ritual had vanished along with traditional gifts of mourning.

Sir Ralph Verney's Will

Sir Ralph's will made on 19 February 1695 showed a similar erosion of custom. Family members were shocked by its three short sentences. The first confirmed that all lands passed 'to John . . . in trust' as part of a previous, normal strict settlement. The second dealt with gifts of money, but only servants received them. Earlier unexecuted wills had contained bequests of money, Van Dyck portraits, and rings to 'noble friends' and relatives.[130] The recipients, however, were old friends and kin who had died by the 1690s. Although Sir Ralph authorized gifts made under separate deeds, it appears he left no new bequests for the next generation. Niece Cary Stewkeley, who had tended Mary Abel, had expected 'a swinging legacy'. But Sir Ralph left John 'all my household stuff, jewels, plate, goods and other of my personal estate whatsoever'.[131]

Recently, Nancy Nicholas had urged John to have Sir Ralph make a new will, because 'neither he nor you did like that which we have in our hands'.[132] Because Sir Ralph was lucid and active at that time, we can only guess why he made no change. His scepticism about custom had been a constant theme before he died, and the absence of legacies was in keeping with changes in mourning and burials. Apparently, Sir Ralph wished to leave John free of charges and encumbrances, in contrast to his own earlier position. This fact illustrates the obsession of many gentry families with dynasticism and primogeniture after the divisions of civil war.

Sir Ralph's will was his last gift to his son. Bequests had always led to family quarrels,[133] but the simplicity of Sir Ralph's will levelled all. Along with other actions, it indicated a lower priority for dependent kin. Sir Ralph had doled out annuities according to his father's wishes. Now his will, like his last gift of venison, transferred power to his son. John inherited with few constraints and the potential to strengthen the Verneys' position.

A chill was in the air that fall, as both hunting season and Sir Ralph's life ended. Kin, tenants, and servants all had reason to fear change, but John had cause for anxiety as well. Because he lived in London, he was relatively unknown. And he had missed an opportunity to insert himself into the country community by acting as host at a public funeral. At the same time, physical and social boundaries were under pressure in the Claydons. John and his gentry neighbours faced challenges from rising middling-sort freeholders and a market economy based upon non-landed forms of wealth. New types of public conduct might be needed to retain the Verneys' influence. If customs that upheld their power were declining, that authority also might be vulnerable to change.

John was well equipped to lead the Verneys. He brought urban networks, business skills, and a knowledge of the market to the family. New forms of social commerce were developing in London, but his father's networks remained strong. A new amalgam would be forged under John's aegis. The question was whether John's London experience would permit this integration without diminution of the Verneys' country position.

2

John Verney: A Younger Son Enters the World of Commerce

The interest[s] of trade and land are the same, for the mutation frequently happens; the moneyed man today is a landed man tomorrow; and the landed man today becomes a moneyed man tomorrow.[1]

When John (1640–1717) inherited at the age of 56, he had lived away from Buckinghamshire since childhood. As a boy, he had found the country 'grievous, dull . . . and mournful' in contrast to 'so jolly a place as London'.[2] This attraction to the capital continued throughout his life, and he eventually found wealth there. But at John's birth, amidst Civil War, his success could hardly have been predicted. He was only a younger son in a financially strapped, royalist family that practised primogeniture.

Fortunately, John was a born entrepreneur with a passionate love of business. Moreover, England was establishing a trading empire that was centred nearby in a booming London. The growth of a commercial revolution at this time is well known. By becoming a merchant and developing financial networks, John pointed the Verneys firmly in the direction that seventeenth-century England was taking. As a younger son, he could not participate fully in the privileges of landed life, but he was free from the constraints imposed upon his elder brother, Mun. John was allowed to roam the Mediterranean, trade in the city, and live by his wits. By 1696, he was flourishing from investment in London's new financial institutions. It is understandable that John was drawn to the metropolis and that he wished to become a merchant. What needs to be explained is how he persuaded his father to underwrite the project.

Growing up after the Civil War

John grew up amidst the disruptions of war and led a turbulent but adventurous childhood. In 1643 Sir Ralph fled to Blois in France with his wife and elder son. Thus, from the beginning, John was treated differently than Mun. Alone in the big house, he roamed through gloomy rooms in the care of servants and aunts. He was tall and thought 'handsome', but he had an imperfection in his speech and the most 'miserably crooked legs'. In 1647 John's mother Mary returned to England. She found her 7-year-old leading an 'ill-ordered' life, where he supped at nine o'clock and ate 'anything he hath a mind to'. Worse yet, Mary reported, 'he hates his book . . . and learns nothing here'. He 'would fain go into France to his father', she wrote Sir Ralph, for she saw that he needed supervision.[3]

In 1647 John was allowed to come to Blois, where his dominant father supervised his breeding. Sir Ralph was determined to give his sons a conventional, English education, albeit in unconventional circumstances, and he demanded self-discipline and responsibility. John practised these habits throughout his life, and they helped him as a merchant and a landowner. John not only physically resembled Sir Ralph, they shared many character traits. Sir Ralph trained him to prize moderation, sobriety, and prudence, and to avoid open emotion. Later, when John lived in London, he claimed he 'went seldom into a tavern' and 'was home every night by 9 p.m'. Even stern Sir Ralph admitted that his son 'lived cleanly and providently'.[4] John's letters were models of self-control, extremely pragmatic, and rarely revealed his feelings.

Both sons were taught that obedience to their demanding Anglican parent was a part of God's plan. 'Disrespect and undutifulness', wrote Mun, 'anger almighty God our heavenly father, and are . . . disobliging to an earthly father.'[5] As an exile among Catholics, Sir Ralph feared any taint of popery, and the boys were bred to revere the Church of England. The superiority of their own religion and heritage was thus taught at an early age. It is likely that John's later arrogance and imperious nature had their roots in his French experience.

Although the boys could not attend Oxford like their father, Sir Ralph searched diligently for suitable tutors. John was 'a very ready witted child', but his scholastic progress was slow. It was not for lack of industry, for he could be found in the early morning 'in his bed with two books together of Latin and French'. A parade of instructors and the constant shifting between French, Latin, and English appear to have overwhelmed him. In fact, John never saw himself as a scholar,[6] a fact of crucial importance when he chose to be a merchant.

Nevertheless, John's life in France exposed him to the 'highly conventionalized codes of civility and politeness which reigned on the continent'. Despite his position as a younger son, John was taught the arts of a gentleman which he enjoyed immensely. 'The viol hath put me in love with all sorts of musics', he declared, and he carried this instrument to Aleppo. John also had dancing and drawing masters, and he adorned his personal papers with architectural sketches.[7]

The art of letter-writing that would loom so large in the Verneys' lives, was taught by a consummate master in Blois. One of the boys' tutors, Claudius Mauger, later wrote English letter-writing manuals. As the boys matured, Sir Ralph insisted that they write regular letters to family members. John was taught to use distinctive modes of address to persons of different age, rank, and gender.[8] But though Sir Ralph respected continental civility, he always remembered that he was an English gentleman and, perhaps because of his father's fate, he detested courtiers. His sons would emulate him in this respect.

John's wide range of reading was certainly formed in this period. Later, his lists of books and dictionaries show that he studied and read Latin, French, and Italian and owned works by Descartes, Montaigne, and Cervantes, as well as classical and religious books. After his return to London, he constantly bought reading material for Sir Ralph, and he became extremely knowledgeable about books and booksellers.[9]

Although not a scholar, he retained a cultivated interest in literature, art, theatre, and music throughout his life. John's exile in France gave him a wider cultural experience than other English boys of his age. Because he was forcefully restricted from indulging in French food, companions, and manners, he also knew about cultural differences.[10] These experiences contributed to a curiosity about other worlds and an openness to new ideas. They surely influenced his decision to become a merchant and to travel to far-off places.

Although the brothers were taught the same values, Sir Ralph groomed them for different futures. After their mother died in 1650, Mun accompanied his father on a grand tour of the continent. John, on the other hand, was left to board with a French pastor's widow. Far from encouraging a close relationship, Sir Ralph wished to keep the boys apart. 'Their age and humours are so different', he wrote, 'that they will do much better asunder.' Sir Ralph could hardly fail to notice Mun's slovenliness. His dissolute character and lack of discipline contrasted with John's careful dress and demeanor. Still, John's intense display of obedience often failed to please his father. John's letters show that he was insecure about his place in the family, especially after his mother's death. Throughout his life he feared losing his father's affection, and long periods of separation only heightened his anxiety. As Sir Ralph aged, however, their relationship grew closer, and the old man openly expressed love. By the time of Sir Ralph's death, John finally had become the favoured heir. No doubt Sir Ralph's disappointment in Mun's debauched life played a role. As recent historians have argued, the Verney letters show that parent/child relationships were a blend of discipline and affection.[11] John realized the significance of family at an early age, and after his years in Aleppo, it became an obsession.

John's faith in his family's importance led to an avid interest in his lineage. In 1674 he excitedly told Mun: 'In a herald's house . . . I found the genealogy of the Verneys from Edward IV's time.' John spent countless hours rereading letters and adding the titles, marriages, occupations, and social status of people who were mentioned in them. By 1692, when he knew of his inheritance, John was compiling volumes of genealogical material, similar to Burke's *Peerage*. These books show that he was enthralled with nobility, unlike his merchant colleague Sir Dudley North, who shunned aristocratic pride. John drew coats of arms in the margins of the documents and updated them until he died.[12] With the help of his neighbour, the antiquarian Browne Willis, he appears to have published a directory of baronets.[13] It is likely that John's reverence for the Verneys' history, genealogy, and records was implanted in Blois. As in other elite families, this proclivity would grow obsessively in successive generations.

Choosing a Career

The family returned to England in 1653, when John was 13 years old. Sir Ralph wished to place him in a traditional Church of England school, but before the Restoration in 1660, this was hard to do. John studied at Barn Elmes with Dr James Fleetwood, the future Bishop of Worcester. After the school was closed by the authorities, John wished to learn mathematics from a Mr Kersey. But from 1656 to 1659, he attended Samuel Turberville's school on the outskirts of London. There he mastered writing, grammar, 'an indifferent Latin', French, and 'command of his viol'. He clearly disliked both Latin and the school and wished to spend time in 'lovely London'. Another younger son who inherited, Sir James Lowther, spoke of country living as 'a poor way'. He too avowed an 'inclination to a life in business in London' that will 'occasion my living there for the most part'.[14]

John repeatedly expressed his own interest in business to Sir Ralph. 'I pray be not angry', he wrote in 1656, but 'if I had the disposing of myself . . . I would go and bind myself an apprentice unto some very good tradesman.' Indeed, Lord Castleton's son, 'whose elder brother was worth £5,000 a year', had just done so. With Verney fortunes in disarray, John knew that he was expected to become financially independent. 'One must have some living now a days', he declared, and 'I do verily think that I am a great deal fitter to be [in] some trade than to be a lawyer.' He pleaded for a more practical schooling where he could learn arithmetic for weight and for measure, 'which ought to be taught rule by rule with the other which is money'.[15]

Although Sir Ralph had considered law for John, in June 1659 he sent him to Mr Rich's school for a commercial education. Over 80 letters in the database describe his experiences in London before his departure to the Levant. 'I would willingly give up all I have to be bound out as other students are,' John wrote, for he wished to be apprenticed to a London merchant. By August, he was learning merchants' accounts and boasting of his progress. John's interest in numbers and calculation placed him in a small but growing vanguard who perceived that they needed numeric skills. As Keith Thomas has shown, numerical training was still hard to obtain at that time, and was thought to be useful only for business. Not until the eighteenth century would more gentry understand that numeracy skills could enhance estate management.[16] John, however, had a unique set of useful talents when he inherited.

John continued to exert pressure upon his father and by September 1659 Sir Ralph asked a merchant, William Wakefield, for advice. Wakefield visited John's school and found him 'perfect' in arithmetic and accounting. He counselled speedy action, for John was already 18, and some men turned down apprentices at that age. Wakefield's own continental trade was 'accounted the surest', but he had not found 'any great good to be done by it'. Barbados and all the islands were lucrative, but 'not to be recommended for a youngster'. Concerning the Indies and Turkey trade, Wakefield declared: 'Not one in three of them thrives, but . . . those which do, it makes them so high that they ask and have £500, sometimes more, with an apprentice'. The 'Turkey' Company was the most influential of all, and Sir Ralph probably thought that John would prosper in the Levant.[17]

After a long search for a suitable master, Sir Ralph paid £400 to apprentice John to Gabriel Roberts (1635–1715), a Levant Company merchant who was knighted in 1678. Unfortunately little of his correspondence survives. The deal was arranged by the alderman, William Love, brother-in-law of Sir Roger Burgoyne, a landowner who was Sir Ralph's friend. Love wrote that £400 was 'the same sum [he] had received from Sir James Harrington's son'. The indenture sealed on 31 December 1659 committed John to Sir Gabriel for seven years to 'faithfully serve his secrets' and to avoid 'fornication . . . matrimony . . . cards, dice, tables . . . taverns or play-houses'. Sir Ralph agreed to provide John's next set of clothes, and he signed a £1,000 bond as security against theft.[18] John now spent his days in Sir Gabriel's warehouse learning to weigh, strip, and measure silks.

Christopher Brooks has shown us that apprenticeship was a social device which instilled commercial ideals as well as skills.[19] Indeed, many of the values that John learned as an apprentice were similar to those of his landed father. John's training as a merchant reinforced these traits, which included a high degree of accountability, a seriousness of purpose, a devotion to order and detail, and a concern for reputation.

In fact, the family had always appreciated John's virtues. His Aunt Gardiner wrote to Sir Ralph with a sense of relief when John became heir. She did not mention Mun's numerous debts, whores, and bastards. She did state that John was 'as good as you can wish him, and like to build up what others has pulled down, for certainly so great a husband has not been in the family for many a year'. Unlike Mun, John considered it 'a thing much against my temper to owe money'. Kin often remarked that John could be depended upon, and Aunt Adams never had 'so punctual a pay master' of her annuity. John's strong work ethic was apparent, for as cousin Pen Stewkeley observed: 'You do not love to sit without a book or a pen in your hand.' His preoccupation with order led him to confess: 'I don't love odd sums' and I 'hate change'. John listed, measured, and counted everything. For example, when he discussed the ubiquitous cold, he declared that he sneezed 'fifty times and some times one hundred times a day'. He probably kept count, for he was not a man to guess at anything.[20]

Yet despite John's attributes which fit him to be a trader, he and his father were taking a risk. A merchant apprentice had to learn many areas of technical knowledge, as a genre of handbooks makes clear. Manuals like *The Merchant's*

Daily Companion provide detailed tables which helped the novice weigh, mark, pack, and value goods. Sample forms, bills, and letters of correspondence try to anticipate every eventuality. Merchants also had to master the complexities of currency values, exchange rates, insurance, and law. *An Essay on the Proper Method for Forming the Man of Business* advises gentle parents that accounting, geometry, navigation, and geography also are important. Its author ran an 'accountants office for qualifying young gentleman for business in Abchurch Lane'. He also provided board, tutors, and classes.[21] Manuals like these tried to give structure to a fluid, developing field. Trade clearly was an uncertain occupation for a raw, untried, gentry youth.

Although becoming a merchant was not easy, a number of factors helped John. One of the most important was his persistent determination to enter trade. Shortly after he became apprenticed, he wrote to his father: 'I am not a little satisfied in this kind of life . . . which you have done me the honour . . . to let me choose.' He hoped that his choice would be 'no less satisfactory to you than if I had become an Inns of Court Gentleman'. Three months later, he trusted nothing would hinder his going beyond sea. 'I assure you (from my heart)', he wrote to Sir Ralph, 'that I never delighted in . . . anything else so much [as] this trade and also in hearing of business both inland and outland.' In 1683, John Henry was similarly 'so prepossest with being for a trade that he matter[ed] not his Latin. . . . ' Years later, Sir Ralph reflected upon John's persistence: 'My youngest son was bent upon it, to be a Turkey Merchant; neither I nor any of his friends could persuade him from it though I ever intended him to the law . . . . I thank God he loves his profession.'[22]

Shifting Attitudes to the Market and the Plight of Younger Sons

Sir Ralph's decision was also influenced by changing attitudes to commerce and gentility. From ancient times, trade involved the crossing of boundaries outside the safe demarcations of household and village. Jean-Christophe Agnew has called commerce a liminal activity, because it bore resonances of uncontrolled exchange and transgression of social boundaries. In medieval England, commerce and profit were severely limited by the Crown, the Church, and the guilds. As town life and trade developed, negative views of the merchant lost strength, but there was no new understanding of economic forces.[23]

During the seventeenth century, however, more people tried to grasp the meaning of economics. Some, like John, were able to embrace new concepts. Others found the changes disruptive and feared social disorder. A new group of writers arose to explain economic principles. In the 1620s, mercantilists described the balance of trade and the need for an alliance between state and commerce. In the 1650s, freer trade was advocated, using Dutch success as a model. In the 1660s and 1670s, pamphlets focused upon interest rates and in the 1690s upon currency and protection.[24]

Lewes Roberts, the father of John's master, and others argued that commerce ennobled the nation and turned landowners' products into profit. These writings assumed the existence of natural economic laws and sanctioned private gain. Sir Ralph, John, and their gentry friends were prone to listen to these ideas. Having lived through a civil war, they could view economic interests as useful bridles against political passions.[25]

By the 1660s, Sir Ralph was ready to apprentice his son in trade. His personal experience with sibling conflict probably affected his decision. John's grandfather Sir Edmund and his elder half-brother Francis had quarrelled fiercely about their inheritances. After fruitlessly petitioning Parliament for redress, Francis abandoned England and died, some say, as a pirate in the Mediterranean. After Sir Ralph's younger brother Tom forged notes, he was sent to Virginia. Tom was in and out of jail most of his life. After the Civil War, Sir Ralph's penniless siblings constantly begged for money. John observed their disastrous situations: all dependent upon Sir Ralph, all in debt. John confessed to his Uncle Henry: 'There is some sympathy between us as younger brothers.' Later in life, he empathized with his Uncle Tom's penury: ''Tis often the fate of gentlemen's younger children', he wrote, 'to be a clog to their families.'[26] John did not want to hang about like his uncles, waiting for handouts from his father.

The Verneys' situation, however, was not uncommon. In 1641, sibling inequities were publicized in *'An Apology for a Younger Brother or a Discourse Providing that Parents may Dispose of Their Estates to Which of Their Children they Please'.* Many an elder son, the author argued, became a 'sinful and shameful creature. . . .' who 'sucks oft times blood . . . of his nearest and dearest . . . brothers and sisters'. Champianus Northtonus in *The Younger Brother's Advocate . . . with Their Petition to the Parliament* denounced fathers who would have younger sons 'gentlemen', but gave them 'little or nothing for the . . . maintenance of it'. The succession crisis that dominated late seventeenth-century politics also raised tensions about inheritance problems. Economic, legal, and demographic trends were partially responsible for the situation. Like other landowners, the Verneys were struggling to rebuild fragile estates. Because they practised primogeniture, younger sons added stress upon already weakened finances. The 'strict settlement' that passed an estate intact from eldest son to eldest son was coming into fashion. In 1662 Sir Ralph used it to negotiate Mun's marriage. But although this type of settlement often gave portions to younger sons, the Verneys' did not do so.[27]

We know that a century of high birth rates ended about 1640, but it is difficult to quantify the numbers of gentry younger brothers after the Restoration. In the 1670s, one writer estimated a minimum of 16,000 younger sons. Contemporaries believed that their employment opportunities had narrowed. 'The trade of the merchant, the military profession, [and] the courtier's life', wrote Ap Roberts, 'advanced many more than now they do.' Two of John's uncles had been soldiers, but opportunities were dwindling. Recently, Uncle Henry had incurred Sir Ralph's wrath by turning down an army command that he deemed not high enough. 'These punctillios are not to be stood upon by younger brothers', wrote Sir Ralph, 'especially at this time when so many persons of worth and honour do take what they can get . . . rather then be left out of all employment.'[28] The numbers of clergymen had also increased rapidly prior to the war and the Church was overcrowded. Law was the alternative that Sir Ralph had in mind for John, but it was competitive and demanded boring schooling. New bureaucratic, military, and professional alternatives were not yet widely available.[29]

Demographic trends that altered inheritance patterns also affected younger sons. Apparently, the landed elite failed to reproduce themselves by a considerable margin in the last quarter of the seventeenth century.[30] John pitied families who were left without an heir, and Sir Ralph was considered lucky to have two sons.[31] This decrease in the numbers of elite offspring eased the position of surviving younger sons by enabling them to inherit estates at the demise of elder brothers. Indeed, John knew at least four Levant merchants who would inherit property because of deaths in the family, and others are cited in apprentice records. Because of this possibility, John's indenture included the guarantee for his father 'for returning your son back to you, if your other should die'.[32] This situation encouraged false hopes and grudges.

Naturally, the insecure position of younger brothers was upsetting to parents. Manuals offered advice to landowners on how to obtain positions for their sons. *The Way to Promotion, or the Young Man's Guide to Preferment* of 1682 is candid and practical. In a series of conversations, a country gentleman despairs of finding occupations for his younger sons: 'All means of thriving by honest pains, study, or industry are bereft to them', he declares. His city friend then analyses every available profession, admitting that most of them are crowded. He describes how to research government records for openings, how to target and make lists of key people who might help, how to give gifts and obtain letters from the great, and how to cultivate clients who might need a professional man. Substantial entry and maintenance costs are itemized for each career. Finally, thirty more menial trades are suggested for gentle sons without funds.[33]

Generally, fathers were told to let children follow their 'inclinations', for different professions required different talents and 'humours'. Obadiah Walker advised young men to put themselves 'in equilibrio' and consider their 'parts, inclinations, bodily health, strength [and] exterior advantages'. In *The Gentleman Instructed*, William Darrell counselled fathers not to give all to the eldest: A 'young gentleman that begins the world without money', he warned, 'ends it without conscience'.[34]

In short, gentry families had tough decisions to make when it came to younger sons. Sir Ralph discussed this topic with Vere Gawdy, who had just apprenticed her son to a Levant merchant, Samuel Barnardiston: 'I confess having but two', he wrote, 'I never intended him that way, but his own importunity (and your example) made me yield to it.' Vere admitted: 'If I could have chose[n] a calling for him, it should not have been into the city, but I have wholly complied with his inclination.'[35] Both parents were willing not only to listen to their sons, but to finance the launching of their careers.

Gentry Younger Sons Enter Trade

In the second half of the seventeenth century, gentry younger sons increasingly entered trade and finance. Yet John and others are omitted from important studies by G. De Krey, H. Horwitz, D. Jones, R. Lang, and P. Dickson. These works sample merchants in particular time periods and limit the pool to men with specific offices or trading incomes. Thus, Jones's *London Overseas Merchants Groups* is confined to those with a £500 minimum trade turnover in 1695, when John and others had substituted investment for trade. Meanwhile, De Krey focuses upon men who held public office. However, gentry sons were likely to avoid corporation positions or livery company admission, revert to non-trade investments, leave trade due to lack of success, or move outside London. Indeed, Levant Company members did not have to become citizens until after the Restoration, and then those living outside London were exempt. John did not hold Corporation office and shifted capital away from commerce in the 1690s, as did the Dashwoods and other families. Not surprisingly, John does not appear in De Krey's thesis and or in many of the subscription lists used by Dickson.[36]

The Verney archive suggests that there were more hybrids like John. In fact, a surprising number of Sir Ralph's country neighbours had sons in commerce. If a circle had been drawn upon a map with Claydon House at its centre, nearby estates with sons or brothers in trade would dominate the area. The group included the first families of the county: the Temples, Dentons, Lees, Hampdens, Busbys, Lovetts, Woodwards, Prices, Lawrences, Maynes, and Duncombes. Furthermore, in 1662, Mun Verney was forced to marry the heiress of a former London merchant. The Earl of Lichfield's younger brother was a ship's captain, Sir John Busby's son became a linen draper, and John's own grandson Kit was apprenticed to 'the greatest merchant' in Cork.[37] Other areas that sent gentle sons into trade from 1650 to 1700 included the West Country, Northamptonshire, and Suffolk.[38]

Although this trend probably reached its high point at the end of the seventeenth century, examples extend into the early eighteenth century. During that time, Squire John Egerton's two sons were attached to merchants in Venice and Holland, while Horatio Townshend's father paid £1,000 for his son's apprenticeship. Although this entry cost was high, he eventually became a South Sea Company director, a Governor of the Bank of England, and a Commissioner of the Excise.[39] One study has found that between the periods 1691–1700 and 1711–1713, the proportion of London apprentices with gentle backgrounds rose from 14.9% to 17.9%. Another finds 22.3% with gentle origins between 1666 and 1720. Richard Grassby's comprehensive study of the London business community shows a pattern of gentle younger sons in trade. Their ability to underwrite the start-up costs of apprenticeship and subsequent demands for capital was crucial. Grassby's statistics and arguments are confirmed in the Verney archive and serve as a guide for the period.[40]

Once in commerce, John followed patterns similar to those of other gentry younger sons. They were usually overseas merchants at the top of the trading hierarchy.[41] Like many other newcomers, John earned fair, but not spectacular, trading profits in Aleppo. He prospered upon his return to London but later put his capital into financial instruments. His marriages also conformed to norms. John married three daughters of London entrepreneurs, but his children's eighteenth-century alliances were with landed families.[42]

The financial and social consequences of these career choices were mixed in terms of benefits. Attaining financial success was often difficult for gentry sons, because they lacked access to city networks. Traditional attitudes lingered and some still believed apprentices lost their gentle status. Richard Baxter's *Compassionate Counsel to all Young Men* warned that rich men's sons were more prone to fall prey to urban vices. By the late seventeenth century, earlier definitions of a gentleman had changed and the Verneys were altering their views about trade.[43]

The title of Edmund Bolton's *The Cities Great Concern, In this Case or Question of Honour and Arms, Whether Apprenticeship Extinguisheth Gentry? Discoursed With a Clear Refutation of the Pernicious Error that it Doth* illustrates their opinions. In 1674, Bolton first reviewed, then disagreed with, a list of treatises that claimed an apprentice lost gentle status. An indenture, Bolton argued, was a civil contract made by a freeborn man whose gentle blood cannot be alienated. Sir Ralph was aware that some did not agree with Bolton and that in France, John would not be 'allowed to wear a sword'. But Sir Ralph vehemently disagreed with this view: 'I despise such idle false stories and believe he may not only wear a sword but use it too. . . . If this were not so, the nobility, as well as the gentry, would not make their younger sons apprentices, as diverse lords have done.' Thomas Watts assured gentle fathers that religion, manners, and 'propriety of expression' can be combined with practical training. He describes a growing class of gentlemen in business, of which John was an early example. John's breeding gave him social graces, while his apprenticeship provided the first steps towards technical expertise.[44]

John's friends and kin accepted his shift from younger son to overseas merchant and then back again to squire. In their eyes, he lost no dignity when he entered the Levant Company. Aunt Gardiner's primary concern was about John's safety, not snobbery. Forty years later she still felt that 'a court place is an uncertainty, a profession is of more advantage to a younger brother, who if he has not learning, had better be a merchant than a courtier'. Sir Ralph's brother-in-law Dr Denton was glad to hear of John's entry into trade. 'I hope he thrives so fast that I may see him Lord Mayor of London', wrote Denton, using a phrase often found in parents' manuals.[45] Not one person suggested loss of gentle status.

Questioning of gentility was less likely to apply to overseas merchants like John. In fact, he was treated with respect during his London apprenticeship. My master 'hath taught me to keep merchants' accounts (for merchants' books) which indeed is not ordinary', he bragged, and he dined with the family at table. Some historians have found that gentle apprentices caused conflict and endured downward social mobility, but this was not the case with John. His portrait, painted before he left for Aleppo, shows an eager young man who is both a merchant and a gentleman (see plate 1).[46] The Verneys' calm acceptance of his entry into trade shows the fluid, more inclusive nature of late seventeenth-century gentility.

Departure for Aleppo

As John's departure drew near, he gathered items for his trip including four hats, two combs, dozens of stockings, twelve pairs of socks and white gloves, two white doublets, caps of laced and satin cloth, twelve handkerchiefs, a cloth winter suit, a silk black suit for summer, six pairs of shoes, one sea chest, one bed rug, and his hat and viol cases. Sir Ralph provided him with Jeremy Taylor's *Holy Living* and *Holy Dying*, and Bishop Andrewes' *Devotions*.[47]

But an ominous event occurred that would have a negative impact on John. Sir Gabriel Roberts' brother William, in whose care John was to be entrusted, decided to leave Aleppo and return to England. Sir Gabriel hoped that John Sheppard, a distant relative of the Verneys, would give John commissions and eventually offer him a partnership. There was no guarantee, however, that this would happen. Anticipating his precarious position, John boldly asked Sir Ralph about his 'intended estate'. 'Children do not . . . catechize their fathers what estates they intend to leave them', Sir Ralph angrily replied. He assumed that John's profits might 'not only keep you but hope you may lay up money'. If you do not 'keep lewd company, and by drinking, gaming, or your own idleness, loose your reputation', Sir Ralph wrote, 'then I shall think nothing too much for you.' Fortunately, John's mother had persuaded Sir Ralph to give him her small Berkshire property at Wasing, but he could expect little else from his father.[48]

John needed money to establish himself in trade, but when he left England, he had little more than £10 in his pocket. Sir Ralph underestimated the capital needs of traders, while John misjudged the problems of winning commissions from Levant merchants. Yet John possessed many skills and virtues needed for merchant success: thrift, honesty, and perseverance; a talent for languages and numbers; family reputation and credit; not to mention a good deal of luck.[49] He also brought a fervour, which his last letter from London betrayed. He proudly repeated Sir Gabriel's 'commission . . . to John Verney now bound for Aleppo

. . . upon the *Dover Merchant*, whom God preserve'. Then he signed his name in bold letters surrounded by huge curlicues. On 30 April 1662, John's ship bore him off to a world of adventure.[50]

Joan Thirsk, Linda Pollock, and Vivienne Larminie have discussed the problems of younger sons, but the topic remains a neglected one.[51] This book considers the freedom of younger sons, as well as their struggles with primogeniture. It suggests that John, and others like him, became agents of change. In his study of gentry emigrants to Virginia, Martin Quitt has argued that younger sons were more likely to create a society that differed from that of their fathers. Many of the Virginians that he described first went to London, where their experiences fostered entrepreneurial views.[52]

Joyce Appleby's 'New Cultural Heroes in the Early National Period' has analysed younger sons' careers in America. She asked how men who had values that might inhibit commerce were able to become business innovators. How did they gain the 'psychological stability and social understanding' to uproot themselves and challenge old ideas? They grew up, she declared, in unstable family circumstances and were driven to create their own successes. Like John, satisfaction with their new lives gave them courage to endure trials. In the process, they prospered and also strengthened their families. Thus, Peter Roebuck credited the rise of the Lowthers to 'the abilities of the younger sons and the fact that the property acquired by them has . . . fallen to the head of the house'.[53]

Finally, Frederick Greenspahn presented younger sons as heroes in *When Brothers Dwell Together: The Prominence of Young Siblings in the Bible*. Younger sons played pivotal roles in scripture, folk tales, and popular literature, despite favouritism towards elder children.[54] These sources help us to understand that younger sons like John, who were not fully integrated into landed society, were more likely to deviate from elite norms. Because they were given more freedom than their elder brothers, they were able to circulate freely about the world, like the coins they were forced to earn. The energy of England's younger sons was thus released to the benefit of her growing commercial empire.

Life as a Levant Company Merchant

John's journey to the Levant took three months, with a stop at Cyprus. Fifty-four letters in the database describe his adventures as an overseas merchant. Always an avid sightseer, John rode nine days on horseback from Leghorn to Pisa and Florence where he saw feast day celebrations. After landing in the port of Scanderoon, he travelled to Aleppo by night with guards to protect him against attack. As he approached the city the next morning, the view was magnificent. Aleppo was one of the foremost trading centres of the Ottoman Empire. It was set atop eight hills and an ancient castle crowned its highest promontory. White buildings capped by towers and cupolas lay inside high walls pierced by ancient gates. Cypress trees and gardens served as green points amidst the whiteness. Since Aleppo was only four miles in compass, John could walk around it in an hour and a quarter. Narrow streets wove crookedly throughout the city lined with covered markets and bazaars.[55]

John was not allowed to enter Aleppo's grand mosque. But he sat upon thick carpets inside cool, colonnaded courtyards of officials and businessmen. Greeks, Armenians, Syrians, and Maronite Christians, as well as Jews and Turks, lived close together. Their walled houses were adorned with bright interior windows, fountains, gardens, and mosaics of the black and white stone quarried outside the city walls. The English 'nation' of merchants resided in their own 'great khan'. John entered it through a fine portal cut with stone roses and a half-foot-thick iron gate covered with nails. Other European merchants, all called 'Franks', and all considered inferior by their hosts, lived in similar isolated khans. Stables, warehouses, and storerooms lay on the ground floor. Above, private chambers opened off a colonnade, giving a feeling of the cloistered monastery.[56] It was a world without women; a world without fathers; a free company of men. John happily joined them as a factor, in hopes of commissions and eventual profit. Here, he would make his first attempt to build the social and business networks that were needed to achieve success.

Englishmen abroad were very sociable, and any new arrival was an excuse for conviviality. Coffee, tobacco, and local wine were plentiful and there were many feasts. In 1676, the Chaplain Henry Teonge was served 'above a hundred princely dishes' on a table more than twenty-four yards long. Many factors kept horses and John rode twice a week. Before sunset, over forty merchants would ride to the Green Plat Valley to shoot duck, hunt, fish, and play handball before eating 'noble dinners' under huge tents. Induction into a genial society, the Knights of Malue, recalled English modes of sociability, whilst set times for prayers and meals lent a flavour of home.[57] John was glad he had brought his viol, for music was enjoyed along with reading from the khan's well-stocked library.[58] This replication of English norms would be emulated by future generations of traders.

But despite these attempts to remain culturally attached to home, John and his colleagues felt isolated. In the mid-1660s, mail from Sir Ralph suddenly stopped, and John heard nothing for two and a half years.[59] John sent pistachios, melon seeds, rare berries, and Turkish habits to his family in return for a periwig, viol strings, a beaver hat, and a crimson velvet saddle. He desperately craved news about kin, especially births, marriages, and deaths. One of his colleagues offered to pay charges on all letters and begged for 'a large map of the whole world . . . of the newest and best description', as well as next year's almanac.[60]

Outside the protected company environment, John encountered new sights, languages, smells, and weather. Because the weather was fine from May to September, the merchants slept 'without any fear of danger or hurt' atop the flat-roofed khan in the 'wholesome' air. They moved freely about the city and observed the dress, customs, and festivals of many peoples. When business was slow, John and nineteen others 'took shipping in an English bottom for Joppa, and from thence to Jerusalem . . . it being the custom for most of our English-men that stay anytime at Aleppo'. This trip further expanded John's experience of different cultures. When he left the khan, however, he faced a hostile, physical environment marked by virulent epidemics. After suffering three months of jaundice, John awoke one day to find his sleeping partner dead of the plague. In the summer of 1669, 150,000 died in Aleppo including a quarter of the English factory, and John lay ill for twenty-five days. A merchant who fled to Scanderoon saw several die atop a mountain pass and he prayed that he might survive.[61]

John arrived in Aleppo when Levant trading conditions were favourable, and he left at their peak.[62] As the Levant trade trebled or even quadrupled in the 1660s, a small number of perhaps fifty factors enjoyed expanding commissions in Aleppo.[63] Their charter protected them from 'unexpert persons' who were 'ignorant' of trade. John was entering a charmed circle, where members voted at frequent local courts.[64]

Nonetheless, business life was fraught with problems. Turkish officials spe-cialized in 'dishonest, wicked, and unfaithful . . . dealings'. John thought they were 'the greatest courtiers of the empire', and his later anti-court views were probably nourished in Ottoman Turkey. Two weeks after John's arrival, English merchants stopped all trade and forbade 'gratuities' until imprisoned Europeans were released. Arbitrary Turkish pressure for money was repeatedly followed by Levant Company efforts to enforce their privileges. John saw that Englishmen were routinely treated with disrespect and often lost control of their affairs. John had the time and distance to gain a perspective about himself and England. The consul at Smyrna, Paul Rycaut, thought the Levant experi-ence gave Englishmen opportunities to 'thank God that thou art born in a country the most free and just in all the world . . . and thus learn to know and prize thy own freedom, by comparison with foreign servitude'.[65]

But were Christian merchants more ethical than the Turks? John had greater troubles with his fellow merchants than he ever had with the Turkish Basha. Sir Gabriel hoped that John might arrange a satisfactory partnership with the merchant John Sheppard whose 12 letters appear in the database. Such an arrangement would permit John to share in profits over and above the small commissions he earned as a factor. Not only did Sheppard balk at a settlement, he and Sir Gabriel's brother William Roberts in England deprived him of promised commissions. They arbitrarily cut John's percentage in half, although they knew it would 'do little more than bear his charges'. Further problems hindered John's success. Most significantly, he lacked connections with London merchants who paid commissions to Levant factors. For example, when William Roberts married into the Dashwood family, fees promised to John were diverted to Roberts' in-laws in Aleppo. John also lacked the permission and capital necessary to conduct his own trading. At first, he made little money,

though he swore 'there are not three in the nation that spend so little'. Embez-
zlement of company moneys by fellow traders in Aleppo made matters worse.
In desperation, John suggested bribing William Roberts with fifty guineas.[66]

Sir Ralph finally spoke to Sir Gabriel, who persuaded friends to give John
commissions. Fortunately, Sir Gabriel was one of the most powerful men in the
Levant Company[67] and he was able to help John from London. Sir Ralph
eventually saw the need to send English merchandise to his son. John could
sell these items in Aleppo, use the money to buy goods, and sell them for a
profit in London. We know Sir Ralph reluctantly sent 'adventures' worth £200
in 1664, £122. 11s. 6d. in 1666, and £200 in 1667. A settlement with Sheppard was
reached in 1668 that gave 3/7 commission to John and 4/7 to Sheppard on
transactions. John now swore he would 'lay up money yearly' and on 28 July
1668, he received the company's liberty to trade on his own account while living
in Aleppo. Despite his problems, John did amass a fortune large enough to set
himself up comfortably in London. From 1662 to 1666, he probably just broke
even. But, Sir Ralph's adventures and increasing commissions had a cumulative
effect, and from 1668 to 1672 he appears to have made money. Because John's
business accounts have not survived, we can only note that he claimed a £6,000
fortune upon his return home. It may have been less, but John's later years in
Aleppo appear to have been profitable, and there are no signs that Sir Ralph
gave John more funds to start his London trading. On the other hand, John's
experience shows the problems faced by gentry sons who lacked city
connections.[68]

Despite John's settlement, he grew anxious in the 1670s, when Sir Gabriel sent
other young men to Aleppo. 'The truth is', wrote John, 'he that takes apprentices (which . . . is the best trade a merchant hath) must send them abroad, and
they are now commonly obliged to do so at the first fingering of . . . the money.'
Moreover, John's partner Sheppard was not to be trusted. As another merchant
put it: 'Mr Sheppard . . . is so much accustomed to such base, shirking tricks
. . . he abuses most of the factory.' Records show that in 1664 the company
seized his goods for non-payment of duties. Sheppard eventually decided to
'make company' for three years with the son of his master Sir Thomas
Bludworth, and then return to England. At this point, John realistically sized
up the situation: 'I am fearful I shall have no employment in this country;
everyone of the merchants whose business I have been concerned in having
other relations or servants on the place of their own.' Sir Gabriel's loss of £400
to a bankrupt merchant in May 1672 was another setback.[69]

Yet other traders' abuses paled in comparison with the bitter stings inflicted
by the Verneys. The contrast between the status of John and Mun was obvious
in their letters. Undisciplined Mun condescendingly lectured John to 'remember you are a gentleman . . . otherwise I shall never own you, for I hate a
poltroon'. He promised money, which he never sent, but only if John followed
'profit rather than pleasure'. After three years without letters from Mun, John
declared: 'I forget not the respect and devoir an after-birth obligeth . . . Tis well

you were not bred a merchant.' He urged Mun to give his sons an estate, 'a thing most of my degree are by law and custom strangers to'.[70] The frustrated feelings of a younger son lay just below the surface of his comments.

But the unkindest cut of all came from his father. In a tersely labelled 'letter to Jack Verney about his not writing', Sir Ralph claimed John was 'negligent in . . . respects and duty'. 'I would sooner choose to die a beggar and dutiful son than live a rich, ungrateful one,' John responded. He was sure his letters had miscarried and yearned 'to be back in good graces—the beloved son of a most loving father'. He begged the continuance of 'fatherly affection to me, whose long absence and new kindred might in any other less generous spirit . . . cause love to faint and turn into remembrance'.[71] John was painfully learning the importance of family.

By 1674 John decided to return to England after twelve years in Aleppo. His letters show that he had confidence in his own abilities, and he planned to establish himself as a merchant in London. The voyage home took him to Leghorn, Genoa, Antibes, Cannes, Marseilles, Lyon, and Paris. After his journey, he made two copies of a travel document entitled: 'Directions to Travel from Leghorn towards England through France'. It listed exact costs for each part of the journey and noted the cheapest routes. But he took time to enjoy 'the pretty, clear-skinned, airy, women' of Marseilles. When he reached Paris he compiled a virtual Baedeker and roamed the city with youthful vitality.[72] There were benefits as well as problems for a free-moving younger son.

John's business ventures in Aleppo influenced his life in many ways, two of which were particularly important. First, John was exposed to a commercial environment marked by bribery and trickery, where one continually had to be on one's guard. In order to survive, John had to trust no one. He learned to wring the last penny from every deal and protect his property above all things. Like Sir Ralph, John led a frugal life and carefully managed his assets. Over time, however, John developed an inordinate obsession about money. After years of trading, John was driven to get the best deal on everything—horses, land, servants, and even wives. After he came into his inheritance it became clear that he was better at managing things than people. When it came to the latter, he was naturally distrustful and assumed trickery. He habitually used agents to perform unpleasant acts and make examples of disobedient individuals. In relationships with kin, tenants, deer stealers, servants, and the poor, John acted more harshly than his father. This fixation upon property created problems, for his stinginess restricted his hospitality. Sir Ralph found these actions self-defeating: 'You will never be the richer for this kind of good husbandry', he warned, as John clashed with others.[73]

John was, however, capable of acts of kindness, provided they concerned something he understood. Hence, he helped his brother's bastard to learn to read, so that he could be apprenticed. And when his gardener's horse was stolen, John offered him money to buy another. Personal property was inviolate and John could commiserate with one who lost it. Likewise, the steward

Coleman, who had helped John since childhood, received kind treatment.[74] But John's largesse was rarely disinterested, for he was not generous by nature, and he would not distribute gifts of venison the way his father had done. Over time, self-interest forced him to curb his greed.

On the other hand, John's experiences affected him positively by giving him benefits particular to cultural intermediaries. When he arrived in the Levant, John was what Paul Siu has called a 'sojourner', who seeks to make a fortune but clings to his own culture. Later in both Aleppo and London, John became what Georg Simmel has described as a merchant 'stranger'—an integral member of the business world who combines inside knowledge with a 'distinct objectivity' due to non-indigenous experience. After he inherited in 1696, John assumed the hybrid status observed by Robert Park: 'a man living and sharing intimately in the cultural life and tradition of two distinct peoples'—in short 'the first cosmopolite and citizen of the world'. John never gave up his gentle origins, but he also felt comfortable in the city. This overlapping duality gave him many advantages.[75]

When John returned from the Levant in 1674, he appears to have been a supremely confident man. Despite failure and isolation, he knew the joys of self-reliance. His time in Aleppo had taught him that he needed city connections in order to be successful. Now he would profit from this experience and build strong merchant networks in London. Yet John did not return solely to a life of trading. He would also renew cherished ties with landed friends and kin.

3

John Verney: Networks of a London Merchant

The Importance of London

When John returned to London in 1674, he found it greatly changed. Parishes within the walls comprised only one-fifth of the greater London area, and the commercial fabric had been rebuilt since the fire of 1666. John was stunned by the city's growth: 'Walking in London differs much from doing so in the country', he complained. 'The roughness of the treading, the rubbing by people, and the bustle of 'em wearies the body and giddies . . . the head.'[1] In 1500 ten continental cities were larger than London; in 1600 there were only two; and by 1700, none. London had the largest percentage of any country's inhabitants, increasing from 5% to 11.5% from 1650 to 1700. While population was levelling off in other parts of England, London's 120,000 to 150,000 inhabitants in 1550 surged from 200,000 to 575,000 in the seventeenth century.[2]

Outside the city walls to the east and north, foreign and domestic workers found jobs created by the massive growth of trade. But the biggest population push occurred in the western fields between the city and Westminster.[3] By 1700 a trading hub of docks, shipping, and industry lay to the east, the city within the walls hugged the middle, while the court and the world of fashion spread to the west.[4]

This spatial picture reveals the capital's multi-dimensional functions that had been evolving over centuries. But by 1700 London was affecting the nation in qualitative and quantitative ways. Its economic development had created a national market and increased agricultural productivity, as well as a rise in real incomes. Moreover, London was the nation's legal, administrative, social, economic, and political centre. Unlike Aleppo, it was located at the heart of a vast, commercial empire.[5] Migration to the capital rose to over 8,000 people per year, and urban attitudes were becoming more 'rational'. The capital was the driving engine for a massive reconfiguration of the nation's wealth, power, and values. No wonder one in six adults decided to live part of his or her life in town.[6]

But though London served the entire nation, it captivated the landed gentry. Many types of documents show their mounting presence: royal proclamations, heralds' visitations, building surveys, parish rate books, records of county feasts, London guidebooks, stewards' correspondence, and manuals for the gentry on how to behave in town. London's growth, however, was considered dangerous by the Crown. Seventeen proclamations from 1596 to 1640 threatened landed families with fines for living in the capital, and some of the Verneys' correspondents were listed as delinquents. These edicts revealed a change in elite residence patterns, especially those of women. For example, in October 1615, Lady [Anne] Newdigate leased a house in Hackney for 'launching her children into polite society'. A proclamation of 1622 called the influx of women 'an innovation and abuse lately crept in'.[7]

The country was so empty, remarked the *Country Gentleman's Vade Mecum*, 'that a true Englishman cannot look into it without . . . pity and concern'. In 1670 Sir William Coventry blamed the gentry's absence for 'decaying rents', and stewards wrote anxiously for direction. Pamphlets claimed that gentleman neglected their estates and lived 'carelessly and voluptuously' in London. Although minor gentry picked up some responsibilities, it was still the duty of major country families to administer the law, help the poor, and provide hospitality.[8]

A city/country debate that accompanied the court/country polemic focused on town corruption.[9] Thus, in 1684, *The Young Gallant's Academy* explained how to elude robberies, graft, and lewd women. Lurid pamphlets, however, inadvertently revealed how attractive London had become, as did spirited defences answering them. *Remarques upon Remarques* . . . lampooned dim-witted squires and praised London's learning and culture, whilst guidebooks offered sightseeing tours, maps, and coach schedules for 'all gentlemen, ladies, merchants, [and] tradesmen, both in city and country'.[10] If even a portion of the approximately 16,000 gentle families came to town, there must have been a large influx.[11]

One inducement was fashionable housing. After years of restrictive building edicts, Charles I reversed Crown policy and opened the West End for development. Aristocrats were permitted to build upon large tracts, provided they adhered to royal standards. In 1630 Covent Garden set the model for a self-contained neighbourhood, with church, market, shops, and houses facing a central square. John's grandfather, Sir Edmund Verney, was one of its first residents, and John was born there in 1640[12] (see plate 16). By 1674 Sir Ralph shared a house with country friends in Lincoln's Inn Fields.

These areas offered lighting, water, sewerage, moderate costs, and short-term leases. In the late 1680s, Sir Richard Temple compared the expenses of leasing a town house for a year at £2,292. 4s. to keeping his country house open for nine months a year, and living three months in town. Country living cost him £2504. 17s. 4d. or an additional £212. 13s. 4d. per year. This was a convincing reason to put the servants on board wages and flee to London. Even residents of northern counties like the Lowthers of Whitehaven were spending as much as nine months in London and made only annual or biannual visits to Cumbria.[13] As John Strype remarked, 'the younger sort' came to London 'to see and shew vanity, and the elder to save the cost and charge of hospitality and housekeeping being . . . for a good portion of the year out of the country. . . . '

Why the Verneys Came to London

The experience of the Verneys confirms this gentry migration. In 1694 Sir Ralph's niece wrote from Claydon: 'This very day you have been gone eight months, which I think is an age.' In June 1696 Sir Ralph spent so much time in town that his housekeeper begged for 'leave to come . . . to London, he staying so long there' himself. John's aunts often discussed changes in the town's population. There was joy in November when 'the town runs a pace', but in July it was 'empty of news as well as people'.[14] Since the 1670s, the Verneys' country neighbours also had been leasing London houses, renting lodgings, or staying with kin. Some attended the Buckinghamshire feasts held in London or sent a buck if they could not be there.[15] Several merchants that John knew would later buy Buckinghamshire estates. In practice, there was constant interaction between city and country friends.[16]

After John inherited, kin censured him for leaving town: ''Tis not in order to settle at Claydon winter and summer', wrote his cousin Nancy Nicholas, 'but that you will winter with your old friends in London.' Yet despite the fact that John moved to the country in 1698 and had to administer his estate, between 1692 and 1717, 3,265 letters in the database were written from London and 2,373 were written to the capital (see Table 3, Appendix II). Although these figures show the importance of London, to meaningfully compare John and Sir Ralph's residence patterns, it is necessary to analyse John's journeys to and from London after 1696.[17] Immediately following his inheritance, John maintained his father's patterns of seven or eight months in London including Christmas. He continued to attend trading company meetings and made his steward come to London. Gradually, the pressures of estate duties and John's political ambitions in the country caused him to redistribute and slightly lessen his time in town. But the time he spent at Claydon remained about the same, for he now stayed in Bath for a month each fall and made regular journeys to his Wasing estate in April and October. After he had moved to Claydon in 1698, he had to find London lodgings. First he stayed in Bloomsbury, then in Holborn, and after 1702 in Covent Garden. When he became involved in politics, however, he felt pressure to attend local court sessions. He still spent at least half the year in London but in shorter chunks of time and travelled to and fro at a hectic pace. The lists of goods he carried back and forth (see plate 21) and the 365 letters written about travel show the complexities and hazards of being a commuter. Only in Bath did John extend his journeys, often without Elizabeth, but sometimes with his son Ralph.

John's residence patterns from 1703 to 1710 are particularly difficult to chart. His children married and they too shuttled between London and the country. Now the family was constantly split in different directions, as we shall see in Chapter 4. John's third wife Elizabeth Baker normally went ahead to ready their town lodgings. Then John would dash to London, often in response to letters from his lawyers, his financial brokers, or his children. His friends and neighbours had similar experiences, based on their own ages, incomes, and healths. But the tone had been set in Sir Ralph's day: people wanted and needed to be in London.

The Verneys openly wrote about the reasons that brought them to town. They included, for example: conversation and sociability; entertainment, culture, and education; consumption; news and gossip; politics, the social season, and the marriage market; medical, legal, financial, and professional services; freedom from family oversight, social mobility, and economic opportunity. Of course, not everyone enjoyed London, but most people knew that vital needs had to be met in town. As Sir Ralph put it: London was 'the fittest place to adjust all matters'.[18]

Family members disagreed, however, about London's effect on health. Some found its air smoky and 'stinking'. But Aunt Adams called Covent Garden her 'beloved' and enjoyed 'her health better in that place than any other'. Elizabeth Palmer conceded that Mrs Dormer in London 'wonders at me to stay in the country, and I . . . wonder at her . . . to leave the fresh air and go up to the dusty town'. The drift to the cleaner western suburbs gradually eased people's fears.[19]

Sir Ralph's only objection to town life was its cost. 'London is a place that affords many fine things', he wrote, 'but they are not to be had without money.' Covent Garden's 'playhouse, Beau Church . . . good company and . . . fine clothes', he warned, required 'a good large income'. Yet everyone enjoyed the capital's sociability. 'The main thing that brings you to London', declared a contemporary manual, 'is for the sake of good conversation.' Verney women hated to be left where the 'dull country affords no diversion'. They realized that London could be the gateway to a fuller, more sociable, life.[20] Margaret Cave's husband did not like London, so she had to humour him to get to town. Her best ploy was to take the stagecoach, bring few servants, and hold down expenses. John's third wife Elizabeth was in London so often that the only way she could keep a maid was to bring her along. Once Parliament dissolved the men might leave, 'but the ladies will not willingly go so soon', admitted John. His son-in-law Thomas Cave summed up the situation: 'London', he wrote, was 'women's heaven'.[21]

The women were tempted by the new shop windows that led to impulse buying. John's aunts bought imported fruits, coffee, and spices, while younger women shopped for textiles and jewellery. These items were also sent to Claydon, diffusing the effect of London's market place. Men also indulged heavily in town luxuries. 'You may sooner light on a horse fit for your service in London than in the country', wrote Sir Ralph's steward. John's gamekeeper vowed never again to buy liveries in the country, since the tailor did 'so ill a thing about my clothes'.[22] Such a mistake was never made on the outfits of John's heir. His clothes trimmed with silk buttons, lace, and silver were made by a London tailor, who stitched for Lord Conway and other aristocrats.

The Verneys were indeed the conspicuous consumers described by John Brewer and others, and they were just as interested in culture. In contrast to the country, where deer hunting reigned supreme, the city was filled with societies of learning, while booksellers produced 'huge catalogues written by town philosophers'. Both Sir Ralph and John were bibiliophiles[23] and when John's son Ralph needed polish, he was sent to London where speech was more refined.[24] The Verneys' portraits were painted by London's most important artists, and the family attended musical events and the theatre.[25] John compiled a list of over 150 plays and saved masses of playbills and advertisements for operas and concerts.[26]

One of the most important reasons to come to London was to slake the thirst for gossip and information. Nancy Nicholas thanked John profusely for his letters: 'Us mortals are in the state (not of innocence) of ignorance, if London did not afford us some news.' John agreed perfectly with Nancy. 'I know not what you would have more', he wrote Mun, 'for you have all the news at . . . London.' Gossip was a staple of life, and there was only one place to get it—in London. The fact that letters from all over Britain came first to London's post office makes a salient point. In part due to the arrangement of roads, London was the information hub of the country. Hence Sir Thomas Cave wrote to John from Leicestershire for election details. John was nearer London, he wrote, and would be 'better supplied with news political'.[27] After 1688, however, letters often were not enough, for annual Parliaments kept John physically in London. Political power had shifted from the countryside to the capital.

The eighteenth-century Verneys also took part in the London marriage market. As each of John's children considered matches, John rushed to London 'that the young ones may see each other and the friends settle'.[28] Marriage settlements were too important to leave to a country attorney. And although Sir Ralph rarely sued others, he often could not leave town because people were suing him. Indeed, the letters cite 106 lawsuits and 120 instances of legal favours. Alexander Denton summed up London's legal importance, when a document required several signatures. Sir Ralph would have to come to town, he wrote: 'It cannot be done in the country.'[29]

The Verneys and their neighbours, the Temples of Stowe, refinanced debts and raised mortgages in London. Both families took advantage of the city's expanding capital markets and falling interest rates.[30] In 1701 John dashed to town on his way from Bath, because his broker could not cash a bond without him.[31]

Medical services were also concentrated in London. The letters contain requests for drugs from city apothecaries, along with 262 references to illness, and 42 to medical favours. Elite childbirths continued to be held in town. Margaret Cave wrote from Leicestershire about her friends' deliveries in London: 'There are several more of our neighbourhood there upon the same occasion, so that we have but a thin neighbourhood at present.' When Sir Edmund Denton contracted venereal disease, he was thought foolish when he left town. In London, John wrote, 'every surgeon hath more experience in the venereal distemper'. The metropolis, he added, was 'the best place for privacy'. The Verneys were sceptical about doctors, but when illness struck they 'hasten[ed] to London'. As Aunt Adams knew: London was 'where what help this world affords is to be had'.[32]

London had a special attraction for people with problems or ambitions: rebels, lovers, dissidents, dreamers, and, of course, younger sons. They came to London for social mobility and economic opportunity, as well as forbidden pleasures, freedom from village restraints, and a stimulating way of life. Women were particularly attracted by London's freedoms. For Mun's daughter Mary, it offered a place for elopement. Surely, Cousin Mary Townsend with her own fortune 'would not have had a shopkeeper in any place but London'. The Verneys' Buckinghamshire neighbour, Lady Atkins was not so lucky. When her husband suspected she had a lover, he refused to let her live in London and locked her up when in town. On the other hand, many a man convinced his wife he had a London lawsuit and instead 'came up to his letchery'. The capital accommodated all types of dissidents. Thus, housekeeper Lillie was not shocked when 'Goody Scot's son turned Roman Catholic in London'.[33]

Economic opportunity, however, was London's most compelling attraction. The story of Dick Whittington was part of a myth of mobility that was linked to the city's rapid growth. For generations, waves of immigrants had arrived with dreams, but now rising incomes and conspicuous consumption gave their fantasies new hope. In 1676, John reported that Alderman Peake had left £40,000, though he had started with less than £40. Others wrote of similar cases without a trace of surprise. No doubt amounts were exaggerated, but social mobility was perceived as a distinct possibility. In 1685, John obtained city office for a Buckingham lawyer as clerk to the Grocers' Company. He also aided a minister's son, who wanted work at the custom-house, or in a brew house, or with a merchant. 'London is the best place in England for a minister', wrote Aunt Adams for her clergyman husband could earn more money there.[34]

Even the Verneys' servants and estate workers migrated to the city. In 1695, John's coachman gave notice 'not to get a better place, but . . . to set up a hackney coach and drive it himself'. 'His wife is a proud woman', wrote John, 'and he hath a little of it himself, and they think it below 'em to be a servant.' Four months later, Mun's country housemaid married a Hatton Garden grocer in order to better her condition.[35] London provided an escape valve for those who wished to improve themselves.

Living in London: Social Life and Networks

John Verney Moves to Hatton Garden (see Appendix IV for network)

When John returned from Aleppo, he stayed with Sir Gabriel Roberts at Carpenters' Hall in the heart of the city. Then he lodged with a wool merchant William Fazackerly on Coleman Street near the Exchange. But though John set himself up as a merchant, he chose not to live among his colleagues like former generations of traders. Nor did he marry a wealthy merchant's daughter, although he had chances to do so.[36]

It is important to see how John's merchant status affected his marriage opportunities. Sir Ralph hoped that John would wed quickly, for he saw 'young merchants have the best offers when they first come over'. He considered John's profession 'as good as most lawyers', who commanded £3,000 or £4,000 portions, and 'as valuable as an office. . . . ' John claimed a fortune of £6,000, yet Mun heard that he was worth £10,000, and Aunt Gardiner was told he had 'but £500 a year and £2,000 in his purse'. In 1679, Sir Ralph valued John's estate at over £1,000 per year, not including trading income. Although we cannot be sure of the sum, John did return from the Levant with his own money. And he established himself in London with his own funds.[37] Unlike Mun who was forced to marry a woman he disliked, John was allowed to choose his spouse, if Sir Ralph approved.

In 1679, John fell in love with 16-year-old Elizabeth Palmer (see plate 3). John described her father as 'an open ingenious person of a mechanick humour', but we would call him one of the 'middling sort'. He lived far outside the walls in the village of Little Chelsea, but he also owned property in Putney, Essex, Hertfordshire, and Leicestershire. Elizabeth's father had refused a gentleman of £100 per year 'who could do nothing but hunt and drink'. It seems that Palmer thought 'a man of trade a better match than most gentlemen with £1,000 per year. . . . The one is bred to nothing but spend his estate, the other knows how to improve it.'[38]

After the couple married in May 1680 they lived with the Palmers, but John hated the long commute to town. It took an hour and a half to get there by land, but he could return by boat if he embarked at the proper stairs. John stayed in London many nights, rather than suffer 'rogues by land, cold by sea, and a dirty walk from Great to Little Chelsea' (see plate 10). It seemed likely that John would settle in the city, after he purchased his freedom. Indeed, he considered a house within the walls on Basinghall Street. It had a parlour, warehouse, cellars, and kitchen below, dining room and two chambers above, necessary houses in the back, and cost £40 per year.[39] Next, John saw a house on Warwick Court with two rooms and closet per floor, offices below stairs, and a yard filled with copper cisterns. Sir Ralph liked a Bury Street house with gardens and a coach house for only £50 per year. John could use the first room for a warehouse, the second for a parlour, and there were no shops on the street, 'only merchants' houses . . . half inhabited by Jews'. Yet these houses, John wrote Sir Ralph, were 'a great distance from your lodgings, Covent Garden, and Little Chelsea'.[40] Proximity to family was important.

John solved his problem by leasing a house in the new development of Hatton Garden which is mentioned in 58 letters. It was just outside the walls near the High Holborn road that linked the city to its north-western outparishes. Lincoln's Inn Fields where his father lodged and Covent Garden where his kin lived were nearby in the West End (see plate 11). Many years later, John repeated his reasons for moving to this location, when he refused to lodge in St James. His old lodgings near Holborn would 'be most convenient', he wrote, 'that being in the middle between the Exchange and Westminster, which are the places where will be my business'.[41] In this neat spatial move, he obtained access to London's business core, its court nucleus, and his kin in new neighbourhoods.

It was not surprising that a social hybrid like John chose to live in a transitional zone outside the walls.[42] There he resided with other liminal groups: actors and theatre-goers; artisans unattached to guilds; and travellers staying in Holborn's inns. Although he had no kin on Hatton Street, the location and price were right.

Hatton Garden was in the parish of St Andrew Holborn, which included Ely Rents and Saffron Hill. The latter was 'a place of small account . . . taken up with the meaner sort of people', but Hatton Garden was a fashionable area. Stow thought its avenues were 'gracefully built and well inhabited by gentry'. Hawksmoor called Hatton Street 'one of the best streets in London', and Guy Miege thought it 'fair and spacious'.[43]

The dwellings had been erected by building-trade speculators according to Lord Hatton's standards. Graceful houses in uniform terraces had twenty-two-foot frontages, two rooms each on three main floors, a basement, attic, back closet, oak staircase, casement windows, and a doorway carved to personal taste. Interiors included ten hearths and were more fashionable than city houses. Merchants and professionals lived side by side with a sprinking of nobles and gentry. By 1693 Hatton Garden had fifteen titled residents, one bishop, two military officers, nineteen esquires, six doctors, and six lawyers.[44]

But adjacent Little Kirby and Cross Streets housed more modest dwellers, and nearby Leather Lane and Hatton Wall led to alleys, brew houses, and workshops. Hatton could not restrain leaseholders from subletting to shopkeepers. But braziers, pewterers, and smiths were not allowed, nor were butchers, fishmongers, or tallow chandlers. John attended the parish church of St Andrew Holborn, but there were plans to build a church on Hatton Street. Perhaps residents were alarmed by three dissenters' chapels behind the yards, one of which held 300 people.[45]

By April 1681, the couple was settled 'at the first wooden balcony on the left hand near Holborn in Hatton Garden'. They rented the house from a lime dealer, Benjamin Cole, and John must have been a tough negotiator. In 1682 his rent was £53. 5s., but by 1688 it was reduced to £45. Before John renewed his lease in 1693, he made Cole alter partitions, make street balusters, and put in fashionable window glass.[46]

John decorated his house in the latest style, and he, not Elizabeth, made decisions, perhaps because of her youth. He hired Mr Smith to 'paint my house and chimney pictures', while Mr Benjamin Stallwood set Dutch tiles around the drawing room hearth. John had a wainscoted parlour, dining room, drawing room, and chamber, but he worried about the gilt leather on the parlour walls, for this was 'the first building work that ever I did'. A nursery was fitted up with hangings and bedstead when Elizabeth became pregnant. After partitions were installed and the furnace was ready to brew beer, John's 'glasses, table, and stands' arrived along with portraits of his father and grandfather. Elizabeth acquired three mirrors, silver plate, twenty-four books, and portraits of John and herself by Godfrey Kneller. Sir Gabriel Roberts helped select tapestries, which were hung in the drawing room by a Quaker upholsterer. But tapestries, tables, and a china cabinet had to be taken out of the spare room when smoke came up from the kitchen below.[47]

Mun felt that John had 'room little enough for your own family and ware-houses', and the cook maid certainly needed more space. She refused to lie 'in the passage room between the two garrets', for 'she never did (nor would) lie in such a damned hole in her life'. In 1680, John put his coachman in livery and purchased horses for a new coach.[48] By 1682/83, his expenses were over £500. Sir Dudley North spent an average of at least £826 from 1677 to 1688, but he had additional costs of public office which John did not incur. At about the same time, Sir Richard Temple and Horatio Townshend, 2nd Viscount were spending over £2,000 annually in London.[49] John's frugality kept costs down, but he was willing to spend money on the accoutrements of a gentleman.

John and Elizabeth appear to have seen themselves first as residents of a neighbourhood community, not of greater London. Self-identity was linked to the space one inhabited, and people were called by the names of their parish or street. Hence John referred to the Nicholases of Covent Garden as 'the Piazza Family'. The city had developed as an amalgam of villages and its neighbour-hoods embraced many sorts of people. In contrast to the eighteenth century, in the 1680s and 1690s there was little residential segregation. Even in the most elegant areas, tradesmen, labourers, and the poor were jammed together with the rich in squares, places, rows, streets, lanes, courts, alleys, and yards, in that order of comfort. Status gradations existed laterally among streets, and also vertically within individual houses: shopkeepers below; servants at the top; household and lodgers in between. Gentry like the Verneys leased houses in fashionable terraces; lesser families rented furnished houses; a floating mass of lodgers crowded into rooms; and servants and apprentices slept in basements and attics. Finally, a virtual army of shopkeepers was dispersed throughout the town.[50]

'Community' may blandly define a social group in a geographic area or convey a positive quality about social relations. Hatton Garden provided a community to John and Elizabeth, in this latter sense. As in Coleman Street, where neighbours rescued John's silk from fire, residents rallied together. John was often interrupted at dinner 'by some gentleman of the neighbourhood about settling grievances of Hatton Garden as to taxing to the poor, watch, etc'. In 1686 there was a house-to-house collection for the French protestants, and a brief was read in the church. If rents rose, residents banded together and demanded reductions. During the Glorious Revolution when the 'mob [was] pulling down houses . . . all men got out arms and lit candles in windows until four a.m.' Hatton Garden exhibited many features of the close country community. John's third wife Elizabeth Baker (see plate 4) lived next door in Hatton Street. And when a neighbour died, John went to the funeral because she was 'buried out of our street'.[51] Citizens served together on vestries and within wards. Thus, street and parish bound people together.

The Urban Way of Life

John's experiences were not limited to Hatton Garden. Just as Sir Ralph's country networks spread out from Middle Claydon, John's city ties reached out from Holborn. John met people of varied ranks, who were literate, numerate, and politically aware. His meeting places were as varied as his acquaintance and included new arenas of public space. As Habermas has suggested, John regularly mingled with other classes in streets and piazzas; in shops and marts like the New Exchange; in parks, walks, and pleasure gardens; in coffee-houses, and taverns, but not apparently clubs; in playhouses and masquerades; in bagnios and brothels.

City contacts were casual, based upon role as well as status, while contract often replaced custom. Lodgers collected mail at a nearby coffee-house, then stepped into a street where encounters were anonymous. Noise and congestion accompanied every step, while shops of all kinds greeted the eye. Indeed, the whole town was a market place for competing products, people, and ideas. London, though itself a cluster of small communities, offered access to diverse public spaces, contact with a mixture of people, participation in urban spectacles, and freedom of movement. 'No place can fit one better', observed Guy Miege about London, 'who delights in a variety of figures and . . . the changes incident to human life'.[52]

John's social life was filled with entertainments, exhibitions, and political dramas. He regularly frequented coffee-houses like Tom's, Gilman's, Knight's, Enderton's, Squire's, and Farr's, but Garraway's and the Rainbow were his favourites. There he socialized with Sir Richard Temple, purchased lottery tickets, conducted business, read the newspapers, and gossiped 'amongst the coffee-house people'.[53] He heard dazzling success stories about men who made fortunes and titillating tales of sexual encounters at masked balls. John waited outside courtiers' entertainments in the courtyard until late at night 'to see them dance . . . with light at all the windows'. Like other young males, he had access to the free-wheeling sex life of the city, and he appears to have fathered a child with a servant shortly before his marriage. Although John denied this charge, he paid £12 to silence his accusers, 'being tender of his reputation and unwilling such a thing should come against him in public upon the stage'. This remark shows the significance of reputation in both commercial and landed milieus.[54]

There were plenty of pleasures, however, that John enjoyed with Elizabeth. They observed the King and his nobles at military spectacles in Hyde Park, and braved crowds to see a 3-year-old speak exotic languages. In 1685 they viewed an East Indian monster with one body growing out of another that was available for investment. In 1684 they went to an art auction at the Banqueting House, but 'great prices' made purchase unthinkable. At Tunbridge Wells, John ostensibly took the waters, but Elizabeth enjoyed the sociability. They saw the Lord Mayor's show 'by land and sea' and followed the King to Windsor.[55]

As they roamed the city, John's religious and political beliefs were moulded by London's environment. Even with so many letters, it is difficult to plumb the Verneys' political and religious convictions, for they were bred to suppress their emotions and adept at masking their thoughts. Moreover, after the Restoration, intense godliness became unfashionable and was identified with political extremism. Indeed, because the Verneys were so politically astute, they hesitated to put beliefs in writing. For all these reasons, there is little direct reference to their faith and politics after the 1660s. Nevertheless, it is wrong to assume that religion was no longer central to their lives. On the contrary, when John returned to London, unresolved problems of Church and state still haunted the Verneys.[56]

To understand John's religion and politics, one must consider those of Sir Ralph, for John was influenced by his father. Sir Ralph was a pious and God-fearing man who bought and read huge quantities of religious tracts. His flight to France was prompted by his loyalty to traditional church governance, but he sided politically with Parliament against his own Royalist father. His Magdalen College training at Oxford left him with puritan leanings and his outward observances were decidedly low church. After the Restoration, however, his Anglicanism became subsumed in a quieter but steadfast faith. By the late seventeenth century, Sir Ralph still believed in providence but made few allusions to Calvinist thought. If a person lived a good life, and showed 'patience and submission', God would grant 'joy and perpetual bliss' in the world to come'.[57]

Sir Ralph's religious and political views were grounded in his love of moderation. After the Civil War, Sir Ralph wished to restore peace to his life, which had been marred by sectarian feuding. The books that he purchased reflected the mid-stream of religious thought. Thus, he gave Jeremy Taylor's guides to John and purchased several copies of *The Whole Duty of Man*. He also kept a stock of 'little prayer books' written by Dr Tenison to give as gifts to friends. This moderate religious position was echoed in Sir Ralph's politics. Unlike Mun, who clung to Whig principles, Sir Ralph refused to take sides during the Exclusion Crisis. And only when the bishops and the Church were threatened, did he finally back the Glorious Revolution.[58]

When John returned to London, the capital was engulfed by religious and political conflict. As it became more violent in the late 1670s, John's opinions underwent change. His early acceptance of dissenters and Whigs shifted to a

more committed Anglicanism and a swing to Tory principles. John's occupation, trading alliances, and ties with the Levant and Royal Africa Companies
contributed to this change.

In fact, John's occupation led not just to toleration, but to intimate socialization with nonconformists. In 1675, he went 'generally to the French Church' and
to Dr Manton's presbyterian meeting house, where attendees were reported to
the authorities. He was present at an Anabaptist wedding, for the bride was kin
to Sir Gabriel Roberts who was probably a dissenter and voted Whig in 1711.
Early on, John opposed laws against nonconformists on both religious and
economic grounds. Such molestation, he wrote in 1676, would be 'prejudicial to
the trade of the city, which is driven by many worthy persons of that opinion'.
But later, as an officer of the Royal Africa Company, he lobbied against free
traders.[59]

After his return from Aleppo, each Tuesday John heard the latitudinarian Dr
Tillotson preach in Pinners Hall. John collected sermons of another moderate,
Dr Edward Stillingfleet, who was chaplain to Sir Ralph's friend Sir Roger
Burgoyne. In 1665, Stillingfleet was made rector of the church of St Andrew
Holborn near Hatton Garden. He later became Dean of St Paul's and Bishop of
Worcester. He performed John and Elizabeth's marriage service and christened
their first child. Latitudinarianism was gathering stength in London, and its
rationality, direct language, and lack of ceremony were likely to appeal to John.
When it came to sermons, John and Sir Ralph agreed they liked them 'short and
plain to common understanding'.[60] As the century waned, John shed his early
interest in dissent and leaned more towards high church principles.[61]

John's experiences during political conflict were as varied as his churchgoing.
He attended spectacles that grew out of the Exclusion Crisis and observed
Parliamentary sessions. In 1679 John saw the Pope burned in effigy from a
seat that cost £10. After the fireworks, the Pope's wax face costing £45 was stored
for another year's use. John immersed himself in the Popish plot, collecting
every scrap of paper about it. At first he believed in the affair but soon he began
to have doubts. He followed or attended state trials, including those of Danby,
Monmouth, Pepys, Titus Oates, and Algernon Sidney. At one trial, he stood so
close behind the Lord Chancellor's chair that he 'could not see the great man's
face'. But he had a good view of dead men's quarters that were impaled on city
gates.[62]

John's early political views emulated Sir Ralph's 'trimming', but he soon
became immersed in party politics. At first, he favoured 'moderate true Church
of England men' and yearned for a Parliament that was 'neither Popish nor
phanatical, but the true medium 'twixt both'. But in August 1679 he denounced
the previous House of Commons that 'wanted nothing but the word 'old cause'
or 'covenant' to play the same (abhorred) game again'. Soon he was supporting
'true Protestants' or 'Church of England men', who were Tory or court candidates. Now he opposed 'the mad separatists', 'noncons', and 'foolish fanaticks'.

Yet although he was a Tory Anglican, he did not actively condone its 'high-flown' branch.[63]

John's membership in a regulated company with close ties to the Crown influenced his political views. He became an official of the Royal Africa Company, with the help of Sir Gabriel Roberts. The two men petitioned Charles II and Parliament for an Africa Company charter and opposed 'factious' Whig interlopers who wanted freer trading. John seldom expressed his political opinions in the 1680s, because it was dangerous to write. Still, his political and religious behaviour grew more partisan as the Whig/Tory conflict mounted.[64]

Social Networks in Covent Garden (see Appendix IV for members)

The diversity of the lives of John and Elizabeth extended to their social networks. In fact, the newly-weds were linked to several neighbourhoods outside the city walls. While John was in Aleppo, the Verneys and their friends had clustered in areas that suited their life styles, life cycles, and pocketbooks. They responded spatially to urban change by choosing different locations for different reasons. Within each neighbourhood, inhabitants developed networks marked by kinship, friendship, and reciprocity. Multiple roles were played by neighbours as creditors, investors, patrons, executors, witnesses, godparents, and pallbearers. As a result, their networks were dense and persistent.

John spent large amounts of time visiting Sir Ralph's Buckinghamshire neighbours and his own kin in Covent Garden. The area, mentioned in 98 letters, embraced the theatrical, artistic, and entertainment communities, as well as London's largest market. Inns, taverns, coffee-houses, baths, brothels, and the Drury Lane Theatre attracted writers, artists, prostitutes, criminals, and a range of London low-life. But on its 'Piazza', large four-storied residences rose above a common arcade. Inside, the nobility, admirals, and bishops lodged amongst the middling sort. Adjacent Russell and James Streets were second-tier genteel streets, but as one receded into back lanes the mix became more spurious. By the 1670s, even the best buildings were subdivided and crammed with lodgers, while shops encroached at ground levels. In 1689 Aunt Gardiner wailed that her closet was becoming a shop, 'so this place will become a place of trade'. In 1683 the house next to hers was searched for 'sixty persons . . . that were suspected for treason'. Worse yet, the scaffolding for Lord Russell's execution was set against Aunt Adams' lodgings.[65]

Covent Garden's rate books show a mix of occupations, incomes, and high turnover, with 'poor and gone' noted next to the names of some titled occupants. But on the 'Piazza', residents might stay for years, and by the 1680s John knew or was related to almost every occupant on the square's north and east sides. In fact, this study shows that the Verneys' Buckinghamshire networks were neatly reproduced in London. It was only natural that friends and kin grasped opportunities to lodge in or rent houses near each other. However, this overlap of city and country residence has been overlooked by historians. From 1636 to 1641, John's grandfather lived at 16–17 in a great double house with a rent of £160 (see plate 16). Each of its four floors were partitioned into a dozen rooms with wainscoting, stock locks, and 'shutting windows' of the latest mode. After the Civil War, the house became too expensive to maintain, and by 1679 Lady Dacres lived there. She proved to be a good connection, for she made a large loan to Sir Ralph. In the late 1680s, Sir Godfrey Kneller moved in, and he painted the Verneys' portraits.[66]

The house next door at 18–19 was occupied by Sir Ralph's intimate Buckinghamshire kin, the Dentons who wrote 83 letters to the Verneys. John and Elizabeth were guests at dinner parties there, hosted by Alexander Denton. In 1686 Sir Ralph and John attended the funeral of their Denton cousin in St Paul's church. John also purchased drugs from the apothecary on the ground floor of Denton's house, who had married a Denton daughter. When the druggist left, his apprentice James St Amand succeeded him 'in both house and trade'. Things were livelier then, for St Amand was a Jacobite and was often arrested on the premises.[67]

Continuing around the corner, John visited Sir Ralph's country neighbour, Sir Richard Temple. In 1676 Temple moved to no. 2 and caused disturbances in St Paul's Church. Fortunately, Sir Peter Lely's Dutch assistant took over Temple's lodgings from 1686 to 1692. Thus, the Verney, Denton, and Temple families, who were so closely connected in the Claydons, maintained their ties in London. They were happy to welcome the merchant and his wife into their Covent Garden society. Naturally, the Temples and Dentons also dined with John in Hatton Garden.[68]

A few doors away, John found his cousins Nancy and George Nicholas. Nancy had been born a Buckinghamshire Denton, and was on intimate terms with John and his wife. Neighbours could be important friends, as Nancy was pleased to discover. Edward Howard, 5th Earl of Carlisle, who lived next door at 13–14, found her husband George a seat in Parliament. Since George had a place at the custom-house, he was in a position to return favours, and he served Carlisle as a trustee.[69] This type of reciprocal patronage based upon neighbourhood was an outgrowth of London's dense residential clusters.

The Nicholases' other next-door neighbour at 10–11, the lawyer Roger North, was closely connected to the Verneys. He was brother to Sir Dudley, John's merchant colleague, kinsman of John's second wife Mary Lawley, and writer of their marriage settlements. At Sir Ralph's request, the Norths lent large amounts of money to his friend, the Earl of Lichfield. In return, John made loans to the Norths.[70] Roger North was also executor to Sir Peter Lely, who lived in the house from 1651 to 1680. The Verneys and the Norths used two neighbourhood craftsmen to execute their family monuments. The carvers, Grinling Gibbons and William Mason, were thus employed in the country by their city neighbours.[71] The Norths let part of their house to lodgers, one of whom was Sir Ralph's friend Dr Henry Paman. John often found Paman there in his dressing gown, and when he died in 1695, Paman left the Norths large bequests of money. It is interesting that the merchant sons of two landed families both spent time at this lively house.[72]

Around the corner, John's two aunts lived upon Sir Ralph's annuities and could only afford lodgings in James Street. A 'John Varney' paid rates for years on a nearby Hart Street residence. Perhaps it was used by Mun's bastard son, for a 'Matthew Varney' was buried in the nearby church. Alternatively, it could have been an investment made by John or a namesake. In either case, John chose not to live near the market, for he preferred the convenience of Hatton Garden.[73] His tight-knit 'Piazza' kin and friends lived like a large extended family, not a nuclear one, and served as patrons, creditors, marriage brokers, pallbearers, and godparents to each other. John clearly preferred to live more privately in Hatton Garden.

Social Networks in Chelsea (see Appendix IV for members)

John was also engaged in the networks of the middling-sort Palmers. The influence of John's in-laws, even after Elizabeth's death, cannot be overemphasized and her father wrote the Verneys 201 letters. Their friends and kin automatically became John's, and by extension, they became Sir Ralph's too. Palmer's father-in-law had retired from the city to the tiny hamlet of Little Chelsea (43 cites), which lay on either side of the Fulham Road between Chelsea and Kensington. Hearth tax lists of the 1670s show twenty-three substantial houses, some with titled occupants. But the area had 'a mixed character' with its 'cottages, terraces, lodging houses, private mad-houses, and schools'. Orchards dotted its fields and robberies were frequent on its isolated roads.[74]

Palmer lived at 252–254 Fulham Road, which he purchased for £350 in 1671. The eighteen-room house had wainscoted walls, brass locks, tiles, and 'a piece of scripture' painted over the hearth. Palmer's son Ralph lived in the house until 1746, when he sold it to John Verney's son, neatly linking the generations.[75] John and Elizabeth attended all the Palmers' social events, including Christmas plum porridge and wedding anniversaries. And Elizabeth remained there for three months after her first lying-in. John's children stayed with the Palmers on a semi-permanent basis, even when John opposed the visits. His in-laws gave the eldest, Betty, such good instruction that she was educated at their home.[76] In contrast, Mun and his cousin Denton sent their daughters to Mr Josiah Priest's nearby school. Elizabeth and John visited both girls there and attended the school's concerts. One of them was probably the first performance of Henry Purcell's *Dido and Aeneas*.[77]

John's Denton and Nicholas cousins of Covent Garden also visited the Palmers. The entire group dined in Chelsea with Lords Cheyne and Lindsey, who also possessed Buckinghamshire estates. Charles Cheyne, 1st Viscount Newhaven owned Chelsea manor and his son William had just married. The newly-wed Cheynes and the newly-wed Verneys dined in Chelsea, as they would later do in the country. Eventually, William Cheyne would become John's Tory mentor.[78]

At the same time, John and Sir Ralph socialized with three middling-sort yeomen of Steeple Claydon who were Elizabeth Palmer's relations. It was like opening Pandora's box, for once one allied with in-laws networks inexorably expanded. Joseph Churchill, Sir Ralph's yeoman tenant from Steeple Claydon, became increasingly important to the Verneys. Because he was Mr Palmer's nephew, he was asked to broker Elizabeth's marriage settlement. Churchill had two brothers who kept shop in the New Exchange and a horde of kin in Fleet Street. He was often in the city and found it convenient to dine in Hatton Garden.[79]

So did another Steeple Claydon neighbour, Captain White, Elizabeth's second relative. White brought along his daughters and his son who was to be apprenticed to a surgeon in the city. White's wife and Mrs Palmer were sisters. But Mrs Palmer had also been a serving woman to one of John's aunts. The Palmers' background was obviously a mixed one, yet their wealth and outward gentility made them acceptable. William Chaloner, a squire from Steeple Claydon, was a third Palmer relation. Originally lord of the manor, he was now heavily in debt to John's father-in-law. Sir Ralph and John socialized with all three relatives and their families at Little Chelsea.[80]

Like Hatton Garden, Chelsea bore elements of a close country community. Palmer's son Ralph married his next-door neighbour. And both the Cheynes and the Palmers placed memorials in the aisle of Chelsea Church. When smallpox came to the Fulham Road, Mrs Palmer put food in the middle of the street for reapers who lived across the way.[81] Yet the Chelsea community was not insular. At the Palmers' house, Sir Ralph and John mingled with old kin and new relations, provincial friends and London acquaintances, the nobility and country gentry, city professionals and the 'middling sort'. It was a far cry from the tight nuclear family confined to bonds with others of similar status. Paradoxically, London's huge size and diversity led to intimate local networks that transcended economic and status categories. In contrast to their country counterparts, Londoners were less confined by rank and developed personal contacts in more uninhibited, intermixed ways.

Working in London—Merchant Life and Networks, 1670–1690

John Verney's Merchant Networks

John's merchant networks were marked by the same diversity as those in the western part of town. The traders in them had hazy backgrounds that often included country origins and they wrote at least 65 letters to the Verneys. Aunt Gardiner's definition of merchants was simple: 'They are commonly rich men.' Gregory King placed them in the wealthiest business group (see Tables 1 and 2, Appendix II),[82] but contemporaries had trouble defining them. John Stow thought they had 'great credit and repute among us . . . their equipage noble . . . many of them honoured by the Prince with knighthood'. He divided the urban social structure into three huge groups, distinguishing merchants from 'handicraftsmen' and common labourers. He also observed three kinds of merchants: those skilled in 'navigation by which the merchandises are brought and carried in and out over the seas; invection [or importation] by which the commodities are gathered into the city . . . ; and negotiation . . . the keeping of a retailing or standing shop'. Defoe subdivided Stowe's handicraftsmen into those who made the goods they sold in contrast to tradesmen who were shopkeepers.[83] There was a great deal of overlap, however, among all these categories.

When the Verneys said 'merchant', they usually meant an overseas trader. Thus, in this study the word 'merchant' also indicates someone trading abroad. Generally, this group experienced a slow start like John, then growth was followed by a levelling off at lower rates of return.[84] Of course, geographic trading area and products made a difference, as did war conditions and foreign competition. Turkey merchants were thought to be members of London's 'greatest company' in terms of wealth and political power.[85]

John obtained his freedom of the Levant Company on 15 December 1674. He was also a member of associations and boards that combined business with socialization, but he never held office in the Corporation of London. Like Sir Gabriel Roberts who paid a £520 fine in 1687 rather than become an Alderman, John avoided partisan politics and confrontations with the Crown.[86] With the help of friends, however, he assumed other positions of authority which gave him access to influential commercial networks. Sir Gabriel's brother William introduced him to the Vintners' Company, where he received his freedom on 21 November 1674. After his induction, John treated the master, wardens, and assistants to an oyster dinner. They went to the Bell in St Nicholas Lane where the meal cost John £3. 9s. He rose to the status of liveryman and junior warden,[87] and served on tax commissions and grand juries.[88] He was now a member of several influential social and business networks.

John was also appointed a Governor of Bridewell, an institution 'for the correction and punishment of idle, vagrant people and strumpets'. In this 'station of great trust and influence', he attended meetings, listened to sermons, and dined with the Governors. One of them, a haberdasher Daniel Baker, lived next door in Hatton Garden and was the father of John's third wife, Elizabeth. Since Baker had been a Governor for some time, it is likely that he helped John obtain the office.[89]

It is hard to think of institutions more prone to dense ties than oligarchic, seventeenth-century trading companies. Colleagues shared both privileges and risks. Pressures from outsiders further united members, especially as 'interlopers' mounted challenges. In 1696 John received a medal via Captain Pickering from a deceased merchant, Benjamin Middleton, for men who had served in foreign countries had special ties. Not surprisingly, merchants' wills formed a thick matrix of reciprocal trustees, guardians, and beneficiaries.[90]

The Vintners' Company was mostly Tory, and both the Levant and Royal Africa Companies opposed Whig interlopers. Still, John's merchant networks included Whigs, Tories, Anglicans, dissenters, Buckinghamshire landowners, foreigners, and even a woman. Angel Harrington, the orphan of a wealthy merchant, lived in John's Hatton Garden neighbourhood. On 3 November 1692 she was admitted to the Levant Company, with the help of Sir Gabriel Roberts. Angel had a £6,000 portion and income from investments in Lincoln-shire and London.[91] In 1695 John, then a widower, proposed to her but she turned him down.

John followed Sir Gabriel Roberts's lead in every aspect of his affairs. Knighted in 1678, Roberts was a leader in the community, rising to Deputy Governor of the Levant Company, Sub Governor of the Royal Africa Company, and Director of the East India Company. When John's trades or investments are found in documents, Sir Gabriel's name is usually in the same source. When Sir Gabriel bought and sold stock or bonds, John often followed suit. Once John's signature was needed as a creditor, and Roberts signed for him. His opinion was sought regarding personal matters, and he served as John's matchmaker more than once.[92]

In return, John journeyed to Hackney to see Sir Gabriel's daughter in a school play, attended his wife's lying-in, and mourned at his son's death. Roberts's kin also had relationships with John. His brother William Roberts, a fellow Vintner, sat with John as an Africa Company Assistant with Sir Gabriel's sons-in-law and a nephew. A 'Guinea Company' court resembled a Roberts family meeting, and John was included in that circle.[93]

John had a variety of merchant allies, many of whom sat in Parliament. Alderman William Love (1618–1689) was a radical Whig politician, while Sir Dudley North (1641–1691) was a Tory. As boys, both North and Verney detested Latin and showed 'a strange bent to traffic'. Both spent years in the Levant, served as Africa Company Assistants, and maintained West-End ties. Like John, Sir Dudley dined in 'exquisite . . . harmony' with 'courtiers, bankers, and divers of the nobility'.[94]

Three life-long merchant friends came from non-gentle families. John Knapp (1638–1710) was the son of a Berkshire farmer. He died owning Buckingham-shire land worth £10,000 after a career as a merchant and an East India Company investor. Knapp became a Tory Common Councilman and in 1697 he registered as a stock broker. His advice about stocks and his help buying Buckinghamshire votes[95] made him valuable in the city and the country. George Torriano and his son Charles played similar varied roles. The father, a cultured linguist, was the author of Anglo-Italian dictionaries and a wealthy marine insurer. He and his son also served John as stockbrokers.[96]

Another father/son team, drapers Simon and Peter Baxter, sent John infor-mation about ships, received dividends, and secured bottomry bonds. In 1706 John called the father 'honest Simon' and invited them both to Middle Claydon. Apparently he considered it appropriate to ask them to his country house. John also associated with men of 'middling-sort' occupations. One Africa Company Court of Assistants included two lawyers, a cooper, linen draper, fustian man, goldsmith, druggist, and sea captain. Although his closest allies were traders, John knew men in these occupations.[97]

John Verney's Trading Activities

On a typical day, John rose at 5 a.m., walked the mile to Islington, and drank the waters for his health. He returned in time to 'meet others at the Exchange at eight o'clock precisely, and thence . . . to two or three merchants' houses, and before ten I must be at [the] custom-house to attend the Commissioners' (see plate 14). Nearby on Fenchurch Street, the Levant Company gathered in Ironmongers' Hall, while the Royal Africa Company met around the corner on Leadenhall Street.[98] It was an easy walk from both halls to Lombard Street, where scriveners and goldsmiths had businesses. John could detour off Lombard Street into Exchange Alley and stop at Jonathan's and Garraway's coffee-houses. This alleyway led to the Royal Exchange, a trading mart of about two hundred shops, where he passed daily through 'the Turkey Walks'[99] (see plate 13). Continuing along Cornhill to Cheapside, John dealt with goldsmiths, drapers, and other retailers. This street took him directly to the bookstalls in St Paul's Churchyard and to the booksellers and silk mercers of Paternoster Row. He often stopped to purchase a volume for his father, before gleaning news by word of mouth inside the aisles of St Paul's Church.[100] As he walked from place to place, he gathered data relating to commerce and his movements were anything but random. Intelligence about trade, ships, and prices was still hard to get, and his walks kept him as informed as possible (see plate 12).

John had a talent for collecting facts and made coded lists of ships, captains, and cargoes. His trading revolved around the arrival and departure of the company's general ships in June and in the autumn. He sent his broadcloths to be cut and pressed and baled them long before the date of sailing. He also drafted bills of exchange when he needed to convert currencies. When ships came in, John hurried to the custom-house to claim goods and pay duties. His cousin George Nicholas was a commissioner and could help John with his problems.[101]

From 1674 to 1685, John regularly sent English cloths to the Levant in return for silk. He also imported cotton, tin, goat's wool, senna, laudanum, pepper, wormseeds, ginger, rhannucho roots, Persian tulips, elephant's teeth, rice, and opium, which 'sleepy drug', he noted, 'may do better than any silk'. Until the mid-1680s, John usually sent three to five shipments a year, some worth over £1,000.[102] Official sources cease after 1685, but letters reveal some trading as late as 1692, at which time he knew he would inherit Claydon.[103] John used at least sixteen different ships hired by the Levant Company and he knew their captains personally.[104] He carefully constructed his city networks, so as to avoid the isolation that had occurred in Aleppo.

John was also involved in the Royal Africa Company. Founded in 1671 'to deal chiefly in negroes', this joint stock monopoly was linked with the Crown.[105] John served on its governing board with Sir Gabriel from 1679 to 1681, from 1686 to 1688, from 1691 to 1692 when stock prices plummeted, and from 1696 to 1697 when its monopoly was challenged.[106] Tuesdays and Thursdays were John's 'Guinea Company' days and he worked from early morning until 9 or 10 p.m.[107]

John was perfectly fitted for the detailed work of an Assistant. In 1680 he investigated a delivery of negroes, some of whom arrived in 'bad condition', but he never mentioned slavery in his letters. He also served on the Committee on Accounts and helped balance the books. Parliamentary lobbying was another duty. In July 1679, he and Sir Gabriel spent the day at Windsor where they had 'discourse with . . . Sunderland and afterwards with His Majesty'. John spent whole days at Parliament during the Exclusion Crisis, but he could not present his petition on behalf of the Company because Charles II prorogued the legislature. 'We go on paying our debts', he complained, 'that if the Company broke, nobody may be sufferers but those that are of it.'[108] John's negative views of the court and its ministers were surely influenced by these disputes.

During his ten years as an Assistant, John received only small annual gratuities for attending 466 Courts of Assistants, 28 General Courts, and hundreds of committee meetings.[109] Information, status, and patronage were the real perquisites of the job, and John probably obtained his black servant, Perry, through the Company. In 1690 Frank White, Elizabeth's Steeple Claydon relative, was appointed Company surgeon. Sir Ralph wrote approvingly of John's position: 'Your employment is so good at the Africa House that I think you do well to continue.'[110] The ability that it gave John to develop networks probably contributed to Sir Ralph's positive attitude.

Yet John's focus on trade declined, even before he became heir to Claydon. War made trading difficult, and John desired safer alternative investments at higher rates of return. In the 1690s, he transferred his energy and assets into new financial channels. Economic developments were primarily responsible for this shift.

Investing in London—Financial Life and Networks, 1690–1720

Although only tiny fragments of John's trading records exist, we can discuss the categories of his income and expenditures. Both depended upon opportunities in London, which changed drastically after the 1690s. A series of economic developments arose which provided new investment opportunities with lower risk and higher rates of return than trade. John accumulated enough wealth to enable future generations of Verneys to obtain land and huge dowries. John, his family, and his gentry friends took part in a 'financial revolution'.

Making Money before the 'Financial Revolution'

John's financial activities must be understood in the context of a shortage of cash, credit, and investment opportunities. Before 1690, even gentry family heads had problems in receiving, transporting, and distributing cash. A cumbersome arrangement called 'the return' arose, whereby local graziers brought funds to the city and were later repaid in the country. Efforts to set up banking facilities and 'supply the want of present money' failed in the 1680s.[111] A debased currency caused havoc and, despite high risk, joint stocks were over-subscribed. In 1676 Sir Ralph begged John to invest money for his friend Vere Gawdy: 'Remember the East India Company' he wrote, 'for I long to have £800 placed there'. Despite John's connections, however, there was 'no hope . . . they having more than they know what to do with'. John tried to put the money in a loan to the Corporation of London, where he was getting 8% interest. But when that was full too, he offered to take the money himself, first at 5% interest, then at 4% when he thought the matter over. In 1681, his own £2,000 in the Corporation was refunded without notice, and he 'knew not where to lodge it'.[112] Lack of investment outlets clearly affected everyone.

Then where did John invest his trading profits in the 1670s and 1680s? John was a part-owner of at least three ships: the *Katherine*, the *Asia*, and the *Princess Anne*.[113] He also shared several marine insurance policies. He made wagers with other merchants about vessels' arrival dates and when the King of France would die.[114] Elizabeth's marriage portion of £3,000 was placed in loans to the City and the Verneys' friends, the Lees. As interest rates fell, John moved in and out of loans, so that he paid a low rate and received a high one. Although he lent to businessmen and the gentry, he could never find enough places for his money and was loath to put it back into trade. In 1687 he had £2,400 on loan at 6%, but was willing to lend up to £4,000 more at 5%. In 1691, John collected £263 in rent from his Wasing property, but in 1689 and 1690 two attempts to buy Buckinghamshire land came to nothing. In the mid-1680s he acquired Battersea real estate[115] and by 1679 he owned seven hundred Africa Company shares. Like Sir Dudley North, he moved assets out of trade after his return to England.[116]

At last, economic developments spurred by war needs provided fresh opportunities. The simultaneous rise of new financial institutions, legislation, instruments, and personnel has been called a 'financial revolution'.[117] The Verney archive reveals a period of investment marked by qualitative and quantitative change. Tied to speculative and intellectual developments concerning science and mathematics, these ventures influenced individual and national experience. New government funds and long-term credit enabled England to finance war and empire. On a personal level, profit was extended to gentry families.

Yet historians have concluded that only a tiny group of businessmen invested. Analysis of subscription lists has confirmed their suspicions that financial innovations affected very few people.[118] The Verney archive, however, suggests that new investment alternatives led to a financial revolution for the Verneys, as well as their gentry, middling-sort, and female friends. Scholars may have missed this linkage by using random ledgers, rigidly categorized subscription lists, and narrow selection criteria. But when personal documents are compared with economic records, 286 investments by a broad range of people emerge into view. East India Company, Million Bank, and Bank of England accounts record the names of the Verneys' middling-sort friends, while investments of unlisted subscribers are revealed in family letters.[119] Male signatures in corporate ledgers were often those of brokers or trustees investing for clients. Indeed, John's banker Henry Hoare and his father-in-law Ralph Palmer both reported mis-named accounts. John insisted that Sir Ralph's investment in the Corporation of London should be put in John's name: 'If it be in a citizen's name', John wrote, 'the Aldermen of that Ward, whence the money was sent in, will have the greater regard to see it reimbursed, for the Aldermen reckon it a piece of honour to have much money sent in.'[120]

The letters are filled with examples that show how women and gentry invested in someone else's name. Wives had particular reason to hide resources and secretly used assets for luxuries, clothes, or sheer survival. Sir Ralph told his landlady to put her money in another's title or else it 'will belong to your husband and his executors'. In a similar spirit, the apothecary, Mary Gape, left a legacy to Mary Finney: 'Pay it not to her husband', she wrote, 'nor to his order, but to the proper hands of the said Mary.'[121] The Verney letters show that in the 1690s both men and women responded to financial innovations.

Making Money after the 'Financial Revolution'

John invested £1,900 in government funds from 1690 to 1693 and £5,400 from 1696 to 1702.[122] He earned as much as 14% interest from government annuities on the lives of his four children and two cousins.[123] In 1695 he bought up the reversion of these annuities which, with income from the Million Lottery, gave him £100 annually for 96 years.[124] John's new investments fascinated his dependent female kin, for the slightest change in their incomes could have critical effects. Aunt Gardiner begged Sir Ralph to invest her savings so that she could 'become quickly a free woman', while her four daughters considered buying annuities. Because they saw 'so many wise men takes these ways to improve what they have', they decided to invest. This statement is important because it shows that new ways of making money were not only noted but emulated. In 1693, the four women gathered up sums from kin and invested in a government fund bearing interest at 6%. A year later, one daughter purchased an annuity which gave her £14 per year, with Sir Ralph acting as broker. Another daughter supported her maid with her proceeds, while a third had but £20 in the world, of which £4 came from her investments. With John's help, his housekeeper also bought an annuity.[125]

Other correspondents were lured by lotteries. And though John viewed those for thread, needles, and pins as 'a very common way to force a trade', he too purchased tickets for the big ones. In new clusters of sociability, Verney women invested together, attended drawings in groups, and gathered to read reports of winning numbers. Nancy Nicholas went to a drawing with twenty-one in her party and 'above 100 numbers to look over'. Cary Stewkeley took part 'to increase my little all I can', while her sisters decided 'to run hazard for their present supplies [of clothes]'. Their mother begged for a ticket, although she was nearly bankrupt. Verney women followed financial opportunities in the newspapers and were able to discuss them intelligently. In 1678 *Advice to the Women and Maidens of London* showed ladies how to keep double accounts. These developments assume importance in the context of English property law. Women normally gave up assets at marriage,[126] but in the 1690s widows, wives, and portionless spinsters could develop financial plans. Even if they had to use males as brokers, kin like John made profits possible.

John chose his own investments carefully, avoiding land banks in the 1690s. He anticipated recoinage and paid debts and taxes to advantage during the conversion. By 1697, he was flush with money, for he received a £3,000 marriage portion in 1692 and another for £3,500 in 1696. Both came from fathers who had made their money as members of his city networks.[127] John's debts were low and he had liquid assets. Hence, from 1698 to 1702 he put £3,000 into the funds.[128] He traded bank and exchequer bills, placed £600 in the East India Company, and made large loans to Buckinghamshire gentry.[129] These transactions helped him to cement alliances with his neighbours.

Let us look at his finances in 1700. The period from 1665 to 1696 was a period of estate consolidation for Sir Ralph. Now, thanks to John's skills, there was cash for expansion. John's two marriage settlements of the 1690s required that he use portions to buy property within 100 miles of London. John now adhered to a financial strategy as multi-dimensional as his networks using city financiers to find investments. In 1701 three men helped him put money in the land tax, while his city and country lawyers looked for mortgages. Simon Baxter searched for bottomry loans, Charles Torriano put £500 into the Million Bank, while the goldsmith Peter Lupart traded bills. As specialized investment fields developed with their own brokers, John put assets into them all. Hence, when Lupart went bankrupt in 1705, only £197 of John's money was affected.[130]

In 1703 when portions were needed for two daughters, John received loans from Ralph Palmer and his cousin George Nicholas. In 1704 he bought land in Steeple Claydon, amassing at least 200 acres.[131] In addition to his Claydon rents of over £2,000 per year, John received a steady stream of city interest income. In 1704 alone, he collected almost £800 from London investments which were only a small portion of his city assets. This study lacks the data to make financial analyses. But if we assume that John was getting a 5% return, his investment capital was at least £4,000. John's city affairs were creating new income for the family, in addition to that which John received from rent.[132] We do not know his income at any particular point in time, but in 1705 he had no portions to pay and would receive £3,000 from his son's marriage settlement.

John's investments in the Royal Africa Company, however, reveal the risky side of London's money market. Like Sir Gabriel Roberts, gentry friends, and his Covent Garden landlord, John purchased the company's stocks and bonds. But after 1691 their value plummeted, setting off calls for money.[133] In 1692 Roger North hesitated to accept John's shares worth £2,350 as security in his marriage settlement. North was wise, for the value of the stock fell in 1693 from 49 on 8 August to 30 on 4 October, when John owned 24 shares. John's account showed £6,000 in 1697, of which he sold £5,000 in February 1698.[134] By 1704 he still had £1,000 in stock, which later fell to £2. By 1713 John's stock was worth only £273. 12s.[135] His financial astuteness was affected by his position as an Assistant and his unrealistic hopes of profit in the Africa trade.

At the end of his life, John put money into land and mortgages, but he always kept some city assets. His financial plan was conservative in its modest amounts, but daring in its breadth and mix of rental income, land purchase, private loans, public funds, lotteries, annuities, and securities of every kind. In short, the financial revolution let John expand his family's fortune. John also helped gentry, servants, and kin to invest. Their names, however, were often obscured through the intentional use of various techniques. Without John's aid, some of his dependent relatives might have experienced bankruptcy.

It was Sir Ralph who insisted that John help his Verney relations, for he saw this as a duty. After Sir Ralph's death, however, John's attitude towards dependent kin changed. In May 1700, he returned Aunt Adams's £500 and refused to help her reinvest it. It was the first indication that he was tired of assisting his kin. Later, he restricted his brokerage activities to his nuclear family and to men and women who were wealthy enough to lend money to him. His letter to Aunt Gardiner's daughters in 1705 sounded the death knell for the paternalism that Sir Ralph had practised. 'I am not in a condition', John declared, 'to maintain poor relations.'[136] At first, the financial revolution created opportunity for John's kin. But although John maintained some of his father's charity, he gradually reduced it. As a result, some female kin were left in a straitened condition.

John Verney's Financial Networks

John's shift from trade to finance not only brought profit, it produced a valuable brokerage network. When John inherited and moved to Claydon House, a group of City financiers helped him to invest. From 1692 to 1717 they wrote him 136 letters. The brokerage business had developed from a mass of scriveners, goldsmiths, and other agents. In the 1620s, goldsmiths began to discount bills of exchange and by 1650 they were taking cash. In Sir Ralph's day, gentry had felt uneasy about such men. John's father-in-law warned him to 'trust never a goldsmith', and in 1676 John wished 'all the bankers broke, they ruining the trade of the whole kingdom'.[137] But by 1681, Sir Ralph told John: 'You do very well to take no more money into your house . . . for tis safer in the goldsmith's shop.'[138] Sir Dudley North changed his mind about them too, and 'when he had left the city and dealt more in trusts and mortgages than in merchandise, he used the shop of Sir Francis Child'. By the 1680s, gentry and merchants kept balances with their goldsmith bankers.[139] While Sir Ralph and John employed John Cogges and Thomas Fowle, Sir Richard Temple dealt with Sir Robert Clayton and 'goldsmith Mr. Child'.[140]

As financial opportunities burgeoned in the 1690s, a new breed of entrepreneurs gathered in London. They saw that profits could be made by acting as brokers and sought licences from the Corporation of London. A City licensing system had been operating since medieval times, but in 1697 admissions procedures were regulated by an Act of Parliament.[141] Brokers were now limited to 100, a fact that showed the fear they inspired as well as their growth. In 1698 they were forced out of their 'walk' on the Royal Exchange, but found a new home in the coffee-houses of Exchange Alley.[142] There they sold and discounted naval bills, bank stock and bills, exchequer orders, and shares and bonds of the joint stock companies. In 1692 John Houghton's *A Collection for the Improvement of Husbandry and Trade* quoted prices of stocks and commmodities. By 1694 it listed sixty offerings.[143]

A growing group of men, initially vendors of plate, now served the gentry as bankers. They included Peter Lupart of the Golden Lion in Lombard Street, and Henry and Richard Hoare of Fleet Street. John kept cash balances in both places, although the Hoares had more responsibility. Lupart, a Dutchman of uncertain background, knew the ins and outs of the exchequer. From 1693 to his bankruptcy in 1705, he purchased stock, collected dividends, placed orders in funds, and sold company bonds. Lupart's broad range of services, however, was not limited to business. In 1698, he found lodgings for John's wife and shopped for her curtains.[144]

When Lupart could not obtain investments, the Hoares stepped in. Their names appear continually in the records of financial institutions. In 1680, John opened an account at Hoare's Bank and kept several thousand pounds there from 1698 to 1705.[145] Lupart and the Hoares did not displace John's earlier advisers. Simon Baxter, who had advised John about ships, now joined the merchants Knapp and Torriano as one of John's stock jobbers. These financiers had a close rapport with John. They told jokes and used coarse language, but they were still invited to Middle Claydon and helped John politically as well. Their relations with John ranged from Lupart's place as a hired inferior to Sir Richard Hoare's equality when they sat together in Parliament. Sir Richard's election in 1710, along with John and 'several of our friends', shows John's city links had only changed, not disappeared.[146]

As John grew older, his financial brokers became more important. He created his own policy of quick risk-taking in a wide array of liquid investments, but they represented him in the city. They played a subtle role in his shift from merchant to squire, for they shielded him from any ugliness that the Stock Exchange might connote. Just as London's integrative power altered the Verneys' social networks, it provided new economic ones as well.

The Verneys' Changing Attitudes and Values

The Verney archive lets us witness a family in the process of cultural change. We have observed John's transformation from gentry younger son to London merchant and have seen the fluid nature of his urban world. John created new metropolitan networks with landed gentry, merchant colleagues, and financiers that overrode social, religious, and political boundaries. In addition, his family gradually absorbed the values of London's urban culture.

Why did the Verneys react in this manner? One reason is that opinions about the market had changed since John had become a merchant. This shift was not solely reflective of the late seventeenth-century moment. In the 1690s, however, a combination of forces converged with new economic opportunities in a time of increasing urbanization. The cultural changes which evolved from this mix are of the greatest interest, for they are usually the hardest to see.

This chapter argues that we can observe such change in the Verneys' response to the metropolis. While the Verneys were sending and receiving gifts of venison, they were also participating in London's market place. Their actions show that they accepted individual gain as a legitimate human endeavour. They were also willing to admit members of non-landed social groups into their lives. This is not say that traditional concepts and institutions were dismantled. Instead, the Verneys assimilated new ideas into their own strong frameworks. It is not necessary to draw a rigid line between a society that focuses upon social relations and one that perceives the value of commerce. Gifts and the market coexisted in the Verneys' lives in a relationship marked by interaction and feedback.[147]

During the seventeenth century, families like the Archers of Warwickshire, the Fitzwilliams of Northamptonshire, the Temples of Stowe, and the Barringtons of Essex, to name a few, invested in the urban market place. In the Verneys' case, we have documents that record their attitudes to their urban environment. In the 1690s, the Verneys constantly talked about trade and money, whereas earlier they had been less vocal. The family clearly realized that their lives were affected by commerce. Thus, in 1692, Sir Ralph prayed for Parliament 'to take the greater care of our trade', while Nancy Nicholas 'rejoice[d] to hear the Turkey fleet was out of danger'.[148] In 1695 Sir Ralph noted that 'coffee beans . . . will . . . be worth 10s. the pound now the East India ships are lost'. Aunt Gardiner was more concerned about the competition with France. She was shocked that the Navy was 'letting the French be masters of the sea'. In 1693 Sir Ralph admitted that trade affected everyone. 'Our merchant losses have been exceeding great,' he wrote. 'Tis also a national loss, as well as the merchant's, for it destroys trading.' This statement was made by a man who, in 1664, did not 'understand the ways of merchants'.[149] Now his views were informed and passionate. The family's view of trade in the 1690s was more positive and definitive than in the 1660s.

Pamphlets credited the improved standing of merchants to their

giving and lending moneys and daughters and intermarriages: the converse and acquaintance thereby gained with persons of highest rank, together with the help of inherent qualities derived from their parents, being mostly the sons of Gentlemen, and the general improvement of the knowledge and the manners of this town. They are . . . become men of such outward parade, and inward accomplishments, that the better sort of them are received by the best gentry.

These words perfectly describe John's experiences and the reasons why he was respected. By the eighteenth century, it was understood that 'formerly trading degraded a gentleman, and now a thriving tradesman becomes a gentleman by the happy returns of his trade'. Lillo, Sprat, and Defoe applauded traders, while conduct books echoed their praise. By 1711 the *Spectator* spoke for many of its readers: 'There are not more useful members in a Commonwealth than merchants. They knit mankind together in a mutual intercourse of good offices.'[150]

Contemporaries recognized these common interests. Yet historians have underplayed them in their desire to show a separate middle-class culture.[151] Studies have suggested that fear of debt produced unique merchant practices: time management, self-discipline, thrift, and double accounting.

But landowners were also anxious about financial and ethical problems. Many of them, like Sir Ralph, improved their estates and supported the reform of manners. Both Sir Ralph and John illustrate the well-known fact that English landlords were open to capitalist ideas. Sir Ralph and his neighbour William Denton experimented with crop rotation, fertilizers, and East India Company investments. At the same time, John and his colleagues ran their businesses in a club-like atmosphere. They relied on kinship networks and based their trading on trust, honour, personal contact, and the oath. These principles may have overlapped with those of the gentry, but they were inherent in the merchant's calling. The trader and the squire shared a material culture of books, legal documents, personal property, and trade marks, if not arms, although many merchants were knighted.[152] An awareness of these shared values led to positive views of merchants.

As the Verneys' opinions about commerce shifted, their attitudes towards money also changed. Letter-writers rarely discussed abstract ideas such as the market economy, but they talked constantly about money and its effects. After the Restoration, declining prices, inflation, shortage of coin, and debasement led to fear about the cash nexus. Money was replacing old measures of value and face-to-face exchange.[153]

It is no wonder that the Verneys had ambivalent attitudes about the moral effects of money. Sir Ralph's letters to John advocated customary limitations on profit. He cautioned John against amassing money 'merely for lucre's sake when you have enough to maintain you like a gentleman'. He warned his son not to pursue a widow solely for her wealth, noting: 'Money is so tempting a commodity that it makes most men's eyes dazzle.' Sir Ralph worried that kin talked of 'will, codicils and money' on their death beds, instead of their souls. In Sir Ralph's eyes, John had an inordinate love of money.[154]

However, conduct books such as *The Gentleman Instructed* disagreed with Sir Ralph: 'Nobility stript of means makes no gentile figure', the manual notes. 'It can't stand without golden supporters.' In 1693 Sir Ralph's sister Pen Osborne declared: 'I am infinitely pleased that you think I have the sort of wisdom as to love money. All persons that love money do preserve themselves and their family from being destroyed.' This creed ran counter to her brother's beliefs, but it perfectly matched those of John and Sir James Lowther, 4th baronet (1673–1755) who 'loved money more than anything else'. John put Pen's philosophy into practice and it strengthened the Verney dynasty.[155]

Still, even John acknowledged certain limits when it came to gain. In 1693 Alderman Gore's contract that supplied stuffing for 20,000 Navy beds drew John's censure. 'Surely the profit is too much', he admitted. Two proverbs in the Verney papers of 1695 show anxiety about gain: 'It is a most difficult thing for a man to use wealth well. Pleasure and riot are attendant of wealth.' In 1700 Aunt Gardiner warned John that his inability to part with money might cost him an election.[156] Unlike their unanimous, positive views of trade, the Verneys' attitudes to money were marked by doubt.

One of the reasons for this confusion lay in the heightened prominence of the market. In the first two decades of the eighteenth century, negative aspects of commercialization became more visible. However, contemporaries made a critical distinction between worthy merchants, like John, and corrupt monied men. Whereas traders created profits for the public good, stock jobbers and money lenders drained the nation, 'their characters dirty as their employment'. These professional speculators were linked to a state run by Whigs. Thus, the rage of party reflected anger against the 'monied interest'—those involved in banking, broking, and public finance. Soon other Whig shareholders were lumped together with professional brokers. The debate looked like a clash between two different groups of people: city men who traded stocks for profit, and country men who did not.[157]

Yet the Verney letters indicate that the boundaries between city investors and squires were often blurred. In 1708 John refused to loan money to his Claydon neighbour, for, he wrote, 'then I should be a monied man whereas I am its reverse, in debt, and consequently a slave to others.' Yet we know that he received over £3,000 in interest from city investments that year. In 1715 John noted that stocks were falling 'which will be a good time now for the money men to purchase. I would I was one of 'em,' he moaned. In practice, however, he bought Bank of England stock up to his death in 1717.[158]

In John's rhetoric, we can sense a society undergoing change. Anxiety about the political order was expressed in terms of dichotomies that helped people deal with issues of church and state. A highly visibile consumer culture added to their fears, for some considered luxury a national sin.[159] These factors made the Verneys feel ambivalent about financiers, in contrast to their positive views of merchants.

Yet although their rhetoric reflected fears, it did not always reveal practice. Despite anxieties, the Verneys embraced financial opportunities. John's worthy example let them place their actions in the context of older concepts. John was not a stock jobber, but a forward-thinking man who preserved his family dynasty. With his experience in mind, the Verneys could view prosperity as a reward for virtue, not as a form of corruption. John's journey from younger son to city merchant and back to Tory squire makes sense if he is seen as an early example of a society en route to gentlemanly capitalism. Descriptions of England's bourgeois aristocrats have been centred upon the country house.[160] The Verney archive now connects them to London's urban culture.

This chapter also allows us to speculate about the impact of the half century culminating in the 1690s. We can think of the relationships between land, trade, and the monied interest as part of a long-term continuum. John's entry into commerce occurred during a formative stage of capitalism, when foundational building blocks were put in place. The 1690s were a particularly creative time when a convergence of trends led to diminishing cultural distinctions between landed and non-landed groups. The rising importance of London, the financial revolution, changing demographic patterns, the availability of a pool of younger sons, and an expansive urban culture created a window of opportunity for men like John.

This study makes no claim that John was typical of his status group, and his experience should not be taken as the norm. More case studies are needed to show the connections between land and commerce over time and in various strata of the elite. However, the attitudes of John and his family help us to understand late seventeeth-century developments, such as the importance of younger sons and the absorption of commercial interests. Further research into the professional lives of younger brothers should demonstrate that John, and others like him, were perceptive 'advance men'. They saw the direction in which society was heading and knew that London was the best place to profit from future developments. Perhaps slightly ahead of their contemporaries in visualizing new modes of behaviour, they were less inhibited by the constraints of landed society.

Long ago, Robert Park observed: 'It is in the mind of the marginal man—where the changes and fusions of culture are going on—that we can best study the processes of civilization and of progress.' Imperial historians have shown that the energy of peripheral elites often led to their conquest of the metropolis. More recently, Natalie Davis has put marginality at the centre of cultural studies, arguing that the 'borderland between cultural deposits . . . allow[s] new growth and surprising hybrids'.[161] These examples teach us that cultural amphibians like John are unusually well suited to showing the processes of historical change.

The Verney case study also encourages us to speculate about the existence of an 'open elite'. Lawrence and Jeanne Stone have argued that after the Restoration landowners closed ranks, creating barriers between city and country. The debate has been vigorously extended into the nineteenth century.[162] Yet the Stones have focused primarily on barriers to merchants in the countryside. In doing so, they may have underestimated London's impact on families like the Verneys.

Because John moved easily in the city and the West End, he makes a perfect lens through which to observe town and country interactions. His experience suggests that boundaries between London and the shires were more fluid than has been imagined. Using London as our laboratory, we can demonstrate that the Verneys' Buckinghamshire networks were reproduced in town. We can also see the mix of elite and bourgeois groups that populated the pages of *The Spectator*. Surely, the accommodation of land and trade is more likely to be found on the streets of London, than in searches for merchant purchases of country estates. Once we accept the fact that the gentry absorbed market values, we can envision the development of a polite urban culture in new ways. With this topic in mind, the next chapter shows how John learned the rules of politeness while he was still a merchant.

Part II

RESPONSE TO LONDON

4

London Modes of Sociability:
The Visit and the Coach

Men and women . . . has always lived for company. Tis hard for them to be confined, conversation being the pleasure of this life.[1]

After John returned to London, he had to learn urban modes of sociability that differed from Sir Ralph's country hospitality. A powerful group of female relations taught John the rules of London's social code. However, his kin rarely mentioned gifts of venison. Instead, conversation focused upon visiting in a coach.

By the late seventeenth century, calling upon one's friends in a carriage became an important expression of London sociability. It was a fashionable way for individuals to gather, and it expressed their power and politeness. It vied with gifts of venison as a symbol of elite culture and revealed a shift in the Verneys' networking methods. Visits were cited in 632 letters from 1692 to 1717 compared with 342 references to gifts. Although there were other modes of town sociability, visits played a significant role in urban life. In the following chapter, this overlooked rite of daily living is used to reveal cultural values. John had to buy a coach and visit friends when he established himself in London. Under his aunts' tutelage, he learned to give and receive hospitality in a 'modish' fashion. Despite family supervision, he sometimes rebelled or made mistakes, but gradually he adopted his aunts' rules.

The Verney archive allows us to reconstruct the body of social knowledge that John had to master. The Verneys referred to what 'the world knew', as did Jonathan Swift, or to what was 'fit' and proper. In fact, there are 222 references which describe a social code. Mentors were essential, for as John's mother-in-law Lady Lawley complained, not everyone showed 'the prick of good breeding'.[2] Polite people did agree, however, that there was an intimate connection between status and manners. Birth gradually became less important as a determinant of rank.[3] Instead, shared norms of public behaviour identified the members of polite society. The use of restrained, but artful, compliment provided a language of courtesy through which social relations were expressed. But although polite conduct was supposed to appear natural, it was a complex art with subtle, concealed methods.[4]

This chapter sheds light on the rise of polite manners that has recently interested historians. Building upon Maurice Agulhon's work on sociability, Dena Goodman and Daniel Gordon have analysed French salon culture and David Shields has described social life in British America. Lawrence Klein has pioneered a discussion of British 'politeness', while Paul Langford has probed the manners of a 'polite and commercial people'.[5] Although it is agreed that eighteenth-century Paris and London witnessed the growth of a civil society, we know little about how it evolved. The story of how John, a merchant, entered London society provides a window into this topic. It provides data about the criteria for gentility and how standards changed over time. Finally, it shows us that a knowledge of urban sociability is central to understanding the Verneys' power.

Sociability, Commerce, and Politeness

The dynamic, urban culture that confronted John was a blend of civic humanism, natural law, and commercial inputs. London was its location, politeness its doctrine, and courtesy manuals its texts. The gentleman, not the courtier, became its ideal type. From Aristotle, the English borrowed moderation and from Cicero, the belief that outward decorum showed inward disposition. Seneca and the Stoics contributed concepts of reciprocity and self-discipline, while Erasmus added a civil education.[6] Gradually, 'politeness' superseded the terms of 'courtesy' and 'civility' that had dominated prescriptive literature. As Norbert Elias has shown us, the rise of court society led to a self-consciousness about manners and a decline in militaristic values.[7]

In addition to these traditional inputs, civic humanism converged with ideas about sociability that were more attuned to commercial life. In the process, a new form of an older gentility appears to have developed in London. The term 'sociability' was coined by natural law theorists early in the eighteenth century when 'society' became a distinctive field outside the state. Given this time frame, it is not surprising that sociability embraced the word 'commerce' in its broadest sense. The two terms were neatly linked by the reciprocal exchanges that took place inside social networks. To contemporaries, commerce meant not only the buying and selling of property according to monetary value. It also signified the reciprocal 'trafficking . . . of conversation, friendship, love and all manner of obligations' amongst diverse individuals.[8]

Letters, gifts, and favours were forms of 'social commerce' that bound individuals together. They are tabulated in Table 4 (Appendix II) along with 826 references to sociability generally.[9] The use of the London marriage market and the sale of titles and offices were additional forms of social commerce. Visiting in a coach, however, affected everyone and was a ubiquitous form of sociability. It had much in common with the competitive self-interest of the stock exchange and the municipal polling place. They were all part of an urban agora, whose distance from the shires has been exaggerated. Indeed, it was the centrality of 'social commerce' to all aspects of life that made the Verneys and their age so sociable.

The Verneys' urban sociability, however, was refined and tamed through the use of polite manners. Rules of proper behaviour were needed in London, where social hierarchies were fluid and the Verneys shared public spaces with an urban propertied class.[10] The declining ability of religion and the court to regulate morals caused anxiety about the social order and led to the reform of manners movement.[11] The rise of a commercial environment necessitated new modes of social interaction to tame self-interest in a polite way. Periodicals such as *The Spectator* and *The Tatler* tried to fill the vacuum and shape a system of public morality.[12] Virtue and commerce, they insisted, could coexist. Later, the Scottish enlightenment would expand this concept and argue that commerce might even polish manners.[13] These arguments allayed fears about luxury, which rose, in part, from Bernard Mandeville's writings.[14] A system of shared polite behaviour might control the market place and counter the inherent fragmentation of urban life.

But though historians agree about the rise of eighteenth-century politeness, it is difficult to define. Because politeness is based upon socially constructed concepts, it is subject to constant change. As Janet Holmes notes: 'Correctly identifying what is perceived as polite behaviour in a culture involves under-standing the society's values.' Furthermore, different social groups and indivi-duals have different norms of politeness.[15] Much depends on who interprets the norms and for what purpose they do so.

The Oxford English Dictionary emphasizes aspects of politeness relating to aesthetics and manners. Lawrence Klein, however, adds the term's social and psychological characteristics that clearly affected the Verneys.[16] He defines politeness broadly as a cultural paradigm—a method of discourse that brought order to society. To this, we should add that politeness reveals gender and power relationships. 'If there is one constant feature of politeness discourse,' writes Peter France, 'it is the place it gives to women.'[17] But politeness can tell us just as much about masculinity, as Michelle Cohen and Philip Carter make clear. We must consider its tendency to emasculate, especially in relation to the French.[18] This notion caused anxiety for the Verneys and made them critical of excessive refinement.

The way in which the Verneys wrote their letters is a good test of what it meant to be polite. The stories that are told in this chapter may also help us to define the term. First, a comparison of Sir Ralph's country entertaining is made with John's London hospitality. It reveals that urban modes of sociability were acquiring their own individuality.

Country and City Hospitality

Sir Ralph Verney was known for his hospitality, which centred on Claydon House. Although he lived in a frugal manner, he entertained liberally. In 1682 Sir Ralph described 'fifteen at our table and eleven servants, in all twenty-six persons'. Moreover, he gave the cook strict instructions to provide guests with 'plenty of everything'. At nearby Stowe, Sir Richard Temple's table was just as bountiful. In 1680, in addition to his family's drink, he provided 'three dozen claret at dinner, ten bottles of sack . . . six bottles more of claret after dinner for men and women below, all the tenants being about ninety'. He still treated the neighbourhood, as well as his own peers, as did his neighbours Browne Willis of Whaddon Hall and Richard Winwood of Ditton Park. Their free-flowing liberality was part of a code of hospitality that considered largesse a duty.[19]

Sir Richard and Lady Temple often arrived at Claydon for dinner without an invitation. In 1694, twenty people 'came in by chance', in time to eat Sir Ralph's gift of venison to Dorothy Bridgeman. At race time, Lady Middleton's house often had company stuffed in it 'as close as peas in a tub', with two or three beds in a row and no room for anyone to be ill. Sir Ralph was expected to make as many visits as he received, and when he entered or left the county, he reinforced his ties through visits. In 1675 he and his elder son Mun made a circular route around the neighbourhood, picking up people along the way on what he called 'our march' around the county. 'I have been from home visiting all this day and go out again tomorrow', he wrote John, 'and so, so, weary and sleepy'.[20]

Sir Ralph instructed Mun in the art of sociability. Hence in 1670, Mun knew it was 'fit' for him to 'get to all major seats' at the New Year. But in 1673, Sir Ralph warned Mun to withdraw himself from an insolent neighbour 'lest he think you seek him'. Because visits were given freely as part of the patronage system, their absence showed a feud in progress. In 1683, however, Sir Ralph moved to London and put his servants on board wages for over thirteen weeks including Christmas. While in town, he dined out every night and often John was invited too. Scores of brief notes setting times and places document these events.[21]

When John married Elizabeth Palmer in 1680, his kin gave him rules for entertaining. In the country the Verneys occupied the top rung of society. But in London they did not move in court circles, though they occasionally attended royal functions or plays. Consequently, it was not necessary for John to give huge banquets, but he often invited guests to dine. In 1681 Sir Ralph praised him for the way he hosted company: 'You treated them as kindred ought to be treated, that is with good plain meat, but not with costly dainties.' In London, a joint could easily be provided by a landlady, and if Sir Ralph sent up produce from the garden, so much the better for the pocketbook. John kept Christmas at the Palmers which saved money. And when John's first child was christened he 'made no more banquet than a cake and . . . wafers'. Gone was the principle of liberality and the duty linked to its provision. A gap was growing between the values underpinning town and country hospitality. Hence John learned patterns of sociability that differed from those at Claydon House. Sir Ralph also accepted these distinctions, for he modified his entertainments when in town.[22]

Still, even in London, food exchange was a key element of social relationships and there are 161 references to dinner parties. Cousin Nancy Nicholas put it well: It was 'kinder to dine' than to visit. In 1681 cousin Nelly Denton showed thoughtfulness when he planned a London dinner. His country housekeeper sent up different foods for different guests, including each of their favourite dishes. Treating friends with courtesy was critical in the city; only the methods differed. Shortly after his marriage, John ordered 'a great leaf to hold twelve or thirteen' for his dining table.[23] Newly married couples had to establish themselves as participants in dining networks. The purchase of the leaf was part of the ritual accompanying John's entry into society.

As in the Claydons, punch bowl and cards were often provided for guests. Yet the Verneys' letters about London parties struck a more racy tone than their country counterparts. Covent Garden dinner conversation at the Dentons' often embarrassed cuckolded guests. And John's cousin, a clergyman, wrote for weeks about putting urine in the wine bottle at Aunt Adams's dinner party.[24] Perhaps it was the same in the country, but the Verneys never wrote about Sir Ralph's gatherings at Claydon House in this vein. The old patriarch had strict ideas about moral conduct. In the freer atmosphere of London, diners may have felt less inhibited. The Verneys' city feasts were acquiring their own characteristics.

The Visit

The Importance of Visiting

It was the simple visit spiced with gossip that became a principal mode of town sociability (see plate 17). Like gifts of deer, visits were more than systems of exchange. They were signifiers of politeness, especially if done in a coach. The Verneys spent more time paying and receiving calls than any other social activity. During a visit, one's speech, carriage, dress, wit, and manners were placed on public exhibition. Visits also could be read by contemporaries as barometers of power relationships. The right to call upon a patron was a public declaration of standing, while the status of one's visitors was another display of influence. Visits fitted perfectly into the Verneys' social code, because they mandated proper self-presentation. Hence, when Aunt Osborne's face was sore and bleeding, she asked her friends for 'leave to come to them with my patch on'. In a similar situation, her kinsman Thomas Gardiner cancelled all visits. 'His face is so broken out', wrote Aunt Gardiner, 'as he cares not to be seen.'[25] Obviously, the whole point of visiting was to be seen in public at one's best.

The visit may also be perceived as a school for manners, where people were initiated into fitness. In 1687 Obadiah Walker's *Of Education* noted that French and Italian parents took children visiting 'to shew them how such demean themselves, and to procure convenient boldness'. During a call, one learned to make the polite conversation that was crucial to gentility. *The Lady's Preceptor* gives readers helpful hints on how to prepare for a visit: 'It would not be at all amiss', it cautions, 'to consider, before-hand, what topics are suitable to the company, and to make yourself . . . mistress of them.' If there is 'a design' to the visit, advises *The Ladies Dictionary*, it is necessary to converse. But if it is made 'only to show ourselves, and let his Lordship know we are alive, we need do no more'. De Courtin's *Rules of Civility* includes sections such as 'how we are to comport our selves when a noble person visits us, and when we are obliged to make returns'.[26]

Visiting also legitimated status, as Lady Denton knew well. In 1706 she refused to receive visitors at her London town house, because its tiny rooms did not reflect her rank. Clearly, she did not wish to have guests unless she could confirm her status. Moreover, when people visited impolitely, conflict often ensued. There was little civility between the Verneys and their neighbours, the Smiths, for Lady Smith did not return Sir Ralph's visits. Nor did she send to see how he fared in 1681, as she rode by Claydon to the races. In 1691 the Verneys quarrelled about politics with their kinsmen the Dentons. Consequently, Sir Edmund Denton forbade visits and would not acknowledge John publicly. The Busbys, however, best understood the importance of visits. They never went to places where they would find the hated Abels, and they made 'that family give them two visits for one'.[27] These examples prove that there were norms for visits, for one had to know the rules to ignore them. Had visits not been so significant, they would not have produced such strong reactions.

London Visiting Patterns

In contrast to lengthy country sojourns, Londoners crammed a mass of visits into a single day. A coach was often borrowed or hired to pay back visits received. A typical morning resembled Aunt Gardiner's travels on 19 September 1693. She managed to see five friends, her tooth drawer, and her oculist, before dinner with John at one o'clock. On 1 March 1694, she visited six sets of people at six separate locations. Evening socializing was just as hectic. On 8 February 1717, Cousin Pen called on John's daughter. Then both women visited the Palmers in Chelsea from five to nine p.m. Later, they played cards with Aunt Adams in Covent Garden and topped off the night at the home of another cousin.[28]

Repeating brief calls sustained a maximum number of city networks. Long distances, on the other hand, made most country-house visits lengthy. In 1697 Aunt Adams felt she acted 'civilly' by remaining only sixteen weeks with country friends. She 'thought it a shame to stay too long with one that was no near relative'. Urban and country visits also placed different emphases upon personal contact. In town, the content of the call was unimportant, as long as politeness was shown by the visitor. Thus Lord Lichfield wrote John: 'If I visit anyone, I will visit you, if only to stop by in the coach and not get out.' The person visited did not need to be at home in order to complete the ceremony. In contrast, the company of country visitors was earnestly desired in order to combat dullness and unite loved ones. In 1709, John's daughter Margaret was 'all chagrin and melancholy' when her guests departed. 'How our spirits will be supported hereafter', she moaned, 'I know not.'[29]

Because society in London had a central core that was wired to a gossip network, constant monitoring of visits was possible. City living also encouraged social display and material values. With increased availability of luxury goods, conspicuous consumption proved that one met certain standards. Clothes, coaches, and liveries became an object of scrutiny, as guests arrived and departed.[30] Thus, visiting grew increasingly like a market, with mounting exchanges among social vendors. There was little trace of Sir Ralph's country philanthropy in these brief public transactions.

City Visits and Verney Women

London women generally had freer social lives than their counterparts in closely monitored villages. When it came to permissible venues, rules had long been established in the country. Sir Ralph knew that his granddaughter Molly might visit a county suitor 'either at or after dinner', but he was uncertain about how to proceed in London. Molly eventually rebelled against country chaperones and ran off to more freedom in town. In 1679 Mun compared his own autonomy with his wife's lack of it in the country. 'When I go up to London', he wrote, 'I shall leave my family here . . . .Neither will I be confined to time or place, for that were to render myself, who am master of a family, a prisoner to it.' In contrast, John's London wives roamed through garden, parks, and promenades without him. They also went to concerts, plays, and spectacles with other women, and visited friends' homes for gossip and cards. In 1679 Lady Mary Newman had the temerity to call on Sir Ralph with her daughter, 'but without the advantage of a husband, since 'tis so modish a thing'.[31] The visit may have masqueraded as a sheltered sanctuary. But when women modified visiting rules, they expanded their control of social space.

John's first and second wives lived solely in London, but after John inherited, the complexities of commuting engendered new patterns. When John was in London, his third wife Elizabeth Baker often made unchaperoned visits from one county to another. She not only stayed with other women, but went sightseeing in county towns and toured country houses like Celia Fiennes. On other occasions, she enjoyed time alone with family and friends. When she came to London, she and John often lodged separately because of crowded conditions. If she did not receive an invitation from friends, she could stay at an inn instead.[32] This freedom was nurtured by London's anonymous environment. In contrast to earlier generations, Elizabeth developed her own gendered visiting patterns.

Finally, John's London wives enjoyed a privacy unknown to country hostesses. Neither Sir Ralph nor Mun stayed with John when in town, for they knew that he 'love[d] to be private within yourself'.[33] Mun's wife Mary in East

Claydon and John's wives in town lived vastly different lives. The visit played a part in this difference.

The Rules of the London Visit

These examples indicate that, by 1700, a London visiting code had evolved. Individuals publicized their visiting days and gave friends the right to call. In 1680 Nancy Nicholas 'accepted' the visits of Sir Peter Lely's daughter. Nancy, in turn, had the right to visit Sir Richard Temple's wife on 'her day'. Proper times for visits had to be considered. Usually, the Verneys received morning calls, dinner was about one, gaming occurred continually, and people visited at night in groups. Some Londoners adopted a later timetable, for there was more than one standard of politeness. Thus, in 1715, the Hills were said to 'lie in bed every day till twelve, go to dinner at six, to supper at twelve, and go on and make great entertainment.'[34] This regimen was unique to London, where activities flourished around the clock.

At every hour, offerings of food were welcome. In 1679, when Ralph Palmer called for sweetmeats, John thought him very 'kind'. And in 1706, Elizabeth Baker treated breakfast guests to two bottles of Rhenish and a pot of chocolate. Despite the demise of sumptuary laws, the clothes in which one visited were regulated. A certain standard of fineness had to be maintained. Some people had to cancel trips due to unsuitable dress. Hence, Isabelle Gardiner made excuses when asked to visit, for 'she knew she must go better in clothes'.[35]

Once a person was accepted as a visitor, the rule of the return was observed. People watched and counted every call to make sure they did not give offence. Hence, Cousin Pen grew 'troubled' when she was visited repeatedly and could return only one call. Aunt Gardiner's daughters were often unable to visit John, because he had not waited on them first. If a visit was attempted when one was not at home, apologies were sent. In 1706 John wrote from Bath to Sir Thomas Tipping: 'I was from home when you favoured me with a visit. But I know your goodness will excuse me, upon consideration that I came here . . . for my health.' Polite people had to anticipate when visits were expected. In 1708 John's son-in-law took his leave before a trip, so that John would not feel slighted. And when a married man left London, friends called upon his spouse. Thus, on 12 July 1693, John's wife received four different sets of kin and was invited to dinner.[36] Not to have entertained her would have been considered impolite.

During the season, visiting greatly increased. In the summer, however, Aunt Adams only drank tea with neighbours, though she yearned to 'meet with gamesters'. Visits were also connected to rites of passage. After lying-in, women received formal visits in bed, but they could not return calls for a month. In 1705 Margaret Cave had so many guests that they had to wait downstairs in the parlour. Four years later, she had fewer callers, but this 'sparse attendance . . . in the ceremonials' meant that fewer returns were required.[37] Weddings provided another excuse for hectic visiting. As Ralph Palmer wrote in 1703, 'a great deal of company . . . attends new-married folks'. Visits were also made prior to and after a death. Before she passed away, Aunt Pen Osborne's status soared, for she was 'much visited by the great ladies'. After John's wife died in 1694, he was 'tied at home by decency', because his mourning clothes had not arrived. Friends could only come to the door, since John lacked proper garments.[38]

Visits relating to patronage also had complex rules. Manuals advised the novice to call regularly upon great men, inquire after their healths, and attend them in times of joy and sorrow. If the patron deigned to return a visit, one must greet the coach in cloak and sword. Eventually, the Whig/Tory struggle led to segregated socialization by political party.[39]

The Tyranny of the London Visit

Although visits required politeness, they could also be cut-throat affairs. Competition over visits by Verney kin was often very fierce. It was like a game of cards played for high stakes. John's aunts continually reproached him for not visiting and complained when he called on others. The lawyer, William Busby, grew anxious when John postponed a visit, for he desired social intimacy.[40] Competition always marked country sociability, but in London it was publicly proclaimed. It cut across all activities from the city to the West End. A market ideology permeated urban social life, just as it dominated business affairs.

Because city visiting was so competitive, some people reacted negatively. Sir Ralph condemned Aunt Gardiner's 'play and extraordinary visiting', while John Evelyn complained about 'the tediousness of visits: which they make here so long, that it is a very tyranny to sit to so little purpose'. Henry Peacham thought 'perpetual visits of vain and useless acquaintance' were one of London's 'snares'. *The Ladies Visiting Day: A Comedy* mocked a city social climber, who was able to forego 'the pleasures of visiting days' only when her husband died. In 1693 a pamphleteer was even more satirical. Visiting with the dead, he claimed, was 'safer and affords more pleasure, because more wit'.[41]

These comments may have reflected male anxiety about the liberating effects of visits upon women. When Elizabeth was invited to Spring Garden without John, she stayed home because of 'wild' female companions.[42] For the majority of people, however, the visit seemed a harmless venue that was more tiresome than dangerous. Thus, visiting was freely extended to women with little awareness of risk. It now became appropriate for ladies to congregate in public. Indeed, the politeness that society required was on display during visiting. Because it was one of the public places where gentility was won or lost, we should see it as a locus of power.

Women interpreted the rules that Peacham and Evelyn hated. They defined its functions, shaped its norms, and excluded men. Other studies have stressed the Verneys' patriarchal nature.[43] In contrast, this study maintains that even closely regulated females had room to manoeuvre.[44] As Verney women interpreted the social code, they constrained men's actions. The following case study has been chosen to show one way in which they did this.

John Verney Learns to Make a Proper Visit

A Narrative Tale

From the moment John returned to London, his aunts guided his conduct. But after he married Elizabeth Palmer, he violated their visiting code. John's problems started in April 1680, when Elizabeth met his family. For weeks the couple visited kin, but they forgot John's Aunt Osborne. She wrote Sir Ralph about her 'kind quarrel' with John and complained that she had not been visited.[45] At the same time, she was saying that John was impolite.

Her letter should have been a signal to John that politeness was important to kin. Instead, he grumbled about rude callers who sandwiched brief stays between visits and rushed off too early: 'They did as gamesters go at backgammon', he wrote Sir Ralph, 'that hit a lot and pass on.' John bridled at this custom but bravely bore gossip about his bride. One guest said Elizabeth 'had ferret eyes . . . and that her face was full of pimples'. 'I never did see but three', John groaned, 'but good manners shall not make me less respectful.' John was learning that gossip was a vital part of visiting, and its presence had to be tolerated.[46]

Despite John's attempts to be accommodating, his post-nuptial visits caused conflict. According to elite practice, the day of John's wedding was concealed. After a private service at Westminster Abbey on 27 May 1680, only the minister and four of Elizabeth's kin dined in Soper Lane at the Rummer. Then the group visited Aunt Gardiner for three hours, but they gave no hint of the marriage. Late that night, the couple wrote Sir Ralph the good news. Until then, all had been shrouded in secrecy. Now, coach after coach of 'jolly company' formed 'a great train to attend the bride'. Even Sir Ralph's landlady visited the Palmers in Chelsea.[47]

John warned his kin that he could not return visits immediately, but on 3 June, Aunt Gardiner found the couple at the home of his cousin Nancy Nicholas. John would regret visiting Nancy, for it caused unpleasantness in the family. Like some of the players at Aunt Gardiner's backgammon table, he had made the wrong move. Three days later, John blundered again by leaving Elizabeth with Nancy while at business in the city. Yet that same day he had written Sir Ralph that he still had no time for visits.[48]

His father's reply was filled with anxiety. He was shocked that John had not left Elizabeth with Aunt Gardiner, 'for both her relation and quality required you should go first to her'. According to the social code, Sir Ralph's titled and oldest sister deserved the first ceremonial visit. John's omission demeaned her status. John assured his father that he would 'pay those formal scores off'. On 9

June after work, he visited Aunt Gardiner and Nancy for a few minutes each. But he also accepted a dinner invitation at Nancy's for the next day.[49]

John defended his behaviour to Sir Ralph by distinguishing a visit from an invitation. He knew that there were different rules for each and that a visit should be unsolicited. Still, he considered neither Elizabeth's stay with Nancy, nor their dinner at her house, 'a visit . . . they being both invitations'. In addition, he had spent three hours with Aunt Gardiner on his wedding day, and if she was angry, he could not help it. But Sir Ralph was unable to condone John's behaviour. You 'did very ill', he told his son: 'You can never excuse it'. He begged John to 'use all the art you can to make up this unhappy breach'. Sir Ralph agreed that Nancy's feast was by invitation, but the day spent informally at her house was a visit, and Elizabeth should have been left with Aunt Gardiner.[50]

The difference between invitations and visits may have been socially constructed, but it was clear to the elder Verneys. John was less concerned with polite behaviour, perhaps due to his absence abroad. He tried to adapt to his position as a married man, but business demands interfered. Worse yet, he appeared to have little reverence for his aunts' social code. Even so, his family was determined to govern him. Unless he wanted to rebel against his kin, he would have to apologize. John was not willing to defy his aunts, although he was testy about the affair. Therefore, on 16 June, he and Elizabeth finally made four formal visits 'to all our friends, though they were not at home'. They stayed half an hour with Aunt Gardiner's daughters and considered their return visits completed. Despite the fact that there was no interaction with Aunt Gardiner herself, she had been publicly honoured by his presence. Although John made no more visits that week, he 'sent my boy among them to know how they do'. He acknowledged his 'ill management and unthoughtfulness . . . never dreaming the consequence'.[51] In the end, John bowed to his aunts' wishes.

Despite John's capitulation, however, family conflict did not subside. A month later, Aunt Gardiner called Nancy Nicholas 'a whore . . . that ugly name' in a seemingly unrelated dispute. But the quarrel between Nancy and Aunt Gardiner over John's visits had merely re-emerged. The result was a breach in family harmony that had serious implications. As Sir Ralph knew: 'Family disputes resemble civil wars, wherein all sides may have reason to complain.'[52] For men like Sir Ralph, who had opposed their fathers in a real civil war, this was no small matter. Perhaps that is why John followed his aunts' visiting code, despite his inclination to rebel.

Similar violations of visiting rules resurfaced in 1681 and 1683, but in each case John quickly made amends. Fifteen years later he was still apologizing to Aunt Gardiner for a perceived slight, this time by his 'giddy-brained' daughters who had not visited her.[53] Clearly, the aunts used visiting to enhance their own status and govern others. Control over manners as a source of women's authority has been concealed from view. John's experience holds it up to the light and exposes hidden female agency.

Interpreting the Tale

Was this just a tale about a petty family quarrel? If so, why was everyone so concerned? At first glance, it seems that one person's criteria for making social calls merely differed from another's. John, Sir Ralph, Nancy, and Aunt Gardiner constructed four interpretations of the same events based upon four different views of the social code.[54] The Verney archive provides numerous accounts of the same incident and shows the merit of this type of analysis. It also demonstrates that 'correct' behaviour altered over time as values changed and gate-keepers vied for dominance.

Despite these explanations, the tale suggests that the distinction between a visit and an invitation was both understood and important. Politeness was not simply a formality but was used to attain status. As the Verneys received John and his bride, they exhibited rank, confirmed networks, and worked out power relationships. John's impolite visits created strife and upset the family's fragile balance of power. When he gave offence and did not accommodate himself to others, he was not acting like a gentleman. John should have admitted at once that different courtesies applied to people of different rank, kinship, and age. Instead, he used personal preference to make decisions and was more concerned about his business and social freedom than with following social norms. The result was family conflict, and since the family was a microcosm of the larger society, this had wider implications.

In fact, neither society nor the family were as stable as they appeared. Cary Gardiner was competing for favour in old age with young women like Nancy Nicholas. A comparison of their assets will clarify this point. John's Aunt Gardiner was Sir Ralph's oldest sister, whose deceased first husband had been a knight. Although she lived in genteel poverty, she still had important political friends. She served Sir Ralph and John as a matchmaker and political adviser. In age, status, and kinship, she outranked Nancy Nicholas, the daughter of Dr William Denton. Aunt Gardiner wrote an amazing 518 letters, but she only received 30 in return from 1692 to 1717.

Cousin Nancy Nicholas hoped to extend her father's intimacy with the Verneys into the next generation through her cousin John. Unlike Aunt Gardiner, she and her husband were rising in status and wealth. She had money for expensive dinners, as well as a coach, both of which Aunt Gardiner lacked, and she wrote 347 letters. Although she only received a fraction in return, both John and Sir Ralph visited her in town and country. Nancy's husband George was a member of Parliament and held a custom-house place. Hence, his political connections were more current than those of Aunt Gardiner. He also served John as executor, offered him large loans, and kept family wills. In a society based upon patronage, the Nicholases had much to offer. They threatened Sir Ralph's sisters, who existed precariously upon family annuities, for when John inherited they would be dependent upon him. As the rivals challenged each other socially, they were, in fact, duelling publicly like men. At the same time, they were scrupulously courteous when they met face to face. Built-in tensions marked the Verneys' London culture, as restraint vied with competitive self-interest.[55] A polite person tried to integrate both qualities in a smooth and graceful manner.

When John dined with the Nicholases, he reinforced their claim to intimacy. Leaving Elizabeth casually with Nancy for the day was even more important. No formal invitation was issued, but John knew that Nancy would willingly share her privacy. In John's London milieu, formal invitations bespoke a less intimate connection than a spontaneous visit. A person who had the right to call without an invitation had a place in the inner ring of a network. In sociologists' terms, the frequency and density of the relationship was considered stronger than others. Most of the world remained outside this central core and were often described as 'strangers'. Thus, Sir Ralph told John not to invite kin to costly dinners, 'for then you use them more like strangers than friends'. He was also firm about the way he wished to be treated: 'I will not dine with you by invitation because you make a stranger of me, but I will come when you least expect me.' Sharing one's meal was an act of intimacy, even sacrifice, and meant more to Sir Ralph than Denton's offering of favourite dishes. Likewise, Elizabeth Palmer's brother pleaded for an intimacy with her son Ralph. 'Always deal freely', he wrote the boy, 'that you would not make a stranger of me'.[56]

Nancy Nicholas wished to enter John's privileged inner ring and therein lay the problem. She encouraged John and his new wife to visit her informally, as well as by invitation. Shortly after their wedding, she told John how much she liked Elizabeth: 'I hope you will not deny me the pleasure of an intimate friendship', she wrote, 'as well as a relation with her.'[57] Because the distinction between informal visiting and formal invitation was understood by all, John's special treatment of Nancy threatened others.

The narrative of John's visits does more than tell a story. It gives an example of how the Verneys constructed social relations in a competitive urban environment. John's visits suggest that an elite urban social code with accepted norms was gradually gathering strength. Yet conflict arose from rival interests, especially those of middling-sort newcomers. Social change put pressure upon old hierarchies and caused tension among kin. But while struggle and self-interest shaped the Verneys' networks, so did the quest for harmony and cooperation. Nancy's longing for friendship played an important role, as did the aunts' true affection. As these strands intermingled, a polite, competitive culture was developing. John's visits reveal its characteristics, as well as its inherent tensions. They also illustrate how women influenced the rise of politeness.

The Coach: A Symbol of Power

Because visiting was a complex act, John still had much to learn. It was not enough to visit quietly on foot; it was more fashionable if done in a carriage. The image of the coach fills books, plays, and verse of the period to such a degree, that it should be regarded as more than a material artefact. As Sir Ralph's venison incorporated country values and transformed gift-giving into a cultural statement, so the coach embodied the spirit of the town and made John's visits polite. Before Sir Ralph died, he sent gifts of venison to confirm his networks. In contrast, John and Elizabeth regularly maintained social ties by exchanging visits in a coach. Both actions were symbolic activities that stabilized social relationships, but the symbol altered as the focus switched to London. In this chapter, the coach appears and reappears, as it did in the letters. We use its everyday journeys to observe cultural values and historical change.

The Coach and its Functions

Although John maintained his father's deer park, he paid far more attention to his coaches. Sir Ralph's old carrier, John Innes, still rumbled down the London road, but his wagon contained few gifts of deer. Now Innes's cart was overtaken by John's gleaming private coach carrying family and friends to town. It was but one of his Lordship's many vehicles, for in 1703 he was elevated to an Irish peerage and became Viscount Fermanagh (see plate 2). His heavy springed vehicle took him to town, a mourning coach served him at funerals, and his light London chariot showed off his family. Of course, London teemed with other transport modes, all of which John used: sedan chairs and hired hackney coaches; river boats, horses, carts, and stage coaches. Yet throughout his life, John bought and sold different types of private carriages. They served many purposes and were not just a form of transport.

For example, John's carriage provided a prestigious place from which to view the not-so-privileged world. Kin jockeyed for space in its cushioned interior. Like the sections of his venison, the coach had its own hierarchy of spatial positions. The owner or person of honour entered first, the next best place was by his right side, then over against him on the other side, and finally in the back.[58] No matter where one sat, a place in John's coach publicly proclaimed status.

The coach also perfectly expressed urban values, like market competition, social mobility, and conspicuous display in public spaces. Because it made a statement about power, status, and wealth, it became a badge of membership in society. Hence, when Sir Edmund Denton was chosen as Knight of the Shire, he quickly 'bought a fine equipage to make a figure'. John carefully decked his own town coach with rich accoutrements: tassels, fringes, brilliantly coloured silk linings, gilded ornaments, and of course, the family coat of arms.[59] Like its liveried coachman, postilion, and outriders, John's coach was outfitted as if it were a person. On special occasions its presence, not John's, was requested, for it served as an extension of its owner's identity.

The coach helped an unknown person to enter London society. The same process was not possible in the country, where personal backgrounds were well-known. Deer were still tied to land ownership, but anyone with cash might buy a coach. Thus, it played the role of a leveller among the Verneys and the wealthy middling sort. By 1694 the status category of a gentleman was linked to coach ownership, as a database at the Centre for Metropolitan History shows.[60] Now, master and mistress used physical display to advertise their place in society.

Coaches also played a part in the patronage system. In 1697 King William III's procession of 'old coaches and poor horses' disgusted John. But in 1714, even John's Tory friends enjoyed a 'noble show' of 206 coaches filled with Whigs with six horses each. Coaches clearly indicated power in an age of party politics.[61]

Finally, the coach reunited fragmented families. When 'the season' replaced its agricultural counterpart as the arbiter of life's rhythms, family members were often separated. Children, wives, friends, and lovers were torn apart like 'limbs' and then reunited by the coach. In February 1711, for example, John lodged alone in London, while his wife visited in Essex, Leicestershire, and Buckinghamshire. Late summer found John enjoying Bath, his wife at her parents' country home, and their daughter Elizabeth with her London grandparents. The Christmas holidays called for a further regrouping.[62] Back and forth the coach plied in overlapping directions, obeying the English goddess of visiting. But its focus was no longer on Claydon House. Its itineraries were governed by London.

The Rise of the Coach

Why did the coach become important at this particular time? Biblical and classical sources had linked coaches to royal ceremonies, war chariots, and processions carrying gods. The Romans had developed sumptuary laws regulating their use and Montaigne associated them with pomp.[63] Greek culture, however, had connected carriages to women and indolence. In 1636 Henry Peacham called coaches 'moving closets of brave ladies and bereft virgins who . . . are unfit to walk the streets' and 'cradles of young children'. Dislike of the effeminate and deplorable roads may have delayed their use.

Nevertheless, by 1585, Stowe noted: 'Little by little they grew usual amongst the nobility and others of sort. . . .' Queen Elizabeth's lavish use of state coaches set an example for courtiers who rushed to purchase their own vehicles. This rise in popularity, however, also caused envy. Watermen and sedan chair carriers vented their fury against the 'sin-guilty coach' and 'hell cart',[64] while municipal decrees tried to limit their numbers. By 1636 there were estimates of over 6,000 private coaches in London.[65] Three hundred licensed hackney coaches for hire in 1650 grew to 700 by 1696, while unlicensed competitors jammed the streets. Coaches were 'a convenience to rich people', an observer noted, 'but . . . a great hindrance to those who . . . go on foot, for the streets being . . . very muddy, the passers-by get terribly bespattered'. As coaches hogged the road, bitter conflicts ensued (see plate 15). In fact, the Verneys' proud kinsman, yeoman Joseph Churchill, was knocked over and killed when he refused to give way to a coach.[66]

By 1673 stage coaches linked London to towns within a twenty-five-mile radius. This development enabled varied ranks of people to ride together. In 1682, John sat with 'a tanners wife on top . . . a cooper in the next degree, and a third person with her sucking child. A reeking scent' groaned John, 'did frequently reach my too sensible nostrils'.[67]

Unfortunately, there were not enough well-maintained highways to accommodate this growth. By the mid-sixteenth century the road system had disintegrated and wheeled traffic was all but impossible, except in the south and east. Even near London, highways were 'a widening circle of mud and misery'. Plagued by accidents, robberies, and even loss of life, travellers made wills before taking a journey. As *The Rules of Civility* put it in 1671, travelling is 'a kind of warfare, accompanied with cares, diligences, and precautions, as well as with down-right labour and fatigue'. Road surfaces were repaired in conjunction with a series of Turnpike Acts starting in 1663. Only in the eighteenth century did they achieve their goals, but roads were at least starting to improve when John returned to London.[68]

Better coach design also led to more comfortable vehicles. Early coaches were merely primitive litters, and carriage bodies suspended on straps did not appear until the sixteenth century. Even then, they were still leather-encased boxes that crashed against every pothole. Royal Society experiments from 1665 to 1667 led to lighter vehicles and by 1670, steel springs finally were in use along with better designed doors and more compact bodies.[69] The eighteenth-century evolution of the coach into a glass, gilt, and leather enclosure contained echoes of a similar enclosure of estates. Both sealed off gentle folk from rude society. Indeed, the coach may be thought of as a secluded private room on wheels that permitted discreet meetings, to say nothing of sexual intercourse.

On the other hand, as the coach grew more opulent, onlookers were encouraged to gaze inside. Lumbering, country giants gave way to a separate group of more graceful town types. In 1714 the Earl of Bridgewater's accounts made a distinction between 'two town coaches' and a 'travelling coach'. In 1689, Sir Richard Temple's bailiff noted similar differences, for Temple's one-ended town chariot 'always hung back'. 'You need a working not a playing chariot', he advised his master. But when he tried to buy one in Northampton, he found that country coaches were 'not so fine' as those made in London.[70]

In fact, town chariots, charettes, and calashes with the top down, gracefully exposed their occupants. Therefore, it is no surprise that London was the place where the coach became a status symbol. It was there that people wished to be seen with their superfluous, expensively clothed attendants. Foreign visitors wrote of carriages with gilded coronets in the corners, 'behind which stand two or three footmen attired in rich liveries'. In 1704 Margaret Cave wrote John about her new, modish coach. 'A glass chariot is an inconvenient way of travelling in . . . August', John responded. 'But tis beauish and that makes amends to your sex, especially when overgrown with pride.' Pepys was at first ashamed to ride in a glass coach, but in 1668 he purchased two black horses and a chariot, 'it being light and will be very genteel'. Once inside, he confessed, 'people did mightily look upon us. . . . It makes us appear great.'[71] Even John Taylor, a spokesman against coaches, succumbed to pride when he rode in one. A coach might be the last thing sold by a bankrupt aristocrat, and a ride in one to execution at Tyburn was a last favour to persons of rank. By 1700 ownership of these showy vehicles had become a requirement for polite families[72] (see plate 19).

Prices, however, soared well above the pre-Restoration average of £20 to £30. In 1642 the Earl of Bedford paid £32. 10s. for a new coach, but by 1682 a smaller chariot cost him £53. 10s., not including £24 for velvet, £14 for fringe, £11 for glasses, and £30 for painting. In 1680, Dudley North paid £45 for his coach and two horses. By 1700, a coach probably required more continuous expense than any other possession, costing at least £50 initially plus £50 for horses, and up to £100 for trimmings.

In 1682/3, for example, £80 out of John's living expenses of £480 went for liveries, coachman, and vehicle maintenance. In 1680 he spent almost £35 for his coach horses. In 1690 John's liveries cost £9. 8s. 6d., while in 1698, he paid over £10. 15s. for silk and fringe alone (see plate 22). Sir Horatio Townsend and Sir Richard Temple made similar large outlays.[73] Sir Richard Temple, 3rd Baronet, tried to save money by refurbishing old coaches and trading in worn ones for new. But the accounts of his son Viscount Cobham show large expenses like the £130 paid to Mr Terrett, a coachmaker. The Verneys' and Temples' Buckinghamshire neighbours had similar problems. In the Chilterns, Lord Cheyne listed expenses from footmen's shoes and stockings to ale for a sick postilion. Meanwhile, in the early 1700s, Lord Bridgewater paid amounts of £49. 15s. 8d. and £66. 4s. 11d. for merely refurbishing his coaches. Fortunately the annual wages of his coachman, postilion, groom, porter, and three footmen were modest: £6 for the coachman, and £3 for the others, though they also received tips, bed, and board. Inventories of coachmakers show the huge number of items and expenses that went into each vehicle.[74] It seems that even frugal families spent lavishly on their coaches.

John Verney Learns to Use a Coach

As with visits, John upheld a polite code that controlled the use of his vehicles. Sir Ralph, on the other hand, had a different attitude towards his coach. He saw it primarily as a means of transport and ignored its ceremonial aspects. By the late seventeenth century, a trip to London took Sir Ralph a little more than a day. He travelled with just a driver and secretary and avoided all signs of pomp. Nor did he fuss with his coach's decoration, but kept the same red and black lining year after year, because it resisted fading. Only the coach's cleanliness interested him. To this end, he hung towels before the windows to keep out dust, used a coach cover, and kept a dust gown in a press ready to wear on trips.[75] As might be expected, Sir Ralph only mentioned coaches in 13 of his letters.

Changing Attitudes to the Coach

Other correspondents referred to coaches in 108 letters, and John mentioned them 81 times. People watched for the latest models and tallied their numbers in mourning parties and royal events. In 1678 John counted 300 coaches bedecked with ladies as Charles II reviewed his troops. In 1696 he saw the Venetian Ambassador attended by 120 carriages. When John married in 1680, he automatically bought a carriage. Everyone knew that a match meant 'the wedding garments are buying and the coach a making'.[76]

As he searched for a house, John counted the number of coaches per street, for he was concerned with status. After he selected his home, John obtained space in a mews for his coach. He knew what type of vehicle he wanted, for he had just helped his cousin Alexander Denton buy one. Denton, who was also courting, bought a velvet-lined vehicle for £60 from a city merchant. The trader had sold it, wrote John, 'because he thinks it too fine for him and hath lately bought a second-hand chariot at £23 without harness'. In 1679 just who appropriately might own a sumptuous coach was still unclear. In 1698 however, a Frenchman noticed that 'diverse of the citizens' houses have port-cocheres to drive in a coach'. By 1709, as *The Tatler* attested, coach ownership had so expanded that there were few restrictions.[77]

When John first bought a carriage in 1680, his father conceded he must 'follow the fashion'. Still, Sir Ralph feared that the rage for flowers in the panels might not 'hold' and that blue linings would fade. Unlike his father, John bought several kinds of vehicles. He often kept his main coach in Sir Ralph's London mews and used his smaller summer chariot until 1 November. When he visited friends in Essex, he rode in his 'light calesh'. Both John and Denton periodically turned in old coaches for new models. Thus, a scant two years after his marriage John bought another new coach, and there were constant outlays for foot lockers, padding, brass plates, and tops that were often stolen.[78]

One reason for buying so many coaches was that John and Denton married several times. Hence in 1695, John again spent days helping the bridegroom Denton select 'scarlet and black striped calamanca lining and liveries'. In return, John was favoured with a haunch of venison. Possession of coach and deer coexisted, but the carriage was the more passionate interest. At John's second marriage to Mary Lawley in 1692, he chose to save money and redecorate his old carriage. 'I have put side glasses to my coach', he informed Sir Ralph, 'and taken off the red tassels from my harness and put on white ones, and also white toppings on the bride's . . . .The arms I have not yet altered, but will shortly, by putting her coat with mine.' After all, Mary would acquire the coach on John's death and her status had to be proclaimed. Sir Ralph grudgingly accepted the change, 'if it be for love liked', but he thought it had looked well enough before.[79] The attitudes of father and son towards coaches were quite different.

Coaches and the Power of Women

Both John and Sir Ralph turned to their female kin for advice about their vehicles. Wives of both the Verneys and Temples normally inherited coaches and used them whenever possible. In 1705 John was 'put to the fatigue' of a stage coach, because his wife needed his carriage.[80] None of the Verney women could present gifts of deer, but the use or loan of the family coach was frequently at their disposal. Since access to a coach offered freedom, the person who controlled it had power. Thus, some elite women were able to grant the gift of independence, if only for a day.

Yet this female control depended upon many factors, including age, rank, wealth, and marital status. Unmarried females, especially spinsters, were usually borrowers. They begged John for his coach in order to take sacraments at church, appear at funerals, conduct marriage negotiations, and, most often, to visit. When Aunt Gardiner was forced to let her coach and coachman go, she lost prestige and autonomy. John's three wives had varied amounts of authority, for they had different skills and shared distinctive stages of John's life cycle. Wealthy widows, on the other hand, often had their own carriages.[81]

Even dependent females possessed power relating to coaches. John's London aunts knew the rules pertaining to polite use of carriages and interpreted them to their own benefit. Elizabeth Baker was particularly adept at commanding who should come to London and who should travel by coach. In 1695 John's aunts fought viciously over whose servant should ride in their sister's funeral cortege. Aunt Gardiner expected her maid to take precedence, and after days of acrimonious conflict, Sir Ralph met her demands. In the 1690s, John's second wife Mary rode with a black servant playing a trumpet and two liveried men on horseback. John had little control over this glittering retinue, which must have been an imposing sight.[82] Mary knew that who looked in and who looked out showed one's social position in a second.

Women played their most powerful role when polite rules were in question. After John's first wife Elizabeth died in 1688, the aunts made Sir Ralph put his coach in mourning for 'tis now a general custom'. Although he grumbled, he followed their commands. However, at the death of John's second wife, Mary Lawley, her mother challenged the Verney aunts. Her coach, she insisted, 'must not be put into mourning for a daughter' for 'that was not the mode'. But John must greatly increase the number of coaches that attended Mary's corpse.[83] Two powerful groups of women fought to have their way in interpreting the social code. Although there were guidelines, the rules were construed differently by different people. Normally, it was women, however, who asserted authority. As they modified the rules, they increased their influence, for Sir Ralph and John usually followed their advice.

As John grew older, however, he spent more time in the country and was less involved with his vehicles. In 1700 he admitted that 'I living mostly in the country, the coach won't be half so much used as if I lived in London'.[84] John was noticing a change that had taken place since his father's generation. Sir Ralph's cumbersome country carriage had given way to fashionable urban vehicles.

But with illness and old age, John abandoned many of his aunts' London rules. Tension between their social code and his autonomy had always lurked beneath the surface, and at Claydon he did as he pleased. He did not send a coach to take Cousin Cary Stewkeley home from Sir Ralph's funeral. And when John's mother-in-law died, he simply rented a vehicle at £15. John retained just enough ceremony to maintain his local position. By 1706 John showed the same informality in his attitude towards visits. Cousin Pen, he wrote, should visit his pregnant daughter Margaret 'without standing upon such trifles as a return'. It was 'not fit' for Margaret to 'go out on the stones of London'. As with coach use, John acted independently, motivated by grumpiness and old age. But he was also asserting his Tory country ideology and a masculine resistance to excessive politeness.[85]

In fact, the Verneys perceived a conflict between manners and morality in continental models of gentility. They observed that polite accommodation often led to loathsome artifice in personal relationships. In an age of commerce, warned *The Gentleman's Library*, 'the greatest part of the conversation of mankind is little else but driving a trade of dissimulation'. If gentlemen continually praised each other, one would never know their true sentiments. Dr Denton swore he wrote to Sir Ralph 'not to flatter', for his praise was 'no compliment . . . but really true'.[86] Nancy Nicholas also vowed that she wrote 'without compliment or lying'. The Verneys knew that in a society based upon patronage, one must distinguish between the two.

But excessive politeness was not just artificial, it had negative implications for national and sexual identity. The proud Verney family wished to create their own cultural standards. As Mun observed, they longed to cease sending 'young gentlemen . . . into France to learn manners . . . .They come back fool as ever, imitating the French mode with so much affectation . . . that in derision we Englishmen are justly styled apes of the French.' These views were consistent with Britain's new commercial and military power vis-à-vis France. They reflected a desire for 'a close . . . natural way of speaking'[87] apparent in eighteenth-century English letter-writing manuals.[88]

Mun's comment also showed an anxiety about French politeness and its effects upon gender relationships. Normally, it was women who pressed men into formalities. Thus, Sir Ralph was critical of Nancy Hobart's courtesies: 'I thought you had known me better . . . than to write me a letter of ceremony', he complained, and prayed that her next would be 'without compliment . . . in plain English, which is the natural language of Buckinghamshire bumpkins'. As Michele Cohen has argued, politeness was perceived to blur gender boundaries 'with its emphasis on softening, pleasing, and polite . . . conversation'. There was fear that this type of seductive contact might cause effeminacy in men, as illustrated by the fop. In the early eighteenth century, the Verneys' desire for French refinement was replaced by an assertion of British manliness along with patriotism and independence.[89] John's resistance in old age to his aunts' rules was one way of declaring his masculinity.

But despite John's small steps of protest, he still worried about politeness. His rented mourning coach had to be 'all new painted'. And, he warned the coach-maker, if his in-laws' coaches were 'handsomer than mine, I shall think you use me very ill'.[90] John's polite urban heritage was not discarded. Coaches remained necessary tools of eighteenth-century power.

Sociability, Power, and Polite Urban Culture

This chapter has examined the Verneys' adaptation to urban pressure in the social sphere. Like John's economic adjustments, his social accommodation was eminently successful. The family's modes of sociability were modified by John's generation. In contrast to Sir Ralph's hospitality and gifts of venison, John's modish visits became statements about urban status. By the early eighteenth century, some people believed that city activities were replacing country rituals. Thus, a rising middling-sort lawyer, Dudley Ryder, who longed to enter society, snobbishly declined to go hunting. He wondered 'how persons can divert themselves in this way to go round the fields for a long time in vain'. With the help of *The Spectator*, the coffee-house, and a reasonably wealthy family, he rose to prominence. Like John, who rarely hunted, one of Ryder's main forms of social activity was an endless round of visits.[91]

Making social calls in a coach helped John, and others like him, to present themselves as polite gentlemen. Verney women also used coaches to maintain their status. But London life gave them freedoms and mobility, as well as new roles and obligations. The existence of separate gendered visiting patterns has received little attention. Yet Elizabeth Baker made her own cross-county itin-eraries.[92] And Aunt Gardiner created her own social arena by restricting her gaming to women. On the other hand, women also controlled the rules of mixed company and persuaded men to observe them. The powers which accrued to Verney women were seldom asserted openly. They had to be wielded, sometimes hidden, with tact. This fact reminds us that a system of inequality dominated society and permitted those small powers to which women clung.

Nevertheless, in contrast to the male monopoly of gifts of deer, women controlled the way they made social calls.

Historians often describe London sociability in terms of separate public and private spheres, each of which reflect gendered functions. For example, coffee-houses are portrayed as public sites for men, where news and political information are shared.[93] In contrast, women in the privacy of the home are assumed to be excluded from significant public space. The Verney archive challenges this rigid model of gender roles and instead finds overlap and complexities.[94] In fact, news was available in ladies' drawing rooms, as was liquid consumption and political gossip. Politics similarly dominated visits, especially before elections. Aunt Gardiner might be chastised for her gambling, but she sent her best political secrets after a day at cards.[95] Her Covent Garden parlour was a site of female sovereignty, with little distinction between public and private spheres.

And when friends took a seat in John's private coach, they were simultaneously on public display. The coach was both a private space and a public attraction, as London prints make clear. Some of them show riders shrouded behind curtains (see plate 18), while others expose their finery to the viewer. Depending upon one's motivation, either strategy could be used to enhance the owner's status.

The terms 'public' and 'private' had a multiplicity of related meanings in the eighteenth century. The definition of 'public' as 'sociable' in contrast to 'solitary' aptly describes the Verneys' visits.[96] The family's coach riding also locates them in Habermas's public sphere. But their venues did not lie in the institutional world of clubs, associations, and rational debate that he envisioned. Instead, the Verneys rode privately in public parks and displayed themselves publicly in the privacy of the home. Despite the lack of a salon culture as in Paris, public and private spaces converged in London drawing rooms.

This chapter also addresses questions about the rise of politeness. It has used visits in a coach as a device to show how the Verneys absorbed social norms. As John's cultural transformation shows, politeness provided a framework for integrating the city and the country in a refined manner. For John, the merchant, politeness meant presenting a proper public figure, showing good breeding, and maintaining harmonious relationships. It required an intent to please his Verney kin and the ability to discriminate between different types of sociability. It also involved a knowledge of deferential norms, including those owed to individuals of different age, gender, and kinship. Since the Aunts were teaching values, not just rules, it meant adapting his own to theirs.

At first, John upset his family's social harmony, and in doing so was impolite. Eventually, he accepted his aunts' visiting norms and the balance was restored. At the same time, he used his coach according to a polite, urban code that acknowledged competition, mobility, and conspicuous display. Because the code was a dynamic one, it was not easy to conform to its dictates. John's efforts to do so were significant. They show he understood that the way individuals formed social relationships affected society as a whole. Conformity like John's helped to dampen anxieties about political, religious, and social divisions. Thus the Verneys' politeness was not merely aesthetic. It was a tool used to attain stability.

But because the code was both polite and competitive, it contained inherent tensions. The Verneys' quarrels over visits are proof of this fact. So are John's later retreats from excessive politeness that declared his masculine independence. At the end of his life, he discarded some of his aunt's visiting rules and all but one of his coaches. Nevertheless, that one remained, for John adhered to those London norms that were needed to ensure politeness. John's ability to transmit his polite code to the next generation and the Claydons would be critical to the Verneys. Chapters 5 and 6 show his success in two key arenas that linked sociability and power—the marriage market and the world of politics.

5

Choosing Partners: The Marriage Market

The Money and the Maidenhead is the subject of our meditation.[1]

Marriage—the Historical and Family Context

At the dawn of the eighteenth century, marriage was on the minds of the Verney family. Indeed, 656 letters in the database deal with marriage, making it the second most cited topic in the collection. Wedlock was an important goal of the London season and a reason for visiting in one's coach. Furthermore, every step of the discourse about 'matches' took place in the public arena. It was heavily laced with gossip and scandal, as narrators assigned monetary and moral value to proposed unions. Even the Verneys' steward received sensational titbits about matches along with his instructions for rent collection.[2] In short, the Verneys and their friends were obsessed with matrimony, like the plays and novels that they enjoyed.

We can see the Verneys' struggles to maintain power by analysing the ways in which they chose marriage partners. By 1700 London's marriage market was the national locus for matchmaking and it influenced the way the Verneys made alliances. Their experience sheds light upon debates about the effects of primogeniture and the strict settlement.[3] This chapter also addresses a range of issues concerning relations inside the family including: expectations, values, and motivations of individual members; the power balances that existed between them; differences based upon gender, birth order, and marital status; and the ways in which individuals internalized or surmounted social constraints.

British family history has been revitalized by the study of gender, with which the topic of marriage is naturally entwined. At first, historians reclaimed women as subjects[4] and questioned whether their status had improved or declined. Some scholars turned back wistfully to a golden economic age.[5] Others described the rise of a private sphere that confined women to a restricted domestic world, leaving the public sphere of business and politics to men.[6] Recently, the rigid boundaries of these spheres for both men and women have been questioned and a vigorous debate flourishes.[7] Still others have looked at the strength of patriarchy and Lawrence Stone's argument that by the eighteenth century, power relationships within the family were easing in the face of 'affectionate individualism'.[8] Miriam Slater confirmed Stone's early chronology by analysing the Verneys' patriarchal behaviour up to the 1650s, but this too has been challenged.[9]

More recently, historians have replaced this teleological approach with more complex models. The field is animated by gender historians who probe notions of masculinity and femininity and ask new questions about gender, class, sex, and power. They have shown that gender roles are socially constructed, historically specific, and used to legitimize power structures.[0] More recently, the work of Tim Hitchcock and others on the cultures of the body and sexuality has led to overarching models about gender. These new approaches help us to see that concepts of gender, sexuality, marriage, demography, family, honour, and politeness are intricately interrelated.[11]

This chapter sheds light upon these topics by analysing the roles, motivations, and power of family members during courtship, negotiations, and the concluding of marriage settlements. Multiple drafts of deeds, wills, codicils, and private letters are used along with final settlements. Hence we see the hopes, fears, feuds, kindnesses, treacheries, and reunions that underpinned the documents. The effects and outcomes of over six generations of marriage settlements are also examined. Did they work out as planned? Who lost or benefited? How were social and personal identities affected? As we eavesdrop on the negotiations, we see that individual goals were in constant tension with those of the larger family. In fact, marriage settlements and wills were discussed in at least 275 and 108 letters, respectively.

This study demonstrates that distinctive points of view were held by the bride, the groom, and their respective families. Different attitudes were likewise found between patriarch and kin, elder son and younger son, and brothers and sisters. Moreover, the positions of heiresses, widows, wives, and spinsters varied. Much attention is given here to the topic of choosing a spouse. For courtship was a special time, set between two periods when a woman was under someone else's 'cover'.[12] Choice was not simply free or not free, leading to happy or unhappy marriages, but placed the young people between two conflicting poles of duty and affection. Seventeenth-century prescriptive literature commanded obedience to husbands and parents.[13] By the eighteenth century, however, some tracts and novels defended both a child's free choice and the familial duties that restricted it. The resulting pressures from conflicting obligations caused great personal anxiety.[14]

Elizabeth Delaval's diary shows the effects of these tensions in the 1670s in her 'meditations . . . concerning my father, some months before I married Mr de Laval'. She knew that she was 'positively commanded by God to honour my Father, and yet without any regard at all to this law of God . . . I fail not with bitterness to censure him for all his failings and to discourse of them to many hearers.' She tried to pay 'an humble and a constant respectful duty' to her father, although her forced marriage caused pain to all those involved.[15] Some Verney children were caught in this same predicament, for despite their parents' supportive statements, there were many instances of pressure. In practice, whether child or parent possessed a veto changed with time and circumstance. But by 1706, Mary Astell still believed: 'A woman indeed can't properly be said to choose, all that is allow'd her, is to refuse or accept what is offer'd.'[16] As we shall see, birth order and gender clearly affected choice. Of course, in non-elite families where so much property was not at stake, children had more freedom.[17]

When it came to selecting partners, wealth was essential, but the Verneys considered other criteria too. Prospective in-laws were judged by their status, religion, social connections, political influence, and place of residence. The young person was evaluated according to age, physical beauty, height and bodily stature, general humour, and especially the ability to get along with in-laws. Sex was of course important, but the prudish Verneys rarely discussed it. Good 'breeding' was usually mentioned as it related to manners and there was interest in music and dancing skills. Women were singled out in relation to house-keeping and the likelihood of a compliant character. Former marriages were a source of concern, as was the likely treatment of stepchildren. For the frugal Verneys, a person's attitude towards spending money was also important, as was equality in age, wealth, and rank.[18] Although individual contexts determined the combinations of the above, these criteria appear on list after list suggesting accepted norms.[19]

Except for a few rebels, love was not the highest concern and was mentioned only 57 times. As Lady Lowther of Ackworth noted, that which 'principally concerns the contentment . . . of young people's lives [is] a full and competent fortune . . . to secure them from debt and make their lives comfortable'. The Verneys often articulated their distrust of passion. Thus John was infatuated with his first wife, Elizabeth Palmer, 'but not so much in love withal as to consent to unreasonable terms'.[20] Aunt Adams wrote of a bride whose fond husband 'scarce stirs out of her chamber. I wish this great fondness may continue', she declared, but 'I fear 'tis too hot to hold.' Yet the Verneys were not devoid of affection. Sir Ralph declared its importance to Mary Eure, whom Mun hoped to marry, and John expressed special love for his second daughter Mary. Although John did not declare his feelings in poetry, like his brother-in-law Ralph Palmer, both men cared deeply for John's children.[21] Most people agreed that in a fragile world, both economic security and affection were desired. In practice, companionate and arranged marriages were not mutually exclusive. The Verneys' voluntary matches were both successes and failures, as were those made under pressure.[22]

The Verneys expressed conventional views about gender roles and relation-ships in 192 letters. The remarks of John's son-in-law Thomas Cave, a hard-hunting country squire, represent the standard views of masculinity and fem-ininity found in conduct books. As we shall see, however, practice often differed from prescription. Cave normally discussed his women and his animals in the same breath. During his wife's pregnancy he complained to John: 'In the night the little brat kicks, my wife coughs and . . . I am put to it to quiet both. . . . With other suffering comes the loss of many of my hounds by the murrin.' Cave also had a chilling view of marriage. 'Matrimony does not relish like hunting', he wrote John's son Ralph, 'of which I have great need.' Cave believed that procreation alone defined a woman's function. In contrast, his own role had many dimensions, especially those associated with landed pursuits.[23]

Sophisticated male Londoners also described women as weak, child-like subjects who needed to be governed. Thus, William Tregea told John: 'I think women are like young birds which fly out but can't find the way home unless the old ones come to be their guide.' His analogy illustrates the dominant social construct that females were dependent by nature and needed male oversight. It also reflects the idea of two separate natures and bodies.[24]

In public, both sexes acknowledged the higher value assigned to males and described women as a group, without differentiation. Cave proudly recalled the song: 'If she be but a woman; what care I', when his newly weaned son was unmoved at the loss of his nurse's 'bubbies'. Sir Ralph prayed that John's second wife Mary would give him 'heir males to hold up your family', and a male friend wished John 'olive branches, and that of the better sort'. Aunt Gardiner, a women of sharp political acumen, admitted that her sex was 'little accounted in our age', while articulate Sarah Henry talked of her 'mean capacity' and Cave described women as 'a sort less esteemed'.[25] But because, Aunt Gardiner was a powerful marriage broker with great self-confidence, we must look for a more nuanced reality.

Indeed, the Verney letters do not confirm that marriage was the goal of everyone who had money. Historians have argued that unmarried women held an insignificant place in the world, and Cave believed that until marriage 'women are never well settled here in England'.[26] As we shall see, however, there were large numbers of bachelors and spinsters, and contemporary pamphlets argued both for and against marriage.[27] Failed negotiations also show that some people preferred to remain single.[28]

Matrimony did give women status and kinship connections, but it offered far less freedom to them than to men. Women operated under a double standard when it came to sex. John's brother Mun acknowledged many bastards and his mistresses openly nursed his wife's children. Even a cautious man like John appears to have fathered an illegitimate child.[29] He probably had at least one affair during his third marriage, as well as connections to London's street women. In 1695 an anonymous lady asked for and received money from John. She was glad to hear that he 'had not left off rambling yet'.[30]

In contrast to upper-class women, Verney men gained increased manhood when they had sexual affairs. When a child was born to widow Wellhead's servant, John hoped the widow's son was the father. 'Twill advance his marriage', John remarked, 'for now they'll say he's a man.' John wrote Mun that their father's maid had married a silly fellow, 'but she'll be good game for John Stewkeley next time he visits Claydon.' For upper-class men, sexual liberty was both assumed and available. Thus Miss Cabell's mother refused to let her daughter marry Thomas Wharton, because she would 'pass for the wife and there be a mistress besides, according to the mode'.[31]

Part of the focus on elite virginity was due to the importance of a legitimate male heir. In addition, wealthy women suffered from the effects of harsh property laws. 'By marriage the husband and wife are one person in law', Blackstone noted. 'That is, the very being or legal existence of the woman is suspended during the marriage.' The wife ceded both her real and personal property, excluding only barest necessities. Her children could be taken from her, and she was unable to make contracts. However, as Amy Erickson, Laura Gowing, and Margot Finn have shown,[32] women found creative ways to attain liberties and even agency.

Before examining how the Verneys chose their partners, it is useful to outline the standard provisions of their settlements. The bride's father gave a cash sum called a portion to the groom's father or his trustees. In return, the bride was granted rights of dower—one-third of the groom's estate. By the mid-seventeenth century, an annual allowance or 'jointure' that was paid during widowhood had replaced dower rights.[33] The relationship between portion and jointure was set by bargaining and varied over time. By the Restoration, the Verneys' contracts were in a form called the strict settlement that had been developed by conveyancers to meet needs of landed clients. Ideally, it ensured that family estates remained in the restricted hands of a life tenant, and not in the possession of a tenant-in-tail, who could do what he liked with the property. Trustees were appointed to guarantee that the estate descended from eldest son to eldest grandson, or other designees. Strict settlements also provided for younger children by earmarking lands or monies to generate portions and annuities. These deeds were usually signed when the eldest son married.[34]

The Verney archive unveils the steps that were taken to effect settlements after the Restoration including: initial manoeuvrings to see, meet, and choose a partner; instruction of a broker who would bring players together; meetings between the bride and groom, followed by courtship visits; a meeting between the two fathers or their agents confined to general discourse, suceeded by visits when the alliance was discussed; strategic moves by lawyers and their clerks who drew up the legal documents. The Verneys' negotiations, and those of other families, often took up to a year.[35] Each family opened with desired terms and presented themselves positively, sometimes employing inflated claims. These were checked by investigators behind the scenes, but with a display of good manners up front. There was often a break-off point that halted negotiations and gave each side time to redefine goals. Hopefully, a face-saving compromise made by lawyers would unite the former adversaries.

The major players were two male family heads, or a trustee or lawyer who spoke for the family. Since women could not sign contracts, their signatures are missing from documents that determined their fate. Trustees served on a reciprocal basis and had designated roles and rewards. The Verneys tipped clerks with money, while lawyers and brokers might receive gifts of venison.[36] Last, and sometimes least important, were the bride and groom.

Male and female marriage brokers were central to the process, for without their services, players remained unconnected. A broker's job demanded mediating skills and a knowledge of social and legal norms. Brokers provided a buffer that saved face if negotiations failed. In the Verneys' case, brokers were likely to be middling-sort agents or dependent women like John's aunts, who had access to the London marriage market. In return they obtained favours, status, and, in Sir Ralph's day, a piece of venison.[37] Brokers played important roles in determining the overall patterns of courtship, negotiation, and settlement. The chronological guide in Appendix IV lists the Verneys' marriages and illustrates these patterns.

Marriage Settlements of the Verneys 1612–1662

The land-centred marriages of John's grandfather, father, and brother helped to save the family's fortunes. The strategy of the royalist courtier, Sir Edmund (1590–1642), had been to marry well and profit from royal income. But when he died, he left debts of almost £7,550 and ten children with inadequate portions. His wife Margaret Denton (1594–1641) came from a well-established family only four miles away in Hillesden. She brought a £2,300 portion, for which she received a jointure of £400 per year, a standard ratio of about 6 to 1. But Sir Edmund's expenses as a member of the royal household far outstripped his court income.[38] In 1636 he married his 16-year-old son Ralph to a 13-year-old orphaned heiress, Mary Blacknall (1616–1650), against her relatives' protests. Sir Edmund had purchased the right to marry her to his son for £1,000 from the Court of Wards. Despite the premature forced marriage, the pair appear to have grown to love each other. In contrast to Sir Edmund's large family, only two of their six children survived.[39] This would have a positive impact on Verney finances.

Sir Ralph's later marriage strategies were influenced by his stressful inheritance in 1642. He was forced to sell most of Mary's outlying jointure lands, but he kept his Claydon lands intact, and from 1665 to his death in 1696 no Verney land was sold. Estate preservation laid a heavy burden on Sir Ralph's nine siblings. His sisters' dowries of £1,000 could not be paid and their marriages were economic disasters. His brothers received pitifully small annuities and constantly begged for money. Although Sir Ralph had a 'personal and perpetual relationship' with his friend Vere Gawdy, he had no land for a jointure and never remarried.[40] The cornerstone of his family strategy was to wed his eldest son Mun to an heiress.

By 1658 Mun longed to marry his cousin Mary Eure, but she refused his advances. 'Tis impossible to force affection', Sir Ralph told Mary, 'and where that's wanting, there can never be true contentment.' Despite these sentiments, he had already selected a more advantageous mate for Mun. Mary Abel (1641–1715), an orphan, was heiress to lands adjacent to Middle Claydon worth £700–800 per year. As Sir Ralph bluntly told Mun, he expected him 'to clear my estate and free my person from my father's creditors'. Mun's marriage, Sir Ralph told his rector, 'was the best and happiest way to make my family flourish'. The match was desired by the Abels, for they were merchant newcomers tainted by London scandal who needed social acceptance.[41]

Mun defended his right to choose a bride. 'Rather than I'll wed anything that I have not an affection for,' he declared, 'I will run the hazard of all the misfortunes that can befall me.' In the end, however, he gave in to his father. 'Her land joins with ours', he told a friend: 'I believe her body will do the same with mine, in case my father be fully satisfied that her estate is absolutely her own without control.' Unfortunately, the couple had conflicting expectations about matrimony. Mun told Mary's maid, who was also 'his wench', that my wife 'must be humble and submissive in all things'. He would be sorely disappointed, as would Mary, who had hoped for an ardent suitor. Instead, Mun neglected her and continued his sexual affairs, while Mary concealed her feelings.[42] Both heiresses and elder sons were expected to make sacrifices.

Sir Ralph proposed various settlements that would give Mun an income from Middle Claydon and the remainder after his death. Sir Ralph wanted a £1,000 annuity in order to pay debts, but Mun secretly urged Mary to hold out for £600 annual maintenance and £2,000 in reversion. Mary did so, but quietly warned her own trustee: 'I'll put no further tie on the estate, because I will be mistress of my own.' The final marriage settlement in 1662 settled a part of Middle Claydon on the couple in return for Mary's East Claydon lands. Mun received about £1,300 and Sir Ralph kept £1,100 from a combined income of about £2,400 per year. The Verneys obtained a valuable piece of property estimated at up to £16,000,[43] while the Abels married far above their station.

Probably to keep Mun from selling his patrimony, in 1662 Sir Ralph used a new conveyancing technique—the strict settlement—developed by Sir Orlando Bridgeman, a friend of both families. Because the Abels owned adjacent land, they were in a strong bargaining position. They insisted that East Claydon should descend to the Verneys only if there were children. A daughter might inherit, but if there were no living heirs, the land would revert to Mary. In 1688, to strengthen the Verneys' claim, Mun persuaded Mary to sign a new agreement. 'In case she died before him without a child, then he was to have it, but if she outlived him and had no child by him, then she might give it whom she pleased.'[44]

Mary's melancholy or 'madness' that developed after the marriage soon cast a pall over the union. Mary appears to have had no such symptoms prior to her wedding and was calm during the bargaining. These facts suggest that her melancholy arose to shield her from an unhappy marriage. Perhaps she used her sickness that caused the Verneys such embarrassment as a weapon against Mun and his kin. Mary had to put up with at least three of Mun's mistresses in her house and his love letters to female servants indicate still more affairs. To have mistresses and seduce maids was common behaviour, but to openly keep them in the household was a violation of social norms.[45]

In 1677 by will, Mun left a house and maintenance for one of his mistresses, Mary's wet nurse, and her son '[whose] name is Matthew Verney'. Mun also bequeathed portions to Mary's children in a separate will.[46] But all three children passed away between 1686 and 1692, and in 1688, Mun died in debt. Death thwarted the Verneys' strict settlement and they lost Mary's lands, until John's son Ralph repurchased them in 1729.[47] Despite harsh laws some heiresses managed to keep their portions. Still, the Abel marriage led to the Verneys' financial recovery that had started with Sir Ralph's own arranged marriage.

John Verney's Settlements with Three City Wives

Sir Ralph had a very different attitude towards the marriage and career of his younger son. In the same year as Mun's forced marriage, John strode off to the Levant. When he returned to London in 1674, he had liabilities as a marriage candidate: his tanned face was pock-marked from disease; his age of 34 might concern younger partners; and his future income was uncertain. Nevertheless, he would marry three wealthy women with London backgrounds: Elizabeth Palmer in 1680, Mary Lawley in 1692, and Elizabeth Baker in 1697. John received enquiries through his aunts from merchant families about his age, religion, and assets. Soon the aunts pushed his interest with a wealthy widow. 'If she be so great a fortune (though she be on the wrong side of fifty)', John wrote, 'that should be no obstruction to a younger brother's advancement.' Yet although the widow was sent a side of venison, the match came to naught.[48]

Although John had more freedom to choose than Mun, Sir Ralph retained a veto. 'I'll never alter my condition', John assured his father, 'without your real good liking and approbation.' For his part, Sir Ralph wished to see John married 'to your own liking and where I may approve of your choice'. John fell in love with 16-year-old Elizabeth Palmer who lived in Little Chelsea. She was discovered by Sir Ralph when visiting Steeple Claydon kin who had fallen upon hard times. Sir Ralph divulged his own marital criteria by describing her as 'handsome enough for a wife . . . tall enough and straight . . . of a jolly good humour, and forward enough, not at all reserved' (see plate 3). Moreover, she played the 'espinetto, organs, [and] guitar, and danceth very well'. John responded candidly in the terminology of his London trade. He was 'ignorant of her fortune . . . person, name, and complexion, and though, if the first be very large that will blind me to the rest, yet if it be but moderate, then the others will necessarily be put into the thoughtful scale for balance'.[49]

Aunt Pen Osborne recalled Elizabeth's mother as 'a pitiful chambermaid to Aunt Isham', for the Palmers were socially inferior to the Verneys. But Aunt Gardiner called her family 'as good as ours, and close by us, and her father a gentleman'. Gossips said that Elizabeth's uncle had left her a £6,000 portion, while they guessed her father had '£800 in land and houses in London, and keeps his coach and hath some thousands in his purse'. 'As to her birth and education', wrote John, 'so they be honest I look after no more.'[50] Birth had become less important to the Verneys, if personal and financial criteria were met.

We have no idea of Elizabeth's views, for she was bred to silence her emotions along with others of her class and only a few letters survive. Sir Ralph told John to 'take her to a window or corner in the same room'. 'Then you can find out her humour . . . before proceeding too far.' By December 1679, John was still 'ignorant of her thoughts', yet his apathy turned to passion after secretly observing her at church, visiting her at home, and taking her to a play. 'No man breathing can have more love for you than myself', he wrote. 'Pray let the three words I wrote in your glass window testify that I love and love EP.' Soon after this admission, the Palmers received a gift of venison with all fees prepaid.[51]

Sir Ralph chose his yeoman tenant Joseph Churchill as 'agent in this business', for he was Elizabeth's first cousin. 'Use him kindly and let him pay nothing', Sir Ralph instructed John. 'He is a sober man and expects nothing but civility.' Palmer asked John questions, 'to try whether I was given to lying', but John answered twice with the truth. In London, where people were unknown, every statement had to be verifed. The Verneys searched the parish register to establish Elizabeth's age and obtained a copy of her uncle's will from the Prerogative Office. Some Palmer kin thought her too young for John, but her father wanted a merchant, not a landowner who might pay debts with her portion.[52] The Palmer settlement set a precedent, for from this time on the Verneys used portions to raise daughters' dowries.

Palmer estimated John's fortune at £500 per year and hoped Sir Ralph would add an equal amount, while John claimed 'my own gotten estate in money is £6,000'. The Verneys asked for a £4,000 portion but agreed to £3,000 'for love's sake' after eight months of negotiations. Palmer demanded that the jointure be given to the bride, her heirs, and 'God knows whom', if John died without issue. Like the Abels, the Palmers wanted more than a lifetime interest in Elizabeth's property.[53]

At this point, negotiations broke off and John's visits were forbidden. The final settlement was a compromise in which £2,000 of the portion was to be paid to Elizabeth, with an additional £2,000 for their children if she was widowed, thus keeping some of the portion for the Verneys. If there were no sons, daughters would receive £3,000 if one, £4,000 if more. As with Mun's settlement, no sums were specified for younger sons.[54] It was the last time that a Verney bride received more than a lifetime interest in her property or claimed the custom of London. The portion was put partly in the Chamber of London, then gift-giving took place. John sent Elizabeth a diamond ring worth £15 and gave cut stones for seals to her parents. The wedding garter was sent to Mun, while the newly-weds, Ralph Palmer, and Sir Ralph's lawyer, all received gifts of venison.[55] The surviving settlement masks the angry disputes that are revealed in personal letters.

Elizabeth was the passion of John's life, as his love letters show. Nancy Nicholas made hints to John about the couple's sex life admitting: 'I ought to ask pardon for meddling in these affairs . . . but 'tis a sort of conversation with you which is very pleasing.' In 1685 John reminded Elizabeth of their intimacy, noting he had not forgotten 'the kicker in the dark'.[56] During Elizabeth's first pregnancy, John made her 'inform him about pains on the inside and when she next kicks', correctly guessing that she would have a girl. After one birth, he held her hand for two hours when she could not sleep.[57]

Although Elizabeth's youthful wants raised eyebrows, Sir Ralph admitted she was 'a kind and loving wife'. When business called John from London, she declared: 'I would not live without you as some . . . do, for all the world.'[58] Her death in 1686 must have been too painful for expression, for it was hardly mentioned. The Palmers soon forgot the bitter negotiations. They cared for John's four children, wrote weekly letters, and treated John as a son throughout his life. Among many other favours, they lent him large sums of money. Elizabeth's brother Ralph served as John's trustee and mentored his nephew Ralph. The Palmers' lavish care of the next generation of Verneys shows the continued importance of in-laws.

Five years later, after failed negotiations with Judith Bridgeman,[59] John wed Mary Lawley, daughter of Sir Francis Lawley, baronet. Lawley's father, a second son, had married an heiress from Hackney, Middesex. Lawley, like John, belonged to the Vintners' Company and had an estate in Staffordshire as well as an interest in the Rainbow coffee-house in London. He served on the Privy Council, as MP for Wenlock and Salop, and as a custom-house commissioner. The family lived in Whitehall 'over the gateway . . . up the Banqueting Hall stairs', and from 1691 to 1697, Lawley held the office of Keeper of the Jewel House. John thought Mary 'handsome enough, and I believe wants no wit . . . and twenty-nine years old'.[60] John's aunt Pen Osborne served as marriage broker and made Mary promise to be 'kind to the childering'. This was an important consideration for a widower with four children. Aunt Osborne felt that since John was now heir, he deserved a baronet's daughter, while Sir Ralph confessed that 'pride and self love' had inspired the match. Aunt Whitmore summed up the Lawleys' motives in a letter to Mary: 'You and I know a great estate is what is set by and coveted in our family.'[61]

Although the fathers met frequently, it took them eleven months to agree. At first, Roger North, the Lawley's lawyer in Covent Garden, refused to accept Royal Africa Company stock as security, but John vowed he could redeem it in 30 days. Already new, more liquid forms of capital were figuring in marriage negotiations.[62] John's second settlement contained some terms similar to his first: a portion of £3,000, a daughter's portion of £3,000 if one, £4,000 if two or more, and no provision for younger sons. But the portion was to be laid out in land near London. And the jointure of £400 was secured on a £3,450 mortgage on Oxfordshire lands and a loan of £2,350 to the Royal Africa Company. There was the usual 7 to 1 ratio between portion and jointure. But unlike the Abels and Palmers, the Lawleys sought only a life interest in Mary's portion, and when she died childless after two years of marriage, they lost their daughter and their money. Perhaps because the Lawleys got so little in return, John sent them £100 for mourning clothes.[63]

As with the Palmers, John's ties with the Lawleys lasted after Mary's death, and they wrote 45 letters to the Verneys. Mary Lawley's sister married a Palmer, while a Lawley granddaughter wed a kinsman of John's son-in-law, Sir Thomas Cave. As in-laws intermarried, kin networks grew dense, bringing social mobility and reciprocal patronage. In 1712 John raised cash for a Mrs Frances Lawley by selling her earrings. He helped the Lawleys with their finances, and they did favours for him.[64] The importance of in-laws cannot be overestimated and was a source of influence for women.

We know little about John's brief second marriage. The couple must have been intimate, for when John saw a suckling child, he alluded to Mary's nickname and 'wisht for some of Mrs Lamb's sweets'. Shortly after Mary's death, an 'Easter Le Gay' wrote to John about a lady with £6,000 who will not 'hear of anyone but a merchant who can make her a jointure'. However, John was wooing an orphan, Angel Harrington, who lived in Hatton Garden. Her father William had belonged to the Mercers' Company and in 1671 he left a personal estate of £5,117. Angel had a £6,000 portion and a large income from investments in Lincolnshire and London. John noted her imperfect nose and 'lowness of stature' but found her 'passable with me at this time of the day'.[65]

When Angel rejected the proposal offered by the matchmaker, Aunt Gardiner, John suspected a ploy for a larger settlement. Angel's fortune, however, was twice that of John's wives and she had other serious reservations. Since John already had an heir, she would never see a son married, for he would not receive money until her death. Moreover, she found John 'of a very near [frugal] temper', which John wrongly thought she would like 'for she is very near herself'. Then, his age was 55 to her 30. Finally, she had promised her own mother never to be a 'stepmother', knowing others who had 'found it ill'. John swore he would quickly 'marry off' his children and added a £100 exchequer annuity to the usual £6,000 to buy land. With Angel's £6,000 in addition to John's, she might expect a jointure of £600 per year plus the annuity.[66]

But Angel had her own gendered perspective. She 'lived . . . within her fortune . . . enjoyed great easiness' and would not 'alter her present contented life'. Nor was she 'willing to lose a[n older] husband' and then raise portions for children out of her jointure. John's response was also influenced by his gender. Because he could not imagine that a woman would wish to stay single, he assumed that she wanted more money.[67] Sir Ralph had a similar opinion: 'Many persons that have money withstand their *markets*', he wrote, 'and can never get so good terms again.' If the match was dropped, John would be 'free to *trade* with any other'. The problem was, he said, that 'women love wealth and honour', but it was the Verneys who wanted Angel's riches. Finally, he advised John to find a £3,000 portion and 'moderate provisos', rather than £6,000 from one 'who will hamper you too much'. Because financially independent woman were rarely encountered, Angel's self-government appeared threatening. Like Angel, Sir Ralph and John prized autonomy but could not recognize the sentiment when it was expressed by a woman. They expected her to give in, but she rejected John, albeit 'with great civility and thankfulness'.[68] Later, John may have recalled Sir Ralph's advice, when he took less money for his son Ralph in return for full control.

As this case shows, gender was responsible for different reactions to the same proposal. Angel's desire not to marry sprang from maternal instincts, joy in a comfortable independence, fear of losing her property, and a desire to protect her children. Yet the Verneys, who were clearly interested in her fortune, saw only a woman's greed for a large settlement. Instead, Angel was exhibiting affection and materialism, deference and strength, truthfulness and artifice, directness and tact. She expressed herself in many ways: as a daughter, sister, future wife, mother, and widow. Her identification with all these roles shaped her decision. Because she lived in London on her own fortune, she had an unusual degree of independence. Her brief story tells us more about gender roles than we can learn from the lengthy settlements of John's wives. Without the Verneys' personal letters, we would never know that she existed.

John made his best financial deal in 1697, when he married his third wife, Elizabeth Baker (see plate 4). Since he inherited a baronetcy in the midst of courtship, he was bargaining from strength. In contrast, his father-in-law Daniel Baker (1628–1700) was a Cheapside merchant, who thanked God 'who me from small beginings hath most wonderfully raised'.[69] By 1692 Baker was living in Hatton Garden next door to John. His family called him 'Alderman', but he did not hold this position in the Corporation of London. Tax records for 1692–4 show that Baker was the richer of the two adjacent households. John served with Daniel as a Governor of Bridewell, probably due to Baker's influence.[70] About 1690, Baker bought an estate in Penn for his son Daniel, only sixteen miles from Middle Claydon. The elder Daniel and his wife were buried there amidst great extravagance. Later, his son Daniel helped John win votes on the Chiltern side of Buckinghamshire.[71] In-laws were integrated naturally into the patronage system.

The elder Baker left an estate of £6,000 to £8,000 that included many London properties. Some of them would go to Elizabeth, since she had wed with parental consent. She would also receive £2,000 and a large quantity of silver from her mother.[72] Sir Ralph sent venison to Miss Baker amidst their marriage negotiations. He yearned to see John settled, but he died before the match was concluded. After Sir Ralph's death, John had an offer from a London marriage broker for a baronet's daughter. But it would have been a breach of etiquette to break off bargaining at this stage.[73]

Steely, cold Elizabeth Baker stood most in contrast to John's first wife, Elizabeth Palmer. Her letters were pithy and to the point. When her marriage negotiations faltered, she wrote John secretly, not for any specific sum of money, but for 'making it secure to me, which I thought nobody could be against'. It was reasonable, she told John, 'to make things firm beforehand, that there needs be no law afterward'. Her actions reflected Lord Halifax's *Advice to a Daughter*: 'Do like a wise minister to an easie prince; First give him the orders you afterwards receive from him.' She made John feel that he had invented her ideas, as Halifax suggested.[74] Elizabeth used this tactic effectively during their twenty-year marriage.

Their final settlement showed the difference in the status of the two families. John contributed only £4,000 to buy land—£2,000 less than he had given the Lawleys. But Daniel Baker had to pay a £3,500 portion—£500 more than in John's other settlements. If John died before the land was purchased, a sum of £200 per annum could be charged against the estate. If that was the amount of Elizabeth's jointure, it was half that given to John's previous spouses and meant a portion/jointure ratio of 17.5 to 1. Although the ratio had now risen to about 10 to 1, this was a poor return for Baker. Elizabeth's daughter would receive £3,500, with £4,500 for two or more. But like Mary Lawley, Elizabeth had no children, so no portions were paid. As usual, there was no provision for younger sons and the Verneys controlled all lands. The Bakers won fewer financial benefits than their predecessors.[75]

The marriage took place on 8 April 1697 in the parish church of St Andrew Holborn. We know little about the couple's sex life, but in 1697, when they came to Middle Claydon, they shared a room only for the first few nights, after which John moved to his own quarters. The pair seemed to be compatible, but John constantly complained about expenses. When it came to money, relations with the entire Baker family were unpleasant. Elizabeth wrote her nephew not to mention sums she had given her brother, for John was 'very mistrustful'. The Bakers made cutting remarks about the Verneys' greed and fought with John about legacies from Elizabeth's parents.[76]

John's will reveals deep family conflict, in contrast to the idealized picture shown in his settlements. He gave Elizabeth an extra £70 per year from the Exchequer, but it ceased if she remarried. In fact, all bequests to her had conditions. Perhaps, expecting discord, John tried to prevent later quarrels. Despite this, Elizabeth fought with the John's kin over a silver coffee pot and the value of wood on her jointure lands. She finally turned over her rights to Wasing for a £220 annuity.[77] Although she was an astute business woman, who actively struggled for privileges, when John died she lost the power that his protection gave her. The health of the dynasty took precedence over individuals including in-laws.

Looking back over the Verneys' early marriage strategies, we see that partners normally were chosen in order to strengthen estates. The family adopted strict settlements and adhered to the laws of primogeniture.[78] Because inheritance customs allowed women as well as men to inherit property, heiresses were in demand. Indeed, the Verneys married heiresses in four consecutive generations. John, a younger son, was the only exception, but even he brought in £9,500 in portions. Habakkuk attributes similar patterns to other families including the Berties, Ashburnhams, Butes, Windsors, Norths, Cecils, and Wentworths. Perhaps those that did so were particularly ambitious and willing to take the risks of paying expensive jointures. They had a sense of family time in which one generation worked for another, and they privileged the nuclear family at the expense of other kin.[79]

The Civil War threatened to destroy the efforts of these families, and for some, marriage was the only means by which estates might be saved. Thus in 1662, Mun was forced to use a strict settlement and wed an heiress. But the Verneys were not yet strong enough to obtain land without giving up some advantages. As a result, some of their spouses retained more than a life interest in their portions. By the 1690s, the Verneys were more powerful and the focus had shifted to London. John's three brides and fathers-in-law had residences in the capital and possessed non-landed wealth. Their money had been earned by men in transitional states with mixed backgrounds, like John: one with a recent office; another with a new landed estate for his heir; a third whose son was a London lawyer. John's early agreements reflected his status as younger brother, but as the heir he commanded better terms. The Verneys' portion/jointure relationship improved with each marriage. Moreover, control was tightened over wives' portions which the Verneys used to buy land, not to pay debts. John's bargaining skills were an asset, for his merchant background helped him to understand the psychology of negotiations.[80]

Most important, the Verneys received great benefits from the effects of demography and chance. By John's generation, early deaths, smaller families, late age of marriage, the absence of demands to pay portions or jointures, and John's unexpected inheritance, all had positive consequences. Sir Ralph had many brothers and sisters who lived to old age, but he and Mary had only two living sons, one of whom, Mun, died suddenly along with his three children. John's first late marriage produced four offspring, but he had none thereafter. Moreover, two of his three wives died soon after marriage. Thus the Verneys clearly illustrated elite population trends: a rising marriage age accompanied by declining nuptiality and fertility. These demographic changes helped the Verneys to recoup their fortunes by limiting the number of charges on their estates that were actually paid. John Broad has shown that from 1646 to 1703 no portions had to be raised, and from 1642–1717 no jointures were disbursed.[81] Yet incoming portions were received, and with only the Abel exception, heiresses' lands were retained. Although settlements did not accomplish some original goals, they were enhanced by unexpected benefits for the Verneys.

The effects of strict settlements upon family members varied according to gender and birth order. Eldest sons and heiresses reaped the greatest rewards, but they also bore larger burdens. John's mother insisted that he inherit her small Berkshire estate in Wasing,[82] but later Verney women made no such demands. Thus the Verney experience supports the theory that post-Restoration younger sons no longer received land. Unlike Mun, however, John had freedom first to marry for love, then for a blend of compatibility, convenience, and money. The fates of his spouses, on the other hand, were dependent upon the relative strengths of their fathers' wealth and status. The silence of his wives amidst a cornucopia of letters indicates the bridling of self-expression that marked their breeding.

The London Marriage Market

Before we compare the Verneys' seventeenth- and eighteenth-century marriage strategies, we must consider the urban marriage market. By 1696 London had become the marriage capital of England. Neither John nor his neighbours negotiated their children's matches in the country, as Sir Edmund, Sir Ralph, and Mun had done. When a deal appeared imminent, their lawyers summoned them quickly to town for fear that their matches might 'go off'. The presence of these lawyers encouraged the shift to the capital, where important legal trends affected marriage practice. The impact of Chancery in protecting women's property rights and the decline of Church courts made a difference. So did innovations like the equity of redemption that encouraged use of mortgages. Long-term credit was crucial to the strict settlement. When money became widely available at lower interest rates, families were able to raise portions without selling estates. The centre for all these services was London.

But it was the magnetic pull of the social and political season that kept families in town. It is helpful to think of the marriage market as a giant laboratory for integrating monied and commercial interests. Non-landed groups, such as merchants and professionals, sought access along with the landed elite. Because of the capital's fluid nature, social boundaries were unclear. Moreover, many of the nation's unsolved dilemmas were being worked out in the capital and marriage was connected to most of them. They included challenges to traditional gender relationships, pressures upon property laws and patriarchy, tension about dissenters, and questions about the monarch's religion, sexual behaviour, and authority. As people gossiped about the morality of prospective marriages, they were simultaneously engaged in a larger discourse about the 'unsettled' social and political order.

One of the most profound debates concerned the future of the patriarchal family.[83] During the Civil War, households saw the break-up of family unity, as kin divided over loyalties. Radical experiments regarding family and communal life styles were accompanied by a flood of tracts, some of them by women.[84]

The sexual abandon of the Restoration court aggravated the situation. At the same time, there was still anxiety about the authority of Church and State that had obvious parallels within the family. Many hoped that the Glorious Revolution finally would produce a stable, patriarchal order. But a decade later, a woman writer, Mary Astell, asked a most disturbing question: 'If absolute sovereignty be not necessary in a state, how comes it be so in a family'?[85] This was a radical thought because it challenged the family's patriarchal foundations. Locke's contract theory also raised uncomfortable notions about the position of women. Although he saw wives as subordinates, he believed that both parents had power over children.[86] By the 1690s, male/female relationships had become 'unsettled' in another new way. Women now owned liquid forms of property such as bank notes, stocks, and annuities. They not only made investments, but willed them to whom they pleased. It is not surprising that self-governing women like Angel Harrington caused confusion.

In short, a sense of social disorder lingered after the Restoration. The search for its resolution may be seen in the Verney letters of the 1690s, especially when marriage was discussed. They suggest a perception of marital experimentation and dysfunction that contrasts with the Verneys' orderly settlements. For example, abduction attempts on young people frightened parents. In 1695, the housekeeper, Mrs Lillie, wrote that six men seized Mr Falls' daughter on her way from church, while a Lincolnshire papist 'catched up and married' a young baronet, who was 'lately come from Eton School and very rich'. There were constant 'stolen marriages' without parental consent at all levels of society. Neighbour Pru Woodfine, who was worth £800 per year, eloped on horseback with an apothecary. Moreover, her three sisters 'married themselves' as well. In 1689 Sir Richard Temple's bailiff hastily moved his shop. The reason for his exodus was that his sister had wed 'against his mind'. The archive confirms the disordery state of matrimony that was finally addressed by legislation in 1753.[87]

The letters also indicate that despite society's wish for parity, class distinctions were not always observed. Hence Sir Charles Gawdy married a countess and his daughter a stone cutter; Lady Busby's singing master tried to marry one of her daughters which, Aunt Gardiner noted, 'is commonly done'; and Sir Francis Compton's marriage to 'a common whore' troubled his family, to say nothing of the Bishop of London.[88] Clauses in wills tying legacies to parental consent bear witness to this danger. Partners in discredited alliances, however, were often criticized not because they married below their social group, but because their incomes declined. A London oculist was thought socially good enough for cousin Peg Woodward, but her family objected on the grounds that he might gamble away his money. Aunt Gardiner decried her niece Cary's Irish marriage, for if she had not disposed of herself, 'she could live like her father's daughter'.[89] Although research is needed to quantify these trends, the Verney letters suggest a fluid marriage market driven by mercenary motives.

When it came to marriage, the Verneys had their share of rebels who challenged models of chastity found in conduct books. Cousin Denton's wife

Hester and Mun's daughter Molly both ran off to London: the first to commit adultery, the second to elope. Hester's money was cut off and she died of poverty in a London garret, while Molly Verney was never forgiven by Sir Ralph. When Aunt Gardiner's daughter Pen Stewkeley admitted she had slept regularly with her sister's fiance, the family considered shipping her to a remote part of England.[90] But after Pen's godmother left her a huge fortune, John quickly wrote a settlement that duped her husband and kept the money in the family. Participants in marital escapades paid a social and an economic price if their families did not forgive them. Although some relented, many did not, because the real sin had been to fly in the face of the family and society.[91] The family/state analogy and the unsolved problems of the Crown's good govern-ance still found resonance in domestic correspondence. But with a little bit of luck, women like Pen Stewkeley kept their reputations and status intact.

Two themes run through all the Verneys' discussions about matrimony: the impact of London and the importance of money to upper-class marriages. Indeed, the Lowthers of Whitehaven viewed London as 'a centre where accurate intelligence could be obtained about the estates of potential fathers-in-law, about sons and heiresses . . . who were entering or in the market, and finally what was the current "rate of exchange"'. This is not to say that there were no other motives or that everyone was affected similarly. Nevertheless, a pattern emerges for the Verneys and their friends after the Restoration. Under the guise of the London season, the ritual of choosing a partner masked a competitive struggle for wealth. Swift called it an 'epidemick' that had been spreading since the 1670s.[92] Many upper-class children were subjected to its predatory rites. In fact, some thought the situation 'more sordid than in France'. Like other activities that marked the London season, such as games and cards, opponents made moves, took risks, and might be checkmated at any time. Aunt Gardiner explained how Cousin Edmund Denton had paid his gambling debts: 'Tony Rowe won of Sir E.D. £6,000 before he married his daughter to him, which debt was to be part of the £10,000 he gave in portion.' Anne Lee's £8,000 portion and large estate went to Thomas Wharton and led to a bitter marriage for Anne.[93]

As in other spheres of life, the Verneys used the market mechanism to attain marital goals. Thus, observers described marriage transactions by borrowing the language of commerce. Nancy Nicholas asked John if he was 'in the loving *trade*', and could provide a match for her niece, while Lady Isabella Wentworth wrote of her daughter's fear of the smallpox: 'She . . . I fear, would be peppered with them should she get them, and then her *market* would be spoiled . . . .' In 1703, a pamphlet used the same images to discuss the position of landed families: 'Matrimony is indeed become a mere *trade*; they carry their daughters to Smithfield, as they do horses, and sell to the highest bidder. . . . They have no way to repair the cracks in the estates, but by marrying of fortunes.' In short, marriage had 'become a trade indeed or traffick'.[94]

This focus upon money heightened existing gender inequalities related to marriage opportunities. In fact, the Verneys repeatedly tell us that males had an advantage. Aunt Gardiner wrote angrily that 'all sorts of men can get wives in our age'. She was shocked that 'a haberdasherer of small ways' not only wooed her daughter, but 'would not marry any woman under £800 to set him up a wholesale trade'. 'Men sets a high value on themselves', she told John, who reminded her that there were plenty of available young widows worth £600 to £1,000 per year. In contrast, women without money were hard-pressed to find a spouse. In 1701 Pen Stewkeley predicted that cousin Hugh's debts would 'be a hindrance to his daughters' marriages. They are all . . . to be liked in every respect, had the father the ready rino, but they may live to be old maids.' Cary Stewkeley was sorry for Mr Duncombe's daughters. She knew their father was 'of that temper . . . that is not willing to part with his money, so they may be without husbands, as well as others'. Daughters of widowed parents found matches especially hard to get. Hence Hugh Stewkeley 'stayed unmarried till he laid up portions for his . . . daughters'.[95]

Dependent kin without dowries who strove to keep gentility suffered more than others. Their first priority, noted Aunt Gardiner, was to prevent 'perishing for want, the saddest of all miseries, which I pray God keep all my relations from that unspeakable affliction'. Poor relations were forced to beg for necessities and practice self-deprecation or undignified toadying. Capable Peg Adams, who cared for Sir Ralph at his death, had to be humble: 'I had rather follow your directions in all things', she wrote him, 'than trust my own discretion which at the best is very small.' Relationships could only be skewed, when poor relations sat waiting for kin to die. Neighbours knew Mrs Duncombe's sister did 'all things to please her, because . . . she is in hopes that when she dies . . . she will give what she has to her and her three daughters'.[96] When money was available, gender and birth order produced varied outcomes. But when there was no dowry, law and inheritance customs reinforced gender stereotypes that assumed feminine humility.

Although Sir Ralph withheld his sisters' portions, when finances improved, he added gifts of money to their tiny annuities. After John inherited, his unmarried cousins hoped that this practice would continue. However, John's idea of charity differed from that of his father. The circle within which he felt responsible for favours tightened to include only his nuclear family and those relatives who were not a financial burden. In 1704 Aunt Gardiners' daughters begged for money to bury their mother. John angrily complained about their debts 'to baker, brewer, grocer, [and] meat woman'. They must 'sooner get a livelihood by working and labour', he advised, 'than run in debt upon uncertainties. . . . I neither will nor can I allow you anything. . . . Pray consider the number of cousins . . . that I have . . . in condition low enough, yet [they] make a shift to live. . . . If I were to maintain them . . . I might soon go a begging.'[97]

John was forsaking the traditional duties of kinship cited in 189 letters, but his kin were forced to thank him for his advice. They deplored their debt, 'we knowing the misery of it', and explained 'how hard it 'tis to get bread'. In 1697 Aunt Adams tried to make John see the plight of poor widows, when he taunted her for love of luxury. 'My great grief', she wrote, 'is want of money to pay my debts and feed my family.' When John refused to invest a small sum for her, she explained how credit affected dependent women: 'If I once fail of paying, they never trust me anymore. It's an easy thing to go over a broken hedge or tread upon that [which] is down.'[98] John's sense of responsibility was waning by the eighteenth century.

If a woman lacked a portion, it was unlikely that she would marry, as Peg Adams knew well: 'As for anybody falling in love with me', she confessed, 'I can't expect that, which have none of that which all the world values; I mean money.' Although she was well-liked and attractive, she was forced to remain a spinster. The most acceptable alternative was to become a gentlewoman companion, who was little more than a servant and had to be 'courteous and modest . . . to all persons' as well as 'humble and submissive to . . . Master and Mistress'. Neglected in most studies, Verney women in this position wrote 257 letters and were mentioned 74 times. Sir Ralph thought such women complained too much. John's cousin Pen Viccars, however, had a different point of view. Rather than be a companion, she wrote, she would 'rather serve hogs'. Her sister Cary Stewkeley who waited on Mary Abel in East Claydon lived in fear of offending Sir Ralph. She bore great responsibility, yet in comparison with the minister's wife and Sir Ralph's housekeeper, she probably had the least freedom. Her reward, she thought, would be a nice legacy, but she received nothing. Lady Gardiner wrote of 'how dutiful Cary was to my dear brother, and how severe he was to her upon any slight occasion . . . and need not tell you what return she has had for her dull and unpleasing life'.[99]

Yet even distasteful places like Cary's were hard to get. In 1709 Aunt Gardiner complained that 'many has put away women as formerly kept them . . . and lessened their servants in all places . . . .There was never more gentlewomen wanting services than now.' She worried particularly about cousin Mary Lloyd: 'As her condition is, she must always trust upon uncertainty . . . and thank god for having such offers of a present livelihood.' When Nancy Nicholas no longer wanted Peg Adams's company, Sir Ralph wrote supportively to Nancy. Peg should not only submit in being deprived of 'those happinesses she enjoyed under your protection', but show thankfulness for past favours.[100] Instead of becoming a 'kept' woman by a male, genteel ladies were 'kept' by wealthier women. In both cases, the inferior female was disposable when services were no longer wanted.

Why was there such a gender disadvantage for those without dowries? The Verneys gave many reasons, including the declining numbers of males due to bachelorhood and war. In 1704 Cornelia Dunk spoke of 'the great slaughter among the men'. The Verneys also blamed a growing number of wealthy bourgeois heiresses with large portions.[101] For example, in 1700 Alderman Chiverton's 'very plain' daughter caught 'a pretty man' with her £30,000 dowry. Four years later, John's banker Henry Hoare gave his eldest daughter to the heir of the Earl of Orrery, along with a £25,000 portion, while his second daughter had £20,000. Total costs for both marriages reached £80,000.[102] Similar astronomical figures were received through the mid-eighteenth century. In 1736 and 1740, John Verney's grandsons received portions of £40,000 and £30,000, while in 1715 and 1737, Anne Halsey and Anna Chambers brought £20,000 and £50,000 to the Temples of Stowe.[103]

Historians have suggested a complex array of causes for these figures including rising incomes, inflation, and land prices; high taxes, falling interest rates, and increased borrowing on mortgages. Like the Verneys, however, they agree that demographic changes had a tremendous impact on family fortunes—too few children could mean biological extinction through lack of an heir, too many could result in economic extinction through an excess of portions and jointures to be paid.[104] Studies of late seventeenth-century London suggest surpluses of 'status-seeking nubile women' due to declining male survival rates, rising male emigration and celibacy, entry of younger sons into professions, and competition from widows and daughters of commercial and professional men.[105]

As Chapter 2 suggested, during the last quarter of the seventeenth century elite families failed to reproduce themselves. Both the Verneys and Temples had no male heir in the eighteenth century. In 1702 Aunt Adams found this circumstance normal: 'Mr Peniston is dead', she reported. 'He has left only two daughters, no son. But he has made his eldest daughter as an elder son. It is said she'll be worth £30,000.' Because Peniston's other daughter was sickly he left her only £300 a year 'believing that if she married she would die' and her money would pass to her spouse. Thus, a large supply of heiresses led to fluid gender boundaries and disadvantaged other women.[106] Let us see how John's children were affected by the London marriage market.

The Settlements of John Verney's Children 1703–1708

In 1696, when John inherited, he had three marriageable daughters: Mary, Margaret, and Elizabeth; and an unwed son Ralph. The eldest, Elizabeth remained a spinster despite her £3,000 dowry. The others married wealthy spouses with landed backgrounds unlike John's wives, but their settlements were negotiated in the London marriage market.

By 1702, 21-year-old Mary, had a suitor, Colonel John Lovett of Kilruderry, Ireland (d. 1710), the second son of a former Levant trader. The Lovetts of Liscombe had owned land near Claydon since the fourteenth century. But Colonel Lovett's late father Christopher had left Buckinghamshire and become Lord Mayor of Dublin. Lovett was a 34-year-old widower, whose first wife was the sister of John Verney's rector. Worse yet, Colonel Lovett lived in Ireland, and a recent match by cousin Cary Denton had brought out family prejudice against the Irish. As Aunt Adams noted: 'I should have had an Englishman with half as much rather than have gone into Ireland.' But Lovett was a wealthy gentleman, so he was still an acceptable candidate. He wrote 83 letters to the Verneys and received at least 27 in return.[107]

Colonel Lovett's courtship was far different from that of Sir Ralph's generation. Lovett declared his passion before money matters had even been discussed. Furthermore, Mary was not John's eldest daughter. 'It must not be so done in our country to give the younger before the older,' observed Aunt Gardiner. As usual, Mary's feelings are unknown, but her stepmother Elizabeth [Baker] wrote to John about 'poor Molly . . . who leaves it wholly to yourself. . . . She shall not be in the least concerned if you break it off . . . so you may do as you please'. Lovett's persistence and Mary's 116 letters suggest that both parties married primarily for love. John could have broken off the match, but he listened to Aunt Gardiner's warning about the surplus of eligible women: 'Our sex is such a drag in our age', she wrote, 'that parents must pass by many objections or [they] will keep their daughters.'[108] John, however, would not accept Lovett until he had evidence of the Colonel's wealth.

Because John could not visit Lovett's property, he asked him to itemize his assets. The Colonel listed £19,650 in lands, houses, and mortgages with an annual income of £1,446. 13s. and £2,500 in stock. John's third wife Elizabeth suggested an Exchequer inquiry and thought Lovett 'short' for not showing his leases. Her demand for collateral security showed both her business sense and her active role. John investigated Lovett so aggressively that one man indignantly refused to help.[109] Integrity might be a point of honour among gentlemen, but marriage negotiators did not rely solely upon a man's word. To do so would have been considered foolish, for social discourse required a veneer of polite manners that could mask unpleasant realities.

Negotiations dragged on for over a year because of John's objections about Mary's jointure. Lovett promised a £400 annuity and £1,000 for future sons, £3,000 if no son and one daughter, and £4,500 if two or more girls. In return, John was to pay a £3,000 portion. Since the standard ratio of portion to jointure had reached 10 to 1, John obtained a good deal at the old ratio of 7.5 to 1. John and Lovett were to purchase £4,000 of English land to act as security for the jointure. Yet when Lovett died suddenly in 1710, much of his estate was lost because of a failed lighthouse venture and a price drop in his East India stock.[110] In contrast to dower rights, women's jointures may have become less secure, when linked to speculative forms of property.[111]

None of the standard letters of congratulation exist for the Lovett match, perhaps because of the more interesting marriage of John's youngest daughter Margaret. While Lovett waited patiently, Thomas Cave was rushed to the altar in less than a month. On 28 January 1703, John's landlord Thomas Cheret of Covent Garden wrote to John of 'an address to Mistress Margaret' by Cave.[112] The affair had started in London, where courtship opportunities abounded without parental knowledge. Secrecy and haste were required, for the groom's father Sir Roger opposed the match and had gone 'out of town this day. . . . How long he shall stay is uncertain.' Sir Roger's displeasure was not surprising, for his heir Thomas could command a greater portion than the Verneys could provide.[113]

The Caves of Stanford Hall near the Northamptonshire/Leicestershire border became landowners in the mid-sixteenth century. John's aunt Peg Elmes nursed Sir Roger Cave's mother at Stanford, while 'paying for her diet', and Thomas Cave and John's son Ralph were at Oxford together. Status and rank were prized by Sir Roger (1655–1703), who rebuilt his house on a grand scale and became a member of Parliament and a baronet. He also made two matches that helped him financially and politically.[114] The first, in 1676, was to Martha, heiress of John Browne of Eydon, Clerk of the Parliament. The second was to Mary, sister of William Bromley, the Tories' Midlands whip, who became Speaker of the House of Commons (1710–1713) and Secretary of State (1713–1714). Because the Speaker regulated Parliamentary business, 'all party men . . . were keenly aware of the importance of controlling or influencing him'. Since John had recently failed to regain Sir Ralph's Parliament seat, he found Thomas Cave's proposal 'very welcome'.[115]

Thomas was a country gentleman who was happiest with his dogs and horses. He believed that 'stinking London will increase any distemper . . . especially when the wandering mind is so much set upon the country'. Yet he rushed to town to vote against repeal of the Occasional Conformity and Schism Acts. Tory country principles were his first priority, and he sat in Parliament with John. He later wrote 259 letters, of which 209 were to his father-in-law.[116]

Margaret's feelings about the marriage are unknown, despite her 145 letters, but the groom wrote of an 'ectasy of joy'. John secretly sent his wife Elizabeth to London to conclude the affair. This was an important responsibility involving large sums of money. She had to buy wine, claret, and sack, approve the groom's present of earrings, purchase the bride's clothes, see lawyers and bankers, and order six pallets and a new hall mat for Claydon. 'I will manage it as frugally as I can', she vowed, but she spent £199. Sir Roger Cave's parson rushed to London to find Thomas. Too late, he was diverted to Windsor, while a coach took the wedding party to the church. 'Mr bridegroom's man does not know where his master was', wrote Elizabeth, 'but I send for him tomorrow before they are up, and then he may tell the parson that he is married and saw them a-bed.'[117]

Elizabeth and Margaret spent a week visiting in their coaches, while the London cousins basked in 'the joy of our new relation'. Margaret's spouse brought glory to her kin, although she had married secretly before her elder sisters. The London aunts reported: 'The private marriage of Mr Cave, unknown to his father, has filled the town with a fresh discourse, and for a time Mrs Temple's marriage sleeps.' The alliance of Temple's sister with a Covent Garden lecturer was now hardly worth discussing. In contrast to Mary's unacknowledged wedding, letters of congratulations poured in. Many claimed to know the amount of Margaret's portion, while others condemned the 'guilt' of the groom's family. After all, the bride and groom's births were equal, and Margaret had a decent, if not sumptuous, portion. 'The world says', Lady

Gardiner reported, 'his father gave him a pitiful allowance for a son whose mother brought him above £20,000.'[118] Gossipers passed harsh judgements when the marriage market's rules were breached.

Then suddenly, in October 1703, Thomas's father died. Letters openly congratulated John and several described the death as 'a revolution'. The analogy between family head and monarch was still used in every day speech by those who had lived through 1688. But Cave's inheritance was subject to charges of £22,000. After the couple moved to Stanford Hall, Cave's family did not socialize with the Verneys. John confessed: 'I think it not proper for us to come when they be there, considering how dearly they love us, and what discourse and nicknames some of 'em give us.'[119]

Meanwhile, John and Cave quarrelled over which lands would be settled upon Margaret. The settlement was not drafted until May 1704, over a year after the marriage. Although portions were rising and the norm was a 10 to 1 ratio, John continued to pay only £3,000, for which Margaret was promised a £600 jointure. The Caves usually limited jointures to £100 per year for each £1,000 of the brides' portion. But Sir Thomas promised to add £300 to Margaret's £300 jointure, reducing the ratio to 5 to 1.[120]

The settlement was threatened by Sir Roger's will and a lawsuit in 1705. Cave's mother, sisters, and brothers demanded £22,000 in portions and the return of Sir Roger's personal estate. The latter was valued at over £7,363 after payment of £1,407 for debts and the funeral and £1,164 in legacies. The family won their portions, but Cave received the personal property. A Parliamentary Act was passed 'to enable Sir Thomas Cave, Baronet, to sell certain lands in the County of Northampton to raise money to pay his brothers' and sisters' portions'. Although the Caves' strict settlement was broken, Sir Thomas, like the Verneys, kept his main estate intact 'being minded to preserve the ancient estate of his family entire'.[121] At her husband's death, Margaret would receive her jewels, plate, furniture, and coach, and an extra £1,000 to be paid six months after his decease. In comparison, John's wife of twenty years, Elizabeth Baker, would receive an additional £70 to be doled out each year. Unlike the Verneys, Cave also reserved portions for younger sons in his will, but they were a fraction of his daughters' inheritances.[122]

In analysing the power relationships of family members, both fathers must be considered. In contrast to Sir Ralph, Cave was a father without power, for his heir was willing to risk marriage without parental consent. Luckily, Sir Thomas had a life interest in his mother's fortune. He may have felt that society would sanction his action and that his father would come around in the end. Before his death, Sir Roger had asked for a £5,000 portion through Verney's tenant Joseph Churchill. By condoning Margaret's secret marriage, John tacitly acknowledged a new social standard that accepted disobedience. When he talked to Sir Thomas about his grandchild saying: 'Bless him and make him an obedient son', John forgot his own previous support of defiant behaviour.[123] Sir Ralph never forgave his granddaughter Molly's elopement. But John condoned the secret marriage of Margaret, since it was made with his consent and gave him a Tory son-in-law. John's ambition overcame the principles of filial obedience, because they were breached in his own favour. The prescriptive model of duty to parents was again discarded.

As to motives, John and Sir Roger were mirror images: one approved of the marriage for all the reasons that the other abhorred it. The Verneys possessed neither an heiress nor politically prominent Tory relations. Partly because of the Whig/Tory competition that reached its height under Queen Anne, the Verneys found the marriage financially and politically desirable. Immediately after the wedding, the Verneys advised Cave 'to apply himself to Mr Bromley, who if he be as good as he is wise may reconcile all'. For a man with a son who was anxious to enter Tory politics, Bromley was a desirable connection. Cave worked with his stepuncle Bromley in Parliament and had influential Tory friends.[124] Only his early death foiled the Verneys' strategy.

John played a reactive role to his daughters' suitors, but he devoted five years of time and energy to choosing a bride for his heir Ralph. Not coincidentally, marriage proposals from London matchmakers followed John's elevation in 1703 to an Irish peerage. John also took Ralph to Bath at this time, which gave the boy additional exposure. The first offer was received when Ralph was age 20. It was brokered by John's former mother-in-law, Lady Lawley. Shortly thereafter, John's London landlord Thomas Cheret wrote about a Mr Hopkins, who needed £6,000. 'He would willingly have one half of it to marry his daughter and the other half his son, and will settle £500 a year in present and £500 more at his decease.' When John showed little interest, Cheret described a 16-year-old lady 'whose education and birth is both honourable and virtuous. Her portion is at least £7,000 down'. Since the lady was Lord Hatton's daughter, sister of Lord Nottingham's wife, there was 'no want of birth nor interest, which is an advantage counted by all'. John rejected her in a passage which revealed his country roots and his father's old distrust of the court: 'Had I a dependency at and from the court, to marry a family that hath a good interest there, might be beneficial. . . . As I am, I value it as a great happiness, or feather, which one may live without.'[125]

Giving clues to his own priorities in November 1703, John described two co-heiresses who had £1,500 between them in land. He was buying Buckingham-shire property and soon received a proposal from the Egertons, who were kin to the Buckinghamshire Lord Lieutenant, Scroop Egerton, 1st Duke of Bridgewater (1681–1745). By 1705 Mrs Anna Tregea emerged as John's chief London marriage broker. Her business kept her so busy that her husband sometimes wrote her letters. They show the raw commerciality of the marriage market and its continuously rising portions.[126]

Mrs Tregea recommended a woman who was 'handsome . . . of great gentility . . . bred to all affairs concerning a house and affairs of good housewifery'. This probably was Lady Henrietta Mordaunt, whose father would 'pay £6,000 on the nail and be obliged to make you an English Viscount', in return for a £700 jointure. By June 1706 the Countess of Monmouth and Peterborough had expressed interest to Mrs Tregea. Meanwhile, Lady Verney reported: 'At Bath, a citizen proposed . . . a young woman . . . with £7,000 down and £8,000 more at her father's death . . . but Mr Verney being indisposed and at Bath for his health, My Lord did not think it seasonable to treat at that time.'[127] In Bath and London, women were appraised like so many acres or shares. Everyone knew that the quotes were inflated and strove to place their candidate in the best light.

By June 1706 Mrs Tregea had switched support to another Egerton relation, Lady Leicester, 'a handsome well-bred young lady with £10,000 in fortune down'. Her uncle promised to make John an English baron in return for £1,200 a year present maintenance or £600 a year with the money in trustees. The latter device had developed to ensure that a women might hold separate property that her husband could not touch.[128] Even though portions had risen astronomically, sweeteners such as titles also had to be added. What is noticeable is that titles were still for sale and played an important role in the London marriage market.

John clearly desired land, not court favours, even though real estate may not have produced the highest return. 'I have lately been so unfortunate in treating with the quality', he wrote Mrs Tregea, 'that as yet I have not recovered assurance enough to attempt on another of the same degree.' 'When I match my son, I'll settle Middle Claydon on him, which is above £2,000 a year, but for the rest of my lands, though I design him all, I'll not settle on him till I die.'[129] John had decided to retain leverage over his heir and to control some lands until his death. To make his point, he told Mrs Tregea about

a rich, handsome widow who was a Lord's daughter worth over £10,000, if not £12,000. . . . My son once did see her . . . but when I proposed it to him, I found him not inclined to the match, and he being chiefly concerned, I had no more to say to it, though I doubt he won't do better; As to the terms, they would have been easy, but if they were but £5 a year, as long as he matches with my approbation, I'd not give 5s. a year from him.[130]

Clearly, Ralph's happiness was important to John, but because he was the heir, he could not have real freedom of choice. Ralph had had at least twelve offers by the fall of 1706, but he was still a bachelor when he left Oxford and was sent straight to London. He would reside in the lodgings of his Uncle Ralph Palmer in the Middle Temple,[131] where he might 'find a good, improving acquaintance in the world and accomplish himself by . . . a little French, fencing &tc, as well as be in the way more of a happy marriage'. John believed that the London marriage market, supplemented by visits to Bath, would eventually provide him with a bride. In town, Palmer served as mentor to the boy and wrote 173 letters, mostly to his nephew.

Within four months of Ralph's arrival, John was negotiating in London with Mr Henry Paschall of Great Baddow Hall, Essex, concerning his co-heiress, Catherine. The Paschalls were an undistinguished family in terms of rank, but in the early sixteenth century, a yeoman John Paschall had acquired large amounts of Essex land.[132] The current squire, an elderly justice of the peace, was an undemanding negotiator. He would readily pass on his estates, providing his debts were paid and his daughter achieved status. John's Aunt Adams had married the rector of Great Baddow and often mentioned the 'two pretty Miss Paschalls'. In February 1707, John told Ralph about Catherine who 'will be the day she marries worth £8,000'. 'If she does not dislike him', John wrote Aunt Adams, 'I shall be very ready to wait on . . . [her] father.' Aunt Adams served as John's broker, but he thought her 'extremely in their interest', so she was falsely told that Ralph knew nothing. Meanwhile, Ralph was required to report anything he could 'fish out of Aunt Adams'.[133] No matter how close the ties, every negotiation contained elements of secrecy. This added risk no doubt heightened the pleasure of success.

In a desperate, last effort, Mrs Tregea switched from Mr Egerton's niece Lady Leicester to his sister. Her parents 'were not for long settlements nor pin-money', she assured John, for this was now a factor. They would make John an English baron and give Ralph 'any place in the civil government' that he desired. Since Mrs Tregea had invested time and trouble, she kept raising the stakes, for she did not want to lose a potential groom. Nevertheless, the Paschall match moved forward. John met Catherine's father in a Fleet Street tavern and offered £1,000 to 'equip' his son. Ralph's uncle, Ralph Palmer, was glad that Ralph 'has now a better liking to when he seemed at first'. This remark suggests that Ralph was being pushed into marriage and had succumbed to family pressure. Palmer told Ralph to take Catherine to the 'enchanting covert of a shady grove . . . to serenade your lady amidst a chorus of nightingales'. Along with this romantic advice, Palmer also sent a list of negotiating points to consider: jointure, maintenance, portions, pin money, and securing Catherine's inheritance in default of issue. The latter point shows the Verneys' possessive attitude towards retaining their brides' portions.[134]

In the background, John conducted his usual meticulous checks and again used yeoman Churchill to appraise house, lands, rents, and even the silver. The question of who should pay an estate debt threatened to stop the match. John accused Mr Paschall of falsifying values and secretly keeping £1,000 for himself. Catherine's jointure would be only 'her own estate and about £400 per year' from the Verneys. In the final strict settlement, Catherine's half of the Great Baddow estate reverted to the Verneys, who might sell it if there were no children. Mr Paschall had to be content with £100 per year, but his debts of £2,200 were paid. John struck near the top of the gentry market and obtained Catherine with at least £8,000 and more to come.[135] After testing the waters for heiresses in the £10,000 to £12,000 range, he preferred to negotiate with a squire who submitted to his will.

Paschall's acres fell into the Verneys' hands at extremely favourable terms. Several clauses restricted Catherine's use of the land and sums for daughters' portions were not specified. Various stages of Ralph's wills remedied this, granting up to £5,000 portions for daughters and lands for younger sons. Catherine might dispose of the furniture in their London town house, but the family portraits, furniture, and Ralph's 'study of books' were tied to Claydon House forever.[136] (See cover for a portrait of Ralph's family.)

The wedding finally took place after a year of arguments. In practice, John arranged the match, although in theory he only had a veto. Ralph had never seen Catherine before their formal interview set up by Aunt Adams. John wrote Ralph, 'I leave this matter to your choice', but Ralph's Uncle Palmer hinted at paternal pressure: 'My nephew . . . has weighed the reasonableness of this matter . . . since your Lordship so kindly leaves the result of it to himself, I doubt not but you mean it so, that in all respects he may continue the same in your favour, opinion, and kindness as he does before, or otherwise I am apt to think he will do nothing.'[137]

John's 'favour, opinion, and kindness' was crucial to Ralph who wanted financial benefits. John's objectives were admittedly economic. Like Sir Ralph, he was uninterested in court living, but desired land and money. Yet John also wanted his heir to be happy and would not force him to make an abhorrent match. Catherine and Ralph seemed to get along well,[138] but Ralph never exhibited the passion of John's first courtship, and because he was less interested in letter-writing, we have fewer clues about his character. If he had been a younger son, his options would have been different. As 1st Earl Verney, however, he would enjoy other compensations.

John's eldest daughter Elizabeth remained a spinster despite suitors, so her £3,000 portion was never paid. Ralph's sons, John (1711–1737) and Ralph (1714–1791) continued the family strategy of marrying heiresses and using strict settlements. Both brothers wed women whose business wealth emanated from London. Indeed, the Verneys' eighteenth-century estate commanded two staggering portions. In 1736 Ralph's eldest son John received a £40,000 portion from Mary, daughter of Josiah Nicholson of Clapham, a Thames Street brewer. In return, Mary's jointure was set at £1,600. When John died in 1737, his younger brother Ralph became 2nd Earl Verney. Three years later, Ralph obtained £30,000 from Mary, heiress of Henry Herring of Mincing Lane, a merchant and director of the Bank of England. John thus had the best of both worlds. In the face of rising portions, he continued to provide his own daughters with only £3,000. His sons and grandsons, however, reaped full benefit from London's 'rage' of marriage and received bloated portions.[139]

A comparison of the Verneys' seventeenth- and eighteenth-century marriage strategies shows both continuity and change. The impact of the London marriage market was important. It created personal freedoms for a few, but led to marriages for money. Although none of John's in-laws lived in London, his children's courtships, negotiations, and wedding ceremonies took place in the capital. Some of their jointures were tied to non-landed wealth earned in the city. John's sons and grandsons became land buyers, and they bought a great deal in the eighteenth century. Thus, the cycle that had begun with seventeenth-century indebtedness and selling of land had now come a full circle. The Paschalls, on the other hand, were downwardly mobile and had different goals. They gave up their land in return for payment of debts and an alliance with a titled family.

The eighteenth-century Verneys maintained a mercenary marriage strategy. After financial status was ascertained, other motives came into play for younger children, but not for the heir. Although Mary's move to Ireland was at first resisted, a combination of love and wealth overcame this obstacle. The Cave match was based upon a different consideration. It shows how the rage of party was intertwined with the scramble for marriage partners. John was willing to sanction disobedience in order to gain political and social advantages. London played a role in his discarding of traditional precepts. It offered Margaret an unsupervised courtship locale and gave John an excuse to condone elopement. Although the London marriage market had known rules, standards had become more permissive.

The Verneys' eighteenth-century offspring except male heirs effectively chose their spouses, although fathers but not mothers retained veto rights. Love-sick suitors could initiate the process, instead of waiting for fathers to agree. All John's daughters were wed in a manner quite different from their grandfathers' day. We have only to contrast Sir Ralph's purchase of his bride Mary Blacknall in 1636 with the secret wedding of his granddaughter Margaret in 1703. Margaret's elopement was worlds apart from the award of her grandmother to her grandfather by the Court of Wards. Before Margaret's elder sisters had married, she wed with her father's blessing and her mother's assistance in duping the groom's father. Not only was there no settlement, it took several years and a lawsuit to arrive at an agreement. Nor did John select the husband of his daughter Mary. Colonel Lovett fell in love before any relatives met or approached Verney. John's eldest daughter Elizabeth never married at all, although she too had a £3,000 portion. Perhaps she was not as attractive as her sisters or did not like her choice of suitors. In addition to freer choice for the bride and groom, other family members played more active roles in the pre-wedding process. Ralph's Uncle Palmer helped to handle his courtship of Catherine Paschall. John's third wife Elizabeth not only organized the secret wedding of her stepdaughter Margaret, she played a role in her own marriage negotiations.

But the London market encouraged matches made for money as well as freedom of choice. The bargaining for John's son Ralph shows this clearly and illustrates the commercial nature of the market. It was no accident that Ralph was sent to London to find a bride, nor that he was regularly taken on trips to Bath to be seen and approached by matchmakers. As heir, Ralph, though loved, was a marketable commodity. John acknowledged this fact when he was offered a portion of £7,000: 'You see the cheapness of the sex', he responded. 'My son . . . is very young and I hope may acquire more if he carry himself discreetly.'[140]

The letters of John's London broker Anna Tregea describe the process by which the marriage market worked. It was marked by a 'rage' of marriage that paralleled that of party. As the search for Ralph's bride progressed, already inflated portions kept rising like bids on Exchange Alley. If the sum was not sufficient to close the deal, pin money or separate property in trust might be added. When possible, titles, offices, and other benefits were dangled to increase competitiveness. The result was a step-by-step escalation of terms that was expected and condoned by society. This bidding reflected a large supply of city and country heiresses, who helped to fuel the inflation.

The existence of such a market was crucial to families like the Verneys. Critics have argued that the strict settlement was not effective, because of private acts, the inclusion of only partial estates, and demographic factors such as the lack of an heir or the death of a father before a son agreed to settle.[141] Despite some of these problems, the Verneys achieved the primary goal of keeping core estates intact. They used the strict settlement and when they lacked male heirs in the eighteenth century, estates were left to women who assumed titles or to men who adopted the family name. Thus, Claydon lands never left the family and were passed on to chosen successors.

Eighteenth-century settlements continued to affect family members in different ways. Thus, the first-born sons of the Verneys, Caves, and Temples made sacrifices to safeguard their patrimonies. John's son Ralph appears to have negotiated only with Tory heiresses, while Sir John Cope's son set another example. His wife, wrote Aunt Gardiner, was 'lame, sickly, a very coarse skin, low and plain. So I suppose her fortune is large, or surely Sir John Cope's father would never have picked her out for his eldest son, who is a pretty gentleman'.[142] Heiresses suffered the same shackles as elder sons. In their case, birth order had a greater impact than gender. Wives saw their properties subsumed by the Verneys and found no pin money in this close-fisted family. The Verneys' jointures were never large. Perhaps in compensation, their wills sometimes liberalized settlements by providing added monies or lands. These grants, however, were hedged with restrictions that constrained wives. Historians have written of the development of separate women's property that gave some women more financial control. Widows and heiresses may have had property in trust. But unless there was a formal separation or a court order, the Verneys' gifts were only willed at death if the husband felt like doing so. Wives like Elizabeth Baker, who desired or expected a windfall, were constrained to toe the line during their spouses' lives. As we have seen, Elizabeth received only an extra £70 per year in contrast to larger bequests to wives of the Caves and Temples.[143]

The Verneys' eighteenth-century settlements also had different effects upon younger brothers and sisters. Except in Catherine Paschall's case, all the Verneys' contracts contained specific sums for daughters that were equal to their mothers' portions. But, although younger sons eventually inherited in every other generation, they received no money in settlements. A sample settlement deed in Sir Orlando Bridgeman's *Conveyances* included sums for daughters, but not for younger sons. It is probable that in many families, portions for younger sons were paid only if there were enough resources to go around. If not, portions for daughters that were needed to make a good match may have come first. For example, the daughter of Sir Daniel Fleming was 'better provided for than the sons', since their sister 'had no career but marriage'. And Elizabeth Delaval knew her father 'would much sooner part with a great sum for my portion, than with a small one to pay my debts'. A daughter with a dowry might make a more advantageous alliance than a younger brother with few prospects. As to younger sons, noted Swift, 'all that can be spared from the heir, or laid up out of the father's estate, is little enough to put off the daughters, and he can expect nothing but his education, and some small matter to set up with'.[144]

This behaviour, though at odds with that of many families, is in keeping with the Verneys' focus upon dynastic ends to the detriment of individuals. Yet other families gave liberally to younger sons, so the Verneys' policy may be unusual. Sir Richard Temple, 3rd Baronet, left his younger sons each £1,000, as well as £6,000 to be split among his daughters, which sum he raised to £8,000 in 1694.[145] This question is even more problematic, because there were no surviving Verney younger sons in this period except those who inherited. It seems reasonable to assume that in comparison with their sisters, some younger brothers received less protection over time. Consequently, they were pressured to become fortune hunters. Cousin Hobart, for example, wept over her son and hoped 'some rich lady may fall in love with him and make him master of a good fortune'. Similarly, Jack Nicholas was told to 'go into orders with all speed' when a living became vacant. He knew that 'the next business must be to get a good fortune with a wife'.[146] While younger sons may have had more freedoms, many were downwardly mobile. One must weigh both benefits and liabilities when assessing their position.

In practice, the Verneys' strict settlements did not automatically protect men or women. Even heiresses with large portions did not always attain a strong family position. This was the case for Catherine Paschall who received only 9 letters. Though she brought land, her settlement terms and place in the family were undistinguished. She was merely the most appropriate and tractable of a series of monied women presented by a London matchmaker. Locke's contract theory with its emphasis on reciprocal obligations had the potential for improving women's lot. For most Verney women, however, this promise was not fulfilled.

Men, Women, and Marriage Strategies

The foregoing section paints a bleak picture of the marriage market and the position of portionless men and women. But some individuals found subtle ways to attain their own ends and to challenge the dominant models of domestic femininity and public masculinity. Historians have suggested a variety of outcomes for the continuous tension which marked early modern gender relationships. In older models, women were increasingly oppressed by a homogeneous group of masculine patriarchs. But the Verney letters suggest a world of fluid complexities regarding both men and women. Surely secret weddings, elopements, madness, passionate love, tender husbands, confirmed bachelors, and strong women do not belong to the world of harsh property laws and controlled marriage settlements. Even in this strict family, we do not find rigid gender models or separate spheres for men and women.

First let us look at the varied roles and lives of Verney women. Due to feminist scholarship, we can see more complexities in their response to patriarchy than we can in the case of men. Verney women exercised power as mothers, kinswomen, consumers, arbiters of gossip, and gatekeepers of sociability. Wives retained close ties with their natural families, as letters of the Palmers, Bakers, Caves, and Temples show. These links were a source of leverage, especially when in-laws were powerful. Thus, political and legal exclusion did not make all Verney women helpless.[147] Nor did they all conform to the standard model of femininity.

In fact, the Verneys had their share of defiant women. Those who eloped challenged the system in a debilitating way. They usually suffered for their mesalliances, but the family did so as well. The elopement of Mun's only surviving child Molly was just such a case. In 1682 Cary Stewkeley warned Sir Ralph that his granddaughter 'cares not to marry for estate'. 'One had better marry to one one loves', declared Molly, after her elopement with John Keeling, 'though one was to eat nothing but bread and cheese'. Keeling defended their clandestine marriage noting 'how many families have been ruined from matches . . . that have married wholly disgreeable to one another'. But Molly was never forgiven, and some said her death might have been averted with proper care.[148] If she had married with her grandfather's approval, her claim to the Abels' East Claydon lands might have worked to the Verneys' advantage. In contrast, Pen Viccars' sexual affairs were forgotten after she inherited riches from her godmother.

In most cases, adulterous women lost their rights to family protection. In the 1670s, Sir Ralph considered sending an unmarried, pregnant relation to the north of England under an assumed name. In the end, she was shipped off to Virginia, where a different demographic situation provided her with a husband.[149] Other family members tried to rebel, but lacked the courage. When John's sister-in-law, Cornelia Palmer, was told to marry a rich, ageing merchant, she protested: 'My inclinations are not at present towards matrimony'. Cornelia gave in to her relatives' pressure and had a tragic marriage.[150] Yet considering the amount of family coercion, it is amazing how many other women had the courage to say no.

There were few powerful Verney matriarchs, as in the Newdigate, Harley, or Churchill families.[151] Nevertheless, one still finds a fear of female disruption in the language of Verney men. Thus when merchants raised the price of corn, Sir Ralph noted: 'The poor women of Banbury, Bicester, Buckingham, Stratford, Winslow, and Aylesbury, did so beat and punch and scratch those men that brought it.' In 1694 John reported that ladies had fought in St James Chapel, Windsor, 'for one hour, pulling on each other's commodes'. Evidently, Sir Ralph and John perceived a female tendency towards riot on the part of both elite and lower-class women.[152]

Men also remarked about how women used their sexuality to entrap lovers and husbands. When Sir Richard Temple married pregnant Mary Knapp, Mun joked about her 'modish education' and 'breeding', punning on the last word. Yet when Mun saw them put to bed he confessed that the bride's 'attractive beauty was powerful enough to make Diogenes the Stoic leave his tub and turn lover'. Men were also apprehensive about liberties of independent women. In 1705 John complained that 'now women go out of doors a month after their delivery'. Sir Thomas Cave worried more about his wife's everyday 'rambling'. He chided her for 'going abroad without acquainting her bedfellow'.[153] These fears may not have been groundless, for elite women assumed freedoms when their husbands were away.

We have the most documentation about John's third wife Elizabeth Baker, whose public and private spheres clearly overlapped. She expressed strong opinions, invested in the city, bred her own animals, and influenced the giving of patronage. She wrote 99 letters and received 49, a high ratio for a female in-law. She ran two homes and used her organizing skills to make John's commuting run smoothly. As Chapter 6 will show, she publicly managed county election activities while John was residing in London.[154] When she spent too much money or misplaced her keys he grew testy, but he trusted her judgement enough to put his daughter's elopement in her hands. In return, she was repaid with increasing authority. The fact that John's kin challenged her rights after John's death is evidence of her strength. They were aware of her power and hoped to end it.

Elizabeth was also able to assist other female relations. She appealed to John's Christian duty to help Uncle Tom's abandoned wife. The woman's request for money was 'lawful', argued Elizabeth, for she had brought a £500 portion and was burdening others with her debts. Elizabeth also interfered effectively when John considered firing her companion, Mary Lloyd. 'It will look very unkind', chided Elizabeth. 'She is your cousin . . . which nothing could be closer but brothers and sisters. And really, if we can't expect some compassion from them which are so nearly related, who must we from?' At the same time, she remembered to be deferential, adding: 'I can't pretend to have any influence over you.'[155] In practice, she obtained power by confessing that she had none, and used his love of family to Mary Lloyd's advantage. Elizabeth's finesse mitigated John's harshness. Strong women played compensatory roles that helped other more dependent women.

Another group of Verney women attained a different type of influence by serving as London marriage brokers. John's aunts benefited in this manner from the market's shift to the capital. Their activity was highly regarded and won Sir Ralph's praise: 'You ladies are so subtle and so versed in intrigues of this nature', he conceded. 'You can order these affairs much better than the Council Board of both Houses of Parliament.' At the same time, he downgraded their work by noting their 'intrigues' and gossip. But gossip had power when it drove up prices and produced financial offers.[156] By drawing analogies between domestic matters and state government, Sir Ralph showed that boundaries between private and public spheres were blurred during matchmaking.

Some elite widows had another type of influence. Verney men often spoke negatively of widows, especially if they were wealthy. John criticized a 'joyful widow with £6,000', even though she endured years with 'a mighty drunken sot'. It was one thing for women to have a bit of pin money and another when they controlled large sums. This may explain Sir Ralph's warning to John when he wooed a widow in 1679: 'Widows cheat more than any.' Several men described them as 'brisk' persons who would not live 'a dull country life'.[157] This language implied a gendered disapproval, for a man with money was not viewed in a negative light. A wife might have contributed a large portion, but as a widow she was seen as a drain on family fortunes. In 1690 Oliver Le Neve used the excuse of a widow's charge on his estate to avoid becoming sheriff of Norfolk. When jointures hindered the Temples of Stowe, Sir Richard's relict Mary Knapp was asked to surrender a part of her annuity to a relative who was interfering with the estate's succession.[158] These cases, whether real or exaggerated, encouraged negative stereotypes of femininity.

Verney women, however, spoke about widows with more awareness of their difficulties. John's daughter Mary believed that widows who remarried 'very seldom do well for themselves'. In her view, male suitors were likely to cheat widows of their money. There was resistance to second marriages for many reasons, including problems caused by new families. Aunt Gardiner hoped widow Pickering would not marry again and make herself 'a sham to her sex', while Aunt Adams worried about Lady Temple. 'If she keeps herself a widow she may be kind to her child. And if she marries, I feel she'll have the fate as most widows have, that is to ruin themselves.'[159]

Recent studies have disagreed about why marriages of widows declined at this time. The Verney archive confirms the view that some widows were unwilling to give up independence, wished to endow children, or preferred to keep property in their own family. Other widows did not remarry because of pressure from kin or because they would lose their jointures if they did so. Lady Temple and John's third wife Elizabeth Baker would suffer financially if they took another husband.[160] Still other widows like the London aunts lived close to the poverty line and were unable to remarry. A cluster of complex pressures affected different types of widows.

Finally, widows were not the only people who resisted marriage. Cornelia Dunk had to be forced to wed, while Nancy Nicholas's niece had a £2,000 portion waiting, but only £50 p.a. until she married. The number of spinsters has been estimated as rising from 10% to 25% for the peerage from 1579 to 1799 and was substantial for other classes in the late seventeenth century.[161] New investment opportunities were one factor that allowed women to remain single. Other women amassed large amounts of property due to the failure of male issue. Equity developments that legalized separate women's property also increased the wealth of women. The fact that many of them were able to bequeath money to other women is a significant development. At the death of Mary Lawley's relation Mrs Bennet, relatives found her 'chairs and stools were stuffed with money', while Cousin Pack was £5,000 richer because her mother died before her father'. Will after Verney will is filled with small legacies or gifts of money from one woman to another. Thus Cousin Paulett's £20 gift was 'a great thing to Kitty' Stewkeley. Perhaps the grandest gesture was Aunt Osborne's legacy to Pen Viccars. After distributing £600 in money and twenty-two gifts, there was still £7,700 left for her god-daughter. Although we may never discover how Pen Osborne amassed it, we know that she controlled annual payments from her estranged husband.[162]

In sum, many of the Verneys' elite female friends acquired financial resources and status. Some avoided matrimony and survived on their own. Others located small, but vital, independent spaces inside their restrictive marriages. Because the Verneys have been depicted an an extremely patriarchal family with few strong women,[163] these are significant findings. Instead of asking whether women's lives were better or worse, we can observe a continuous tension between individual and corporate interests for both men and women.

When it comes to men, however, there is more difficulty in perceiving gender roles. Historians have been criticized for writing solely about males, but we know little about the complexities of masculininity and what it meant to be manly.[164] In England, where elite society was based upon patriarchy and primogeniture, masculinity was central to society. Elder sons and heirs, in particular, had to fit into an established model of manly behaviour that created burdens as well as privileges. As we have seen, the principal means by which the Verneys preserved and increased their estates was through the marriages of elder sons.[165] A cyclical pattern emerges when five generations—Sir Edmund, Sir Ralph, Mun and John, Ralph, and his sons John and Ralph—are viewed as a whole. First, the family faced debt after the Civil War. The heir rebuilt the family fortune through a variety of techniques. His son consolidated gains and left his own heir in an enviable position. One constant persisted in every generation—marriage of the heir to an heiress. As in other elite families, a dynastic mindset was implanted through use of the strict settlement. Thus Verney sons were bound to their fathers' wishes by hoops of steel forged out of shared values.[166]

Until we know more about the development and varieties of masculinities, we can only make conjectures about why more elder sons did not rebel and what effects primogeniture and patriarchy had upon them and their younger brothers. Of course, there were economic reasons for elder sons to marry as told, but not everyone complied and fathers behaved differently too. We do know that after 1600 the percentage of bachelors was at least between 20% and 26%. The number of those who never married may have reached a peak in the 1670s and 1680s, rising to about 27%. The Marriage Duty Act of 1695 with its 1s. duty on bachelors infers that there were large numbers of single men, as do pamphlets, both satirical and serious.[167]

The coexistence of patriarchy, primogeniture, and a large number of bachelors raises unaddressed questions about birth order and masculinity. For example, were bachelors mainly younger sons without funds or recalcitrant elder brothers? Did younger sons remain unmarried solely for economic reasons? Did they have a tendency to become fops or members of London's homosexual 'molly' culture?[168] Were post-Restoration libertines and rakes more likely to be rebellious younger sons or their elder brothers? Why did these and other alternate masculine subcultures become more noticeable at this time?

Several themes discussed in this book are linked to these questions. For example, did London have an impact upon elite masculinity and produce different modes of sexuality than in the country? How did demographic, legal, and cultural developments affect identities of landed and urban fathers, elder sons, younger brothers, and bachelors? In what ways did the gentlemanly code of honour and politeness effect the masculinity of these groups?

Answers to these questions are beyond the scope of this study. The Verney letters do show us, however, that duty to one's father and one's family honour were so important that they often overrode other factors. In this regard, elder sons had a special responsibility to show self-discipline and to perpetuate the family estate and name. For them, being masculine was in part a group stereotype that meant sacrificing individual values to those of the greater society.[169] To produce this mentality, sons were educated with care. Even John, who entered trade, was bred to become a gentleman. He too was provided with manly accoutrements: a civic humanism crowned by studying Latin; training in sports and physical recreation; broad learning based upon access to libraries and travel; pride in honour and morality; and a healthy dose of genealogy. The breeding of John's heir Ralph included a horse to make his life 'delightful'. He was educated in the all-male environments of boarding schools, Merton College, Oxford, and the Middle Temple, where he could meet 'sober, young gentlemen' and live a life of manly virtue, if not sexual morality. Bonds between father and son were reinforced by constant letter-writing. The use of dependent female kin as governesses, who were commanded by the family head, may have further contributed to filial deference.[170]

At the same time, paternal pressures supplemented voluntary actions of elite children. Primogeniture was a given, from which one's place in life was derived. But family heads found ways to attain more freedom with their estates. Sir Ralph withheld valuable lands from Mun's settlement, as did John from that of his son Ralph. With the exception of John's small Berkshire property, their were no provisions for younger sons. Wills restored the balance, but they had to be patiently awaited. Examples of disinherited sons were reminders of parental authority. After Mun's generation, however, patriarchal power was delicately used. No children were forced to marry against their wishes, but they knew that parents had the right of veto.

Over time, certain traits and behavioural strategies were passed on from father to son in elite families like the Verneys, Temples, and Caves. Each family head combined a marriage policy that preserved estates with a variety of strategies, depending upon the time and circumstances. Sir Edmund Verney took the courtier's route, but his attempts to make money from office failed. From that time on, each generation shunned the court. Sir Ralph rebuilt the family fortunes through estate improvement, frugal living, and debt consolidation. Both he and John avoided forms of conspicuous consumption that ravaged other families such as a prolonged grand tour, extensive house building, and expensive gardens. Thus, each generation kept the core estate intact, as did Sir Thomas Cave and Sir Richard Temple. It was in later generations who inherited wealth that over-expenditure would wreak havoc.

John's son Ralph (1683–1752) became a land buyer, buttressed by his wife's estate and his father's city money. In 1717 he assumed his father's Irish viscountcy and in 1743 he received an Irish earldom. When his eldest son John died in 1737 leaving only a daughter, a Verney younger son once again inherited. This son Ralph (1714–1791) became 2nd Earl Verney. He crippled the estate with enormous house building expenditures and died in debt without issue. Like Mr Peniston who 'made his eldest daughter as an elder son' and left her all he had, the 2nd Earl's niece Mary was created Baroness Fermanagh. Thus she was able to inherit the estate and gender boundaries were blurred.

Mary pulled down her uncle's new house and died unmarried in 1810 (see plate 7). She left the estate to Catherine Calvert, her half-sister by her mother's second marriage to Richard Calvert. Catherine and her husband Reverend Robert Wright assumed the name of Verney. When Catherine died without issue in 1827, she left Claydon to a distant cousin, Sir Harry Calvert. Calvert, a baronet without an estate, was unrelated to the Verneys. When Sir Harry inherited Claydon in 1827, he too changed his name to Verney. Again, a substitute for a direct male heir was found to preserve estates. This book has emphasized the importance of dynasticism. Because it was so significant, it overrode gender and lineage considerations.[171]

The Verney pattern of marrying heiresses was not unusual for elite families. The Townshends of Norfolk experienced a similar cycle. So did the Temples of Stowe. In 1673 the steward of Sir Richard Temple (1634–1697) recognized the third baronet's responsibility to marry an heiress: 'There is wanting what all families have', he wrote, 'a marriage portion to free you from a straight condition, that . . . you might enjoy the whole at your pleasure as a gentleman ought to do.' Sir Richard found his heiress, repeating an old family pattern. Like John, Sir Richard selected his bride from the market place, marrying wealthy

Mary Knapp, daughter of Henry Knapp of South Stoke, Oxfordshire.[172] His son Richard Temple, Viscount Cobham (1675–1749) wed Anne Halsey, sole daughter and heiress of a brewer Edmund Halsey. Halsey had come penniless to London, married his employer's daughter, and become sole owner of James Child's brewery. Anne's £20,000 portion allowed Cobham to rebuild his house and construct magnificent gardens. She received a £1,400 jointure and £400 at her own disposal.[173] Both the Temples and the Verneys needed lucrative marriages to underwrite their spending.

Again like the Verneys, Cobham had no heir. Although a distant male relative was anxious to succeed, Cobham was determined to pass on his estate more directly. He therefore arranged a marriage for his sister Hester with Richard Grenville of nearby Wotton. Cobham's lands were then left to Hester, who was later created Countess Temple. Again like Baroness Verney and Mr Penison's daughter, she became a substitute for a male heir. Her son hyphenated his name to Grenville-Temple and later became Earl Temple. In 1737 he married Anna, 'a fortune of £50,000', the daughter of a merchant, Thomas Chambers, who bought his estate with the proceeds of a West Indies fortune. It was rumoured that she was of 'black ancestry', and that his uncle and mother had forced the union. By this time, at least six heiresses had married into the family. Furthermore, the Temples, like the Verneys, used surname substitution to achieve dynastic continuity.

In the cases of both the Verneys and the Temples, eldest sons or their surrogates in every generation fulfilled their masculine responsibilities and received substantial marriage portions. Only the combination of strategies used by the male head to supplement wives' portions differed. John Verney lived prudently, avoided court connections, and confined himself to local Tory politics. The Temples would take an alternate court route by participating in national patronage networks and Whig Government ministries. Both families understood that marriage for money was a reliable component of their family strategies.[174]

PLATE 1. John Verney, a Young Merchant by Gerard Van Soest [mid-17th century]

PLATE 2. John Verney, 1st Viscount Fermanagh attributed to Thomas Murray [c.1707]

PLATE 3. Elizabeth Palmer after Sir Peter Lely, 1st wife of John Verney, d.1686

PLATE 4. Elizabeth Baker attributed to Thomas Murray, 3rd wife of John Verney, d.1736

PLATE 5. Sir Ralph Verney, 1st Baronet, father of John Verney by Sir Peter Lely, d.1696

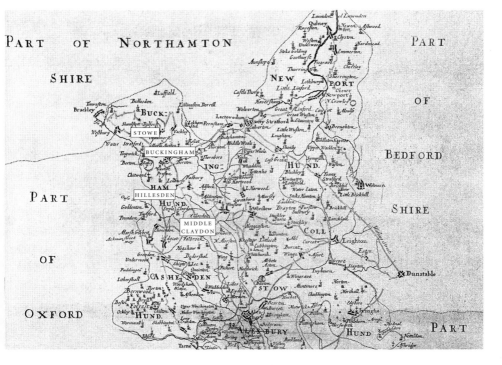

THE OLD MANSION AT MIDDLE CLAYDON.

NORTH

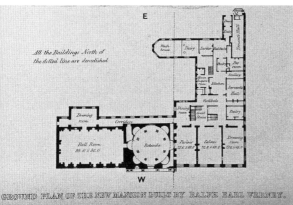

E

All the Buildings North of
the dotted line are demolished

W

GROUND PLAN OF THE NEW MANSION BUILT BY RALPH EARL VERNEY.

PLATE 6. Map of Buckinghamshire by Robert Morden [1695]. Note how the Verney, Denton, and Temple estates at Middle Claydon, Hillesden, and Stowe encircle the Parliamentary borough of Buckingham in the north-west corner.

PLATE 7. The Old Mansion at Middle Claydon and A Ground Plan of the New Mansion Built by Ralph, 2nd Earl Verney in the Eighteenth Century from George Lipscomb, *The History and Antiquities of the County of Buckingham* (London, 1847, vol. i, facing page 186)

PLATE 8. Stagg Hunting, Viz Chopping at his Head from Richard Blome, *The Gentleman's Recreation* (London, 1686, following page 84)

PLATE 9. The Last Horse Race Run Before Charles II by Frances Barlow, 1687

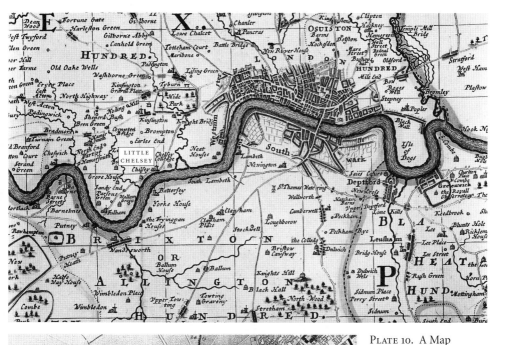

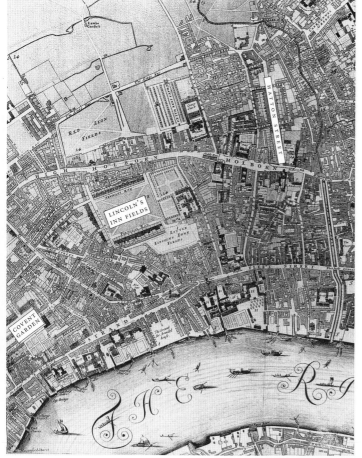

PLATE 10. A Map Containing the Towns, Villages, Gentlemen's Houses, Roads, Rivers & Other Remarks for 20 Miles Round by William Knight, c.1700. Note the western village of 'Little Chelsey' where John Verney's in-laws lived, far from the city to the east.

PLATE 11. London . . . Actually Survey'd by William Morgan, 1681–2 with Covent Garden, Lincoln's Inn Fields, and Hatton Garden. Note the proximity of John Verney in Hatton Street near Holborn to Sir Ralph in Lincoln's Inn Fields and to kin in Covent Garden. John chose to be 'in the middle between the Exchange and Westminster, which the places where my business'

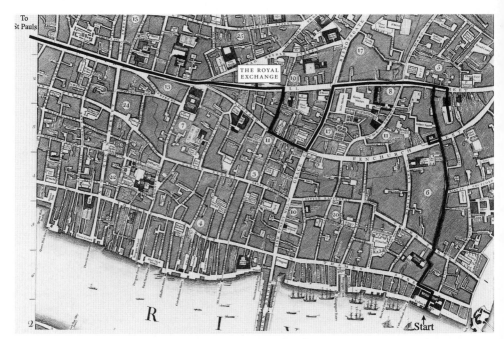

PLATE 12. John Verney's City Walk: A Plan of the Cities of London and Westminster and Borough of Southwark . . . from an Actual Survey taken by John Rocque, 1746. The Royal Exchange is marked by a square in the upper-middle section of this map. See page 73

PLATE 13. South-West
P . . .

THE ROYAL
EXCHANGE

To
St Pauls

Start

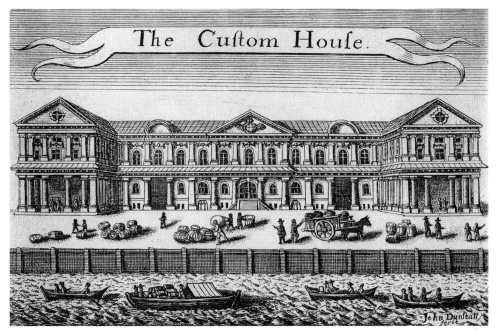

PLATE 14. John Dunstall's View of the Custom House (Wren's 1674 building) from Morden and Lea's Prospects, *c.*1690

PLATE 15. Temple Barr du Côté du Couchant from James Beeverell, *Les Delices de la Grand Bretagne, & de L'Ireland* (1707, vol. iv, facing page 834). Note the coach hogging the road

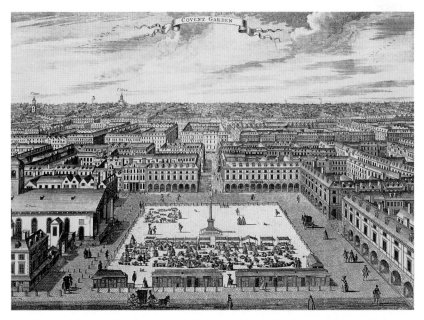

PLATE 16. 'Covent Garden': A Bird's-eye View of the Piazza and Market, Sutton Nicholls del. et sculp., 1720. The Verneys, Dentons, and Temples lived on the east side of the Piazza. A coach drives by Sir Edmund Verney's double house on the corner of Russell Street on the right-hand side of this map.

PLATE 17. The Tea-Table [c.1710]

PLATE 18. Coach at 'The South Prospect of the Church of St. Clement's Danes' in the Strand. J. Kip del. et sculp., 1715

PLATE 19. Coach Rank in front of 'Montague House' in Great Russell St. as rebuilt in 1687. J. Bowles del. et sculp., 1714

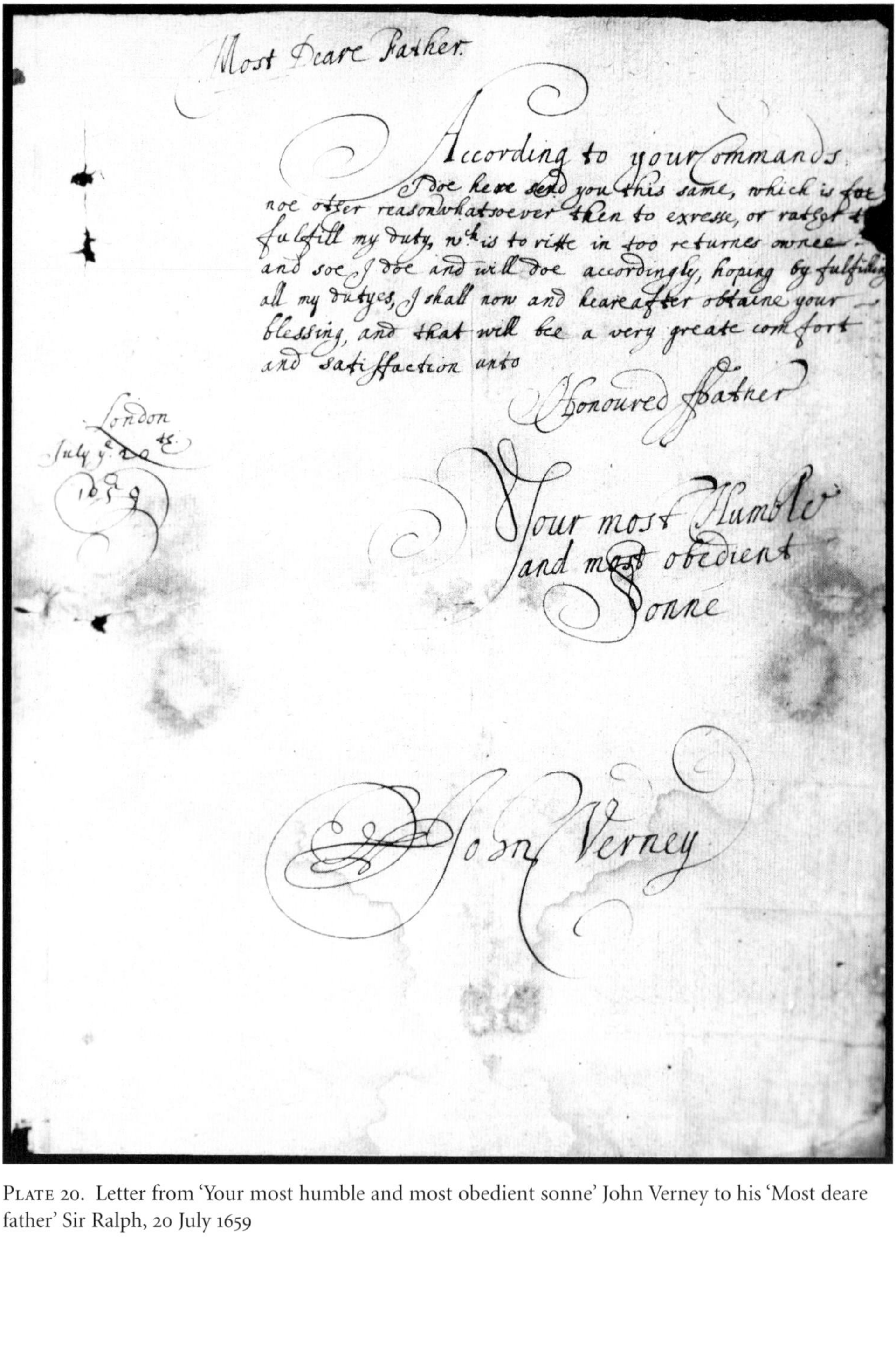

Most Deare Father.

According to your commands
I doe here send you this same, which is for
noe otter reason whatsoever then to exresse, or rather to
fulfill my duty, w:ch is to ritte in too returnes onnce
and soe I doe and will doe accordingly, hoping by fulfiling
all my dutyes, I shall now and heareafter obtaine your
blessing, and that will bee a very greate comfort
and satiffaction unto

Honoured Father

Your most Humble
and most obedient
Sonne

London
July y:e 20
1659

John Verney

PLATE 20. Letter from 'Your most humble and most obedient sonne' John Verney to his 'Most deare father' Sir Ralph, 20 July 1659

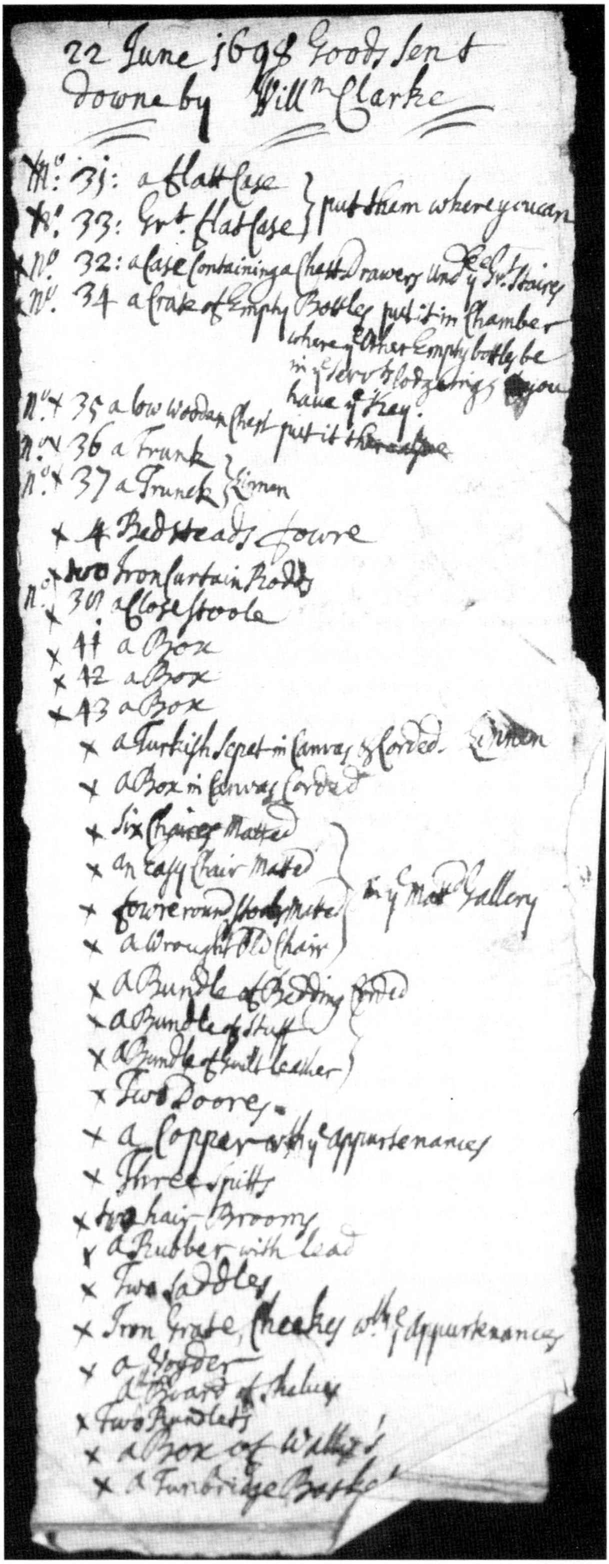

22 June 1698 Goods sent
downe by Willm Clarke

No: 31: a flatt Case } put them where you can
No: 33: Grt. flatt Case }
No: 32: a Case Containing a Chest of Drawers Under ye Back Staires
No. 34 a Crate of Empty Bottles put it in Chamber
where ye Other Empty bottles be
in ye Serv: Lodgings you
have ye Key.
No. 35 a low Wooden Chest } put it there also
No. 36 a Trunk }
No. 37 a Trunck Linnen
4 Bedsteads fowre
two Iron Curtain Rodds
No. 38 a Close stoole
41 a Box
42 a Box
43 a Box
a Turkish Carpet in Canvas & Corded. Linnen
a Box in Canvas Corded
Six Chaires Matted
an easy Chair Matted
fowre round stools Matted } in ye Matted Gallery
a Wrought Old Chair
a Bundle of Bedding Corded
a Bundle of Stuff
a Bundle of Gilt Leather
Two Doores
a Copper with ye appurtenances
Three spitts
two hair Brooms
a Rubber with lead
Two Saddles
Iron Grate, Cheekes with ye Appurtenances
a Fender
a Board of Shelves
Two Bradlets
a Box of Willis
a Tunbridge Basket

Plate 21. List of Goods sent from London to Claydon House, Buckinghamshire, 22 June 1698

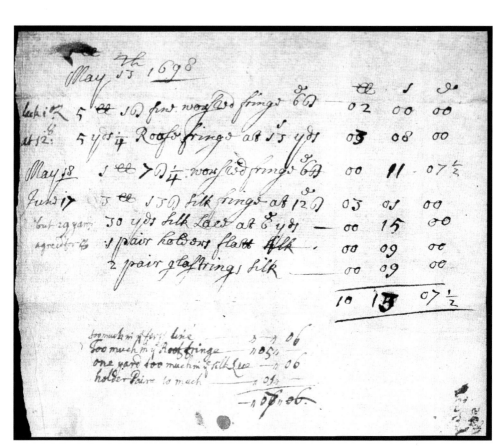

PLATE 22. Fringemaker's Bill for John Verney's Coach for £10 15s. 7.5d. John notes that he was charged 'too much' and was deducting 7s. 6d.

6

Party Politics and Power:
The Verneys and the Temples

I am always for peace.

Sir Ralph Verney,
2 January 1691[1]

The Temples of Stowe and the Verneys of Claydon may have had similar marriage strategies, but when it came to politics they were as different as day and night. This was startling, for with their kinsmen the Dentons of Hillesden, the families formed an interdependent network that had persisted over generations. Chapter 1 examined the Buckinghamshire community as Sir Ralph lay dying. It showed the gentry gathered in the ritual of the hunt, exchanging gifts of venison. This chapter ends with the death of Sir Ralph's son John. We see the Buckinghamshire community gathered in the ritual of the election, bestowing gifts of patronage.[2]

For centuries, hospitality and shared governance by the gentry and their neighbours had tempered religious and political conflict. By the eighteenth century, however, the Verneys were participating in new forms of electoral politics that divided the gentry community. Country custom was especially affected by the growth of political parties, which led to a shift of power from the localities to the national centre. The Verneys' experience in county and borough elections was affected by the rise of a strong central government, new opportunities for national patronage, the dominance of annual Parliaments, and absenteeism of the greater gentry.[3]

In response to these factors, the eighteenth-century Verneys and their neighbours embraced a competitive political culture. This chapter compares Sir Ralph's non-partisan activities based on old forms of social relationships with the party politics of his son John and the Temples of Stowe. It shows that sociability and power were intertwined and when politics changed, so did modes of sociability. During the rage of party, politics permeated every aspect of the Verneys' lives. In keeping with their perception, this study maintains that political behaviour and events took place in everyday social activities.

At elections the community gathered together and performed a series of rites. Social practices that were embedded in the election process went through three stages. In the first stage during the sixteenth century, candidates used food and drink to thank supporters after elections, thus displaying hospitality and reuniting the community. Elements of this stage coexisted with new conditions that had roots as early as the 1620s, but became more widespread by the 1640s. By the late 1670s, the intrusion of national politics had led to bitterly contested local elections. During this second stage, treating was done before and after the poll, while the use of cash and bribery became more openly acceptable. At the same time, old social relations came under strain. A bitter, social rift developed between the Verneys, Temples, and Dentons. As a result, their social code based upon kinship, honour, and communally selected candidates was severely undermined.[4] Part 1 of this chapter analyses the political acitivities of the Verneys, Temples, and Dentons from 1679 to 1690.

From the 1690s through Queen Anne's reign, a third more competitive stage evolved. It was characterized by a virulent rage of party cited in 214 letters and a sharply expanding electorate of 2,500 to 4,500 voters. Former, fluid gentry alliances hardened into Whig and Tory parties. The votes of an expanding group of middling-sort freeholders now became critical. The result was a fissured gentry community, whose sociability was segregrated by party. Hotly contested horseraces, followed by Whig and Tory balls, replaced communal dining at local hunts.[5] It is telling that John was not even invited to the funeral of his kinsman Sir Edmund Denton, although he had served as his guardian. This snub would have been unimaginable to earlier members of both families.

A new generation of county leaders emerged, whose politics differed from those of their fathers. Sir Ralph Verney, Baronet (1613–1696), Sir Alexander Denton, Knight (1654–1698), Sir Richard Temple, 3rd Baronet (1634–1697), Philip Wharton, 4th Baron Wharton (1613–1696), and Charles Cheyne, Viscount Newhaven (1625–1698) all died within a few years of each other. Part 2 examines the political careers of their sons from 1690 to 1715. It compares the alternative routes taken by the Tory Verneys and Cheynes with those of the Whig Temples, Dentons, and Whartons. In doing so, it addresses the rise and rage of party, the political influence of women, and the question of eighteenth-century stability. While Sir Ralph Verney shunned partisan politics in the seventeenth century, his son John built a local Tory power base and brought new forms of sociability to Claydon House. But although John adapted to a commercialized political culture, he did not attain the same national power and offices as Sir Richard Temple and his son Viscount Cobham.

The story ends with a decision by local Whigs and Tories to join temporarily in a political compact. Party feuds undermined social networks, but conflict always existed within a framework of common gentry interests. This type of compromise was rejected by John's son-in-law, Sir Thomas Cave, a Leicestershire baronet (1682–1719) with Jacobite tendencies. These different paths demonstrate the political choices open to post-Restoration families.

Mark Kishlansky, Geoffrey Holmes, and others have analysed Buckinghamshire politics in detail. Indeed, there were many contested elections in its six boroughs (Aylesbury, Amersham, Buckingham, Marlow, Wendover, and

Wycombe) and there were seven County contests between 1700 and 1714.[6] Instead, I have chosen to focus upon how sociability and power were connected and how partisan strife affected social and cultural relationships. The existence of many poll books helps to make this approach fruitful. A summary of Buckinghamshire politicians and events is found in Appendix V.

PART 1: SIR RALPH VERNEY (1613–1696)
AND SIR RICHARD TEMPLE (1634–1697)

The Country Community

The Verneys, Temples, and Dentons had shared bonds of friendship, kinship, and neighbourhood since time out of mind. While the Verneys' presence in Buckinghamshire dated back to the thirteenth century, the Dentons were well-established by the end of the fifteenth. The Temples, though late-comers in the sixteenth century, quickly rose to prominence.[7] Ties of intermarriage entwined the three families and they served each other as godparents, pallbearers, and trustees. Sir Alexander Denton repeatedly assured Sir Ralph that he made no political decision without seeking his advice. Sir Ralph, on his part, counselled his sons to keep close ties with neighbours, 'especially those that are next you'.[8]

The three families not only exchanged venison, they served together as members of Parliament, justices of the peace, deputy lieutenants, and tax commissioners. Sir Alexander Denton, Sir Ralph Verney, and Sir Peter Temple had sat in the Long Parliament. Although county landowners generally supported the Parliamentarians, a minority were Royalists including Sir Ralph's father Edmund and Sir Alexander Denton. Sir Ralph first sided with Parliament, but in 1643 he fled to France. Meanwhile, Denton died in custody after the Parliamentarians burned down his house. In contrast, Sir Peter Temple resisted ship money collection and backed Parliament.[9]

The authority of the old county families was easily reasserted after a period of retreat during the Cromwellian interlude. Since there were few resident peers, the gentry controlled political life. Although there were no large county towns, six market boroughs had a growing number of urban freeholders and sent two members to Parliament. Local lawyers and middling-sort voters in these centres were becoming more politically active.[10]

The gentry's commitment to mediate local conflict fostered political stability. However, the county was a breeding ground for independent congregations. Buckinghamshire had a tradition of Lollardy and Puritanism, and from 1669 to 1690 Quakers flourished in Aylesbury, Biddlesden, and Amersham. On the upper side of the county there were sixteen meetings, while eighteen sites were listed under the Toleration Act.[11] Sir Ralph and most of his gentry neighbours supported the established Church, but they also displayed toleration. Although the dissenter Robert Stopp was not allowed to preach in Middle

Claydon, Sir Ralph refused to 'make strict inquiries what he doth in other places, so as it be not too near me'. Dissenting ministers turned to Verney for help when imprisoned, and because he refused to encourage informers, some called him 'a favourer of fanaticks'. Sir Richard Temple summarized the feelings of the local gentry: 'They never were for persecuting men for conscience sake and hope they shall always live in peace with their neighbours.'[12]

In addition to mediating religious conflict, the gentry tried to resolve land disputes for the 'preservation of good neighbourhood and friendship'. In the 1670s, the Verneys quarrelled about enclosure with the Dormers of Lee and their Busby in-laws. Thus, when Sir Robert Dormer inherited, Sir Ralph told Mun to observe condolence calls, send compliments, and 'court the friendship' of Dormer. To cement ties, Sir Ralph and Mun celebrated a birth, settled a border dispute, and jointly licensed alehouses with the Dormers and Busbys.[13]

Similar attempts were made to ease political disputes. After a violent election in 1679, Mun took care to dine with his Dormer and Busby adversaries. The meal was a political event as well as a social occasion, for Mun was reworking the threads of community consensus. As tensions mounted during the Exclusion Crisis, fear of conflict haunted Mun. After Sir John Busby removed Temple's brother-in-law from the Commission of the Peace, Mun felt 'a strangeness between us for a great while'. 'Our country is like to be divided into feuds', he warned 'which . . . may prove fatal'.[14]

Rural peace, however, was disturbed most often by poor relationships with tenants. After his father's unhappy experience at court, Sir Ralph made Claydon the centre of his concerns. Daily letters to and from Sir Ralph's steward William Coleman were filled with news of tenants: their farming methods, financial problems, social behaviour, and family affairs. In contrast, Sir Richard's letters to his steward William Chaplyn dealt mainly with ensuring that Buckingham remained Temple's pocket borough. Sir Richard prodded Chaplyn to stir up the town burgesses and embarked upon a grandiose building plan to increase his prestige. Stowe and its gardens would become a showcase for political power and a source of cash from rents and wood sales.[15]

Yet although Chaplyn had less time to devote to local peace, he still had to deal with tenants. His relations with them, he admitted, were a 'perpetual contest here about freebords and trees, presenting the minister, keeping leys . . . taking game . . . continually fishing the river and .. withholding of custom from the mill'. Both Temple and Verney voiced concern about middling-sort yeomen who were called 'rising' men. Arrears in rent were also a problem. Sir Ralph disliked seizing a man's land, for his cousin Denton had been 'a great loser by it'. This is not to say that Sir Ralph was an easy landlord, for he squeezed every penny he could out of tenants until arrears rose at the end of the seventeenth century.[16]

Obviously, there would always be conflicts between landlord and tenants. But Sir Ralph and Sir Richard had grown up in a community that depended upon the gentry to preserve the peace. By the late 1670s, however, as national politics grew more partisan, the Temples reacted differently from the Verneys. Their divergent paths help us to understand their changing political culture.

Sir Ralph Verney and Sir Richard Temple (1679–1696)

Sir Ralph Verney and Sir Richard Temple held opposing views about politics. Opportunistic, ambitious, and a risk-taker, Temple was an active, fracas-loving politician. In the 1661 Cavalier Parliament, for example, he had 263 committee appointments, 32 tellerships, and made over 200 recorded speeches. Temple had been a member for Buckingham borough since 1659, with only one brief interlude. His ancestors had amassed huge amounts of land through 'a strong acquisitive instinct backed by remorseless litigation'. By the time of John Temple (1542–1603), the family had become prominent in Buckinghamshire. In 1653 Sir Richard inherited an estate worth £6,000 per year, but extravagance and war had led to debts of over £26,000. By the late seventeenth century, however, Temple, like Sir Ralph, had used London's financial institutions to rebuild the family's finances.[17]

Though formerly a Parliamentarian, Sir Richard brought little political baggage and he was willing to use any means to achieve power. Although at first he opposed the Crown, he soon turned to the court party. He changed patrons many times, but by 1675 he was supporting the King's chief minister, Thomas Osborne, Earl of Danby (1632–1712). During the Exclusion Crisis, Shaftesbury tellingly called Temple 'thrice vile'. Temple's strategy led to lucrative offices including a Board of Customs' place worth £2,000 a year.[18] Although he was twice dismissed from this post, in 1686 he obtained a £1,200 pension. 'In all governments, steady to none', wrote an opponent, while others thought him 'a nimble-tongued fellow' and 'the subject of . . . raillery'. 'I find he will be Vicar of Bray still, let who will reign', said an observer. 'Though all hate him, he gets what he aims at.'[19]

If Temple switched sides easily, Sir Ralph was consistent to a fault. He regarded Parliamentary service as a family duty, for a Verney had been a member since 1472. Sir Ralph represented Aylesbury in both Long and Short Parliaments, but in 1661 and 1679 he refused to stand. In 1681, 1685, and 1689, Sir Ralph reluctantly joined Temple in representing Buckingham. The key to his politics lay in his love of moderation and his view that religious and political morality were tightly linked. Because he was as sober and frugal publicly as he was in private, he would not debauch voters with drink. This position annoyed Temple, who was prepared to spend liberally in exchange for votes.[20]

Sir Ralph's attitude towards bribery and corruption placed him in the 'country' camp, but he disliked partisan politics. Not surprisingly, his reactions to the Exclusion Crisis and Popish Plot were cautious and conservative. In 1678 he and Dr William Denton hoped that the Commons would draw up only 'a representation, (a remonstrance savours too much of 1641)'. In 1679 he and Mun believed that the present Parliament should 'not drive so furiously to overturn things as the late Parliament hath done'. Both men were unwilling to put aside a divinely endowed prince, for 'no mortal ought to disinherit whom God almighty makes heir'.[21]

But neither would Sir Ralph endorse James II's absolutist behaviour. Verney's removal from the county bench in 1686, the same year that Temple received a pension; Verney's dismissal from the lieutenancy in 1688; and his refusal to answer the three questions about the Penal Laws and Test Act, contrast with Temple's toadying to the court for a Buckingham Charter.[22]

The Rise of Party

Before the 1690s, political labels and affiliations remained fluid. Sir Ralph's family traditionally had court connections, but he was more comfortable with 'country' principles. Temple was usually listed as a member of the court party, but he was also called a 'less violent Whig'.[23] If partisan allegiance was still unclear, however, by the mid-1670s the term 'party' had crept into the Verneys' vocabulary. At first it was used pejoratively to describe opponents, because party was considered a divisive concept. Because the Verneys had Tory inclinations, there are many references to the Whig party, but few to that of the Tories. In this early phase, the Verneys spoke of parties in terms of court and country and used references to religious categories. Thus, in 1677 John wrote that 'the court *party*' was ousted by Sir Thomas Player of 'the non-conforming *party*' because 'the fanaticks' had left church early to vote. Sir Ralph also called Player's followers 'the Godly *party*', using a term employed to describe Puritans. In 1678 Mun was upset that there would be no war with France: 'Those men', he declared, 'who were of the court *party* and tack about now and vote for the country, should have done it sooner.'[24]

During the Exclusion Crisis, references to party mounted, often in relation to the Earl of Shaftesbury. Aunt Gardiner saw the King's slight to Essex, Shaftesbury, and other leaders as 'a slight to their whole *party*. . . . The King despises all the other *party* can do'. In 1681 the Verneys first defined party as a source of finance. Thus, Mun discussed actions of the candidates Sir Peter Tyrrell and Charles Blount, noting: 'Some say (but I don't believe it) that these expenses upon Buckingham people are defrayed by a club of their *party*.' After Blount lost, it was reported that he would not stand again and 'has writ to his *party* to that effect'.[25]

By 1681 the Verneys used the terms 'Whig' and 'Tory' more often. In 1682 Dr Denton complained about the 'rogue Whigs' in London. In the same year, Temple's steward William Chaplyn indentified Whigs as 'a sort of people ready to oppose the concerns of such people they call Tories'. While references to Whig and Tory parties continued through the 1680s, the language of court and country persisted along with religious terms. What was significant to the

Verneys was that party politics now meant contested elections and the use of money to buy votes. By 1690 the Verneys feared that a party as a group might give money to candidates. Aunt Gardiner was disgusted that 'the whole *party* of the Whigs' funded candidates, but '*our party*' did not. She now identified herself with one of two evolving groups. Two criteria appear to be significant: a shared body of ideas about Church and State, and some amount of centrally imposed organization. The recognition of these elements by contemporaries supports historians who argue that the seeds of party were planted during the Exclusion Crisis.[26]

Buckinghamshire Elections and the Country Community (1679–1690)

Both the Temples and the Verneys had ancient ties with Buckingham borough. A review of their efforts to win its Parliamentary seat shows that partisan politics led to new patterns of social relations between individuals, families, and burgesses. The borough lay in the arms of the Ouse River, only two and a half miles from Stowe and six from Middle Claydon (see plate 6). Castle ruins perched upon a hill, while numerous inns catered to about 800 families.[27] The Dentons owned a manor in town and endowed a free school in 1540, but there were few other amenities. Four guilds—the mercers, tanners, butchers, and merchant taylors—admitted freemen, but by 1660 trade was declining. The status of county town had been lost to Aylesbury, along with the right to hold quarter sessions, winter assizes, and county elections. Because the town hall had burned down, there was no jail and sheds had to be erected for summer assizes.[28]

By the 1670s, however, a rising middling sort were striving to improve the town's trade and by 1690, fifty-six occupations were noted. Local entrepreneurs annoyed Temple with their independent ways, especially Henry Robinson. In 1670 Robinson built an assembly room in Castle Street for the gentry. He laid out a bowling green on Castle Hill, and in 1679 he set up a stage coach to London. Along with his inn, he provided a new range of services and grew powerful in the town.[29]

Under a charter granted in 1554, thirteen burgesses nominated two of their number for bailiff, from which the freemen elected one every May Day. Vacancies were filled by the burgesses, who enjoyed a closed corporate oligarchy. They claimed the sole right to elect members of Parliament, but since 1660, the freemen or 'populace', had challenged this entitlement.[30] Because most elections went to a poll and results were often disputed, candidates had to woo both burgesses and the populace. Violence and petitions for a wider franchise marked the polls in Buckingham and the open town of Aylesbury. The burgesses hoped to obtain money for a town hall in order to regain the status of 'county town'. They played off one candidate against another in return for promises to finance the building.

Between 1660 and 1690, Sir Richard Temple won six of seven Parliamentary elections, and he was the town's High Steward. In February and August 1679, borough elections were influenced by the Exclusion Crisis and problems of Danby's court party. Despite urgent pleas, Sir Ralph refused to stand with Temple because of the 'certainty of the charge and the great uncertainty of their [Parliament] sitting'. Temple stood with Danby's son Edward Osborne, Viscount Latimer (1654–1689) against the new 'country' interest of Sir Peter Tyrrell and Thomas Wharton. Temple 'set the taps a running all over the town'. If he wins, Denton wrote Sir Ralph, 'twill be by bribery'. There was stone throwing and sword fighting at the poll, and the Duke of Buckingham intervened against Temple. As a result there was a double return which meant that Tyrrell was elected by the mass of freeholders and Temple was chosen by the thirteen burgesses. Temple's appeal was denied and he lost his Buckingham seat, while Wharton won for the county in spite of court interference. 'It is plain by the elections', wrote Mun, 'the country for the most part . . . which way it inclines. . . . Therefore the court may do well not to irritate the people over much.'[31]

In the next election that August, Sir Ralph again refused to stand, but this time Temple and Latimer prevailed. The county election, however, was won by Wharton and John Hampden with the aid of bribery.[32] After the 1679 contests, both sides produced pamphlets, ballads, and lawsuits. Religious issues were stressed and there were outbursts against popery. There was also anger about Temple's use of patronage, for one burgess's son had received a custom-house place, while another was recommended to Eton School by both Temple and Latimer.[33] Although each party manipulated the facts, the Verneys recognized authors' agendas. Thus, John found *A Letter from a Freeholder of Buckinghamshire to a Friend in London* 'pretty near to truth, but not altogether'. And Mun thought *A Strange Monster in Stowe Woods* 'so sharp upon Sir Richard Temple because I doubt too true'. Moreover, the Verneys knew that *A Mild but Searching Expostulary Letter from the Plain-dealing farmers . . . to the Men of Buckingham*, was a 'scurrilous . . . railing letter (pretended) from farmers'. Another account cited 'people crying through this town "no Timber Temple"', however Sir Ralph wrote in the margin: 'but by few'.[34]

In the wake of this tumult, the election for bailiff on May Day turned violent. Henry Robinson, now accused of writing ballads, led a mob who broke open the municipal chest, examined the charter, and declared that 'freemen have voices. . . .'[35] Pressure was mounting for a broader definition of the franchise.

In 1681 Sir Ralph finally agreed to stand with Temple against Peter Tyrrell and the deist Charles Blount, whose religion caused Verney anxiety. Sir Ralph reluctantly agreed to pay for treating the burgesses and their wives, and for half the costs of treating the populace, but only on election day. Sir Ralph did not expect or seek the popular vote. 'I do not trade with them', he admitted, and 'would rather lose it than get it by excessive drinking.' If the populace were admitted to the poll, he warned Temple, 'it will . . . be construed that you admit of their right to elect'. Sir Ralph's notions about the franchise were mixed with ethical principles which motivated his actions. Temple and Verney won with eight burgesses each, but the popular vote totalled 239 for Tyrrell, 238 for Temple, 207 for Blount, and only 181 for Verney.[36]

In 1684 the Crown attacked the borough's charter. Temple convinced the burgesses to give up their old constitution by dangling promises of exclusive franchise. Recently, Robinson had built a cockpit, fountains, and gardens on Castle Hill, which he swore was 'worth two assizes to the town'. Temple tried to remove him from the Corporation, for his entrepreneurism made him too popular.[37]

The new charter was a victory for Temple, who was made High Steward for life. Voting rights were limited to a mayor and twelve aldermen. Some of Temple's enemies were excluded from the Corporation, but Robinson's kinsman was made a Justice of the Peace.[38] Court politics intruded upon town government, yet local challenges to Temple persisted.

The death of Charles II in 1685 brought another tumultuous election, analysed in Mark Kishlansky's *Parliamentary Selection*. One reason for Verney's candidacy was the meddling of Lord Chief Justice Jeffreys. Verney's letters also reveal cultural factors that underpinned the election including Buckingham's growing civic consciousness, and the importance of community memory. Although Temple had a secure majority, Verney could count on only six burgesses. As a result, Temple threatened to stand with Sir Alexander Denton (1654–1998). Sir Ralph finally agreed to treat both men and women, 'they having done it frequently on the other side'. A self-perpetuating spiral was drawing money into the town and commercializing the election process. Now Sir Ralph at last agreed to finance the town hall, if it was done in another's name to 'colour the bribe'. Justice William Busby, however, told the burgesses that he disliked 'the selling of voices'. As they auctioned off their votes, he warned, they sold 'their country, their religion and all things'.[39] Although the poll had become a market place, a vote still had sanctity. Verney and Temple won the election, but at a price.

The burgesses' motives were clearly selfish, but in the context of the borough's problems, they appear more complex. The absence of a hall and county status retarded investment and income. Moreover, when the mayor refused to give his vote until a town hall was secured, he swore 'he should not be frighted out of his judgment'.[40] He and other middling-sort burgesses wanted to maintain their independence. As Busby had suggested, a vote signified municipal pride.

Community memory sustained this feeling by recalling the smallest gentry slights. Dr Denton believed that some aldermen still remembered the 'taking away of assizes' by Sir Ralph's grandfather. The Ethersay family, which included the mayor, nursed memories of Sir Ralph's decisions as Justice. They did not forget that he had refused to save their charter. Nor had he 'sweetened the town' with trade or ale. They remembered that Mun once failed to speak to Jack Ethersay, the attorney, and did not give him wine as he passed Mun's house.

Jack also declared that Sir Ralph had called Buckingham 'a nest of bastards and beggars'. Ethersay 'stands much upon the honour of his family', wrote John, 'ever formerly the best in that town'. The Verneys should have understood Jack's family pride. Yet John found the Ethersays rude and passionate. To him, they were 'hot-headed people that can't speak sense'.[41] A dialogue between middling-sort burgesses and local gentry had not yet been opened. Partisanship hampered listening and drowned out any conversation that might have taken place.

During the 1685 county election, the Ethersays worked with Jeffreys to prevent Thomas Wharton's re-election. Jeffreys publicly called Sir Ralph a trimmer, or 'one on both sides', because he previously had voted for Wharton. Jeffreys's action shows the significance of partisan politics, for he objected to voting for an individual, rather than for a side. Wharton and Tyrrell were country Whigs, who were challenging court candidates. Consequently, Sir Ralph wisely obtained a release from his promise to vote for Wharton. Then he reluctantly used old ties with the Earl of Clarendon to make sure he still had the King's favour. In 1685 Sir Ralph could not remain a viable candidate without a patron at court.

James II's pressure on Parliament grew in the late 1680s. Sir Ralph served on committees for preventing clandestine marriages, relieving debtors, and building churches. But he refused to answer all three questions on the repeal of the Penal Laws and the Test Act and was put out of the magistracy and lieutenancy. Even Temple lost his offices and Robinson temporarily became Mayor. But to Temple, he was still 'a mean, rude, debauched fellow unfit for society, much less governance'. Sir Richard's own late support of William of Orange brought him open ridicule.[42]

After the Glorious Revolution of 1688, the old charter was returned and in 1689, Verney and Temple stood again. Although Sir Ralph had helped finance a new town hall, he still refused to treat the populace.[43] Temple asked Sir Ralph's godson Alexander to stand instead of Verney, but when he refused, Verney and Temple won the election.[44] By publicly deserting his kinsman, Temple broke the social code and his word. During the Convention Parliament, Sir Ralph agreed with the Lords that the throne was not vacant, and his name was put on a black list. Sir Richard who took the opposite view now decided to get rid of Verney. Only nine days before the next election, Sir Ralph discovered that Denton was standing with Temple. Recently, when Denton's wife had run away with a lover, Sir Ralph had dropped everything to help his godson. The betrayal of Denton and Temple was so shocking that the Whigs were rumoured to have withdrawn to 'let the three kinsmen fight it out'. 'Odious' stories falsely accused Sir Ralph of sending money to King James in exile. Despite a life time of peacemaking, Verney now faced a public family feud.[45]

The night before the election, Sir Alexander Denton visited Claydon House and Verney agreed to withdraw. Sir Ralph privately told John: 'The truth is, I had not voices enough to carry it . . . but keep that to yourself.' Temple and Denton publicly discarded kinship in a community that prized memory. 'These are men that never consider past obligations', wrote John, 'they are altogether for the present.'[46] The definition of a gentleman was undergoing change.

Sir Ralph's sister Cary Gardiner vowed she'd rather see a cobbler win than Denton. His niece Nancy Nicholas, née Denton, thought that 'the break between the Verneys . . . and the Dentons would break her fathers' heart'. Indeed, how was one to act in such a circumstance? Would visiting proceed as usual? Lady Gardiner said she could never look upon Denton 'as a man of any principles, honour, or goodness'. Still, he was the head of her mother's family, so she would 'endeavour to be civil'. The kinship code had been violated, but a veneer of politeness was expected.[47]

Several months later, Denton called upon John, who 'had been better pleased if he had spared his civility. . . . ' When Sir Ralph was forced to write to Denton about Deputy Lieutenant's business, he crossed out the word 'dear' before 'cousin' and inserted a cooler 'good'. 'I am always for peace' had been his personal motto. In contrast, his son John would enter a world of political parties where 'trimmers' were abhorred. On the same day as Denton's victory, the aunts complained that 'the Whigs fund purses to make Parliament men. . . . '[48] New forms of public conduct were evolving as old and new values clashed. Sir Ralph represented an earlier stage of politics based upon masculine honour and fierce loyalty to kin. Now partisan concerns were overriding the family and its values. A successful candidate would have to treat the populace both before and after the election. The Verneys were embarking upon a third stage of electoral politics when kin were no longer automatically members of political networks. Part 2 describes their competitive political culture at the dawn of a new century.

PART 2: SIR JOHN VERNEY (1640–1717) AND SIR RICHARD TEMPLE (1675–1749)

> I am out of all patience with these villainous rogues, the Tories, and hate 'em worse than ever . . . I hope . . . this Parliament will cool their courage . . . by lopping off some of the heads of 'em and hanging up some of the scurrilous mob.
>
> Richard Tighe, 15 May 1715[49]

Fathers and sons, deaths and inheritances; one had ever followed the other for the Verneys, Temples, and Dentons. Yet the old generational wheel turned with unusual synchronization between 1696 and 1699, when all three family heads died in succession: John Verney, 2nd Baronet (1640–1717), inherited in 1696 and was created Viscount Fermanagh in 1703; Richard Temple, 4th Baronet (1675–1749), inherited in 1697, and was created Viscount Cobham in 1718; Sir Edmund Denton (1676–1714) inherited in 1698, and was created a baronet in 1699.[50] On the other side of the county, two more deaths influenced Buckinghamshire's political future. Philip Wharton, 4th Baron Wharton (1613–1696), a presbyterian of Wooburn and Upper Winchendon, had sought Sir Ralph's help when in the Tower and made Verney a trustee of his heir's marriage settlement.[51] In 1696 Wharton's estate fell to his son Thomas (1648–1715), created Viscount Winchendon and Earl of Wharton in 1706 and Marquess of Wharton and Malmesbury in 1714. Wharton had 'the greatest interest of any man in Buckinghamshire', although his power extended 'all over the country'. He soon became one of the most powerful Whig leaders in England. Locally, Wharton was supported by dissenters as well as by powerful Whig peers. Only three of his letters survive in the Verney archive, but he is discussed 142 times.[52]

One of Thomas Wharton's allies, William Cheyne (1657–1728), later 2nd Viscount Newhaven, inherited Buckinghamshire and Chelsea estates in 1698. William's father Charles, Viscount Newhaven (1625–1698), had powerful court connections. But William strayed from his father's court politics and allied himself with Thomas Wharton. They quarrelled, however, over a choice of candidates, as Verney and Temple had done. Their enmity was so severe that it culminated in a duel. Cheyne eventually reverted to Toryism and became its Buckinghamshire leader.[53] He mobilized the Anglican clergy and Tory gentry in opposition to Wharton. When John inherited, Cheyne was a knight of the shire and he soon became Verney's mentor. He wrote at least 43 letters to John, received 29 in return, and is cited 91 times.

John Verney enters the Country Community

John entered the country community at a time when party allegiances were hardening. Although he had avoided London office, he now wished to consolidate, even increase, the Verneys' political power. This meant regaining his father's Buckingham seat or standing for the more prestigious county seat. His merchant experience gave him skills that were easily transferable to politics: a hardened practicality when dealing with opponents; a keen sense of bargaining; and a wordly-wise attitude towards men and money. As a merchant, he had tolerated dissenters, but by 1696 he saw them as a threat to the monarchy and the Church. He was now a committed Tory Anglican with a dislike for courtiers and was far more partisan than Sir Ralph had been. He knew that he must establish his own ties with his father's country community. He could resolve conflict peaceably like Sir Ralph, or he could adopt new methods of governance.

John's entry into country society lets us examine local power relationships and ask questions about authority and resistance. The Verneys clearly respected informal power, even when specific rights were withheld.[54] In 1696, however, John felt the need to assert his formal authority and to publicly distinguish himself from his father.

Immediately after Sir Ralph's death, John sent a Parliament Act describing rent seizures to his East Claydon steward, Anthony Dover. Dover declared himself 'ignorant in such matters, for my master never seized but once in my time'. The Middle Claydon steward, William Coleman, was told to get signed warrants for tenants' arrears. Once the rent was collected, John could grant leases to someone else. Other leases were tightened and the rent was raised. 'Whatever . . . happened before', John declared, 'that's no rule to me'. He was determined to run his estate like a business and to hire workmen as needed, not as formerly by the year. No more wood was sold on trust and economies were enacted. If his cook kept feeding people, John noted, he would have nothing left. Hence, in 1698 he ordered 'nothing given away at the door. . . . '[55]

This break with a long charitable tradition was a public declaration of change. In John's eyes, requests for favours were in fact challenges to his authority by 'saucy, impertinent, tenants'. Thus, he instructed Coleman not to reimburse a farmer's repairs because 'he thinks it a test to ask it of me.' He would not be put off with 'fresh flamms', he told Coleman. 'I must be severe to some or I shall be abused by all' and considered 'a great fool'. Ironically, concern for public opinion caused him to flout it, and he developed a pattern of retaliation against uncooperative men. First, the steward or attorneys established that money was owed to John; then they demanded it and threatened arrest. John punished wrongdoers as an example to the parish. But his country agents buffered him from evictions, just as his City brokers distanced him from Exchange Alley.[56] In time, he learned to compromise, especially after losing elections. Thus Coleman stopped John from jailing a thief whose father always voted for the Verneys.[57] Still John seldom gave venison or alms to the community and was not so concerned with local peace.

Because John's policies violated custom, he was faced with acts of insubordination which are cited in 153 letters. When a household servant stole a furnace, John demanded its return to 'make an example'. Although there was proof of neighbours' complicity, neither furnace nor informers could be found. When a second theft followed, Coleman was told to search houses whenever John was robbed. At the same time, the park was so beset with poachers that Coleman feared 'the watchers are in fault'. In June 1697, men with blackened faces robbed and tied up a tenant. John's authority was being tested and since he was then a Parliamentary candidate, the acts had political meaning. Antagonism to John was displayed by a range of social groups: lesser gentry, clergymen, yeomen farmers, tenants, servants, and labourers. For example, while John was in London, squires Abel and Duncombe stirred up farmers about contested land rights. Someone also convinced a valuable tenant not to sign a lease. In nearby Adington, when the parson Sherrier refused to resign upon demand, a Mr Carter paid his bail. Tenants were also contesting manorial justice. 'If at the court the orders are made to please the freeholders, they will keep them', warned Coleman. 'If not they will soon break . . . any promises they now make.'[58] If these promises recalled Temple's broken election vows to Verney, it was not a coincidence.

Claydon villagers likewise banded together to thwart John. They blocked an incoming tailor who threatened others of that trade and prevented a widow's eviction. Bankrupt tenants gave stock to each other before notifying John, while in 1697 'prating tenants' threatened to bring on a tax penalty. In a case of intervillage rivalry, John learned that fifty mowers started at 9 p.m. and mowed all night and day so that 'the grass should not be my right'.[59]

Servants and workmen also found ways to express independence. When Sir Ralph failed to leave a legacy to the housekeeper Mrs Lillie, she complained openly to John. Others left service to better themselves and some labourers would not work on feast days. Steeple Claydon men refused to haul coals, while others demanded increased travel expenses, and John King never worked for 'under one shilling per day'. Gardener Stapp told John to 'provide yourself with another gardener' when his tasks were increased, while other workers hid their marriages from Sir Ralph and John. Carpenter Willy Scarlet was 'warned out' of the village, after he took John's horse without permission to take possession of lands outside Claydon. This was an act of a 'rising man', whose independence was viewed as a threat.[60] John's steward handled the warning, thus buffering John from conflict.

Landlords could always prevail by calling in debts or seizing land, but these acts bore risks. In 1695 Simon Mayne's Aylesbury election was in doubt, yet he foolishly prosecuted local men for poaching. He forgot to reflect, wrote Sir Ralph, that 'the poorest of them has as good a voice as the richest'. Some freeholders pressed John directly before elections for leases at lower rates. By the eighteenth century, E. P. Thompson's field of force that constrained patriarchal power had reared its head in the Claydons. Thompson's claim that eighteenth-century stability was often a surface phenomenon, riddled by subterranean tension and conflict is confirmed by the Verney letters.[61]

Altered political conditions were a major cause of rebellious behaviour. After 1688, annual parliaments, frequent elections, a growing central government, and the impact of London combined to produce a new political climate. Partisan issues and centralized methods dominated local campaigns even more than in the past. An expanding military and professional bureacracy offered new patronage opportunities that Whigs like Temple and Wharton seized.[62] Both Cheyne and Wharton became Lords Lieutenant of the county, for that office had become more important. Under Charles II, justices of the peace had been expelled. Now they were subject to removal by party bosses. The balance of power was shifting from the provinces to the national centre.[63]

These changes led to new trends in electoral politics. Like the London marriage market and the Stock Exchange, campaigns were based upon open payments of money. A frugal man like Sir Ralph was unlikely to be elected. Geoffrey Holmes has suggested that although county elections now might cost over £1,000, boroughs required only a few hundred. But amounts varied with income, location, and ambition. From a yearly income of about £16,000, Wharton spent at least £80,000 on elections over time, £12,000 in 1705 alone.

Even when he was not standing, Cheyne liberally bankrolled Tory candidates and paid for poll clerks, poll books, poll booths, chair carriers, local officials' fees, transport, music, and the poor. To forestall corruption charges, market-based techniques were used: sham commercial deals, tax payments on behalf of voters, the giving of goods, and the issuing of bonds and securities. Money was openly bestowed, sometimes for signed pledges of support.[64]

Electioneering described in 80 letters became more highly organized. Candidates checked poll books, compiled voter lists, used door to door canvassing, and wrote circular letters begging votes from landowners and their tenants. Party chiefs sent squads of agents with specific targets to pre-assigned areas. Advance men and regional whips established priorities based upon numerical forecasts. Transportation was supplied to Londoners and outliers who owned local property. Freeholds were purchased before elections, as in the case of John's son-in-law Sir Thomas Cave. The services of wives and local brokers were essential when candidates were in London. Aunt Gardiner told John to hire Mr Woodward, 'he knowing men of a second rank'. Feedback and reports to party bosses crowned the whole process.[65]

Despite this organization, the fissuring of landlords into two parties provoked independent behaviour by a growing electorate. After Sir Ralph's death, Buckinghamshire freeholders increased from 2,645 in 1700, to 3,554 in 1701, and 4,519 in 1705. While enclosed Middle Claydon maintained its 3 voters, there were 6 East Claydon voters in 1700/1 and 18 in 1710. Steeple Claydon poll books record 28 voters in 1700/1, 34 in 1701, 40 in 1705, 44 in 1710. The electors of Buckingham borough rose from 40 in 1700/1 to 49 in 1701, 74 in 1705, 79 in 1710, and 85 in 1713. If this growing electorate often made partisan choices, the floating vote remained high at 13% in both 1705 and 1710.[66] Political strife gave voters leverage among rival candidates and they used it to advantage. It is possible that the Buckinghamshire electorate divided gentry power even more forcefully than William Speck, Geoffrey Holmes, and J. H. Plumb have indicated.[67]

Some historians have claimed that Buckinghamshire landholders were particularly effective in controlling tenants' votes.[68] These studies may have exaggerated landed authority by oversimplifying the situation. Unenclosed villages such as Steeple and East Claydon were less vulnerable to party pressure than those in Wharton's neighbourhood, while market towns such as Aylesbury presented a different situation. The size and location of a landlord's estate, the number of his tenants, his residential patterns, political weight, zeal, and even health, all affected elite power. The Verney letters confirm that middling-sort freeholders used votes to obtain favours. Once support was given, the voter felt entitled to year-round patronage. Thus Browne Willis apologized to John for asking to have a child touched by Queen Anne. The father believes, wrote Willis, 'like other country fellows, which notion we can't beat out of them, that he has a title to your lordships favour'.

The systematic use of brokers, along with a growing electorate, new campaign techniques, and a highly organized party structure marked the political world of the eighteenth-century Verneys and Temples. The two families, however, adopted different strategies, parties, and principles. An analysis of their political activities shows how their paths diverged.

The Verneys and the Temples: A Study in Political Contrasts (1696–1717)

By the time John inherited in 1696, former alliances were coalescing into Whig and Tory parties. Party labels were assigned to most landowners whose views were locally known. John's Tory Anglican sympathies and his alliance with Lord Cheyne separated him from the Whig Temples and Dentons. In 1698, he challenged them in an effort to regain his father's Buckingham seat. John also stood for Parliament as a Tory on six other occasions: unsuccessfully for the county seat in 1696, 1698, 1700/1; successfully for the county in 1710 and 1713; successfully in 1713 and 1715 for Amersham. His quest for office fell into three phases. From 1696 to 1701, John lost four consecutive elections. He therefore withdrew his candidacy and changed his strategies and goals. From 1702 to 1710, he gradually built a local power base as a justice of the peace and friend to Lord Cheyne. He shed his father's reluctance to treat voters and brought a new sociability to Claydon House. In 1710, national trends catapulted him to a Parliament seat and a place in the Tory network. When the Whigs won in 1714, however, the same trends swept him out of power.

But in 1696, when John inherited, these events could not have been foreseen. Barely two months after Sir Ralph's death, he naively stood for the county. He felt that his 'family name' would bring success, although he was 'a stranger in the country'. 'You can never do it with less charge and more advantage [than] now', advised Nancy Nicholas. Although women could not vote, they played important roles. John was told that his neighbour Mrs Pigott 'gives life to your cause' and East Claydon women helped as well. More important, the London aunts wrote to influential friends and sent reports of Wharton's intrigues. Sometimes they were more informed about country candidates than either John or Sir Ralph.[69] London was indeed the centre for political information.

The yeoman Joseph Churchill provided a different type of assistance by rousing tenants and speaking at markets. Meanwhile, the lawyer William Busby gave John a practical course in politics. He urged John to settle at Claydon House and to contact Lord Cheyne 'for he is a Church of England man . . . and hath good interest'. He also sent John a list of local gentry and suggested how each one should be approached. John must try to get his neighbours' promises, or at least avoid animosity. If a man was for you, he might sway his tenants, but if he was against you, they would have a hard time giving support. A 'leading man' in each town should provide transportation, for many would 'not stir from home unless they have a driver'. John should ride to the poll with many followers, wrote Busby, 'that you may not come off with dishonour'.[70]

But John entered the campaign too late and was soundly thrashed at the polls. At first he spent little money, but the cause was stinginess, not morality. Wharton lavishly supported John's opponents with Christmas hospitality. In contrast, John concealed his arrival until 26 December. Temple treated the Buckingham burgesses with food and drink, but John never sent them a word. Some one should have told him to 'go into the country, lay aside the merchant, and spend and speak like a gentleman'.[71] Urban values might erode hospitality in town, but a country gentleman was expected to be generous. John's miserliness had always conflicted with the gentry code of liberality, but in the Claydons it was even more apparent.

John's behaviour stood in stark contrast to that of his rivals, the Temples. Sir Richard's son, the future Viscount Cobham (1675–1749), knew the importance of sociability and its relationship to political power. He placed Stowe at the heart of his public life, when he was not in London. As he entertained his neighbours, social and political affairs converged. But in 1696 John did not yet speak the language of courtesy that was needed to build an interest. He was ill-at-ease in his circular letters that he wrote to request votes. They were penned 'without compliment', he admitted, 'for I'm not good at that'. Not surprisingly, John came in a poor third with 263 votes compared to 863 for the winner. Party alliances and the weather added to John's loss, but frugality sealed his fate.[72]

In 1698 John seized a second opportunity to stand for the county. Wharton's brother Goodwin and Sir Roger Hill hoped to win both places. But Cheyne's kinsman Robert Harley and his country party were challenging Wharton. Even housekeeper Lillie wrote John with complaints about the land tax and corruption. John saw that Cheyne, who was based in the southern Chilterns, needed a northern Vale man to drain second votes from Wharton. Though he expected defeat, he agreed to stand with Cheyne, whose Church and Tory principles matched his own. 'I am willing to receive a baulk', John wrote Cheyne, 'so I may be serviceable to you.' He was inserting himself in the Tory patronage loop, which later would reward him.[73]

After 'many gentleman and . . . freeholders' asked John to stand, he finally moved to the country. As in town, John adapted to social norms after a period of acculturation. He learned to provide country hospitality in ways that differed from those of his father. This time, it was his third wife, Londoner Elizabeth Baker, who helped to shape his conduct. She convinced him to entertain and loan money to the local gentry, although there was always tension about expense between husband and wife. John's 114 circular letters requesting votes became more graceful.[74] He was learning the value of polite courtesies, as well as sociability.

John lost the county election but polled 926 votes compared with 263 in 1696. This was a stunning achievement, for Goodwin Wharton polled only 970 and Cheyne won with 1557. Many copies of the totals were printed to publicize John's accomplishment. Cheyne vowed to help John in the next election and sent regards to Elizabeth from himself and his wife. In this case, social recognition for both sexes followed political victory. John was now invited to Cheyne's country house in order to inspect the poll. The list was rearranged 'with every man placed in his respective parish and every parish in its respective hundred', in hopes of detecting fraud. Cheyne also circulated copies of recent election laws to enhance party effectiveness.[75]

At the same time, against Cheyne's wishes, John let pride cloud his political judgement about Buckingham borough. Since 1690, when Alexander Denton had replaced Sir Ralph as MP, there had been little warmth between the Verneys, Temples, and Dentons. Still, in 1698, Temple's heir had promised to vote for John in the county election. As the poll book shows, however, he voted for the Whigs. In 1698, when Sir Edmund Denton inherited Hillesden, relations grew even cooler. His father's will of 1688 had made John his trustee and guardian.[76] Now Sir Edmund's lawyers forced John to cede this trust. After this happened, John decided to challenge Sir Edmund Denton for his deceased father's Buckingham seat. Cheyne feared that 'an opposition . . . between kindred and neighbours might break the interest of the country' and hand the seat to the Whigs.

Unfortunately the Ethersay family, who despised the Verneys, now controlled Buckingham's burgesses. Their rumours of John's supposed illness forced him to send a health certificate from London. Even friends told Elizabeth to stop courting the burgesses, for they would never vote for Verney. John hoped that Mrs Egerton might sway her Bridgewater kin, because 'women does often prevail in these affairs'. Unfortunately, Lady Wharton was helping Denton and Temple, which made their whole family feel 'great'. Thus, the power of women to influence votes was again a factor. In the end, Temple and Denton carried the day. The concurrent poaching in John's park was probably related to the poll.[77]

From that day on, the family 'breach' or 'wound' was openly admitted. Sir Edmund was not so 'civil' to come to John's coach when he sent to see him. Denton even prevented one of his aunts from visiting her Verney kin. John's aunts hoped that Denton would leave 'that party . . . opposite . . . you', which his father had always 'abhorred'. In 1699 they were shocked to hear that Temple and young Denton had met with Wharton. Denton now planned to 'court Winchendon and . . . this Lord will guide him'. Formerly, kin had served as political mentors, but now strangers were assuming that role. The rift assumed a permanence that even death could not dissolve. When Sir Edmund died in 1714, John admitted: 'Neither our coach nor any from our house were there, we not being sent to, as the others were.'[78] This example shows how party politics had eroded old patterns of sociability.

After John's defeat in 1699, his thoughts returned to the county seat and he secretly agreed to stand with Cheyne. Religion played a crucial role, for Wharton was a presbyterian. Aunt Gardiner feared that Quakers and Anabaptists would not vote for high-leaning Anglicans like Verney and Cheyne. She perceived that as old alliances coalesced into Whig and Tory parties, unresolved problems of

Church and State were re-emerging. For example, in 1701 the Tories hoped that God would 'preserve the church and kingdom', because their opponents were 'all for war with France' and 'would cast out the bishops'. By 1705, Ralph Palmer fretted about 'the preservation of the Church in this time of danger'. Church and State, he wrote, 'were so interwoven that one could not be safe without the other'. In 1710, when John and Sir Henry Seymour stood for Parliament, they called themselves 'genuine sons of the Church of England'. By 1714 John conceded that his Anglican commitment precluded office: 'I am too much for the Church of England', he stated, 'to be put into any, so I shall live quietly under my own vine and remain an honest Sacheverellian'.[79]

But surely Whigs also were in favour of a strong Church and monarchy, though their visions of both differed. The Whigs believed that the Buckinghamshire Tories undermined the 'excellent constitution in both Church and State'. In 1713 the Whigs campaigned in the Claydons with the slogan of 'liberty and property, no French Government, no Pretender'. Both parties were addressing problems of Church and State and showing how they would protect these institutions. The Verneys longed for one established religion and felt that Wharton's party was 'against the Church'. In 1713 they marked voting lists 'Church side' and 'Whig-side', automatically linking Whigs with dissent. But Whigs felt that toleration and their financial programmes strengthened the monarchy as well as the Church.[80]

By the eighteenth century, John and Cheyne were standing for the county seat as committed Anglican Tories. But in November 1700, they discovered that John's Whig neighbour Robert Dormer stood against them. Dormer's candidacy had been planned at his country house with Lord and Lady Wharton and the Duke of Shrewsbury. The setting was indicative of the country house sociability at the heart of Wharton's technique. Dormer could not possibly win, wrote Cheyne, so the 'trick' is 'to divide our interests'. In 1698 John had done so well in the northern Vale that now he and Cheyne might prevail. Unfortunately, Dormer's court connections and ties to tenants in the Claydons would drain away votes, and freeholders were 'much divided in their opinions'. John supported a Lace Act and vowed integrity against corruption. But rumours that Cheyne had voted for 'taking away . . . liberty of conscience' alienated dissenters.[81]

John soon found that his closest neighbours were pre-engaged by the Whigs. Mr Knollys assumed that John would not stand, because 'the Claydons were almost all for Mr. Dormer'. When John and Sir Edmund quarrelled publicly, it made matters worse. Although John's attitude to money had improved, he did not spend like Dormer, and cash was fuelling the race. John was warned to 'treat as others do, that they may see you value money no more than they do'. This philosophy was hard to accept, for John suspected that voters 'promise everybody, so that their votes are uncertain until . . . in the poll books'. Although party control was mounting, there was still a floating vote.[82]

As Wharton hoped, John polled a humiliating 705 to Cheyne's 1,853, Goodwin

Wharton's 1,604, and Dormer's 1,209. But although John's vote plummeted in the Whig-dominated villages near Claydon, it rose sharply in Cheyne's neighbourhood. Denton and Temple voted for both Whigs, as did Thomas Tipping to whom John had just lent £1,000. Cheyne swore Verney's kinsman Joseph Churchill had voted for Dormer. A Joseph Churchill in Steeple Claydon did vote for the Whigs, but another, who was certainly John's tenant, plumped solely for Verney. This was an act of loyalty, for as John knew: 'Freeholders hereabouts think if they give but one voice they don't maintain their right.'[83]

In 1702, however, when John was not a candidate, Churchill would not vote as Verney directed, protesting: 'Voices ought to be free'. John vengefully called in a bond of Churchill's, although the money was not yet due. Joseph had not expected such action and complained of injustice. In John's view, however, Churchill's behaviour was 'opposite to the friendship, relation, and neighbourhood of our families'. In 1690 Alexander Denton had trampled upon these same ties when he seized Sir Ralph's Parliament seat. John held Churchill no less responsible than Denton for his actions. 'When a freeholder rents land of me', he wrote, 'one voice is partly my due, though not altogether for the land.' The two men were discussing the definition of property, about which Locke had so recently written. Was a man's property embodied only in his estate, or was it freely possessed in his person, rights, and liberties?[84] The relationship of landlords and tenants all over England was inextricably entwined with this issue. Although some voters still deferred to landlords, this could no longer be assumed.

From 1701 to 1710, a humiliated John refused to be a candidate. During that time, no Tory stood with Cheyne, who in 1701 lost to Wharton and Dormer. In 1702 Cheyne regained his seat as Queen Anne took the throne, but John grumpily refused to 'intermeddle' and gave Wharton and Cheyne each a vote.[85] John had been made Justice of the Peace and of the Quorum in 1700 and a deputy lieutenant in 1701. With Cheyne Lord Lieutenant in 1702, John received his Irish title as Viscount Fermanagh in 1703, surely a reward for his previous campaigns.[86]

For the next eight years, John worked steadily to increase his local power. In 1704 he bought Steeple Claydon land, served on the Commission for Charitable Uses, and entertained at the Quainton races. He favoured a bill to make army officers serve with their men, rather than remain in England. Still, he refused to stand against Dormer and Temple. In 1705 Cheyne asked John for 'but one vote . . . not giving the second'. John, however, voted for Dormer as well, and Cheyne lost the election despite his attempts to shield Quakers from forced oaths. Verney's growing local authority was evident in the 1705 poll. His influence helped the Tory antiquarian, Browne Willis, to seize Temple's Buckingham seat. Willis's ten fawning letters to his patron confirm John's new authority. By 1706 Verney was one of Ashenden hundred's two Justices, which gave him authority over his neighbours. John stayed home that year to attend sessions, while his family went to London. He openly proclaimed his

Tory principles, noting: 'those who receive benefit by public taxes' should not sit in Parliament. He agreed with those who condemned the 'inexcusable immorality of occasional conformity'.[87]

When Cheyne entered the House of Lords in 1708, the Whigs Denton and Richard Hampden stood unopposed. John continued to gain power locally. In 1708 he served as godparent to three children of nearby gentry. In 1709 he was able to help the Earl of Lichfield through his position as Tax Commissioner, but refused a summons to the Irish Parliament. In 1710 Dr John Cockman summarized John's transformation from London merchant to Tory politician: 'He lives now at an extravagant rate and gains ground in these parts.' Cockman thought John would be successful if an election came his way. The London merchant had shed his frugal fixations and was destined for political prominence.[88]

Fortunately for John, the national mood now swung back towards the Tories. The economic effects of war and the breakdown of peace talks caused widespread disaffection. John's brother-in-law Samuel Baker believed 'our divisions . . . are now . . . grown to a greater height than has been known these many years'. He felt they were 'occasioned chiefly by the proceedings against Dr. Sacheverell which set all people . . . against one another with great heat on both sides'.

In August, the Tories gathered as usual in Aylesbury, not in a country house the way the Whigs did. They chose John and Sir Henry Seymour to oppose Richard Hampden and Sir Edmund Denton. For the first time since 1701, they now had two candidates. 'I pray . . . make the Quakers for us', Cheyne begged Harley, who gave him national support from London. A win now seemed possible and John worked with partisan zeal. He bought meat from local burgesses and withheld bark from a tanner in order to change his vote. In addition to treating voters, John offered them lucrative financial deals. With the help of a former merchant John Knapp, now a local squire, John bought £186 of turnpike debts from shopkeepers in Stony Stratford. The men had gained little on their investment and desperately needed cash. In an inversion of his fathers' morality, John outlined 'my thoughts as to bribery'. His concern was not about ethics, but that no sums were to be paid until all poll books were checked. His use of printed forms to record the tax transfers shows that market techniques were condoned.[89] It was only prudent to use commercial methods in towns with a floating electorate. Thirty Stony Stratford voters chose the Tories, while thirty-one voted for the Whigs. Since only sixty-two votes (out of 8,565) separated top and bottom candidates, John's turnpike expenses were well spent. Not surprisingly, in 1712, the same tax deal was repeated in Great Brickhill.

John's election expenses of almost £800 included transportation, building an outhouse at the poll, and sums for ringers, musicians, and officials. John even reimbursed a poor man who lost a horse in the turmoil. Final votes were 2,161 for Verney, 2,157 for Denton, 2,148 for Hampden and 2,099 for Seymour.[90] National trends and the support of the Tory party finally brought John to

Parliament. Ironically, two cousins who were estranged by party shared their county's highest honour. The Tories also won the Buckingham seat, where 51 of 79 borough electors voted for John. The 'sedulous . . . art' of John's wife Elizabeth was publicly praised by Cheyne. He dined with her family at nearby Penn and hoped 'mightily to see her in the Chilterns'. Reactions to the election showed party rage. 'The spirit of a Commonwealth swelled those . . . rascals to such a height', wrote Tory cousin Verney Lloyd, that they 'forgot there was . . . the Queen in being or a church to be supported'. Whigs denounced local Tories, whose descent 'into the same dangerous paths of . . . forty-one' would surely lead to French 'universal monarchy and a popish pretender'.[91]

Denton immediately bought a fine coach and dined with Temple in London. The latter was a member of the Kit Kat Club and a host to Pope, Vanbrugh, and Congreve. In contrast, John avoided high living but took lodgings closer to the House of Commmons. Entering Parliament at age 70 and plagued by gout, stone, and deafness, his activity was bound to be restricted. But despite leaves of absence, he attended most of his first session. A member of the October Club, he dined at the Fountain Tavern in the Strand in November, reporting: 'I don't know of one Whig amongst us.' His name appeared on several lists as a Tory in 1710 and 1712. The next year his attendance waned and he missed committee meetings. In April however he presented the Buckingham address to the Queen urging peace in Europe.[92]

Because of John's Tory principles, it grew harder for him to socialize with Whig friends. Adolphus Oughton had regularly visited Claydon since he attended Oxford with John's son Ralph. Now his arguments at dinner 'to persuade you to Whiggism' provoked his hosts' anger. Soon Oughton was spending all his time at court. By 1708 the Verneys admitted that there was little contact 'where there was such intimacy' in the past.

Town drawing rooms also broke into camps, along with groups of diners. In 1714 the Earl of Sunderland left Lord Halifax's table when Harley's 'wand' appeared.[93] Whigs felt most comfortable reading a Whig paper at their own coffee-houses and clubs. Yet John scorned 'the Kit Cat Club and all their toasts, who are rather honorary than handsome'. *The Spectator* mocked this severed sociability by describing different coloured face patches on Whig and Tory women. Indeed, all the matches planned for John's son Ralph appear to have been with Tories. Although we do not know how many courtships were halted because of different party ties, they probably were not encouraged. In 1716 the sister of Sir Thomas Cave's political rival married a Tory without her brother's knowledge. Cave reported the brother 'dumbfounded', for her fortune was now in Tory hands.[94]

Social segregation also spilled into sports events, where party competition was fierce. As early as 1683, John noted that Tories at the Hatson Races would not contribute to the plate. By 1702 entertainments after the Quainton races had become segregated by party. The Whartons, Dormers, and Dentons danced all night at Hillesden, but the Verneys were not invited. After 1710, the Verneys always described races in party terms. 'The Whigs have the best horses', Cave complained in 1712, 'since they have all the money.' He refused to go to the Brackley races, because Brackley was a Whig town. In 1716 the Tory horse might have won there, 'but the other three (all Whigs) combined to make him lose it'.[95] With four candidates at the polls and four horses on the track, party conflict was evident.

Moreover, the next generation grew up in a socially divisive climate. When John's grandson Lovett was called a 'little Whig' at school, he asked to go to Claydon where he was sure to 'be a Tory'. In 1712 John's granddaughter Margaret Cave constructed her own Tory creed. Each day she drank 'a health to Claydon, Stanford, the Queen and Church, to Dr. Sacheverell and her maid'. Her father sent John a list of Tory pallbearers, who served at Lord Denbigh's funeral. Lady Chandos noted the same segregation at her husband's burial. Finally, Mrs Price's death in childbirth was described as 'a loss to our party'. Partisan rage passed to one's children and pervaded life's passages. It may have reached a climax in 1710, when 'wicked . . . Whigs . . . rang bells for joy' at the false news of John's death.[96]

But although John was isolated from Whig friends, he was engulfed by Tory supplicants. Paradoxically, John was more constrained after his 1710 victory, for he was obligated to supporters. A pattern of calling in debts after elections had arisen over time. Hence, Thomas Newman needed £500 after voting Tory, and John was forced to help. In 1712 John had to rent land to the Tripletts, because of 'a good many voices in that family'. Moreover, treating throughout the year was no longer a question of choice. Thus, in 1712, John reported: 'Our house is everyday very full of country people, that it's like an election time.'[97]

In addition to indulging voters, John also had to give patronage. Four hundred and seven transactions between patrons and clients are noted in Table 4 (Appendix II). After the 1710 election, almost every letter requested favours: land tax and excise offices, military commissions, benefices, and touching for the Queen's evil. After John's win, Cheyne quickly sent John a roll of proposed tax commissioners. Together they would 'put out and put in as you please, till we have a perfect list'. Cheyne played the patronage game with his kinsman Harley, requesting offices for local voters. 'Your Lordship has it every day in your power to satisfy my small ambition', he declared, when he lost his own place as Clerk of the Pipes. He begged Harley to get it restored for life or to make him 'Comptroller General of . . . the customs till Her Majesty shall please to provide better . . .' But despite Cheyne's example, John refused to humour voters. In contrast, Denton sent newspapers and 'votes' to a Chesham club of freeholders, while he was 'out of Parliament as well as in'. Without a similar supply of news, Cheyne warned John, a Tory 'club of your friends' who met every Friday would soon 'desert'. Despite Cheyne's prodding, however, John did not honour this request.[98]

More seriously, John failed to build the network of national patrons that had now become essential. When he needed an exemption from the expensive office of sheriff, John admitted: 'I have no friend at court.' He had to plead with a London friend to get him off the list. Even at the height of John's authority, his support remained locally-based. His country ideology and dislike of the court hampered him as a patron and led to disappointed clients. Thus, John baulked at soliciting the Duke of Shrewsbury because they were not personally acquainted. It is 'unmannerly', he told his petitioner, 'to write to one so much above me'. In fact, he had few patrons to connect him to the centre. When John failed to get Mr Bates a living, Elizabeth consoled him: 'Nobody can do more than lies in their power and he is satisfied as your friend.' One doubts, however, that Mr Bates was as content as Elizabeth.[99] In 1711 Cousin Verney Lloyd asked John to make him a Lieutenant Colonel, but John's contacts in the military were slim. Temple, on the other hand, pursued an army career and soon led a Flanders regiment. He became a Lieutenant General, Colonel of the 1st Dragoons, Constable of Windsor Castle, a member of the Privy Council, and Buckinghamshire's Lord Lieutenant. Thus, when a neighbour Edward Andrewes wanted an army promotion for his son, he was told to write Temple an 'obliging letter . . . for he is looked upon as a very great man'.[100]

As Wharton and Temple built national networks, they retained those in the county. Local brokers were bought with favours and both parties vied for their support. A case in point was the attorney Nicholas Merwin, who supervised elections as undersheriff and wrote the Verneys 139 letters. Although both John and Sir Richard employed Merwin as a lawyer, Verney fought with him and rebuked him publicly at the 1713 assizes. In contrast, Temple found Merwin a Buckingham office. Merwin then signed a pledge to resign his post if Sir Richard was dissatisfied. It was obviously in Merwin's interest to assist Temple and the Whigs.[101] This flaw in John's patronage abilities reduced his long-term chances for success. It was one reason for the Verneys' lesser position in comparison to the Temples.

The Election of 1713 and the Role of Women in Politics

In 1713 John still had authority and he wished to stand again. The May Day Buckingham poll for bailiff raised hopes for a Tory county victory. A white flag with the arms of John, Elizabeth, and the borough was marched into town by drummers. Garlanded women bore pictures of Queen Anne and Sacheverell and the streets rang with 'no low Church, no presbyterians'. The Whigs gave six maypoles but to no avail.[102]

In order to find John a running mate, Cheyne invited a group of Tories to his country house. They chose Cheyne's cousin John Fleetwood as the second candidate. Before the meeting, Elizabeth coached John on how to act, for she had watched how Lord Cheyne ate and dressed when he visited Claydon. She made John take servants to wait behind his chair, for she knew he must be careful about status. Although he did not 'take that state . . . at home', she wrote, 'it looks well abroad'.[103] It was hard to maintain deference and also serve as tutor, but Elizabeth tactfully governed John. She instructed him in country sociability, as his aunts had done in town.

When John returned to London, Elizabeth and the steward, now Charles Chaloner, managed voters.[104] The Tories were superbly organized and used market-based techniques. The party whip, Thomas Prior, sent John a list of non-resident voters who would be driven to the polls. Since Prior also acted as Cave's Leicestershire agent, it appears that there was inter-county cooperation. Cheyne welded the candidates' stewards and his own man of business into an efficient canvassing team. They covered every hundred systematically, armed with poll books and local agents. Their goal was to contact large numbers of freeholders, especially those whose votes might be changed. An exhausted Chaloner came home briefly, but only to bring in the 'spoiling' hay.[105]

Meanwhile Elizabeth was left to manage the estate and to entertain voters alone. Although she had helped John before, during the 1713 campaign she reshaped Claydon House hospitality. Her actions reflected new notions of neighbourhood and duty. As Whig/Tory competition sharpened, hospitality succumbed to political pressures. Party rivalry was only one factor, but its effects on sociability were important. John no longer provided tenants with brimming hogsheads, as his father had done. Voters, however, were another matter. As Elizabeth told John: 'Substantial freeholders . . . can't be denied eating and drinking.'[106]

Elizabeth was a worldy London woman, who understood that John must purchase votes. The market place dominated the Buckinghamshire hustings and commercial principles applied there too. In 1712 John wrote testily from London about her costly visits. 'Yet I must go or they will take it ill', she replied, for she grasped local realities. Elizabeth saw that she must not only visit neighbours, she also had to open Claydon House. She must satisy local custom and liberally give food, drink, and money. Prior to the poll, she had 'to dress a great deal', and she sent guineas and her coach to Whitsun Ales. Morris dancers and sword bearers performed at the house, while 'A Verney, A Fleetwood' filled the air. In contrast to Sir Ralph's day, mobs of varied ranks filled Claydon's rooms: one hundred revellers on one day; forty Bottle Claydon people on another. John complained that she hosted 400 people each day and 'everyday . . . the noise of . . . drums, trumpet, haut boy, pipes, or fiddles'. Elizabeth's moods ranged from exhilaration to exhaustion, for with Chaloner gone, there was no one to collect rents. She was miserable when she heard that Lichfield forgot to write to his tenants who now refused to vote for John. On one occasion she admitted crying, as Lady Denton was known to do. But usually she maintained control and felt satisfaction when she changed a vote.[107]

Clearly, the Whig/Tory conflict forced John and Elizabeth to entertain differently from Sir Ralph. The old man had hosted burgesses whom he knew well, but he refused to treat the general populace. His reluctant election favours were a small part of a wider generosity, based upon honour and reputation. In contrast, John and Elizabeth entertained the local 'mob' indiscriminately, in part because of Parliament's increased political significance. Their hospitality bore an increasing resemblance to London's booming market place. By hosting neighbours solely for partisan purposes, they divided the community, instead of uniting it. Moreover, John and his family gave just enough hospitality to maintain their country position, while other social activities were transferred to London.[108]

Despite his poor Parliamentary attendance record, John and Fleetwood polled 2,018 and 2,061 votes, respectively, for the county seat, compared with Hampden's 1,942 and Denton's 1,907. Prominent Tories in London spread news of John's 'great victory', which was 'mortifying' to the Whigs. John's son-in-law Cave won in Leicester, where the balls included 'not one dissenter'.[109] John also stood and won at Amersham, where he spent over £100. It is hard to determine John's county expenses, but they were probably close to £500. Cheyne's expenditures totalled at least £643, including 'housekeeping extraordinary' for Cousin Fleetwood. A great deal of money was spent on transporting voters from Chelsea, Fulham, and Covent Garden. 'Your friends in London left no stone unturned', wrote an ally. Country and city divisions dissolved at the poll.

Accounts of 10s. for 'other freeholders who took no money' confirm that direct cash payments were normal. A Tory agent summed up the situation: 'I doubt whoever lives to another election will find it more expensive every time than [the] other, for those that may be ashamed to ask demand money for their time and expenses.'[110] John's largesse did not extend to Cheyne's agent Mr Robartes, who was given '£0 0s. 0d . . . for the care and pains taken with the election'.[111] Robartes's angry letters show that discourse between patrons and brokers was often strained.

John received no invitations to the Whig balls at Stowe and Hillesden. After Cave's election, friends filled Stanford Hall 'to make a ball, though not like Stowe . . . our people being all Tories'. After the victory, Elizabeth made a triumphant tour without John: first to her family in Penn; then sightseeing to Windsor; finally a visit with Cheyne and 'brother Fleetwood'. Her call at Lord Portland's house was especially satisfying, for Elizabeth was honoured publicly. 'If I'd been a queen, I could not have had greater civility', she wrote John. 'The ladies called us all by our names and you would have thought that they had known us seven years.' This welcome brought her self-esteem, for she was accepted without John. He sourly commented that her visiting would 'tire all the gentry in the Chilterns'.[112] Perhaps he did not wish her to acquire honour in public without his aid. Elizabeth's political work increased her own status. It also challenged the prevailing model of feminine domesticity and public masculinity.

In theory, Elizabeth should not have been visible in the political arena at all. Nor should 52 letters mention women in politics. Gender defined the right to govern and vote, and only men had those privileges. Women, like servants, the landless, and the poor, were not included in this all-male world. The dominant metaphor describing the hustings was war and martial power. Soldiers assembled to do battle at the poll, while triumphant candidates wrote about victories. Cave thought that John's 1713 win over 'the mighty Prince of the Whigs' excelled that of Mannheim. Parent/child and husband/wife analogies described the relationships of candidates to the electorate. The male contestant assumed the role of the benevolent patriarch, while fickle voters had childlike or feminine characteristics. Hence Cheyne had made 'the country his child', and would treat it kindly. And when he plied his militia men with drink, he was said to 'caress the freeholders'. John was told not to worry when he stood for the first time: 'Should you lose . . . 'tis no more disgrace than to be denied by a fair lady'. Thus, gendered terms defined one's political status.[113]

Yet this terminology concealed the fact that women took part in elections. Wives ran campaigns, aunts wrote letters for votes, and daughters influenced husbands. In practice, women at many places in the social scale had to be wooed. Hence John counted on Mrs. Egerton to sway her powerful kinsmen, while the steward treated the burgesses' ladies. 'If their wives don't keep them tight', wrote Mun, 'you must go among the other women.' A candidate in a Buckingham poll was told to 'plough' with the burgesses' 'heifers'. Negative allusions to females, especially in times of danger, were testimony to their political presence. Thus in 1714, as the Whigs took power, John angrily referred to their women. The Whig interest, he wrote, 'was not achieved by merit, but 'by means of their wives or daughters'.[114] Rigid notions of gender were again being challenged.

Of course, there was never any mention of formal political rights for women, but the Verneys respected subtle forms of influence. As with visits in a coach, when the country house was used for political activities, private and public spheres intersected. This overlap enabled women to enter the political arena in socially accepted spaces. Although some may not have wished for this respon-sibility, women like Elizabeth had to assume political duties when their husbands were in town. Sociability became more critical when John entered politics and the problems of commuting brought about a new division of labour. When John made long stays in London, Elizabeth assumed burdensome country duties. In return, she received praise, invitations, and increased status. More often, however, she played her political role in hidden and indirect ways. Elizabeth had to become a political broker, whether she liked it or not.[115]

The Whig/Tory 1715 Compromise

Immediately after his victory, John became ill and was inactive in the next Parliament. Yet poor health was not the only reason that he refused to stand at Queen Anne's death. Elizabeth privately told Cheyne that John 'did not think himself kindly us'd last time in relation to Amersham'. James Herbert had been given John's Amersham seat, which the Verneys assumed would go to John's son

Ralph. 'I, having been at above £100 charge', John fumed, 'I think a relation of mine might have been the person.' Since 'Mr Verney was wished joy of the borough by abundance in this county', there had been a painful loss of face. In truth, John did not have the authority to give Ralph his second seat, due to lack of national connections and his sole reliance upon Cheyne. John's anger, age, and illness again led to Parliamentary inactivity, but he sent proxies and received the 'votes'. It was 'a cordial to me', he declared, 'to see the Schism Bill passed'.[116]

Meanwhile, in the face of Tory successes, Wharton had problems finding Whig candidates. Richard Hampden agreed to stand with Richard Grenville for the county seat, but then he withdrew. With no candidate in sight, Wharton offered the Tories a compact, to which Cheyne too hastily agreed. The Whig Richard Grenville and the Tory John Fleetwood were to be presented jointly to the voters. Wharton wrote with relief that 'rather than lose both, we were glad at last of having one'.[117]

Some scholars have viewed this pact as proof of elite consensus and hegemony over voters.[118] In contrast, others have confirmed the vitality of local popular politics, especially in the areas of politics and religion. The rise of political parties, the pressure of dissent, and the impact of popular culture have been treated by Tim Harris, Steven Pincus, Mark Goldie, Nicholas Rogers, and others.[119] When Whig and Tory letters about the pact are integrated chronologically, we see that conflict always lay just below the surface in Buckinghamshire.

Contested elections had existed locally since at least the 1670s, albeit in a framework of consensus. Candidates tried to control the electorate, which in turn used its leverage to exploit the candidates. A cycle of conflict developed that divided families, villages, and towns. By 1714, the situation had grown chaotic, as the language of the pact reveals. Its goal was to eliminate 'the division and uneasiness the county has . . . laid under, upon account of elections'.[120] As proof of this disorder, gentry on both sides refused to accept the pact. When Hampden defied Wharton publicly, Tories suspected a plot 'to fling out . . . Fleetwood'.[121] Neither party wanted Grenville, and dissenters threatened to give Hampden single votes.[122] An outraged electorate, stirred up by Hampden, protested that their right to choose was threatened.

Hampden's appeal to the people, Cheyne feared, was 'founded upon the old principle of making them . . . judges of our actions'. He believed that voters' rights were not jeopardized by his own 'liberty . . . to recommend a candidate and make him as many votes as my interest and my purse can procure'. John offered the same arguments to his tenants. 'Noble Lords', John advised them, have 'often served their country and best know who is fittest. . . . They do not impose but recommend the two to their choice. . . . If everyone or every town should set up their friend, what a confusion it would make'. Someone posted false declarations that John stood for Parliament and Cheyne confessed that the county was 'in ferment'.[123]

At the end of 1714, a second compromise agreement was concluded. Hampden replaced Grenville as the Whig's county candidate and Grenville stood for Wendover. Wharton admitted that the change was made 'to pacify the uneasiness of the freeholders'. The county was so 'incensed at the agreement of one Whig and one Tory', wrote John, that a man who knew how to 'manage' voters might scuttle the affair. The Tory, James Herbert, who had received John's Amersham seat, sent 500 letters announcing his candidacy. He was 'more inclined to war than peace' and desperately wanted to stand.[124] Although the second pact held, the electorate had affected its terms by putting pressure upon both parties.

The compromise was possible because of specific events and a practical grasp of politics by party leaders. Specific events included: the Hanoverian succession; fear of a Jacobite invasion; government interference in local politics; failure of parties to find candidates; and the growing inability of even Wharton to control party members. Both sides saw that they must 'quiet the minds of the people' after a period of unusual political excess.[125] Far from being an example of gentry authority, the pact showed that conflict and consensus coexisited in a fragile equilibrium.

The Buckinghamshire case sheds light upon the national decline of the rage of party. Clearly, the Whig/Tory conflict was based upon different beliefs about Church and State. Like a feud, however, it was 'a stylized . . . conflict' that conferred structure upon the society within which the two parties shared power.[126] Both sides expressed themselves in terms of the same dichotomies, rituals, goals, and rhetoric. Although the parties espoused different doctrines, they operated within the same system, used similar methods, and supported the political arrangements of the status quo.

After the Hanoverian Succession, however, the Tories faced new political realities. John took a safe seat at Amersham in 1715, but the Whigs soon seized power, and John was not reappointed as a deputy lieutenant. Unlike Temple or Verney, Sir Thomas Cave followed a third path. He filled his letters with coded images of dogs and horses, probably anticipating a Jacobite rebellion. 'The dog is young, but ready to go', Cave wrote on 26 October. 'Name is Beau, born near Cumberland. Now in arms'. Ralph Palmer described Cave's 'dangerous epistles' some of which were written in special ink. They 'fright me out of my wits', Palmer wrote. 'He is enough to bring anyone to N[ew]g[at]e'. Cave denounced Buckinghamshire's 1714 election pact noting: 'We stoutly rejected all such pusillanimous compositions.' He preferred the 'total extirpation' of the Church of England's invaders, whom he called 'Luther and Calvin'.[127]

Was Sir Thomas Cave a Jacobite? John's friend Richard Tighe defined the term: 'Whatever Protestant does not . . . protect and defend his King . . . his religion, laws, and liberty, I shall reckon him a Jacobite, and that he only waits for a favourable opportunity to declare for the Pretender.' Paul Monod has provided another definition. In his eyes, Jacobites experienced a particular *mentalité* and way of life. They privately honoured the Stuart monarchy through toasts and other rituals of everyday devotion. In the process, they accumulated treasured artefacts. Cave fits Monod's profile, and probably Richard Tighe's as well. Although there is no evidence of actual collaboration, Cave sympathized with the rebels. John, on the other hand, accepted the Hanoverian succession. When the Scots rose at Braemar, John hoped 'brave Argyle will prevent the bluebonnets from troubling us in old England'. As to the rebels, John wrote: 'I took 'em to be wiser men than to cabal for anti-Christ, but if they are guilty I hope their punishment will be accordingly.'[128]

In 1715 John's Whig brother-in-law Daniel Baker cleared John of any Jacobite taint: 'You have too good an estate and are too much a Protestant and lover of the country than to embark in any such wicked design as to bring in the Pretender.' Although John's name appeared on a list of Jacobite supporters, Baker's analysis rings true. At age 75, the city merchant had become a 'lover of the country' and a committed Anglican squire. One of his last acts was to vote against the Septennial Bill, affirming his country ideology. But he also bought Bank of England stock just four months before he died.[129] John's personal life integrated elements of a market philosophy with his family's landed heritage. These two final acts proclaimed his Janus-faced accommodation of the city and the country.

By 1715 the ritual of election had supplanted the ritual of the hunt as the locus of power. At Sir Ralph's death in 1696, the mantle of authority had passed to his son John through the distribution of gifts of venison. After John's death in 1717, his son Ralph crowned his inheritance with his own election to John's Amersham seat. Shortly before the poll, Ralph's steward Charles Chaloner killed a buck, so that the electorate might feast upon Verney bounty. The majesty of the deer still spoke of kings at sport and bore resonances of authority. Although the election concluded with venison, the mechanics of power had shifted to the use of hard cash.

John saved the family with his financial skills, but neither he nor his son or grandson was as politically successful as the Temples. The Verneys' achilles' heel lay in their failure to develop national patronage networks. The Temples, on the other hand, attained national power through their social and political alliances. With the Hanoverian succession, Denton and Temple received lucrative government offices and Lady Denton took a house in St James's. In Buckingham borough, Whigs reclaimed both seats, one of which went to a former brewer, Cobham's father-in-law, Edmund Halsey.[130] Richard Temple, Viscount Cobham, turned Stowe into one of England's premier country houses that attracted government ministers and titled landowners, as well as London's intellectual elite. After the marriage of Temple's sister to her neighbour Richard Grenville, the family soared to new heights and their son became Earl Temple. The merger created a mighty dynasty and a series of brilliant ministers, including the Pitts.[131] The Temple's Whig strategy was clearly the wave of the future.

John's son Ralph, 2nd Viscount Fermanagh (1683–1752), inherited a healthy estate along with a Parliament seat. Due to his father's strategies, he was able to buy land. Eventually, he too became a Whig and in 1743 he received an Irish earldom. A generation later, his younger son Ralph became 2nd Earl Verney (1714–1791). The 2nd Earl tried to compete with Stowe by building a grandiose addition to Claydon House. But although he and his brother married heiresses, he bankrupted the family as he built his reception rooms. His niece, Mary, tore down most of his splendid architecture before her death in 1810[132] (see plate 7). The Temples later suffered the same demise through the same financial extravagance, although they too tried to fend off the inevitable through name changing. Both families ran out of funds needed to maintain their treasured houses. The National Trust now runs Claydon House and Stowe Gardens, while the house at Stowe is a public school. History shows us that even long-lived dynasties eventually suffer decline. The most valuable possession of the Verney family has turned out to be their papers.

Conclusion

The challenges that families endure are continuous over the centuries: birth, death, and marriage; health and sickness; how to earn a living. These topics pervade our letters, as they did those of the Verneys. We too search for strategies that provide family stability and a civil society. Social networks and patronage are still crucial; they just take different and expanded forms. Families still attempt to maintain power by adopting fashionable modes of behaviour, while individuals struggle for independence from corporate and social restraints.

Family life styles are still influenced by a spreading urban culture. Its imprint has transfigured the countryside, as fragile greenbelts disappear. Indeed, the sweep of market values now extends globally, as well as nationally. Commuters to the city centre live in village properties or weekend retreats, bridging gaps between town and country. The privilege of enjoying both urban and provincial worlds is still a sign of success.

The Verneys still live in Claydon House and preserve their letters. Yet the history of this remarkably stable family has also been marked by conflict. The Verneys' conduct books and marriage settlements give a tidy picture of family life. Actual life experience, however, also shows marital dysfunction and experimentation, disregard of class distinctions, and angry quarrels. This was especially true for relatives outside the nuclear family, whose lives are usually difficult to track.

For the Verneys, family position and power were dependent upon a wide range of interacting variables — not just whether one was old or young, rich or poor, male or female. Power within the family was affected by one's strength, health, ambition, intellect, and proximity to the family head. Moreover, the position of wives varied according to their age, wealth, social skills, and family connections. The birth-order of children was very important, with strong distinctions between elder and younger sons, not just between sons and daughters. Gender provided more than one rigid model or role. Life's fortunes were extremely varied for widows, gentlewomen companions, wives, and daughters, with or without portions. Both male and female dependent kin found survival precarious. But many used political, business, or social skills as downpayments for future annuities.

Younger sons often found ways to achieve personal goals. They appear to have had more freedom than heirs in choosing wives and occupations. Sir Ralph quickly crushed Mun's wanderlusts, but John was allowed to adventure across the globe. This study suggests that as society grew more urban, younger sons were important agents of change. Their professional skills advanced Britain's power and saved financially strapped families like the Verneys. Elder sons had more power, wealth, and status but sometimes paid a heavy price for their privileges.

Verney women dealt imaginatively with family constraints. They may have been more intimately involved in finance than we have imagined. On the whole, urban women had more independence and mobility than their country cousins. They controlled the social code, defined its functions, and decoded its rules. As they did so, they delicately exerted power over John and Sir Ralph.

The rage of party that politicized every aspect of life gave women opportunities in public affairs. As an efficient wife of a member of Parliament, Elizabeth Baker was reponsibile for election activities. Like many other women of her class, boundaries between private and public aspects of her life overlapped. A broader definition of public and private space as well as sociability and power offers two major benefits. We can look at the Verneys' world in a way that is closer to the way that they did. We can also make more connections by dissolving cultural boundaries.

This blur between borders is most easily observed in London's fluid, anonymous environment. Both the Temples and the Verneys understood that to be in London was itself an essential strategy. In their eyes, the city and the country formed one interdependent world with intertwining roots and interests. London residence also led to changing patterns of social relationships. The coach and the visit, not gifts of venison, became primary symbols of metropolitan culture. London in-laws intermarried with each other and retained influence over several generations, but social relations with kin became more selective in response to market imperatives. Some relatives lost their influence when they made too many financial demands. Charity and hospitality still existed but were less automatically given and more narrowly defined.

Yet despite changes brought about by London's impact, most Verney men and women internalized family values. Pockets of individual independence might exist, but the dynastic vision remained strong. This study has asked the question why and how some families retained power? The Verneys' vision of themselves as links in the chain of a continuous dynasty is a final, but overlooked, source of strength. To put it simply, the Verneys and the Temples knew who they were. When there were no direct heirs, both families insisted upon name changes in order to retain the family surname. Part of the strength of families like the Verneys lay in their silent, neatly beribboned stacks of documents placed in the quiet privacy of their muniment rooms. Letters, genealogies, deeds, and estate papers gave these families a history, permanence, and physical space. After the chaos of the Civil War period, the construction of an ordered family memory bore an overarching significance that is difficult for us to comprehend. It was no accident that the Verneys saved and organized their family history, piling up the largest collection of personal letters in

England and perhaps Europe, nor that a voluminous mass of Temple documents still exist in the Huntington Library in California. In our own day, the Verneys' sense of self-importance may appear to be an obsession. In the seventeenth and eighteenth centuries, it helped to ensure their survival.

Appendix I. Research Design and the Sociability Database

This study and its database show that sociability lay at the heart of a society based upon personal connections. The database was constructed around a younger son, John Verney (1640–1717), his father Sir Ralph Verney (1613–1696), and their social networks. It started with the construction of a broad sociability model which asked *who* interacted with *whom* in *what activities* and through *what type of interaction*. This model was chosen to bring order to a huge mass of data and to connect people, events, and topics. Database fields were chosen to answer questions posed by the model.

A record was created for every document found on reels 46 through 56 of the microfilmed *Claydon House Papers*. These reels begin in July 1692 when John knew that he would inherit the Claydon estate and end in August 1717, two months after he died. This section of the database contains 7,018 records. Reels 16 through 45 were sampled for the years 1660 to 1691, with emphasis on the period from 1674 to 1688 when John settled in London. 1,096 documents were added to the database from these reels including all letters from John, and others from Sir Ralph, his elder son Edmund (Mun), and selected letter-writers. In addition, the following papers were indexed according to the same fields of information: approximately 2,000 papers at Claydon House including wills, settlements, and estate correspondence; approximately 1,500 of the Temple family's Stowe papers at the Huntington Library; papers from London and Buckinghamshire record offices, and a broad array of secondary sources.

Searchable fields of the database include: microfilm reel and number; document date; place from which the document was written; names of writer and recipient; abbreviations of letter-writers' names used in endnote citations. These abbreviations linked each record in the main database to a separate but related 'people' database of 202 persons who were in the inner circle of John's networks. The 'people' database automatically inserted each person's occupation, social status, and kinship to John into the main database. Occupation and status categories were difficult to assign because people's lives were multi-functional. For example, John was listed as a merchant but later rose to a viscount. Furthermore, many of John's merchant friends became financiers in the 1690s, professions were just developing, and women were identified by their husband's status. As a result, merchants, professionals, and single women were probably undercounted. More important, this book argues that status was extremely fluid in this period. Hence there is probably overlap in most categories.

With these caveats in mind, I have used the categories of Gregory King, a Herald of the College of Arms, in his table of social status and occupations published in 1696 (G. Barnett (ed.), 'Scheme of the Income and Expense of the Several Families of England, Calculated for the Year 1688', in *Two Tracts by Gregory King* (Baltimore, 1936), 31). Financiers (including goldsmith bankers and stock brokers), servants, and women have been added by the author, as shown in Table 1 (see Appendix II). Table 2 shows the number of Verney letters according to King's categories and lists the status, occupation, kinship, and gender of the 202 people in John Verney's inner circle.

Subjects cited in letters were indexed according to a list based upon US Library of Congress headings and the indexes to six published volumes of Verney letters. Up to fifty subjects could be assigned to each record. Table 6 shows frequently mentioned subjects and the number of letters which cite them. Nine fields indexed social interactions such as patronage, visiting, gift giving, dining, and favours. They are listed in Table 4. Other fields indexed location of letter-writers (see Table 3) and types of microfilmed papers including bills, thank you, and begging letters (see Table 5). Finally, a field indexed names of people cited in each letter. From this large universe, a list of family names was drawn up for further archival research (see Appendix III). Biographical sketches of people who appear most frequently in the text are found in Appendix IV. Citations and abbreviations to the Verney Papers are located in Appendix VI.

Appendix II. Tables

Table 1. **Gregory King's social status and occupation categories**

Gregory King's term	My term used in tables
Social status categories	
Temporal lords, baronets, knights	[Duke/Marq/Earl/Vi/Bt/Kt]
Spiritual lords	Bishops
Esquires and gentlemen	Gentry/gentlemen
[Wives/daughters]	[Status of husband/father]
Occupation categories	
Persons in offices	Officeholders
Merchants and traders by sea	Merchants
Persons in the law . . .	Lawyers
Clergy men	Clergymen
Freeholders and farmers	Freeholders/farmers
Persons in science and liberal arts	
Medical practitioners . . . apothecaries	Doctors/apothecaries
Educators . . .	Educators
Shopkeepers and tradesmen	Shopkeepers
Artisans and handicrafts	Artisans/craftsmen
Military/naval officers and men	Military men
[Men of finance]	[Financiers]
[Wives/daughters — all categories]	[Occupation of husband/father]
[Gentlewomen companions]	[Gentlewomen companions]
[Servants]	[Servants]
Labourers	Workmen
Cottages, paupers, vagrants	Poor

[ ] Brackets indicate a category added by the author to Gregory King's list

Source: G. Barnett (ed.), 'Scheme of the Income and Expense of the Several Families of England, Calculated for the Year 1688', in *Two Tracts by Gregory King* (Baltimore, 1936), 31.

Table 2. **Number of letters and letter-writers by status, occupation, kinship, gender, 1692–1717**

	Number of letters from	Number of letters to
Social status		
Marquess	2	1
Earl	22	11
Viscount	40	31
Viscount/wife	4	0
Baronet	615	1,357
Baronet/wife	158	26
Titled/wife	43	5
Knight	70	26
Knight/wife	564	35
Gentry/gentleman	240	517
Gentry/daughter	44	4
Gentry/wife	383	29
TOTAL RECORDS WITH STATUS	2,185	2,042
Occupation		
Officeholder	29	8
JOHN VERNEY, MERCHANT	1,450	3,576
Merchant	64	18
Merchant/wife	108	72
Merchant/daughter	19	0
Lawyer	489	152
Lawyer/wife	21	3
Clergyman	108	41
Clergy/wife	329	63
Clergy/daughter	0	0
Freeholder/farmer	263	20
Freeholder/farmer/wife	3	0
Doctor	24	5
Apothecary	3	0
Educator	13	1
Shopkeeper	100	29
Artisan/craftsman	25	4
Military man	99	31
Military/wife	116	13
Financier	135	170
Financier/wife	1	0
Gentlewoman/companion	257	15
Servant	579	266
Workman	2	0
TOTAL RECORDS WITH OCCUPATION	4,237 (60%)	4,487 (64%)
TOTAL RECORDS WITH STATUS	2,185 (32%)	2,042 (29%)
UNKNOWN	596 (8%)	489 (7%)
TOTAL RECORDS 1692–1717	7,018 (100%)	7,018 (100%)

John Verney's inner circle: 155 men, 47 women	Number of writers
People with status: 57 men, 33 women	90 (45%)
People with occupations: 98 men, 14 women	112 (55%)
Kin: 44 men, 33 women	77 (38%)
Non-kin: 111 men, 14 women	125 (62%)

Table 3. **Number of letters by location of writers, 1692–1717**

Location	Number of letters from	Number of letters to
London	3,265	2,373
Countryside	2,870	3,779
Ireland	62	21
France	5	0
Italy	3	0
New York	1	0
Switzerland	1	0
Virginia	1	2
RECORDS BY LOCATION	6,208	6,175 (100%)

Table 4. **Social interactions mentioned in letters, 1692–1717**

Type of sociability	Number of interactions
Financial favours	898
Sociability, generally	826
Visiting	632
Patronage	407
Social favours	378
Gift-giving	342
Dining	161
Legal favours	120
Religious favours	55
Medical favours	42
TOTAL	3,861

Table 5. **Specific types of Verney Papers on microfilm, 1692–1717**

Document type	Number of documents
Acquittances for debt	29
Begging letters	59
Bills for goods and services	72
Coded letters	6
Congratulations	67
Corn Accounts	33
Inventories	26
Foreign languages, letters in	6
Legal documents	38
Lists	42
Love Letters	15
Newsletters	15
Playing card	1
Receipts for moneys paid	160
Receipts for money received	66
Recipes	10
Thank you letters	79
Verses	16
Wood sales	24
Workmen's accounts	38

Table 6. **Selected subjects mentioned in letters, 1692–1717**

Subjects	Number of letters	Subjects	Number of letters
Annuities	67	Kin	189
Bath	56	Land	196
Blessing	63	Landlords	178
Books	56	Lawyers	120
Bribery	87	Legislation	162
Charity	92	Letter-writing	236
Children	116	London life	313
Christening	51	Lottery	85
Clergy	109	Love	57
Coach	165	Marriage	656
Coffee-house	57	Military	81
Country life	212	Money	81
Covent Garden	81	Mourning	65
Crime	114	Neighbourhood	57
Custom	119	News	166
Death	247	Office	292
Dining	130	Parliament	95
Drinking	104	Patronage	330
Education	119	Prayer	56
Elections	570	Pregnancy	61
Family	112	Races	67
Feuds	115	Religion	152
Finances	684	Rent	140
Food	141	Servants	426
Garden	53	Ships	51
Gentlewomen/ companions	74	Shopkeepers	88
Gifts	362	Social code	222
Gift/venison	166	Social status	90
Godparents	58	Social structure	82
Goldsmiths	88	Taxes	139
Gossip	73	Trade	53
Horses	99	Transport/travel	365
Hospitality	85	Values	130
Illness	229	Venison	236
Independence	134	Visiting	449
Inheritance	85	War	100
In-laws	101	Whig/Tory conflict	249
Investments	286	Wills	108
Jacobitism	100	Women	192
Justice of peace	85		

APPENDIX III. BIOGRAPHICAL FILES: FAMILIES CITED IN THE VERNEY PAPERS

Abdy*
Abel
Adams
Backwell*
Baker*
Bate
Bateman*
Baxter*
Blackmore*
Bludworth*
Bridgeman
Busby
Butterfield
Cave
Chaloner
Cheret*
Cogges*
Cooke*
Cheyne
Churchill
Coleman

Dashwood*
Denton
Dormer
Drake
Duncombe
Egerton
Fowles*
Gape*
Gardiner
Gelsthorpe*
Grenville
Grimes
Hampden
Harrington*
Herbert
Hill
Hoare*
Hobart
Innes
Keeling*
Knapp

Lawley
Lee
Ligo
Love*
Lovett
Lowndes
Lupart*
Luttrell*
Merwin
Nicholas
North*
Palmer*
Palmes
Paltock*
Paman*
Paschall
Paulden*
Pigott
Porter
Price
Roberts*

Seaton
Sheppard
Sherrier
St Amand*
Stanton*
Stewkeley
Temple
Tipping
Torriano*
Tregea*
Tufnell
Tyringham
Tyrrell
Viccars*
Wettenhall*
Wharton
White
Winwood
Woodward

* Families living, working, or writing primarily from London

Appendix IV. Biographical Guide: The Verneys and their Correspondents (by Generation and Proximity to the Family Head)

Sir Edmund Verney's Generation

Sir Edmund Verney (1590–1642) knight of Middle Claydon, Bucks., son of Sir Edmund, knight of Penley, Herts. (1535–1600) by his 3rd wife Mary Blakeney. He was knight-marshal and standard bearer to Charles I and died at the battle of Edgehill.

Margaret Denton (1594–1641) daughter of Sir Thomas Denton and Susan Temple of Hillesden, Bucks. She married Sir Edmund in 1612 with a £2,300 portion and a jointure of £400 per year. Four surviving sons, six daughters.

Sir Ralph Verney's Generation

Sir Ralph Verney (1613–1696) knight and 1st Baronet (1661), eldest son and heir of Sir Edmund. He sided with the Parliamentarians, but fled to France in 1643. After his return to England, he dominated the family, served as MP, rebuilt the Verney estate, and established the family archive.

Mary Blacknell (1616–1650) Sir Ralph's wife and heiress of John Blacknall. Her marriage at age 13 took place after payment of £1,000 to the Court of Wards. Most of her estates were sold by the Verneys. She journeyed from exile in France to lobby for Sir Ralph's sequestered estate. Two surviving sons.

Thomas Verney (1615–1707) Sir Ralph's wayward brother. He was sent to Virginia, but returned to a life of misdeeds and debt. Sir Ralph's other brothers died by 1671.

Penelope Osborne (1622–1695) Sir Ralph's money-loving sister and estranged wife of Sir John Osborne, knight. She left a fortune to her niece Penelope Stewkeley, but stirred up trouble among kin.

Cary Gardiner (1626–1704) Sir Ralph's sister and widow of John Stewkeley and Sir Thomas Gardiner, knight. She gambled, gossiped, raised a large family on a tiny annuity from Sir Ralph, and interpreted the London social code for the Verneys.

Mary Lloyd (1628–1684) Sir Ralph's sister married Robert Lloyd. Her daughter Mary took degrading posts as a gentlewoman companion.

Elizabeth Adams (1633–1721) Sir Ralph's youngest sister and wife of Revd Charles Adams of Great Baddow, Essex. She sent Sir Ralph delicacies from Covent Garden and was one of his matchmakers.

Sir Richard Temple (1634–1697) 3rd Baronet, Sir Ralph's kinsman, neighbour, and political opponent. He controlled the borough of Buckingham and built a grand house at Stowe.

William Coleman/Charles Chaloner stewards to Sir Ralph and John.

Elizabeth Lillie housekeeper to Sir Ralph and John.

Charles Hodges secretary to Sir Ralph, later a court official.

John Verney's Generation

JOHN VERNEY (1640–1717) 2nd Baronet and 1st Viscount Fermanagh (1703), younger son of Sir Ralph. Apprenticed as a merchant, he traded in the Levant from 1662 to 1674. A London merchant from 1674 to 1696, he inherited Middle Claydon. He became a Tory MP and expanded the family's fortunes. Three wives, four children.

ELIZABETH PALMER (1664–1686) 1st wife of John Verney, daughter of RALPH PALMER, of Little Chelsea, Middlesex. She married in 1680 with £3,000. Her Claydon kin yeoman JOSEPH CHURCHILL, Captain WILLIAM WHITE, and WILLIAM CHALONER, Esq. entered the Verneys' social networks. Three daughters, one son.

MARY LAWLEY (1661–1694) 2nd wife of John Verney (1692), daughter of SIR FRANCIS LAWLEY, baronet, keeper of the royal jewel house, and part-owner of the Rainbow coffee-house. She brought a £3,000 portion, but died before claiming her £400 jointure. No surviving children.

ELIZABETH BAKER (1678–1736) 3rd wife of John Verney, daughter of DANIEL BAKER (1628–1700) haberdasher of London and Governor of the Bridewell. She married in 1697 with a £3,500 portion but fought with the Verney family after John's death. No children.

DANIEL BAKER II (1659–1727) John's brother-in-law inherited a small Buckinghamshire estate and helped John Verney to win votes. His sister SARAH married NARCISSUS LUTTRELL.

RALPH PALMER II (d. 1746) John's brother-in-law retained influence over John Verney's children after his sister's death. A member of the Middle Temple, he gave legal advice to the Verneys.

EDMUND VERNEY (1636–1688) John's elder brother and Sir Ralph's heir. A spendthrift and adulterer, he died before his father. Sir Ralph forced him to marry the daughter of a wealthy neighbour.

MARY ABEL (1641–1715) Edmund's wife (1662) and orphaned heiress of WILLIAM ABEL, a London vintner, later of East Claydon. She brought adjacent lands worth £700–£800 per year, but they reverted to the Abels. Her reputed mental illness was probably a result of her unhappy marriage. Two sons and one daughter died early.

PEG ADAMS John Verney's capable London cousin who tended Sir Ralph at his death. She never married because she had no dowry.

CARY STEWKELEY John's cousin waited on Mary Abel. She expected a 'swinging' legacy, but received nothing.

PEN STEWKELEY John's cousin became pregnant by her sister's intended husband. After receiving a fortune from her aunt, John arranged her marriage to WILLIAM VICCARS, a London clergyman.

JOHN STEWKELEY John's cousin and friend. He died penniless but avoided prison by evading his creditors.

NANCY NICHOLAS John's cousin and daughter of Dr William Denton of Hillesden. She and her husband GEORGE NICHOLAS, an MP and Customs Commissioner, competed with John's aunts for favours.

WILLIAM BUSBY/NICHOLAS MERWIN John's country lawyers.

SIR GABRIEL ROBERTS (1635–1715) John's master, official of the Levant, East India, and Royal Africa Companies. He was knighted in 1678 but avoided public office.

HENRY HOARE (1677–1725) John's banker of Fleet Street with his father, MP and Lord Mayor of London, SIR RICHARD HOARE (1648–1718). Henry established the family seat at Stourton, Wiltshire.

PETER LUPART Dutchman, John's banker, Golden Lion, Lombard St.

SIR EDMUND DENTON (1676–1714) John Verney's Whig rival, son of SIR ALEXANDER DENTON of Hillesden (1654–1698). He became an MP and 1st Baronet. John was not invited to his funeral.

SIR RICHARD TEMPLE (1675–1749) 4th Baronet (1697) Baron (1714) and Viscount Cobham (1718). John's Whig rival held high military and government offices and controlled Buckingham borough.

THOMAS WHARTON (1648–1715) Viscount Winchendon and Earl of Wharton (1706) Marquess of Wharton and Malmesbury (1714). Became one of the most powerful Whig leaders in England.

WILLIAM CHEYNE (1657–1728) 2nd Viscount Newhaven. John's political mentor inherited Buckinghamshire and Chelsea estates in 1698 from CHARLES CHEYNE (1625–1698). Tory leader in Bucks.

EDWARD HENRY LEE (1663–1716) Earl of Lichfield, husband of Lady Charlotte Fitzroy, illegitimate daughter of Charles II. Son of Sir Ralph's friend, Sir Francis Henry Lee, and Tory ally of John.

John Verney's Covent Garden Network

Sir Richard Temple, Sir Alexander Denton, Buckinghamshire kin. Roger North, lawyer.
  Sir Dudley North, Levant merchant.
Sir Godfrey Kneller, Sir Peter Lely, artists.
Grinling Gibbons, William Mason, craftsmen.
Aunts Cary Gardiner, Elizabeth Adams, and their many children.
Nancy Nicholas, cousin. George Nicholas, MP and customs officer.
Mr Gape, James St Amand, apothecaries.
Mr Thomas Cheret, Dutch landlord and shopkeeper.

John Verney's Chelsea Network

Lords Cheyne and Lindsey, Chelsea and Bucks. landowners.
Ralph Palmer and his middling-sort family.
Elizabeth Palmer, John's first wife.
Joseph Churchill/family, Steeple Claydon yeoman, Palmer's nephew.
Captain William White/family, Steeple Claydon, Palmer kin.
William Chaloner/family, Steeple Claydon landowner, Palmer kin.
Covent Garden cousins.
Josiah Priest, schoolmaster.

John Verney's Hatton Garden Network

John Verney/family.

Daniel Baker, haberdasher and Governor of the Bridewell.
Elizabeth Baker, John's third wife.
William Harrington, merchant.
Angel Harrington, his daughter, courted by John Verney.
Peter Gelsthorpe, apothecary.
Dr Edward Stillingfleet, rector, church of St Andrew Holborn.
Mr Lovett, linen draper. Kin to John's son-in-law and his parson.

John Verney's City Network

Sir Gabriel Roberts/family, John's master and friend.
Henry Hoare, Peter Lupart, John's goldsmith bankers.
Sir Dudley North, William Love, William Roberts, Walter Bludworth, John Sheppard, John's merchant colleagues.
Simon/George Baxter, Charles/George Torriano, John Knapp, John's financial brokers.
A host of London lawyers.

Ralph Verney II's Generation

RALPH VERNEY II (1683–1752) John's heir, became 2nd Viscount (1717) and 1st Earl Verney (1743). He compliantly married a landed heiress. He and his sons became land buyers.

CATHERINE PASCHALL (d. 1748) Ralph II's wife, co-heiress of Henry Paschall of Great Baddow, Essex. She married in 1708, bringing a large landed estate. Two sons, two daughters.

ELIZABETH VERNEY (1681–1767) John's eldest daughter had a £3,000 portion and several suitors, but never married.

MARY VERNEY (1682–1769) John's beloved second daughter married in 1703 with a £3,000 portion and £400 jointure. Lived in Ireland.

COLONEL JOHN LOVETT (d. 1710), Mary Verney's husband came from an old Bucks. family, but his father became a Levant merchant. Lovett's investments left his widow with financial problems.

MARGARET VERNEY (1685–1774), John's proud youngest daughter. She eloped in 1703 without a marriage settlement. Later she was promised a £600 jointure in return for a £3,000 portion.

SIR THOMAS CAVE (1682–1719) Margaret Verney's husband, 3rd Baronet of Stanford Hall, Leics., son of SIR ROGER CAVE (1655–1703). Country gentleman and Tory MP with his father-in-law.

Later Generations at Claydon House

JOHN VERNEY (1711–1737), Eldest son of Ralph, 1st Earl Verney. Married Mary Nicholson. Died before inheriting.

MARY NICHOLSON (d. 1789), heiress of JOSIAH NICHOLSON of Clapham, a Thames Street brewer. She married John with a £40,000 portion and a £1,600 jointure. Their daughter MARY was created Baroness Fermanagh. Mary Nicholson Verney later married RICHARD CALVERT.

RALPH VERNEY (1714–1791) 2nd Earl Verney and younger son inherited in 1752. Married Mary Herring. He built grand ballrooms but died in debt, having squandered the family fortune.

MARY HERRING (1716–1791) heiress of HENRY HERRING, merchant of Mincing Lane and director of the Bank of England. She married Ralph, 2nd Earl Verney in 1740 with £30,000. No children.

MARY VERNEY (1737–1810) daughter of John Verney and Mary Nicholson, created Baroness Fermanagh. Tore down her uncle's reception rooms and died unmarried.

CATHERINE CALVERT (d. 1827) daughter of Mary Nicholson and Richard Calvert and half-sister to Baroness Fermanagh. Catherine and her husband Robert Wright, Rector of Middle Claydon, assumed the name of Verney when she succeeded to Claydon.

SIR HARRY CALVERT (1763–1826) a distant cousin created 1st baronet 1818.

SIR HARRY CALVERT (1801–1894) 2nd baronet. Adopted the name of Verney on inheriting Claydon in 1827. After he discovered the archive, his second wife Frances Parthenope published abstracts of the letters with her stepdaughter Margaret Maria.

Appendix V. Buckinghamshire Politicians and Events Cited in Chapter 6

Sir Edmund Verney (1590–1642) Knight Marshal, standard bearer to Charles I. 1642 killed on the battlefield at Edgehill.

MP Buckingham 1624, Aylesbury 1628, Wycombe 1640

Sir Ralph Verney (1613–1696) 1st Baronet

MP Aylesbury 1640 (Apr.); 1640 (Nov.)–22 Sept. 1645
MP Buckingham 1681, 1685, 1689 with Sir Richard Temple

1643	After siding with Parliament, flees to France
1653	Returns to England
1661, 1679	Refuses to stand for Parliament
1681	Wins Buckingham seat with Sir Richard Temple. Defeats Peter Tyrrell and deist Charles Blount
1685	Wins election with Temple. Finally agrees to finance a town hall. James II accedes to the throne
1686	Is put out of magistracy
1688	Glorious Revolution. Votes throne is not vacant
1689	Wins election with Temple, after Alexander Denton refuses to stand
1690	Withdraws from Buckingham election because he 'had not voices enough to carry it'
1696	Death of Sir Ralph

Sir Richard Temple (1634–1697) 3rd Baronet

MP Warwickshire 1654
MP Buckingham 1659, 1660, 1661, 1679 (Oct.), 1681, 1685, 1690, 1695–10 May 1697

1660–75	Switches sides. By 1675 a court follower of Danby
1672	Gets custom-house place with £2,000 salary
1679	(Feb.) Stands with Danby's son, Viscount Latimer. Loses in double return to Peter Tyrrell
	(Oct.) Regains Buckingham seat
1681–97	Controls Buckingham Borough
1684	Gets new Charter for Buckingham
1686	Gets £1,200 pension
1688	Supports William III extremely late
1689	Wins election with Verney but leaning towards Denton
1690	Stands with Denton and wins
1695	Holds seat until his death in 1697

John Verney (1640–1717) Viscount Fermanagh

MP Buckinghamshire 1710, 1713
MP Amersham 1715–23 June 1717

1696	(Sept.) Sir Ralph Verney dies. John inherits. He has become a staunch Tory Anglican
	(Dec.) John unsuccessfully stands for the county. Loses with 263 votes to Hill and Neale
1697	Sir Richard Temple dies
1698	John unsuccessfully stands for the county, but with 926 votes. Lord Cheyne wins and becomes John's patron
	Sir Alexander Denton dies. John forced to resign as Edmund Denton's trustee. Fails to recapture Buckingham seat from sons of Temple and Denton
1700/1	(Jan.) Loses county election with 1,209 votes in last place. Whig Robert Dormer takes away votes
1701	(Dec.) John refuses to stand
1702–8	John builds a local power base as JP. Refuses to stand for Parliament. Whigs and Wharton control county
1710	(Oct.) John in first place with 2,161 votes wins county election with Whig Sir Edmund Denton. Defeats Whig Hampden and Tory Seymour
1713	(Sept.) John with 2,018 votes wins county election with Tory Fleetwood. Defeats Whigs Hampden and Denton. Wins at Amersham. Wife Elizabeth plays important role
1714	(Aug.) Queen Anne dies.
	(Sept.) Proclamation of George I, Jacobite uprising
1714/15	John refuses to stand for county. Whig Hampden and Tory Fleetwood presented in compromise to voters. John takes safe seat at Amersham
1717	(June) John dies. Ralph replaces his father at Amersham

WILLIAM CHEYNE (1657–1728) 2nd Viscount Newhaven of Chesham Bois. Bucks. Tory leader and John's mentor.

MP Amersham 1681, 1685, 1701 (Dec.), 1705–1 May 1707
MP Appleby 1689 (July), 1690
MP Buckinghamshire 1696 (Feb.), 1698, 1701 (Feb.), 1702

Lord Lieut. Bucks. 1702, 1712–14

THOMAS WHARTON (1648–1715) created Viscount Winchendon and Earl of Wharton in 1706 and Marquess of Wharton and Malmesbury in 1714. One of the most powerful Whigs in England.

MP Wendover 1673 (Mar.)
MP Buckinghamshire 1679 (Mar.), 1679 (Oct.), 1681, 1685, 1689, 1690, 1695–6 (Feb.)

Lord Lieut. Oxon. 1697–1702, Bucks. 1702, Ireland 1708–10

RICHARD TEMPLE (1675–1749) Baron Cobham (1714) and Viscount Cobham (1718). High military offices, member of the Privy Council 1716, Constable of Windsor Castle 1716–23, Governor of Jersey, 1723–49, independent Whig member of 'boy patriots'.

MP Buckinghamshire 1704–8
MP Buckingham 1697–1702, 1708–13

Lord Lieut. Bucks. 1728–38

RALPH VERNEY (1683–1752) 2nd Viscount Fermanagh. First a Tory, then a government supporter.

MP Amersham 10 July 1717–27
MP Wendover 1741–4 Oct. 1752

RALPH VERNEY (1714–91) 2nd Earl Verney, a government supporter

MP Wendover 17 Jan. 1753–61
MP Carmarthen 1761–8
MP Buckinghamshire 1768–84; 1790–31 Mar. 1791

Appendix VI. The Verney Papers: Citations and Abbreviations

All references to the Verney papers are to microfilmed documents in the Princeton University Library entitled *Claydon House Letters*, unless preceded by CH for papers at Claydon House (see below). Citations include the microfilm reel number, the sequential number of the document as found on that reel, lower case abbreviations for the correspondents as they are found in the author's database, and the date of the document. For example, the third letter on microfilm reel number 55 from Ralph Verney to John Verney on 1 March 1714 appears as follows: 55–3, rv/jv, Mar. 1 1714. If the correspondent's name is not abbreviated in the database, the full surname is given in the citation. A list of abbreviations used in citations to the Verney Papers is displayed below. Temple family papers in the Stowe Collection at the Huntington Library have their own catalogue numbers, but have been abbreviated and formatted as above.

Original papers at Claydon House are preceded by CH followed by its catalogue number at the time of research: for example CH 1/73. In most cases, numbers are those found in S. Ranson, *The Verney Papers Catalogued for the Claydon House Trust* (1994). If not, they date from on-site visits prior to publication of the catalogue. Dating of all papers has been modernized to start the year on the 1st day of the year, while the month precedes the day and year. Spelling and punctuation have been modernized.

Abbreviations Used in Citations to the Verney Papers

adov	Dover, Anthony	cper	Pery, Colonel
anor	North, Anne	cpv	Verney, Catherine
aoug	Oughton, Adolphus	cst	Stewkeley, Cary
atal	Talbot, Anne	ctor	Torriano, Charles
atre	Tregea, Anna	cww	White, Captain William
awoo	Woodward, Anne	db	Baker, Daniel
ba	Adams, Bell	db2	Baker 2, Daniel
bb	Backwell, Barnaby	db3	Baker 3, Daniel
bh	Hoare, Benjamin	dbri	Bridgeman, Dorothy
bkni	Knight, Bez	dfus	Fust, Dick
bl	Lovett, Betty	dhol	Hollaway, Deborah
bmor	Morland, Benjamin	dn	Nicholas, Denton
bv	Verney, Betty	drp	Paman, Dr
bwil	Willis, Browne	dsea	Seaton, Daniel
cbur	Burgoyne, Constance	ea	Adams, Elizabeth
cc	Chaloner, Charles	eb	Backwell, Edward
cdun	Dunk, Cornelia	ebat	Bate, Edward
cgai	Gainsford, Captain	ebv	Verney, Elizabeth B.
cho	Hodges, Charles	eden	Denton, Edmund
cl	Lovett, Colonel	eico	East India Co.
colb	Beaumont, Colonel	elan	Lane, Edward

eli	Lillie, Elizabeth		kst	Stewkeley, Kitty
epea	Pearce, Edward		lbri	Bridgewater, Lord
epv	Verney, Elizabeth P.		lc	Cheyne, Lord
etv	Verney, Elizabeth T.		lg	Gardiner, Lady
ewoo	Wooton, Edward		llaw	Lawley, Lady
flaw	Lawley, Francis		llin	Lindsey, Lord
flig	Ligo, Francis		llit	Litchfield, Lord
flut	Luttrell, Francis		lpor	Porter, Lettice
fshe	Sherrington, Ferdinando		lshe	Sheppard, Luce
ftyr	Tyringham, Frances		ltho	Thompson, Leon
fwil	Willis, Francis		lylin	Lindsey, Lady
gn	Nicholas, George		mav	Verney, Mary A.
gpal	Palmes, Guy		mc	Cave, Margaret
gtor	Torriano, George		mco	Cooke, Miles
hbel	Bell, Henry		mgap	Gape, Mr
hch	Churchill, Henry		mgln	Glenham, Mr
hh	Hoare, Henry		mgro	Grosvenor, Mr
hlaw	Lawley, Hester		mk	Keeling, Molly
hlp	Palmer, Hester		ml	Lovett, Mary
hpas	Paschall, Henry		mlld	Lloyd, Mary
hst	Stewkeley, Hugh		mlv	Verney, Mary L.
hsta	Starkey, Helena		mmil	Millward, Mr
ht	Tyrrell, Harry		mmin	Minshull, Mr
htas	Tash, Hatton		mpal	Palmes, Mary
htee	Teeme, Henry		munv	Verney, Edmund
icom	Comyns, I.		mwhi	Whitmore, Mary
ist	Isabelle, Stewkeley		mwick	Wickham, Mrs
jabd	Abdy, Jenny		nden	Denton, Nelly
jbak	Baker, Jack		nhob	Hobart, N.
jbro	Brooks, John		nlut	Luttrell, Narcissus
jbu	Busby, John		nm	Merwin, Nicholas
jcar	Cary, John		nmar	Martin, Nicholas
jchu	Churchill, Joseph		nn	Nicholas, Nancy
jchu2	Churchill 2, Joseph		pa	Adams, Peg
jd	Deere, John		pbax	Baxter, Peter
jfle	Fleetwood, Jonathan		pg	Gardiner, Peg
jher	Heron, John		pgel	Gelthorpe, Peter
jhol	Holland, John		pl	Lupart, Peter
jk	Keeling, John		po	Osborne, Penelope
jke	Kent, John		pt	Tyrrell, Peter
jkna	Knapp, John		ptya	Tyam, Peregrine
jmar	Markham, Joseph		pv	Viccars, Pen
jn	Nicholas, Jack		rac	Royal Africa Co.
jo	Osborne, John		rbur	Burgoyne, Roger
jshe	Sheppard, John		rdor	Dormer, Robert
jst	Stewkeley, John		rglo	Glover, Robert
jv	Verney, John		rgre	Grenville, Richard
kshu	Shuckburough, Katherine		rh	Hoare, Richard

rham	Hampden, Richard	tsmi	Smith, Thomas
rhil	Hill, Roger	tt	Tyrrell, Thomas
rlaw	Lawley, Richard	ttip	Tipping, Thomas
rlow	Lowndes, Robert	tv	Verney, Thomas
rp	Palmer, Ralph	twat	Watson, Thomas
rp2	Palmer 2, Ralph	twet	Wettenhall, Thomas
rpau	Paulden, Rebecca	twha	Wharton, Thomas
rpol	Pollard, Ralph	vgaw	Gaudy, Vere
rpri	Price, Roger	vlld	Lloyd, Verney
rtig	Tighe, Richard	wa	Abel, William
rtoo	Tooke, Robert	wblu	Bludworth, Walter
rv	Verney, Ralph	wbus	Busby, William
rv2	Verney 2, Ralph	wbut	Butterfield, William
sbax	Baxter, Simon	wc	Coleman, William
sgr	Roberts, Sir Gabriel	wcha	Chaloner, William
shar	Harcourt, Simon	wchap	Chaplyn, William
shf	Foster, Humphrey	wd	Denton, William
smal	Mallard, Sarah	wfal	Fall, William
srt	Temple, Richard	wgro	Grosvenor, William
stuf	Tufnell, Samuel	wlaw	Lawley, William
swal	Wallis, Stephen	wlov	Love, William
tbu	Busby, Thomas	wlow	Lowndes, William
tc	Cave, Thomas	wmas	Mason, William
tchap	Chapman, Thomas	wpag	Page, William
tche	Cheret, Thomas	wpri	Price, William
tdun	Dunk, Thomas	wro	Roades, William
tfre	Freeman, Thomas	wst	Stewkeley, William
tg	Gardiner, Thomas	wsta	Stanton, William
tgri	Grimes, Thomas	wtho	Thoroughgood, William
tlaw	Lawley, Thomas	wtow	Townsend, William
tnew	Newman, Thomas	wv	Viccars, William
tpig	Pigott, Thomas	wwak	Wakefield, William
tro	Roades, Thomas		

NOTES

Notes to Introduction

1. 49-266, pa/jv, Sept. 25 1696; G. Brumell, *A Short Account of the Franking System in the Post Office, 1652–1840* (Bournemouth, 1936); BL Add. MS 72517.
2. 49-227, cst/jv, Aug. 11 1696; 49-223, pa/jv, Aug. 9 1696; 49-225, pa/jv, Aug. 11 1696; 49-257, pa/jv, Sept. 18 1696.
3. Jane Austen/J. Edward Austen, Dec 16 1816; C. Tomalin, *Jane Austen* (Viking, 1997), 28.
4. S. Whyman, 'Land and Trade Revisited: The Case of John Verney, London Merchant and Baronet', *London Journal*, 22 (1997), 16–32 and Chs. 1 and 3.
5. J. Habermas, *The Structural Transformation of the Public Sphere* (Cambridge, Mass., 1989).
6. For county studies, see P. Jenkins, *The Making of a Ruling Class* (Cambridge, 1983); P. Roebuck, *Yorkshire Baronets 1640–1760* (Oxford, 1980); J. Johnson, *The Gloucestershire Gentry* (Gloucester, 1989). For family studies, see J. Beckett, *The Rise and Fall of the Grenvilles* (Manchester, 1994); J. Rosenheim, *The Townshends of Raynham* (Middletown, Conn, 1989); J. Plumb, 'The Walpoles, Father and Son', in *Studies in Social History*, (New York, 1955), 179–207.
7. R. Williams, *The Country and the City* (1973), 61–71.
8. F. Verney (ed.), *Memoirs of the Verney Family* (1892), vol. i, pp. xi–xii.
9. NRA 21959, S. Ranson, *The Verney Papers Catalogued for the Claydon House Trust*, 1994. For the microfilm, see the Buckinghamshire Record Office, British Library, and Firestone Library, Princeton University. See the bibliography for other works about the family.
10. H. Bennet, *The Pastons and their England* (Cambridge, 1968), 125. Amounts for servants' annuities are cut out of deeds in DH 1/214–218, 1673–1698. I thank Susan Ranson for this reference. 38-11, munv/rv, Aug. 31 1683; 39–30, jv, [Jan. 1685?]; examples in BL Add. MS 71573.
11. G. Barnett (ed.), 'Scheme of the Income and Expense of the Several Families of England, Calculated for the year 1688', *Two Tracts by Gregory King* (Baltimore, 1936), 31. Letters to and from those whose status is unknown comprise 8% and 7%, respectively. Assignments to categories were based on those most used in letters. Unless noted otherwise, numbers of letters and citations to people and subjects refer to the main database of 7,018 records from 1692 to 1717.
12. 55-590, rp2/rv2, Sept. 23 1715; BL Add. MS 72515, Aug. 17 1687.
13. G. Mosse, *The Image of Man* (Oxford and New York, 1996); M. Cohen, *Fashioning Masculinity* (1996); M. Roper and J. Tosh, *Manful Assertions* (1991).
14. 46-177, rv/lg, Oct. 30 1692; P. Spacks, *Gossip* (New York, 1985).
15. S. Penton, *The Gentleman Instructed* (1688), 59; 54–135, rp2/rv2, Oct. 13 1709; J. Goody, *The Logic of Writing and the Organization of Society* (Cambridge, 1986), 20; 41-19, jst/rv, Oct. 6 1686; 32-47, T. Stafford/rv, Dec 2 1678; 46-518, lg/rv June 7 1693.
16. 51-631, lg/jv, Dec 16 1701; 49-382, eli/rv, Feb. 23 1695; 49-275, eli/jv, Sept. 29 1696; 50-440,

ist/jv, July 12 1698; 50-654, ea/jv, June 19 1699; 51-229, ea/jv, Apr. 2 1700. For similar generational differences, compare the letters of Anne, Lady Strafford in BL Add. MS 22226 with fo. 159 from her mother and fos. 80 and 299 from her mother-in-law.

17. 48-18, mc/rv, Oct. 23 1694; HL Stowe MS STT 1911, A. Temple/J. Mellifont, [Oct. 7, *c*.1695]; 50-637, P. Tyam/jv, May 1699; 51-12, Edward Norgrave/ebv, July 22 1699; examples in BL Add. MS 72515.

18. C. Geertz, 'Thick Description', in *The Interpretation of Cultures* (New York, 1973), 3–30; L. Hunt (ed.), *The New Cultural History* (Berkeley, 1989); V. Turner, *Dramas, Fields and Metaphors* (Ithaca, New York, 1974); P. Burke, *Varieties of Cultural History* (Cambridge, 1997). For a definition of narrative, see L. Stone, 'The Revival of Narrative', *Past and Present*, 85 (1979), 3–24.

19. M. Byrne (ed.), *The Lisle Letters* (Chicago, 1983), p. xxv; J. Oates, 'Tennessee in the Stoned Age', *Times Literary Supplement*, Apr. 19 1991, 8; J. Swift in the introduction to *Letters Written by Sir W. Temple . . . 1665–72* (1700), i, A3ʳ.

20. 51-545, ea/jv, Aug. 22 1700; 51-72, lg/jv, Sept. 27 1699; 46-338, tv/jv, Feb. 2 1693; 50-173, nn/jv, Oct. 5 1697.

21. A. Macfarlane, *The Family Life of Ralph Josselin* (Cambridge, 1970); R. Isaac, *The Transformation of Virginia 1740–1790* (Chapel Hill, NC, 1982); G. Dening, *Islands and Beaches* (Honolulu, 1980); E. Ladurie, *Montaillou* (New York, 1978). For other ways to depict networks, see Ch. 1 for social network analysis and E. Ladurie, *The Mind and Method of the Historian* (Chicago, 1981), 143.

22. J. Broad, 'Sir Ralph Verney and his Estates 1630–1696', D. Phil. thesis (Oxford, 1973) and 'Gentry Finances and the Civil War: The Case of the Buckinghamshire Verneys', *EcHR* 2nd series, 32 (1979), 183–200.

23. M. Slater, *Family Life in the Seventeenth Century: The Verneys of Claydon House* (1984); J. Bruce (ed.), *Notes of Proceedings of the Long Parliament* (Camden Society, 31; 1845) and *Letters and Papers of the Verney Family down to . . . 1639* (Camden Society, 56; 1853); A. Horwood (ed.), *The MSS of Sir Harry Verney, Bart. at Claydon House . . .* (Historical Manuscript Commission, 7; 1879), xiv, 433–509. For six volumes of abstracts, see F. and M. Verney (eds.), *Memoirs of the Verney Family*, 4 vols. (1892–99), with later editions in 1904, 1912, 1925, 1970; M. Verney (ed.), *The Verney Letters of the Eighteenth Century . . .*, 2 vols. (1930).

24. S. Whyman '"Paper Visits"', in *Epistolary Selves* (Aldershot, 1999); M. Manley, *Court Intrigues, in a Collection of Original Letters . . .* (1711); Del Chevalier, *Five Love Letters from a Nun to a Cavalier* (1693); C. Gildon, *The Post-Boy Robb'd of his Mail*, 2nd edn. (1706); [A. Behn], *Love-Letters between a Noble-man and his Sister* (1684); M. Cavendish, *CCXI. Sociable Letters . . .* (1664); R. Day, *Told in Letters* (Ann Arbor, 1966), 237–70; S. Richardson, *Pamela or Virtue Rewarded* (1740).

25. *Familiar and Courtly Letters to Persons of Honour and Quality by Monsieur Voiture . . .* (1701), i; M. Motley, 'Educating the English Gentleman Abroad', *History of Education*, 23 (1994), 251. Book lists in 49-486, [1697?]; 49-637, Apr. 21 1697; 50-279, [Jan. 1698?]; 48-104, jv/rv, Dec 6 1694.

26. T. Elliott, *State Papers Domestic Concerning the Post Office . . .* (1964); B. Austen, *English Provincial Posts 1633–1840* (1978); *The Post Office: An Historical Summary* (1911); D. Cressy, *Literacy and the Social Order* (Cambridge, 1980), 129, 176; K. Shevelow, *Women and Print Culture* (1989), 30; G. Greer *et al.*, *Kissing the Rod* (1988), introduction, 1–31.

27. 52-628, ml/jv, Nov. 18 1704; L. Butterfield, *Adams Family Correspondence* (Cambridge, Mass., 1963), vol. i, p. xxiii.

28. C. Steedman, *Past Tenses* (1992), 11; I. Watt, *The Rise of the Novel* (Berkeley, 1957), 74–6, 177.

29. J. Black, 'Eighteenth-Century English Politics', *Albion*, 28 (1996), 607–33; M. Foucault, *Power and Knowledge* (New York, 1977); M. Wiesner, *Women and Gender in Early Modern Europe* (Cambridge, 1993), 239; E. Chalus, 'Women in English Political Life 1754–1790', D. Phil. thesis (Oxford, 1997).

30. J. Beckett, *Coal and Tobacco* (Cambridge, 1981), 10–11; H. Wyld, *A History of Modern Colloquial English* (Oxford, 1936), 162–5.

31. For the gentry, see J. Rosenheim, *The Emergence of a Ruling Order* (1998); F. Heal and C. Holmes, *The Gentry in England and Wales 1500–1700* (Stanford, Calif., 1994); L. and J. Stone, *An Open Elite?* (Oxford, 1984); G. Mingay, *The Gentry* (1976).

32. N. Davis, 'The Shapes of Social History', *Storia Della Storiografia*, 17 (1990), 228–34 and 'On the Lame', *American Historical Review*, 93 (1988), 572–603; J. Goodman, *Stories of Scottsboro* (New York, 1994); H. White, *Metahistory* (Baltimore, 1973); P. Noble, *That Noble Dream* (New York, 1988).

33. E. Grendi, 'Micro-analisi e Storia Sociale', *Quaderni Storici*, 35 (1977), 506-20; E. Muir, 'Introduction: Observing Trifles', in E. Muir and R. Guido (eds.), *The Lost People of Europe* (Baltimore, 1991), p. xiv.

34. C. Brant, 'Eighteenth-Century Letters', D. Phil. thesis (Oxford, 1988); J. Altman, *Epistolarity* (Columbus, Oh., 1982); B. Redford, *The Converse of the Pen* (Chicago, 1986); [S. Johnson], *The Rambler*, no. 158, Sat. Aug. 31 1751; 49-211, nn/rv, July 28 1696. See also Ch. 4.

35. P. Spacks, 'Borderlands', *Georgia Review*, 37 (1983), 811; M. Hunt, *The Middling Sort* (Berkeley, 1996), 10.

Notes to Chapter 1

1. 32-134, munv/jv, May Day 1679; 35-25, jv/rv, Mar. 14 1680; 29-15, rv/munv, Feb. 3 1676; 37-11, jv/rv, Oct. 19 1682; 29-20, rv/munv, Feb. 17 1676;39-40, rv/wc, Feb. 27 1685; B. Henning, *The House of Commons 1660–1690* (1983), iii. 635.

2. 33-11, rv/jv, July 14 1679; J. Broad, 'Gentry Finances and the Civil War: The Case of the Buckinghamshire Verneys', *EcHR*, 2nd series, 32 (1979), 183–200; M. Slater, *Family Life in the Seventeenth Century: The Verneys of Claydon House* (1984), 12–15; Cambridge University Library, Sel 2. 114–126; P. Hopkins, 'The Verney Collection of Popish Plot Pamphlets', *Bulletin of the Friends of the Cambridge University Library*, 9 (1988), 5–15.

3. I adopt this definition used by J. Eales, *Puritans and Roundheads* (Cambridge, 1990), 16.

4. NRA 21959, S. Ranson, *The Verney Papers Catalogued for the Claydon House Trust* (1994), p. iii gives 1463 for Verney's mayoralty. R. Gibbs, *Worthies of Buckinghamshire* (Aylesbury, 1888), 385–9; G. Lipscomb, *The History and Antiquities of the County of Buckingham* (1831), i. 174–98; M. Holmes, *The Country House Described: An Index . . .* (1986). The Verneys lived in London and Hertfordshire until 1620.

5. Bodl 270. e. 891, Lady Verney, 'The House of Claydon and its Inhabitants' and 'Three Centuries of Family Portraits' (1891), 15–24, 25–55; The National Trust, *Claydon House, Buckinghamshire* (1984), 27, 31; M. Verney, 'Claydon House', *Records of*

Buckinghamshire, 5 (1878), 419–20; Lipscomb, *History and Antiquities*, i. 186. Descriptions of the estate throughout the book have been reconstructed from maps and plans at Claydon House.

6. Slater, *Family Life*, 7–12; CH Deed, Francis, Earl of Bedford and Sir Edmund Verney, Nov. 1 1634; L. Stone *The Crisis of the Aristocracy 1558–1641* (1965), 634. When Edmund died, Charles I owed him £1,500.

7. F. Verney, *Memoirs of the Verney Family* (1892), i. 1–18, ii. 148–85, 382–419; Slater, *Family Life*, 11–18; J. Broad, 'The Verneys and the Sequestrators in the Civil Wars, 1642–1656', *Records of Buckinghamshire*, 27 (1985), 1–9; J. Bruce (ed.), *Notes of Proceedings of the Long Parliament* (Camden Society, 31; 1845).

8. Broad, 'Gentry Finances'; CH 7/37, Debt schedule, [c.1653]; Slater, *Family Life*, 19–24.

9. Sir Ralph had resided in London since Nov. 21 1695. 48-591, rv/jv, Nov. 19 1695; 49-155, rv/jv, July 5 1696; CH 4/5/49/78, rv/wc, June 20 1696; 49-95, wc/jv, Apr. 25 1696; 49-179, eli/jv, June 14 1696; 49-253, eli/jv, Sept. 6 1696; 50-329, jv/wc, Mar. 30 1698; 49-260, cho/jv, Sept. 14 1696.

10. 48-513, rv/jv, Sept. 15 1696; 49-46, jv/wc, Feb. 13 1695; 49-103, rv/jv, Apr. 15 1696; Berks CRO D/EMt/T1–7; E. Wrigley, 'A Simple Model of London's Importance 1650–1750', *Past and Present*, 37 (1967), 44–70.

11. PRO SP 105/152, fo. 388; PRO SP 105/153, fo. 343.

12. GH MS 15201/5, fo. 241; GH MS 15333/5–6; 48-423, jv/rv, Aug. 8 1695; 49-124, C. Todd/jv, Mar. 26 1696; PRO T70/78–88.

13. 49-217, jv/rv, July 30 1696;49-208, jv/rv, July 23 1696; BL Add. MS 29572, fo. 46; BL Add. MS 22226, fo. 9, for examples of the Hattons and Wentworths.

14. 49-88, lg/rv, May 5 1696; 49-129, jv/rv, Mar. 23 1696; [G.E.C.], *The Complete Peerage* (1929), vii. 614–15, 644–5; Henning, *House of Commons*, ii. 717; 46-319, jcar/rv, Jan. 23 1693; 46-312, rv/jv, Jan. 19 1693. Lichfield was a non-juror.

15. CSPD [March] 1696, 110; 49-106, jv/wc, Apr. 29 1696; 49-251, Answer of Sir Ralph Verney, 1696; CH 1/111a, b, CH 2/60, Marriage settlement deeds, June 30, July 1 1662; 49-177, jv/wc, June 17 1696; *CSPD*, June 27 1696, 248; 49-425, mco/rv, June 1696.

16. 49-197, jv/rv, July 16 1696; 49-198, jv/rv, July 18 1696; 49-161, jv/rv, July 21 1696; S. Baxter, *The Development of the Treasury 1660–1702* (1957), 157–65; *CSPD*, May 28 1697, July 9 1697, 174–6, 240; CH 4/5/48/95, rv/wc, Mar. 27 1695; 48-140, wc/rv, Feb. 3 1695; 48-239, wc/rv, Mar. 31 1695; 49-193, rv/jv, July 12 1696.

17. 49-215, jv/rv, Aug. 11 1696.

18. S. Birmingham, *Buckinghamshire: A Genealogical Bibliography* (1993); W. Berry, *County Geneologies: Pedigrees of Buckinghamshire Families* (1837); A. Everitt, *The Community of Kent and the Great Rebellion* (Leicester, 1966); J. Morrill, *The Revolt of the Provinces* (1976), but see A. Hughes, 'Local History and the Origins of the Civil War', in R. Cust and A. Hughes (eds.), *Conflict in Early Stuart England* (1989), 224–53.

19. L. Stone, 'Social Mobility in England 1500–1700', *Past and Present*, 33 (1966), 16–55; K. Wrightson, 'The Social Order of Early Modern England', in L. Bonfield *et al.* (eds.), *The World We have Gained* (Oxford, 1986), 190–1.

20. Hughes, 'Local History', 234–5; C. Herrup, *The Common Peace* (Cambridge, 1987); CH 4/5/58/19–22, nm/jv, Apr. 1709; CH 4/5/59/9, jchu/jv, Dec. 27 1707.

21. M. Beresford, 'Glebe Terriers and Open-Field Buckinghamshire', *Records of Buckinghamshire*, 16 (1953–4), 12–13; V. Burden, *Chiltern Villages* (Bourne End, 1972); J. Camp, *Portrait of Buckinghamshire* (1972); A. Davies, *Buckinghamshire* (Cambridge, 1914); G. Eland, *In Bucks* (Aylesbury, 1923) and *Shardeloes Papers of the*

Seventeenth and Eighteenth Centuries (1947); M. Fraser, *Companion into Buckinghamshire* (1950); W. James and J. Malcolm, *General View of the Agriculture of the County of Buckingham* . . . (1794); L. Hepple and A. Dogget, *The Chilterns* (Chichester, 1992); W. Kennet, *Parochial Antiquities* . . . (Oxford, 1695); W. Page (ed.), *Victoria History of Buckinghamshire* (1905–27); J. Peel, *Buckinghamshire Footpaths* (1947); M. Reed, *A History of Buckinghamshire* (Chichester, 1993); J. Sheahan, *History and Topography of Buckingham* (1862); A. Uttley, *Buckinghamshire* (1950).

22. 49-246, wc, Aug. 31 1696; BL Stowe MS 802, fo. 2, *c.*1637-40 lists 42 assessments. PRO E179/80/354 (damaged) and PRO E179/324 cite Hearth Tax returns for 37 households in 1662 and 2 exemption lists of 13 and 14 names. Broad ('Sir Ralph Verney and his Estates', 165–6) estimates 204–229 inhabitants based on these figures and 248 people on the Compton Census of 148 communicants and 1 Nonconformist. Bodl Willis MS 1, fos. 707–8; Bodl Willis MS 1, fo. 651; J. Broad (ed.), *Buckinghamshire Dissent and Parish Life 1669–1712* (Buckinghamshire Record Society, 28; 1993), 205; A. Whiteman (ed.), *The Compton Census of 1676* (Records of Social and Economic History, New Series, 8; 1986); 'The Verney Tomb at Middle Claydon', *Records of Buckinghamshire*, 16 (1955-6), 66-82.

23. William Coleman paid £2. 9*s*. to the almshouse for 15 weeks on Jan. 13 1695. E. Brinkworth (ed.), *Episcopal Visitation Book for the Archdeaconry of Buckingham 1662* (Buckinghamshire Record Society, 7; 1947), 44; CH 4/5/57/15, wc/jv, May 14 1704; CH 4/5/56/5, jv/wc, May 12 1703; CH 1/137 Sir Ralph Verney's cancelled will, July 27 1653; Bodl Willis MS 1, fos. 707–8; Broad (ed.), *Buckinghamshire Dissent*, 205.

24. CH 4/5/50/76, wc/jv, Feb. 20 1698; 51-493, jv, Oct. 10 1702; 53-392, nm/jv, Apr. 22 1707; 54-394, jv/rv2, Jan. 18 1711; Broad, 'Sir Ralph Verney and his Estates', 163, 169; CH 12/1/1, 'Map of woods and meadows in Middle Claydon; for Sir Ralph Verney surveyed by George Sergeant' [n.d. *c.*1670] and CH 12/1/2, 'Map of Claydon House and surrounding lands', 1654 shows cottages of Ralph Roades and John Andrews.

25. Broad, 'Sir Ralph Verney and his Estates', 159–63, 231–4; Beresford, 'Glebe Terriers', 10, 11, 16. Demesne lands were enclosed by 1600. Some enclosures in 1613, 1614, 1620, 1623, 1629, 1630, 1635 met with local resistance. The process was completed between 1653 and 1656.

26. CH 2/976, Will, Thomas Grimes, Dec. 1 1721; 46-310, wc/rv, Jan. 16 1693; 49-530, wc/jv, Jan. 30 1697; 49-610, jv/wc, Mar. 25 1697; 50-55, jv/wc, June 16 1697; Broad, 'Sir Ralph Verney and his Estates', 169, 191–4.

27. Broad, 'Sir Ralph Verney and his Estates', 167–8, 178, 213. In the late 1690s, men and a few women were paid day rates that varied seasonally for 1–6 days per week. In Nov. 1696, a carpenter received 4*s*. 8*d*. for four days, a brick maker was paid 5*s*. 4*d*. for four days, and an unskilled labourer received 2*s*. 8*d*. for four days. 49-303, wc/jv, Nov. 7 1696; 49-310, wc/jv, Nov. 14 1696; 49-316, wc/jv, Nov. 21 1696; 49-322, wc/jv, Nov. 28 1696. Women earned 4*d*. per day in 1697 for breaking clods and haymaking. Men received the same amounts for these tasks, but also had higher paying jobs. 49-584, wc/jv, Mar. 13 1697; 49-597, wc/jv, Mar. 20 1697; 50-71, wc/jv, June 26 1697; 56-13, cc/jv, June 15 1717.

28. CH 4/5/37/38, wc/rv, Apr. 29 1684; Broad, 'Sir Ralph Verney and his Estates', 166–7. Numbers of servants letters include only part of the estate correspondence at Claydon House, and are thus undercounted.

29. CH 4/5/49/1, rv/wc, Mar. 25 1696; CH 4/5/49/5, wc/rv, Mar. 29 1696; CH 4/5/49/9, rv/wc, Apr. 1 1696; CH 4/5/49/22, rv/wc, Apr. 9 1696.
30. CH 4/5/49/42, rv/wc, May 6 1696; 49-133, cst/rv, Mar. 13 1696; CH 4/5/49/20, rv/wc, Apr. 8 1696.
31. Bodl Willis MS 8, fos. 151–6 gives abstracts of freeholder lists for 1698, 1700/1, 1701. Bodl Gough Bucks 1/3–5 contains poll books for 1705, 1710, 1713. Poll books with numbers of voters for Steeple, Middle, and East Claydon are Bucks CRO D/C/3/61, 1685, incomplete; Bucks CRO D/X 933, 1700/1: MC (3), EC (9), SC (28); Bucks CRO D/X 933, 1701: MC (0), EC (15), SC (33); Bucks CRO D/X 933, 1702: MC (2), EC (10), SC (36); GH Poll Book, 1705: MC (2), EC (15), SC (40); Bucks CRO D/MH/40/1, 1710: MC (3), EC (18), SC (44); Bucks CRO PB 1/17/1, 1713: MC (1), EC (16), SC (43); GH Poll Book and Bucks CRO D/DR/12/39, 1722: MC (2), EC (12), SC (33).
32. J. Broad, 'The Verneys as Enclosing Landlords 1600–1800', in J. Chartres and D. Hey (eds.), *English Rural Society 1500–1800* (Cambridge, 1990), 27–53; Broad (ed.), *Buckinghamshire Dissent*, 37, 90, 204–5.
33. 22-8 and CH 4/5/58/12, Petitions from the parishioners of Steeple Claydon, Sept. 23 1668 and [n.d.]; 49-56, rv/wc, June 10 1696; 49-173, rv/wc, June 17 1696; 54-559, ebv/jv, Mar. 15 1712; Broad (ed.), *Buckinghamshire Dissent*, 90.
34. 49-419, cho/jv, Sept. 20 1696.
35. CH 4/5/50/12, jchu/jv, Mar. 30 1697; 49-187, jv/rv, July 8 1696; 48-257, wc/rv, May 13 1695; CH 4/5/54/11, wc/jv, June 1 1701; Bucks CRO D/A/T/54. D/X/171/50. Churchill wrote many more letters prior to 1692.
36. 49-263, rv/jv, Sept. 20 1696; W. Le Hardy and G. Rickett (eds.), *Calendar to the Sessions Records County of Buckingham 1694–1705* (Aylesbury, 1936), ii. 454; 52-191, ebat/jv, Feb. 25 1703; 49-200, rv/jv, July 19 1696; 49-187, jv/rv, July 8 1696; PRO PROB 11/488, fo. 103.
37. 49-12, cst/rv, Feb. 2 1696; 49-120, cst/rv, Mar. 29 1696; Le Hardy and Rickett (eds.), *Calendar*, ii. 334; 46-348, wc/rv, Mar. 6 1693; 49-59, cst/rv, June 7 1696; 51-676, lg/jv, Feb. 26 1702; 51-690, lg/jv, Mar. 26 1702; 54-345, J. Hotchkiss/jv, Dec. 12 1710; *CSPD*, Feb. 15 1702, 519; 49-34, cst/rv, Jan. 3 1696; 49-404, pa/jv, Sept. 20 1696.
38. 49-405, pa/jv, Sept. 22 1696; 49-257, pa/jv, Sept. 18 1696; 49-100, lg/rv, Apr. 21 1696; C. Morris (ed.), *The Journeys of Celia Fiennes* (1947), 29–30; B. Willis, *The History and Antiquities of the Town, Hundred, and Deanery of Buckingham* (1755), 42–43, and *Notitia Parliamentaria* (1715), 91; Henning, *House of Commons*, iii. 634–5.
39. 50-568, ebv/wc, Dec. 1698; 51-368, rpri/jv, Dec. 30 1700; CH 4/5/58/36, cc/jv, May 5 1705/6; 55-110, nm/jv, May 3 1713; 55-112, nm/jv, May 3 1713; 55-332, jv/rv2, May 18 1714; 50-526, jv, Letter to the bailiff and burgesses of Buckingham', Oct. 25 1698.
40. 31-9, rv/munv, Jan. 10 1678; Whiteman (ed.), *Compton Census*, 368; Broad (ed.), *Buckinghamshire Dissent*, xxvii, 90, 204–6 finds dissenters in $\frac{3}{4}$ of the parishes by 1700–10, yet they rarely totalled over 10%.
41. Bucks CRO D/X 2/27, Richard Grenville's notebook, c.1640; BL Stowe 802, Richard Grenville's Bucks assessments, c.1637-40; A. Johnson, 'Buckinghamshire 1640–1660', MA thesis (Swansea, 1963), 8, 13, 15; Bodl Willis MS 8; Bucks CRO D/X 2/27; HL STTM 5/14, 'The Value of Each P[er]sons Estate . . . April 2, 1660'; BL Stowe MS 802; C. Bonsey and J. Jenkins (eds.), *Ship Money Papers and Richard Grenville's Notebook* (Buckinghamshire Record Society, 13; 1965), 96, 98; Broad, 'Sir Ralph Verney and his Estates', 214–17 and 'Gentry Finances', 198. For gentry lists, see Bodl Top Bucks MS

C1, fo. 166; Bodl Willis MS 30; Bodl Gough Bucks MS 4, fo. 92ᵛ; HL STTM 5/23, Deputy Lieutenants, Oct. 1662; 49-271, jv/wc, Sept. 26 1696.

42. J. Broad, 'Whigs and Deer Stealers in Other Guises', *Past and Present*, 119 (1988), 56–72; 49-258, cst/jv, Sept. 13 1696. John's lists of Buckinghamshire nobility are in CH 14/68, 69, Notebooks, 1693–1710, 1652–1749. Figures for titled people include family members who wrote many letters. This tends to magnify the numbers.

43. Broad, 'Sir Ralph Verney and his Estates', 272; Author's database.

44. 48-86, lg/rv, Dec. 11 1694; 52-16, lg/jv, July 21 1702; 46-251, jv/rv, Dec. 14 1692; 46-257, jv/rv, Dec. 17 1692; 46-571, jv/rv, July 5 1693; WM H468-495; WM H802, fo. 6ᵛ, Jan. 16 1684 shows Sir Richard Temple caused disturbances in Covent Garden Church.

45. GH MS 4256, fo. 129; CLRO MS 83, fo. 7 and MS 42, fo. 3.; 48-624, cst/rv, Dec. 22 1695; CH 11/22/1–2, Middle Claydon parish registers, 1632–56, 1657–1722.

46. 42-9, L. Porter/wd, June 16 1687; M. Verney, *Memoirs of the Verney Family* (1970), iv. 9; CH 15/16, Newsletters 1626–92 sent to Sir Ralph from James Hicke, Henry Muddiman, and others: 1665–7, 1676–9, 1681, 1688–92. Table 3 underestimates Sir Ralph's foreign correspondence which took place prior to 1692.

47. 49-254, pa/jv, Sept. 6 1696.

48. J. Brewer, *The Sinews of Power* (1988); P. Jenkins, *The Making of a Ruling Class* (Cambridge, 1983); J. Rosenheim, *The Townshends of Raynham* (Middletown, Conn., 1989).

49. J. Manwood, *A Treatise of the Laws of the Forest*, 3rd edn. (1665); [W. Nelson,] *The Laws of England Concerning the Game . . .* (1727); *The Statutes at Large Made for the Preservation of the Game* (1726); T. Cunningham, *A New Treatise on the Laws for Preservation of the Game . . .*, 2nd edn. (1766); E. Thompson, *Whigs and Hunters* (Harmondsworth, 1977); Broad, 'Whigs and Deer Stealers', 55–72; E. Shirley, *Some Account of English Deer Parks* (1867); P. Rogers, 'The Waltham Blacks and the Black Act', *Historical Journal*, 17 (1974), 465–86; E. Cruickshanks and H. Erskine-Hill, 'The Waltham Black Act and Jacobitism', *Journal of British Studies*, 24 (1985), 358–65. A Jacobite broadsheet showing George I as a deer whose parts were to be distributed after the kill in PRO SP 35/33/53 is described by Broad in 'Whigs and Deer-Stealers', 69.

50. 47-470, jcar/rv, July 3 1694; 49-194, lg/rv, July 14 1696.

51. Lichfield took up residence in the lodge in the park in 1699. In 1705 he sold the rangership to the Duke of Marlborough for £6,000 and presumably his interest in the Lieutenancy of Woodstock given to him by the King on his marriage to 12-year-old Charlotte Fitzroy, illegitimate daughter of Charles II. CH 14/49, Lee Pedigree made by John Verney in book of documents, n.d.; Page, *Victoria History of Buckinghamshire*, iv. 101; Lipscomb, *History and Antiquities* ii. 404–6; [G.E.C.], *The Complete Peerage*, vii. 644–5; PRO C. 104/109/2, llit/John Cary, Nov. 28 1695.

52. 46-319, jcar/rv, Jan. 23 1693; 46-312, rv/jv, Jan. 19 1693.

53. 46-319, jcar/rv, Jan. 23 1693; 48-109, jcar/rv, Dec. 5 1694; 47-54, jcar/rv, Sept. 9 1693; 47-55, rv/jcar, Sept. 11 1693; 47-232 to 235, jcar/rv, Dec. 4, 9, 19, 21 1693.

54. CH 4/5/49/80, jchu/rv, June 25 1696; 49-249, jcar/rv, Sept. 3 1696; 49-184, jchu/rv, June 14 1696; 49-421, rv/jv, Sept. 13 1696; 49-188, rv/jv, July 16 1696.

55. 49-208, jv/rv, July 23 1696;49-220, lg/rv, Aug. 5 1696; 49-239, lg/jv, Aug. 18 1696; 49-209, lg/rv, July 29 1696; 48-531, lg/rv, Sept. 4 1695; 50-458, lg/jv, July 27 1698; 51-72, lg/jv, Sept. 27 1699; 51-91, lg/jv, Oct. 3 1699; 46-363, lg/rv, Mar. 14 1693; 48-297, jv/lg, June 12 1695; 48-291, rv/jv, June 17 1695.

56. 49-48, lg/rv, July 14 1696; 49-202, lg/rv, July 21 1696; 49-220, lg/rv, Aug. 5 1696; 49-262, lg/rv, Sept. 16 1696.

57. W. Munk (ed.), *The Roll of the Royal College of Physicians of London*, 2nd edn. (1878), i. 467–9; GH *Index to Middlesex Polls, 1705, 1714, 1768*; 48-420, ea/rv, Aug. 7 1695; 53-505, ea/jv, Oct. 9 1706; 49-213, ea/rv, July 28 1696.

58. F. Fisher, 'The Development of London as a Centre of Conspicuous Consumption', in E. Carus-Wilson (ed.), *Essays in Economic History* (1962), ii. 197-207; L. Weatherill, *Consumer Behaviour and Material Culture in Britain 1660–1760* (1988); 49-201, ea/rv, July 21 1696; 49-226, ea/rv, Aug. 11 1696; 49-263, rv/jv, Sept. 20 1696; 49-261, ea/rv, Sept. 15 1696; 49-232, ea/rv, Aug. 18 1696.

59. CH 4/5/43/41, wc/rv, Dec. 28 1690; 48-347, rv/jv, July 21 1695; CH 4/5/43/65, W. Marshall/rv, Jan. 20 1690/1; 49-214, jv/rv, July 29 1696; 48-583, jv/rv, Nov. 13, 1695; 47-158, rv/jv, Nov. 5 1693; 42-6, rv/rpau, June 12 1687; 49-103, rv/jv, Apr. 15 1696.

60. 49-208, jv/rv, July 23 1696. See Ch. 5.

61. 49-210, rv/jv, July 26 1696; 46-186, ea/rv, Nov. 8 1692; 47-611, jv/rv, Sept. 15 1694; 48-27, lg/rv, Oct. 30 1694; 47-626, lg/rv, Sept. 24 1694; 47-637, ea/rv, Oct. 2 1694; 48-85, jv/rv, Dec. 7 1694; 48-20, ea/rv, Oct. 23 1694; 48-25, nn/jv, Oct. 27 1694; 49-217, jv/rv, July 30 1696.

62. 49-214, jv/rv, July 29 1696; D. Coleman, *Sir John Banks: Baronet and Businessman* (Oxford, 1963), 157; Baxter, *Development of the Treasury*, 157–65; *CSPD*, July 9 1697, 240.

63. George Nicholas received £500 per year from the Custom-house. CH 14/68, John Verney's lists of offices, n.d.; 49-210, rv/jv, July 26 1696; 49-245, nn/jv, Aug. 29 1696; 49-169, nn/rv, June 22 1696; 49-212, nn/rv, July 28 1696; 49-211, July 28 1696.

64. 49-214, jv/rv, July 29 1696; 47-525, pa/rv, Aug. 8 1694; 49-219, ea/rv, Aug. 4 1696; 49-225, pa/jv, Aug. 11 1696; 51-397, pv/jv, Feb. 19 1701.

65. 49-210, rv/jv, July 26 1696; 49-222, jv/rv, Aug. 8 1696; 49-214, rv/jv, July 29 1696.

66. 49-249, jcar/rv, Sept. 3 1696; 49-264, cst/jv, Sept. 22 1696; 49-265, pa/jv, Sept. 24 1696; CH 1/133 Will of Sir Ralph Verney made Feb. 19 1694/5, PCC May 10 1701; CH 1/147 Will of John Verney, Viscount Fermanagh made June 23 1713, PCC July 31 1717. PRO wills are PROB 11/460, fo. 73 (Ralph) and PROB 11/558, fo. 134 (John).

67. 49-73, rv/wc, May 29 1696; 49-75, rv/wc, May 27 1696; N. Tadmor, 'The Concept of the Household-Family in Eighteenth-Century England', *Past and Present*, 151 (1996), 111–40.

68. 49-250, rv/jv, Sept. 6 1696; 49-253, eli/jv, Sept. 6 1696; 47-246, eli/rv, Jan. 27 1694.

69. 48-504, jv/rv, Sept. 21 1695. Mr George Horsenell in CLRO MSS 83, fo. 7 and 42, fo. 3. was taxed £1. 10s. on real property and 12s. on personal property in 1692/3; £6. 8s. on real property and £2. 8s. on personal property in 1693/4 (only slightly less than John Verney). GH MS 4251, fo. 131 cites Horsenell at St Andrew Holborn Vestry meetings. For family monuments, see J. Strype, *A Survey of the Cities of London and Westminster . . .* (1720), i, book 3, 251.

70. 49-266, pa/jv, Sept. 25 1696; 48-119, eli/rv, Jan. 12 1695; 49-16, cho/wc, Jan. 29 1696; 47-165, cho/rv, Nov. 5 1693; 47-307, pv/rv, Feb. 23 1694; 47-196, lg/rv, Dec. 12 1693.

71. Coleman knew about Hodges's family in 1695, but the Verneys were ignorant until 1706. 48-592, cho/wc, Nov. 27 1695; 53-305, jv/pv, Dec. 8 1706; 53-303, ea/jv, Dec. 12 1706; CH 1/218, Lease, Feb. 27 1692; 50-379, jv/wc, May 28 1698; 51-570, lg/jv, Nov. 16 1700; 52-120, cst/jv, Dec. 24 1702.

72. 49-420, cho/jv, Sept. 6 1696; CLRO, CF28/1; CLRO, MS 74, fo. 5. A 25-year-old

bachelor, he was assessed £1. 4s. for real estate and £1. 2s. 6d. for personal goods in 1695. His servant Simon Wallis was probably related to John's servant Stephen Wallis.

73. 51-225, cho/jv, Mar. 26 1700; 53-378, jv/tc, Apr. 6 1707; 49-549, eli/jv, Feb. 14 1697; 52-269, cl/jv, Sept. 24 1703; 49-585, jv/wc, Mar. 9 1697; 50-334, jv/wc, Apr. 6 1698; 51-18, jv/pl, July 29 1699.

74. 49-417, rv/jv, Sept. 17 1696; 49-403, pa/jv, Sept. 17 1696.

75. M. Mauss, *The Gift*, trans. I. Cunnison (New York, 1967); G. Duby, *The Early Growth of the European Economy* (Ithaca, New York, 1974); S. Kettering, 'Gift-giving and Patronage in Early Modern France', *French History*, 2 (1988), 131–51; R. Titmuss, *The Gift Relationship* (New York, 1972); N. Davis, 'Art and Society in the Gifts of Montaigne', *Representations*, 12 (1985), 24–32 and 'Beyond the Market: Books as Gifts in Sixteenth-Century France', *Transactions of the Royal Historical Society*, 5th series, 33 (1983), 69–87.

76. Quoted in D. Hainsworth, *Stewards, Lords, and People* (Cambridge, 1992), 122.

77. Seneca, *On Benefits*, trans. T. Lodge (1899); L. Peck, *Court Patronage and Corruption in Early Stuart England* (Boston, 1990), 12–14; O. Walker, *Of Education* (Oxford, 1687).

78. 49-211, nn/jv, July 28 1696; C. Levi-Strauss, *The Elementary Structures of Kinship* (Boston, 1969); G. McCracken, 'The Exchange of Children in Tudor England', *Journal of Family History*, 8 (1983), 303–13; M. Sahlins, 'The Spirit of the Gift', *Stone Age Economics* (Chicago, 1981), 149–83.

79. 33-99, rv/jv, Nov. 20 1679; 34-121, rv/jv, 1680.

80. Social network theorists use computer programs such as the SAS Software System to place individuals in networks. S. Berkowitz, *An Introduction to Structural Analysis* (Toronto, 1982); D. Knoke and J. Kuklinski, *Network Analysis* (Beverley Hills, Calif., 1982); J. Mitchell (ed.), *Social Networks in Urban Situations* (Manchester, 1969); C. Wetherell, 'Network Analysis Comes of Age', *Journal of Interdisciplinary History*, 19 (1989), 645–51; R. Milardo, *Families and Social Networks* (1988). Helpful works by sociologists include: E. Bott, *Family and Social Networks* (1957) and J. Boissevain, *Friends of my Friends* (Oxford, 1974). For historical studies, see A. Macfarlane, *The Family Life of Ralph Josselin* (Cambridge, 1970); E. Ladurie, *Montaillou* (New York, 1978); P. Bearman, 'Relations into Rhetorics', Ph.D. thesis (Harvard, 1985); D. and A. Rutman, *A Place in Time, Explicatus* (New York, 1984).

81. 32-92, rv/jv, July 16 1681.

82. 34-132, wgro/jv, [July?] 1680.

83. P. Beckford, *Thoughts on Hunting* (Sarum, 1782), 10; J. Addison, *The Sir Roger de Coverley Papers from The Spectator 1711–1712* (New York, 1945); D. Birley, *Sport and the Making of Britain* (Manchester, 1993); D. Brailsford, *Sport, Time, and Society* (New York, 1991); R. Holt, *Sport and the British* (Oxford, 1989); R. Manning, *Hunters and Poachers* (Oxford, 1993).

84. C. Geertz, 'Deep Play', *The Interpretation of Cultures* (New York, 1973), 448.

85. Edward of Norwich, *The Master of the Game*, ed. W. and F. Baille-Grohman (1904), 152; J. Giles, *The Compleat Sportsman* (1718), 86; R. Blome, *The Gentleman's Recreation* (1686), 79; Manning, *Hunters and Poachers*, 12; *The Noble Arte of Venerie or Hunting* (1575), 43.

86. A powder of the heart bone was said to aid cardiac complaints and women in labour, while the deer's marrow soothed gout and tumours. Water in which its genitals were immersed cured kidney and urine problems. Classical chemists ground stag's antlers

for use against dysentery, colic, and jaundice and hung them on animals as a protection against witchcraft and the evil eye. *The Noble Arte*, 39–40; Blome, *The Gentleman's Recreation*, 67, 85; Edward of Norwich, *The Master of the Game*, 154.

87. Deer supposedly lured, killed, and ate snakes, then healed themselves by voiding after running to spread out the venom. *The Noble Arte*, 41.

88. Aristotle and Pliny said that the deer buried one of his antlers as a gift to nature so 'man shall hardly find it'. *The Noble Arte*, 42; Edward of Norwich, *The Master of the Game*, 20, 154. Blome, *The Gentleman's Recreation*, 79; J. Evelyn, *A Character of England* (1659), 68.

89. Manwood, *A Treatise of the Laws of the Forest*, 107; [Nelson], *The Laws of England Concerning the Game*, preface, 1; J. Strayer (ed.), 'Hunting and Fowling, Western Europe', *The Dictionary of the Middle Ages* (New York, 1985), vi. 356; Edward of Norwich, *The Master of the Game*, 169 ; Shirley, *Some Account of English Deer Parks*, 27–8.

90. For example, Gratius the Faliscan, *Cynegeticon or a Poem of Hunting*, trans. Christopher Wase (1654); W. Somerville, *The Chace, A Poem* (1735); O. Goldsmith, *The Haunch of Venison* (1776); *Cynegetica or Essays on Sporting* (1733); J. Musters, *Hunting Songs and Poems* (Nottingham, n.d.); *British Sporting Paintings, 1650–1850* (1974). *La Chasse de Gaston Phoebus, Compte de Foix* (Paris, 1854) was the source for English translations and variations including Edward of Norwich, *The Master of the Game* and W. Twici, *The Art of Hunting*, ed. H. Dryden (Northampton, 1908).

91. W. Dix, 'The Hunting Library of Laurence Roberts Carton '07', *Princeton University Library Chronicle*, 15 (1953), 43–5; L. Wright (comp.), *Sporting Books in the Huntington Library* (San Marino, Calif., 1937). Two manuals written close to Ralph Verney's death are: N. Cox, *The Gentleman's Recreation*, 4th edn. (1697) and Blome, *The Gentleman's Recreation*. Some of Blome's subscribers were friends of the Verneys from merchant families like the Bludworths, Claytons, Joliffes, and Dashwoods.

92. Edward of Norwich, *The Master of the Game*, 151; Manwood, *A Treatise of the Laws*, 107, 298–9; G[ervase] M[arkham], *Country Contentments or the Husbandman's Recreations*, 6th edn. (1649).

93. *The Noble Arte*, preface, A5; Edward of Norwich, *The Master of the Game*, 4; K. Thomas, *Man and the Natural World* (New York, 1983), 22, 161–2; Somerville, *The Chace*, 6.

94. Hunting removed man from the 'besotting sensualities and wicked debaucheries of the city' which included 'women, wine, and a bawdy play'. Cox, *The Gentleman's Recreation*, 23.

95. Edward of Norwich, *The Master of the Game*, 22, 93–102. The same descriptions of hunting rituals appear in manuals from the 14th–18th centuries, often due to pirating from earlier books. Men and deer had their own 'quality', as did huntsmen, houndskeepers, antlers, body parts, dogs, and even musical calls. Cox, *The Gentleman's Recreation*, 76. Twici, *The Art of Hunting*, 89; Shirley, *Some Account of English Deer Parks*, 27–51.

96. Edward of Norwich, *The Master of the Game*, 99, 126–9. This part of the ceremony was called the curee. After the throat was cut, the hounds were given the flesh 'to make them in love with a deer' (Blome, *The Gentleman's Recreation*, 84). The best person of quality would 'draw . . . the knife leisurely along the very middle of the belly' (Cox, *The Gentleman's Recreation*, 75) and undo him so daintily that no blood would dirty his unturned sleeves. Then he would take a 'hearty draught' of wine,

wash the guts, and dip them with bread into the blood. 'Gentlefolk with switches' held back the dogs who ate the mess in hierarchical order. D. Madden (ed.), *The Diary of Master William Silence* (1907).

97. Edward of Norwich, *The Master of the Game*, 128.

98. Blome, *The Gentleman's Recreation*, 85; Thomas, *Man and the Natural World*, 29; 39-10, jcar/rv, July 29 1684.

99. A. Cross, *Eighteenth Century Documents Relating to the Royal Forests* (New York, 1928); P. Pettit, *The Royal Forests of Northamptonshire* (Northamptonshire Record Society, 23; 1968); G. Turner (ed.), *Select Pleas of the Forest* (Selden Society, 13; 1901); C. Young, *The Royal Forests of Medieval England* (Leicester, 1979).

100. Cox, *The Gentleman's Recreation*, 7; Giles, *The Compleat Sportsman*, 66; Shirley, *Some Account of English Deer Parks*, 28–9. Shirley noted at least 700 parks on Saxton's maps from 1575 to 1580, while Thomas in *Man and the Natural Man*, 201 estimated 800.

101. 24-10, munv/jv, Jan. 1 1672; CH 4/5/35, wc/rv, Jan. 14 1683; HL STT 782, Finch/srt, Aug. 13 1690; HL STT 94, P. Bertie/srt, Aug. 5 1682; HL STT 271, wchap/srt, Dec. 3 1682; HL STT 272, wchap/srt, Dec. 8 1682; HL STT 374, wchap/srt, Apr. 28 1688; Shirley, *Some Account of English Deer Parks*, 127.

102. HL EL 8612, Licence from John Lord Lovelace to the Earl of Bridgewater, June 13 1689; HL EL 10680, 'A List of the Gentlemen that used to have Venison', Thoresby Park, June 27 1726; BL Add. 32703. fo. 376, Lord Mansel/Thomas Pelham Holles, Duke of Newcastle, Oct. 22 1744; J. Sainty (comp.), 'Lists of Lieutenants of the Counties of England and Wales', *Lists and Indexes* (Special Series, 12; 1979); PRO SP 44/274, fo. 172, Warrants of venison, June 18 1696.

103. In Sir Ralph's day, a poacher paid £20 for coursing deer, £30 for each one killed, or spent one year in prison and a day in the pillory. J. Locke, *The Second Treatise of Government* (1952); 3–4 William & Mary 10, *Statutes at Large* (1726); HL EL 34/C/3, P. Bamford, *The Compleat Keeper*, [1693]. The £100 freehold needed to hunt was fifty times the amount needed to vote. W. Holdsworth, *A History of English Law* (1956), i. 108; *CSPD*, July 20 1683, 173.

104. 49-177, mco/rv, June 17 1696; *CSPD*, June 27 1696, 248. The pardon was granted on July 8 1697, *CSPD*, July 9 1697, July 23 1697, 238, 263–4.

105. HL STT 386 and 388, wchap/srt, June 14 and June 21 1688; 50-64, rpol/jv, June 12 1698; 50-352, jv/wc, Apr. 30 1698; Thompson, *Whigs and Hunters*; D. Hay, P. Linebaugh, and E. Thompson (eds.), *Albion's Fatal Tree* (New York, 1975); V. Turner, *Dramas, Fields and Metaphors* (Ithaca, New York, 1974); Thomas, *Man and the Natural World*, 9, 49.

106. M. Hunt, *The Middling Sort* (Berkeley, 1996); D. Wahrman, *Imagining the Middle Class* (Cambridge, 1995); J. Barry and C. Brooks (eds.), *The Middling Sort of People* (Basingstoke, 1994).

107. 33-96, rv/jv, Nov. 13 1679; 31-71, jv/rv, Aug. 5 1678.

108. J. Goring and J. Wake (eds.), *Northamptonshire Lieutenancy Papers . . . 1580–1614* (Northamptonshire Record Society, 27; 1975); M. St Clare Byrne (ed.), *The Lisle Letters* (Harmondsworth, 1985); L. Stone, 'Terrible Times', *New Republic*, May 5 1982, 24–38; J. Sainty, 'A Reform in the Tenure of Offices during the Reign of Charles II', *Historical Research*, 41 (1968), 150–71 and *Lieutenants of Counties 1585–1642* (1970).

109. W. Prest, 'Judicial Corruption in Early Modern England', *Past and Present*, 133

(1991), 67–195; G. Aylmer, 'From Office-Holding to Civil Service', *Transactions of the Royal Historical Society*, 5th Series, 30 (1980), 106.

110. 33-9, rv/jv, July 12 1679; 33-23, rv/jv, July 24 1679; 35-18, rv/wc, Jan. 27 1681; 35-43, rv/jv, Apr. 18 1681; 47-532, rv/jv, Aug. 14 1694.

111. P. Dickson, *The Financial Revolution in England* (1967).

112. HL STT 272, wchap/srt, Dec. 8 1682. Does brought up to 40s. each. Thompson, *Whigs and Hunters*, 159.

113. 47-470, jcar/rv, July 3 1694.

114. K. Polanyi, *The Great Transformation* (Boston, 1957), C. MacPherson, *The Political Theory of Possessive Individualism* (Oxford, 1962), and the work of Natalie Davis, but see F. Braudel, *Civilization and Capitalism*, trans. S. Reynolds (1981); T. Haskell and R. Teichgraeber (eds.), *The Culture of the Market* (Cambridge, 1993), 3–4, 15–16.

115. P. Metcalf and R. Huntington, *Celebrations of Death* (Cambridge, 1991); A. van Gennep, *The Rites of Passage* (Chicago, 1964), 146–65; R. Houlbrooke (ed.), *Death, Ritual, and Bereavement* (1989); P. Muret, *Rites of Funeral, Ancient and Modern . . .* (1683).

116. CH 1/133; C. Gittings, *Death, Burial, and the Individual in Early Modern Europe* (1984), 87, 192; L. Stone, *The Crisis of the Aristocracy 1558–1641* (1967), 265–6; E. Ashmole, *Notes of Preparations for the Funeral of a Noble Person*, n.d., 738–41; F. Sandford, *The Order and Ceremonies Used for the Solemn Interment of . . . George, Duke of Albemarle* (1670).

117. Gittings, *Death*, 166, 188–215; *The Book of Common Prayer* (1696); W. Frere and F. Proctor, *A New History of the Book of Common Prayer* (1901), 186; D. Cressy, 'Death and the Social Order', *Continuity and Change*, 5 (1990), 99–119 and *Birth, Marriage, and Death* (Oxford and New York, 1997); E. Barnard, *A Seventeenth-Century Country Gentleman* (Cambridge, 1948), 79–81. See the elaborate funeral of Daniel Baker in 1700 (Bucks CRO D/X 1351/30).

118. 49-266, pa/jv, Sept. 25 1696; 49-263, rv/jv, Sept. 20 1696; 49-249, jcar/rv, Sept. 3 1696; 49-257, pa/jv, Sept. 18 1696; 49-405, pa/jv, Sept. 22 1696; 49-268, cst/jv, Sept. 24 1696; 49-265, pa/jv, Sept. 24 1696; L. Beier, 'The Good Death in Seventeenth-Century England' in Houlbrooke (ed.), *Death, Ritual and Bereavement*, 43–61; 37-16, rv/jv, Nov. 9 1682; 40-49, rv/W. Smith, Feb. 17 1686; 36-18, rv/wd, Nov. 19 1681; P. Aries, *Western Attitudes toward Death*, trans. P. Ranum (Baltimore, 1974).

119. 49-287, lg/jv, Oct. 15 1696; 49-290, pg/jv, Oct. 27 1696; 49-266, pa/jv, Sept. 25 1696; 49-271, jv/wc, Sept. 26 1696; 49-415, jv/wc, Sept. 30 1696; CH 11/22/2, Middle Claydon Parish Register, 1657–1722; Bucks CRO PR 52/12/1, Middle Claydon overseers account book with 'Burials in Woolen 1680–1730'.

120. 49-271, jv/wc, Sept. 26 1696; 48-502, rv/jv, Sept. 24 1695; Sir A. Wagner, *Heralds of England* (1967), 302–3; Gittings, *Death*, 96; 47-530, W. Wilkins/jv, Aug. 24 1694; 49-415, jv/wc, Sept. 30 1696; 49-414, jv/wc, Oct. 1 1696; 49-416, jv/wc, Oct. 3 1696. The funeral was held on Oct. 9, 16 days after Sir Ralph died.

121. PRO PROB 11/460, fo. 73; CH 1/133. The underlining is my own. CH 1/134, Unexecuted will of 1650; CH 1/135-6, Codicil to will of Sir Ralph with schedule of debts discharged since making the will in 1643, and of bonds 1649–52 dated Oct. 25 1652; CH 1/137, Cancelled will dated July 27 1653; CH 14/49, Fragment of will, [1680?]. Sir Richard Temple also wished to be buried 'without funeral pomp or ceremony'. HL STTP 14/11.

122. 49-271, jv/wc, Sept. 26 1696; 43-10, rv/jv, Sept. 4 1688. The 1693 funeral of the

Winwoods had been just as private. 'Scarce anybody in the country knew they were to come and a tenant had to open the vault for the corpse . . . . The body never was set in the church and [there were] as little prayers as could be said.' Some local women went into the Winwood's house, but since no one was at home, they did not stay. 46-365, eli/rv, Mar. 18 1693; 47-338, cst/rv, Mar. 18 1693 (misdated 1694); 32-145, rv/jv, June 2 1679; 32-146, jv/rv, June 5 1679; 50-454, ttip, jv, Aug. 4 1698.

123. 49-272, lg/rv, Sept. 27 1696.
124. 49-275, eli/jv, Sept. 29 1696; 49-152, cst/rv, Feb. 16 1696; 49-383, eli/rv, Feb. 23 1695; 49-273, pa/jv, Sept. 28 1696.
125. 49-258, cst/jv, Sept. 13 1696; 49-403, pa/jv, Sept. 17 1696.
126. CH 14/49, Draft notice of Sir Ralph Verney's death by John in a book of documents, n.d. He lists his father's accomplishments in the following order: justice of the peace, deputy lieutenant, and last, member of Parliament.
127. 49-416, jv/wc, Oct. 3 1696; 49-282, cst/rv, Oct. 12 1696; 49-287, lg/jv, Oct. 15 1696; 49-279, lg/jv, Oct. 6 1696.
128. 49-636, jv/wc, Apr. 21 1697; 49-301, T. Wettenhall/jv, Oct. 1696; 49-466, jv/tv, Dec. 12 1696.
129. 49-294, nn/jv, Oct. 24 1696.
130. CH1/133; CH 1/134-37; CH 14/49. See Ch. 5 for the strict settlement.
131. 49-377, nn/jv, Dec. 31 1696; 49-317, eli/jv, Nov. 22 1696; CH 1/133. Even if records of legacies were lost, the letters do not indicate any gifts. Writers' anger confirms this analysis. See CH 1/205-434 for mortgages and charges upon the estate, 1665–1906. The only legacies appear to be annuities for servants and a charge for £500 to pay to Elizabeth Adams, revised 1692. CH 1/126, Lease in trust, Nov. 3 1692, July 9 1700, and CH 1/205-7. I thank Susan Ranson for citations regarding this point.
132. 49-245, nn/jv, Aug. 29 1696.
133. By publicly giving legacies according to status, Pen Osborne angered those of low rank. 48-471, ea/rv, Aug. 27 1695; 49-473, 'A List of the Legacies left by the Lady Pen Osborne', n.d.; 48-473, lg/rv, Aug. 25 1695; 48-464, 'A Note of the Legacies given by my Sister Osborne by her Will' received Aug. 21 1695.

Notes to Chapter 2

1. 'Some Thoughts Concerning the Better Security of our Trade and Navigation', 1695, 4, quoted in J. Appleby, *Economic Thought and Ideology in Seventeenth-Century England* (Princeton, 1978), 177.
2. 16-8, jv/mun, Apr. 8 1659.
3. 8-5, mbv/rv, Mar. 4 1647; 8-8, mbv/rv, Aug. 10 1647; 8-7, mbv/rv, Feb. 11 1647.
4. 33-50, jv/rv, Sept. 1 1679; 33-24, jv/rv, July 24 1679; 33-97, jv/rv, Nov. 17 1679; 35-62, rv/jv, May 16 1681.
5. 41-49, munv/munv2, Mar. 15 1687.
6. 8-8, mbv/rv, Aug. 10 1647; 11-9, lshe/rv, May 28 1651; 11-10, lshe/rv, July 9 1651; 11-12, lshe/rv, Aug. 10 1651; M. Motley, 'Educating the English Gentleman Abroad: The Verney Family in Seventeenth-Century France and Holland', *History of Education*, 23 (1994), 243–56.
7. M. Verney, *Memoirs of the Verney Family* (1970), iii. 363; 18-21, jv/rv, Apr. 28, 1662; Motley, 'Educating the English Gentleman', 244, 250; CH 14/19–49, Genealogical papers.

8. C. Mauger, *Mauger's Letters Written upon Several Subjects* (1671) and *French and English Letters . . .* (1676); C. Bouton, *Les Grammaires francaises de Claude Mauger à l'usage anglais* (Paris, 1972); Motley, 'Educating the English Gentleman', 251; K. Lambley, *The Teaching and Cultivation of the French Language in England during Tudor and Stuart Times* (Manchester, 1920).

9. Book lists: 49-486, [1697?]; 49-637, Apr. 21 1697; 50-279, [1698?]; 51-455, [1701?].

10. 11-14, lshe/rv, Sept. 8 1651; 11-16, jv/rv, Sept. 8 1651; Motley, 'Educating the English Gentleman', 245.

11. M. Verney, *Memoirs*, iii. 79, 364; 33-116, rv/jv, [Dec. 1679]; L. Stone, *The Family, Sex, and Marriage in England* (1979); S. Mendelson, 'Debate: The Weightiest Business', *Past & Present*, 85 (1979), 126–35; L. Pollock, *Forgotten Children* (Cambridge, 1983).

12. 38-11, munv/rv, Aug. 31 1683; 35-85, nhob/rv, June 16 1681; CH 14/19–49 (July 9 1674), 68, 69; R. Grassby, *The English Gentleman in Trade* (Oxford, 1994), 177.

13. CH 15/6 'Faults in the Book of Mr Verney's of Descents of Baronets, Comments of Mr Le Neve', Sept. 24, 1694; CH 14/20–27, Notebooks, [*c*.1690–1715]; 55-337, wv/jv, June 17 1714. Although letters discuss the book, no title or copy has been found.

14. 28-49, jv/rv, Sept. 2 1675; M. Verney, *Memoirs*, iii. 358–60, 366–7; Bodl Eng Misc. MS c. 2, fo. 3, B. Willis, Library Catalogue, 1710–20 cites a copy of Kersey's *Algebra*. 16-6, jv/munv, Apr. 8 1659; J. Beckett, *Coal and Tobacco* (Cambridge, 1981), 16.

15. M. Verney, *Memoirs*, iii. 366–8.

16. 16-13, jv/rv, July 6 1659; 16-16, jv/rv, Aug. 10 1659. Levant merchant, George Boddington, born in 1646, also left his Latin school and learned accounts. GH MS 10, 823/1, fos. 9, 19, 38, Boddington family personal papers; K. Thomas, 'Numeracy in Early Modern England', *Transactions of the Royal Historical Society*, 37 (1987), 111–12.

17. 16-23, W. Wakefield/rv, Sept. 19 1659; R. Grassby, 'English Merchant Capitalism in the Late Seventeenth Century', *Past and Present*, 46 (1970), 87–107.

18. 16-28, rbur/rv, Dec. 13 1659; B. Henning, *The House of Commons 1660–1690* (1983), ii. 760–4; J. Woodhead, *The Rulers of London 1660–1689* (1965), 110; 16-31, Indenture, Dec. 31 1659; 16-30, 'Copy of bond of £1,000 sealed to Mr Roberts when Jack was bound apprentice', Dec. 31 1659.

19. C. Brooks, 'Apprenticeship, Social Mobility, and the Middling Sort, 1550–1800', in J. Barry and C. Brooks (eds.), *The Middling Sort of People* (Basingstoke, 1994), 52–83; P. Seaver, 'Declining Status in an Aspiring Age', in B. Kunze and D. Brautigam (eds.), *Court, Country, and Culture* (Rochester, NY, 1992), 129–47; I. Ben-Amos, *Adolescence and Youth in Early Modern England* (New Haven, 1995); A. Brink (ed.), *The Life of the Reverend Mr George Trosse* (Montreal, 1974); C. Trenchard, *A Cap of Gray Hairs . . .* (1671). [J. Barnard], *A Present for an Apprentice* (1740) is a later version of Trenchard's text.

20. 44-24, lg/rv, Mar. 5 1690; 53-203, jv/pl, Mar. 15 1706; 52-641, ea/jv, Dec. 11 1704; 51-397, pv/jv, Feb. 19 1701; 48-73, jv/rv, Nov. 28 1694; CH 4/5/57/8, jv/wc, May 6 1704; 33-95, jv/rv, Nov. 10 1679.

21. *The Merchant's Daily Companion* (1684); J. Marius, *Advice Concerning Bills of Exchange* (1700); *An Arithmologia, Being a Mirror, Breviate, Treasure, Mate, for Merchants, Bankers, Tradesmen, Mechanicks . . .* (1693); J. Giles, *Lex Mercatoria: or the Merchants' Companion . . .* (1718); *The Freemen of London's Necessary and Useful Companion . . .* (1706); T. Watts, *An Essay on the Proper Method for Forming the Man of Business . . .* (1716); J. Rogers, *The Early History of the Law of Bills and Notes* (Cambridge, 1995), 96.

22. 17-2, jv/rv, Feb. 1 1660; 17-4, jv/rv, Mar. 14 1660; Bodl MS Eng Letts E29, fo. 24, Letter to Matthew Henry, May 7 1683; 21-8, rv/Monsieur Pappin, May 29 1667.

23. J. Agnew, *Worlds Apart* (Cambridge, 1986), 18–24; J. Baldwin, *Masters, Princes, and Merchants* (Princeton, 1970), i. 262; B. Nelson, *The Idea of Usury* (Princeton, 1949); R. Tawney, *Religion and the Rise of Capitalism* (New York, 1947), 39; R. de Roover, 'Scholastic Attitude toward Trade and Entrepreneurship', in J. Kirshner (ed.), *Business, Banking, and Economic Thought* (Chicago, 1974), 336–45; J. Le Goff, 'Merchant's Time and Church's Time in the Middle Ages', in *Time, Work and Culture in the Middle Ages* (Chicago, 1980).

24. J. Eatwell (ed.), *The New Palgrave: A Dictionary of Economics* (1987), iii. 445. *The Oxford English Dictionary*, 2nd edn. (Oxford, 1989), iii. 522; S. Schama, *The Embarrassment of Riches* (New York, 1987), 287, 295–8. This section follows J. Appleby's chronology in *Economic Thought and Ideology.*

25. L. Roberts, 'The Treasure of Traffic', 1641 in J. McCulloch (ed.), *Early English Tracts on Commerce* (Cambridge, 1952), 49–114; A. Hirschman, *The Passions and the Interests* (Princeton, 1977).

26. F. Verney, *Memoirs*, i. 60–8; 23-20, jv/H. Verney, Jan. 30 1670; 33-32, jv/rv, July 31 1679; L. Gragg, 'A Vagabond in Paradise', *History Today*, 45 (1995), 40–6.

27. [J. Ap Roberts], *An Apology for a Younger Brother . . .* (Oxford, 1641), 53; C. Northtonus, *The Younger Brother's Advocate . . .* (1654/5), 4; *The Beau Defeated: Or the Lucky Younger Brother, A Comedy* ([1700]); [J. Brydall], *Jus Primogeniti* (1699); J. Thirsk, 'Younger Sons in the Seventeenth Century', *History*, 54 (1969), 358–77; L. Pollock, 'Younger Sons in Tudor and Stuart England', *History Today*, 34 (1989), 23–9. For settlements, see Ch. 5.

28. E. Chamberlayne in *Angliae Notitia*, 10th edn. (1677), 285 estimates 6,000 esquires and 6,000 gentleman had about £400 per year in land. In 1707 G. Miege cited the same 6,000 gentleman as well as 14,000 younger brothers in *The Present State of Great Britain* (1707), 263; [Ap Roberts], *An Apology*, 29; 17-9, rv/munv, July 23 1660.

29. G. Holmes, *Augustan England: Professions, State, and Society 1680–1730* (1982); P. Corfield, *Power and the Professions in Britain, 1700–1850* (New York, 1995); J. Habakkuk, *Marriage, Debt, and the Estates System* (Oxford, 1994), 108–17.

30. 44-22, jv/rv, Mar. 1 1690; T. Hollingsworth, 'Demography of the British Peerage', *Population Studies*, 18 (1964), Supplement, i–108; R. Porter, *English Society in the Eighteenth Century* (Harmondsworth, 1982), 27.

31. For example, the Pigotts of Doddershall. 52-720, jv/rv, Mar. 22 1705; Bodl Willis MS. 19, fos. 98–9; Bodl Pigott MS b. 4, fo. 1; G. Lipscomb, *The History and Antiquities of the County of Buckingham* (1831), i. 406; G. Eland, *Papers from an Iron Chest at Doddershall, Bucks* (Aylesbury, 1937).

32. 30-3, jv/rv/, Nov. 1676; 39-12, jv/rv, 11 Aug. 1684; 41-21, jv/rv, Oct. 20 1686; 50-173, nn/jv, Oct. 5 1697; 16-28, rbur/rv Dec. 13 1659; CLRO, Mayor's Court Decrees, Box 255E, Oct. 22 1661 and Mayor's Court Interrogatories, 6/120A&B, *Thomas Wilson* v. *Edward Harris*, Sept. 1661.

33. *The Way to Promotion, or the Young Man's Guide to Preferment* (1682), 4, 82; T. Powell, *Tom of All Trades* (1631); [S. Penton], *The Guardian's Instruction* (1688). Richard Grassby has analysed the costs and benefits in *The English Gentleman in Trade*.

34. O. Walker, *Of Education* (Oxford, 1687), 214. W. Darrell, *The Gentleman Instructed*, 4th edn. (1709), 152.

35. 16-17, rv/vgaw, Aug. 11 1659.

36. H. Horwitz, 'The Mess of the Middle Class Revisited', *Continuity and Change*, 2 (1987), 263–96; D. Jones, 'London Overseas Merchant Groups at the End of the Seventeenth Century . . .', D. Phil. thesis (Oxford, 1970) and 'London Merchants and the Crisis of the 1690s' in P. Clark and P. Slack (eds.), *Crisis and Order in English Towns 1500–1700* (1972); R. Lang, 'London's Aldermen in Business: 1600–26', *Guildhall Miscellany*, 3 (1971), 242–65; P. Dickson, *The Financial Revolution in England* (1967); Bodl D. D. Dashwood MS A. 1/6, c. 1, May 7 1690; G. De Krey, 'Trade, Religion, and Politics in London in the Reign of William III', Ph.D. thesis (Princeton, 1978).

37. Temple: 23-19, munv/jv, June 26 1670; 29-10, rv/munv, Jan. 10 1676; 30-8, rv/jv, Dec. 4 1676; 31-73, jv/munv, Aug. 8 1678; PRO PROB 11/353, fo. 42; S. Anderson, *An English Consul in Turkey: Paul Rycaut at Smyrna 1667–1678* (Oxford, 1989,) 106–8; T. Prime, *Some Account of the Temple Family* (New York, 1887); Lipscomb, *History and Antiquities*, iii, 86. Denton: 51-432, lg/jv, Apr. 9 1701; 51-588, ea/jv, Dec. 3 1700; 51-642, jv, Draft deed, [n.d.]; Lipscomb, *History and Antiquities*, iii, 17–18; Bodl Willis MS 19, fos. 33–6. Lee: CH 14/49, Lee pedigree; 22-3, jv/rv, Mar. 25 1668; 23-10, jv/rv, Aug. 5 1669; Bodl Willis MS 8, fo. 15; Bodl Willis MS 19, fos. 81–2; Bodl Top Bucks MS c. 1, fos. 83–6, 239ᵛ, 246. Hampden: PRO PROB 11/396, fo. 98; Anderson, *An English Consul*, 271, Lipscomb, *History and Antiquities*, ii. 374. Busby: 38-66, jv/rv, June 5 1684 and 38-69, June 12 1684; 38-68, rv/jv, June 9 1684; 47-64, rv/jv, Sept. 17 1693; 54-343, jv/rv2, Dec. 5 1710; Bodl Willis MS 8, fo. 137. Lovett: 54-294, ml/jv, Sept. 6 1710. Woodward: 42-68, rv/jv, July 22 1688; Bodl Willis MS 8, fo. 48. Price: 31-40, jv/rv, [n.d.]; Lipscomb, *History and Antiquities*, iii. 142; PRO PROB 11/485, fo. 227. Lawrence: J. & G. Matthews (eds.), *Abstracts of Probate Acts in the Prerogative Court of Canterbury* (1903), 339; PRO PROB 11/179, fo. 12; Bodl Willis MS 8, fo. 29. Mayne: PRO PROB 11/603, fo. 96; Bodl Willis MS 19, fos. 89–90. Duncombe: Bodl Willis MS 19, fos. 39–40. Lichfield: CH 14/49, Pedigree, #10.

38. R. Grassby, 'Social Mobility and Business Enterprise in Seventeenth-Century England', in D. Pennington and K. Thomas (eds.), *Puritans and Revolutionaries* (Oxford, 1978), 356–7; Anderson, *An English Consul*, 75.

39. H. Perkin, *The Origins of Modern English Society 1780–1880* (1969), 43; J. Rosenheim, *The Townshends of Raynham* (Middletown, Conn., 1989), 107–10, 118, 217.

40. M. Kitch, 'Capital and Kingdom', in A. Beier and R. Finlay (eds.), *London 1500–1700* (1986), 246; P. Earle, 'Age and Accumulation in the London Business Community 1665–1720', in N. McKendrick and R. Outhwaite (eds.), *Business Life and Public Policy* (Cambridge, 1986), 44–5, 53–4; R. Grassby, *The Business Community of Seventeenth-Century England* (Cambridge, 1995).

41. *The Way to Promotion*, 86; D. Defoe, *The Complete English Tradesman*, (Gloucester, 1987), 7.

42. 33-114, rv/jv, Dec. 4 1679; R. Grassby, 'The Personal Wealth of the Business Community in Seventeenth-Century England', *EcHR*, 2nd series, 23 (1970), 220–34, and 'The Rate of Profit in Seventeenth-Century England', *English Historical Review*, 84 (1969), 721–51; N. Rogers, 'Money, Land and Lineage', *Social History*, 4 (1979), 444–6. Earle (('Age and Accumulation', 53) estimates a median fortune of £3,200 for a sample of London sole traders, 1665–1720.

43. Grassby, 'Social Mobility', 367; Seaver, 'Declining Status', 129–47; R. Baxter, *Compassionate Counsel to All Young Men* (1691), 34, 158.

44. *The Cities Great Concern*, (1674), 8–10, 50–1 (wrongly attributed to John Philpot and

first published under the title of *The Cities Advocate* in 1629); 31-30, rv/unknown, Mar. 21 1678; Watts, *An Essay on the Proper Method*, 35.

45. For example, 44-24, lg/rv, Mar. 5 1690; 16-14, lg/rv, July 13 1659; 16-19, lg/rv, Aug. 16 1659; 51-587, lg/jv, Dec. 3 1700; 23-12, wd/rv, Aug. 25 1669. *The Way to Promotion, or the Young Man's Guide to Preferment* (1682), preface, A4–5 states that if a son is 'diligent and careful . . . he may in time come to the preferment of being Lord Mayor of London'.

46. 17-2, jv/rv, Feb. 1 1660; 17-3, jv/rv, Mar. 6 1660; Seaver, 'Declining Status'; Brooks, *The Middling Sort of People*, 52–83; 18-9, jv/rv, Jan. 23 1662; 18-13, jv/rv, Mar. 26 1662.

47. 18-5, jv/rv, Jan. 16 1662; 18-17, jv/rv, Apr. 26 1662; 18-19, jv/rv, Dec. 25 1662; 18-18, rv, 'Books bought for Jack, Apr. 26 1662 at 8s. 6d'; J. Taylor, *The Rule and Exercises of Holy Living* (1658) and *The Rule and Exercises of Holy Dying* (1663); L. Andrewes, *Holy Devotions* (1655).

48. 17-15, wlov/rv, Dec. 10 1661; 18-5, jv/rv, Jan. 16 1662; 18-6, rv/jv, Jan. 20 1662; Berks CRO D/EMt/T1/1–7, Wasing deeds; 49-46, jv/wc, Feb. 13 1695; 49-103, rv/jv, Apr. 15 1696.

49. 18-16, rv, For Jack's Voyage, Apr. 27 1662; Grassby in 'Social Mobility' gives an analysis of the barriers facing gentry younger sons. Far from being privileged, they often lacked capital, connections, and skills.

50. 18-22, jv/munv, Apr. 30 1662; 18-15, jv/rv, Apr. 2 1662; 18-13, jv/rv, Mar. 26 1662.

51. Thirsk, 'Younger Sons in the Seventeenth Century', 358–77; Pollock, 'Younger Sons in Tudor and Stuart England', 23–9; V. Larminie, *Wealth, Kinship, and Culture* (Woodbridge, Suffolk, 1995), 194; F. Heal and C. Holmes, *The Gentry in England and Wales 1500–1700* (Stanford, Calif., 1994), 51; D. Hainsworth, 'Manor House to Counting House', in F. Mc Gregor and N. Wright (eds.), *European History and its Historians* (Adelaide, 1977), 66–74.

52. E. Green, *Birth Order, Parental Interest, and Acadmic Achievement* (San Francisco, 1978); M. Hoopes and J. Harper, *Birth Order, Roles, and Sibling Patterns in Individual Family Therapy* (Rockville, Md., 1987); M. Sandmaier, *Original Kin* (New York, 1994); M. Quitt, 'Immigrant Origins of the Virginia Gentry', *William and Mary Quarterly*, 45 (1988), 629–55. *Continuity and Change*, 7 (1992), gives historical case studies of the effects of birth-order.

53. J. Appleby, 'New Cultural Heroes in the Early National Period', in T. Haskell and R. Teichgraeber (eds.), *The Culture of the Market* (Cambridge, 1993), 163–88; F. Sulloway in *Born to Rebel* (New York, 1996), 356–7; P. Roebuck, *Yorkshire Baronets 1640–1760* (Oxford, 1980), 295.

54. F. Greenspahn, *When Brothers Dwell Together* (New York, 1994), 29–84, 92–3, 107.

55. 18-23, jv/rv, June 30 1662; 18-24, jv/rv, June 26 1662; PRO SP 110/73, fo. 87; H. Teonge, *The Diary of Henry Teonge* (1927), 105, 158; J. de Thévenot, *The Travels of Monsieur de Thévenot into the Levant*, 2nd part (1687), 30–9; A. Russell, *A Natural History of Aleppo* (1756), 5–6.

56. Thevenot, *Travels*, 32; Russell, *Natural History*, 5, 132–3, 135.

57. Teonge, *Diary*, 153, 146; PRO SP 110/73, fos. 111–12; 26-1, jv/rv, May 6 1673; A. Wood, *A History of the Levant Company* (Oxford, 1935), 241–2; H. Maundrell, *A Journal from Aleppo to Jerusalem . . . 1697*, 5th edn. (Oxford, 1732), 148–9, addendum, 9–10.

58. G. Ambrose, 'The Levant Company: Mainly from 1640–1753', B. Litt. thesis, (Oxford, 1932), 196; Wood (*History of the Levant Company*, 242–3) estimates 228 volumes in the

Levant Company library in 1688. A stamp from this library is in the Princeton University Library's copy of Alexander Russell's *A Natural History of Aleppo* (1756).

59. 20-12, jv/rv, Feb. 15 1666; 21-5, jv/rv, June 10 1667. John's letter of May 25 1666 was received on Oct. 5 1666. But his letter written several months earlier on Feb. 15 1666 did not arrive until April 5 1667. Some letters were never received.

60. 18-26, jv/munv, Aug. 20 1662; 18-27, jv/rv, Oct. 22 1662; 19-2, munv/jv, May 23 1663; 19-6, jv, June 20 1663; 20-10, jv/rv, Jan. 16 1666; 22-3, jv/rv, Mar. 25 1668; 22-11, jv/rv, Jan. 30 1670; 23-18, jv/munv, Jan. 30 1670; 23-19, munv/jv, June 26 1670; PRO SP 110/73, fos. 82–3.

61. Russell, *Natural History*, 10, 13; Thevenot, *Travels*, 30; A. Hill, *A Full and Just Account of the Present State of the Ottoman Empire* (1733); J. Dumont, *A New Voyage to the Levant* (1696); 19-1, dfus/rv, Apr. 1 1663; 22-10, jv/rv, Jan. 18 1669; 23-10, jv/rv, Aug. 5 1669; Wood, *History of the Levant Company*, 246; PRO SP 110/73, fos. 42–3; 23-11, jv/rv, Sept. 9 1669.

62. Wood, *History of the Levant Company*, 95. Ambrose ('The Levant Company', 129–30, 253) considers 1675 to be the peak time for Levant traders.

63. 38 individuals attended the Court of Assistants on Sept. 11 1662 (PRO SP 110/56 fo. 177). In 1669 he notes 12 Englishmen or $\frac{1}{4}$ of the factory died of plague in 23-10, jv/rv, Aug. 5 1669; 23-11, jv/rv, Sept. 9 1669. R. Davis (*Aleppo and Devonshire Square* (1967), 3) estimates 30 or 40 firms with 50 leaders or partners plus clerks and officials in 1680. Teonge (p. 153) cites 60 seated at a feast in the 1670s, with others standing. There are 15 signatures on the Levant company oath for 1663, and 30 for 1664 in PRO SP 110/56, fo. 212. Ambrose cites 364 members in 1676 (p. 45). However, Sonia Anderson (*An English Consul*, 72 n. 24) points out that the total noted in PRO SP 110/73, fos. 269–75 was actually 346. Verney is cited in fo. 274.

64. 18-28, jv, Turkey Company charter, 3rd Jacobi; Ambrose, 'The Levant Company', 33, 38. PRO SP 110/56 contains the minutes of Aleppo courts from 1659 to 1665.

65. PRO SP 110/56, fos. 177, 235; 20-10, jv/rv, Jan. 16 1666; P. Rycaut, *The Present State of the Ottoman Empire*, 3rd edn. (1670), n. p. (in epistle to reader preceding text.)

66. 19-4, jv/rv, June 20 1663; 19-10, rv/unknown, n.d.; 19-13, jv/rv, July 25 1664; 20-4, jv/rv, March 1665; 21-5, jv/rv, June 10 1667. Wood (*History of the Levant Company*, 215) notes that Levant factors received a 3% commission, but CH 4/5/21/25 indicates that John was getting less in 1664. Davis (*Aleppo and Devonshire Square*, 82) states that factors usually signed a partnership after one year to share profits, with the predecessor returning to England.

67. CLRO MS 7, fos. 15, 39, Assessments, All Hallows, London Wall, 1695; PRO PROB 11/545, fo. 57; K. Davies, *The Royal Africa Company* (1957), 386; J. Woodhead, *The Rulers of London 1660–1689* (1965), 139. Appointed London Alderman by Royal Commission in 1687, he fined to receive a discharge. A. Beaven, *The Aldermen of the City of London* (1913), i. 77; ii. 111; GH MS 11593/1, fo. 153, Grocers' Company Register of Apprentices, July 1646; CLRO MS 92, fo. 293, *Repertories of Aldermen*, June 29 1687.

68. CH 4/5/21/25, Dec. 31 1667; 21-5, jv/rv, June 10 1667; 20-2, rv/jv, Dec. 19 1664; 22-3, jv/rv, Mar. 25 1688; PRO SP 105/152, fo. 388, Court minutes; 33-114, rv/jv, Dec. 4 1679.

69. 24-5, jv/rv, June 10 1671; PRO SP 110/73, fo. 96; PRO SP 110/56, fo. 262; 25-2, jv/rv, May 20 1672.

70. 19-2, munv/jv, May 23 1663; 19-3, munv/jv, June 12 1663; 24-3, jv/munv, Apr. 5 1671; 26-3, jv/munv, May 8 1673.

71. 22-7, rv/jv, Aug. 27 1668; 22-10, jv/rv, Jan. 18 1669; 23-1, jv/rv, Apr. 2 1669; 25-1, jv/rv, Feb. 25 1672.
72. In Paris, John saw palaces, houses of the nobility, tombs, gardens, churches, 'hospitals of incurable men and women', the 'polishing glass house' and 'all the curiosities as well as beasts, fowl . . . and of course the Louvre'. 27-1, jv, n.d. [1674].
73. CH 4/5/56/26, jv/wc, June 30 1703 (endorsed June 13); 38-48, rv/jv, Mar. 31 1684.
74. 44-58, jv/rv, Nov. 12 1690; 49-75, rv/wc, May 27 1696; CH 4/5/54/6, jv/wc, May 21 1701.
75. P. Siu, 'The Sojourner', *American Journal of Sociology*, 58 (1952), 34–44; G. Simmel, 'The Stranger', in D. Levine (ed.), *Georg Simmel: On Individuality and Social Forms, Selected Writings* (Chicago, 1971), 143–9; L. Harman, *The Modern Stranger: On Language and Membership* (Berlin, 1988), 19–26; R, Park, 'Human Migration and the Marginal Man', in R. Sennett (ed.), *Classic Essays on the Culture of Cities* (Englewood Cliffs, NJ, 1969) 131–42; E. Stonequist, *The Marginal Man* (New York, 1937).

Notes to Chapter 3

1. 40-27, jv/rv, May 22 1685.
2. E. Wrigley, 'Urban Growth and Agricultural Change', *Journal of Interdisciplinary History*, 15 (1985), 688 and 'A Simple Model of London's Importance 1650-1750', *Past and Present*, 37 (1967); R. Porter, *London: A Social History* (Cambridge, Mass., 1994), 131; A. Beier and R. Finlay (eds.), *London 1500–1700* (1986); V. Harding, 'The Population of London, 1500–1750', *London Journal*, 15 (1990), 111–28; J. Strype, *A Survey of the Cities of London and Westminster . . . by John Stow*, 2 vols. (1720).
3. P. Corfield and N. Harte (eds.), *London and the English Economy 1500–1700* (1990); F. Fisher, 'London as an "Engine of Economic Growth"', in P. Clark (ed.), *The Early Modern Town* (1976), 205–15.
4. For contrasting views of urban geography, see G. Sjoberg, 'The Nature of the Pre-Industrial City', in Clark (ed.), *The Early Modern Town*, 43–52; J. Vance, Jr., 'Land Assignment in the Pre-capitalist, Capitalist, and Post Capitalist City', *Economic Geography*, 47 (1971), 101–20; M. Power, 'The East and West in Early-Modern London', in E. Ives *et al.* (eds.), *Wealth and Power in Tudor England* (1978), 167–85; E. Jones, 'London in the Early Seventeenth Century', *London Journal*, 6 (1980), 123–33.
5. N. Brett-James, *The Growth of Stuart London* (1935); D. Glass, 'Socio-economic Status and Occupations in the City of London at the End of the Seventeenth Century', in Clark (ed.), *The Early Modern Town*, 216–32; L. Stone, 'The Residential Development of the West End of London in the Seventeenth Century', in B. Malament (ed.), *After the Reformation* (Philadelphia, 1980), 167–212.
6. Wrigley, 'A Simple Model', 44–70, 49. For urbanization see J. De Vries, *European Urbanization* (Cambridge, 1984); E. Lampard, 'The Nature of Urbanization', in A. Fraser and A. Sutcliffe (eds.), *The Pursuit of Urban History* (1983); A. van der Woude *et al.* (eds.), *Urbanization in History* (Oxford, 1990). For relationships between London and the provinces, see P. Borsay, 'The London Connection', *London Journal*, 19 (1994), 21–35; J. Barry, 'Provincial Town Culture 1640–1780', in J. Pittock and A. Wear (eds.), *Interpretation and Cultural History* (1991), 198–234; P. Corfield, *The Impact of English Towns, 1700–1800* (Oxford, 1982).
7. F. Heal, 'The Crown, the Gentry, and London', in C. Cross *et al.* (eds.), *Law and Government under the Tudors* (Cambridge, 1988), 211–26; J. Larkin (ed.), *Stuart Royal*

Proclamations (Oxford, 1973), Dec. 22 1622, i. 563; GH Proc. 1. 30; Bodl Bankes MSS 14 and 62; V. Larminie, *Wealth, Kinship, and Culture* (Woodbridge, Suffolk, 1995), 122–3.

8. *The Country Gentleman's Vade Mecum* (1699), 7; Sir W. Coventry, 'On the Decay of Rents', in J. Thirsk and J. Cooper (eds.), *Seventeenth-Century Economic Documents* (Oxford, 1972), 79–84; D. Hainsworth, *Stewards, Lords, and People* (Cambridge, 1992); D. Hainsworth and C. Walker (eds.), *The Correspondence of Lord Fitzwilliam of Milton and Frances Guybon, his Steward 1697–1709* (Northampton, 1990); P. Roebuck, 'Absentee Landownership in the Late Seventeenth and Early Eighteenth Centuries', *Agricultural History Review*, 21 (1973), 1–17; J. Beckett, 'Absentee Landownership in the Later Seventeenth and Early Eighteenth Centuries', *Northern History*, 19 (1983), 87–107; *Remarques upon the Humours and Conversations of the Town* (1673), 83, 85–6; J. Rosenheim, 'County Governance and Elite Withdrawal in Norfolk', in A. Beier *et al.* (eds.), *The First Modern Society* (Cambridge, 1989), 95–125; G. Laurence, *The Duty of a Steward to his Lord* (1727).

9. T. Dekker, *The Seven Deadly Sins*, ed. E. Arber (Westminster, 1895); [J. Parke], *A Warning to London in Particular* (1679); [S. Vincent], *The Young Gallant's Academy* (1674); *Humours and Conversations of the Town* (1693); *A Guide for Malt-Worms* ([1715?]); *The Character of a Town Gallant* (1675); *Hell upon Earth or the Town in An Uproar* (1985); N. Ward, *The London-Spy Compleat* (1924); [J. Breues], *The Fortune Hunters* (1754); P. Corfield, 'Walking the City Streets', *Journal of Urban History*, 16 (1990), 132–74; A. Weitzman, 'Eighteenth-Century London: Urban Paradise or Fallen City?', *Journal of the History of Ideas*, 36 (1975), 469–80.

10. *Remarques upon Remarques* (1673); *A New View of London* (1708); E. Jones, *A Trip through London*, 5th edn. (1718); W. Stow, *Remarks on London* (1722), preface; *The New Guide to London, or Directions to Strangers*, 2nd edn. (1726); *A New Review of London* (1728); [J.] Pote, *The Foreigners' Guide*, 2nd edn. (1729); *A Compleat Guide to All Persons Who have any Trade . . . with the City of London* (1740).

11. J. Grant, 'The Gentry in London in the Reign of Charles I', *University of Birmingham History Journal*, 8 (1962), 197–202; F. Fisher, 'The Development of London as a Centre of Conspicuous Consumption', in E. Carus-Wilson (ed.), *Essays in Economic History* (1962), ii. 203–4; F. Heal and C. Holmes, *The Gentry in England and Wales 1500–1700* (Stanford, Calif., 1994), 312.

12. J. Smuts, 'The Court and its Neighbourhood', *Journal of British Studies*, 30 (1991), 124–9; CH Deed, lease between Francis, Earl of Bedford, and Sir Edmund Verney, Nov. 1 1634; LCC, *Survey of London*, (1970), xxxvi. 74–5, 97, 370–7; J. Bruce (ed.), *Letters and Papers of the Verney Family . . .* , 1st Series, (Camden Society, 56; 1853), 172; *Archaeologia*, 23 (1853), 194–6.

13. 46-40, jv/rv, July 27 1692; J. Summerson, *Georgian London* (1962); Stone, 'The Residential Development', 180–1, 186, 191–5, 207; Strype, *A Survey*, ii, appendix, ch. 1, 6; HL STTF 59/4, [c.1680]; J. Beckett, *Coal and Tobacco* (Cambridge, 1981), 13, 26.

14. 47-482, cst/rv, July 15 1694; 47-154, jv/rv, Nov. 1 1693; 51-477, ea/jv, July 27 1701; 42-42, rp1/jv, Dec. 13 1697.

15. 49-179, eli/jv, June 14 1696; 32-137, jv/munv, May 19, 1679; 34-56, jv/rv, May 6 1680; 34-62, May 10 1680. 41-28, munv/jv, Nov. 14 1686; 41-35, munv/jv, Nov. 28 1686; N. Key, 'The Political Culture and Political Rhetoric of County Feasts and Feast Sermons 1654–1714', *Journal of British Studies*, 33 (1994), 223–56. See Bodl Rawl MS Letters 50, fos. 218–347 for the Whartons in London.

16. 35-60, rv/jv, May 12 1681; 40-55, jv/rv, Mar. 24 1686; 41-26, jv/rv, Nov. 8 1686; 45-30, jv/

rv, Dec. 12 1691; G. Holmes, 'The Achievement of Stability', in J. Cannon (ed.), *The Whig Ascendancy* (1981), 14–15; D. Jones, *War and Economy in the Age of William III and Marlborough* (Oxford, 1988), Appendix 2, 330–31.

17. 50-559, nn/jv, July 28 1698.

18. 48-537, rv/jv, Oct. 1 1695.

19. 33-10, mun/jv, July 14 1679; 47-91, rv/jv, Oct. 1 1693; 52-464, tc/jv, July 17 1704; 37-10, jv/ rv, Oct. 16 1682; J. Landers, *Death and the Metropolis* (Cambridge, 1993), 354; 46-41, pa/rv, July 26 1692; 56-63, ebv/jv, May 22 1716; 53-12, rp2/jv, June 30 1707.

20. 33-55, rv/jv, May 2 1681; 50-210, jv/ea, Oct. 24 1697; *The Country Gentleman's Vade Mecum*, 2–3; 48-361, nn/jv, June 17 1695.

21. 54-353, mc/jv, Apr. 9 1711; 54-364, ebv/jv, Dec. 10 1710; 53-571, jv/tc, Apr. 17 1708; 54-112, tc/jv, July 19 1709.

22. 50-15, pg/jv, May 17 1697; D. Davis, *Fairs, Shops, and Supermarkets* (Toronto, 1966), 102; R. Burridge, *A New Review of London* (1722), A2; 46-10, jv/rv, July 6 1692; 46-286, 'Mary Verney's bills', May–July 1692; 54-299, cpv/rv2, Sept. 10 1710; 46-445, wc/rv, Apr. 30 1693; 50-366, rpol/jv, May 15 1698.

23. 52-430, ebv/rv2, Mar. 3 1704. N. Mc Kendrick *et al.* (eds.), *The Birth of a Consumer Society* (1983); J. Brewer and R. Porter (eds.), *The World of Goods* (1993); A. Bermingham and J. Brewer (eds.), *The Consumption of Culture 1600–1800* (1993); *Remarques upon Remarques*, A5^v, 34–5; W. Gough, *Londinium Triumphans* (1682); 32-17, jv/rv, Oct. 24 1678; 32-33, jv/rv, Nov. 28 1678.

24. 53-173, rp2/jv, Feb. 11 1706; *Remarques upon Remarques*, 89–92; H. Wyld, *A History of Modern Colloquial English*, 3rd edn. (Oxford, 1936), 4, 163; A. Bryson, 'Concepts of Civility in England 1560–1685', D. Phil. thesis (Oxford, 1984), 313–20; [H. Felton], *A Dissertation on Reading the Classics and Forming a Just Style* (1713); I. Watts, *The Art of Reading and Writing English* (1721).

25. 31-46, W. Fall/rv, [May 1684?]; 37-28, epv/jv, [Feb. 1682?]; 38-56, jv/rv, May 1 1684; 50-59, jv/wc, June 17 1695; 50-376, jv/wc, May 25 1698; 18-21, jv/rv, Apr. 28 1662.

26. CH 15/17–20, Printed playbills 1692–4 included *Henry II, The Indian Emperor, Theodosium, or the Force of Love*, and *All for Love*; CH 15/26, Printed advertisements and notices, 1641–1712; CH 14/49. The list included works by John Dryden, Nathaniel Lee, Elkaniah Settle, Thomas Shadwell, Thomas Otway, Fletcher and Beaumont, Shakespeare, Thomas Duffet, and George Etheridge.

27. 48-81, nn/jv, June 4 1695; 16-6, jv/mun, Apr. 8 1659; F. Levy, 'How Information Spread 1550–1640', *Journal of British Studies*, 21 (1982), 11–34; R. Cust, 'News and Politics in Early Seventeenth-Century England', *Past and Present*, 112 (1986), 60–90; *The Post Office: An Historical Summary* (1911), 5; 55-20, tc/jv, Dec. 14 1712.

28. 53-266, jv, atre, Oct. 15 1706; 51-698, ebv/jv, Mar. 28 1702; 53-234, rp2/rv2, June 23 1706; 52-375, jv/tc, Jan. 23 1704. In May and June 1703, Nicholas Blundell plied back and forth to London during settlement negotiations. R. Houlbrooke (ed.), *English Family Life, 1576–1716* (Oxford, 1988), 41–2.

29. 51-125, nmar/jv, Nov. 9 1699; 49-175, rv/jv, July 17 1696; 47-159, aden/rv, Nov. 4 1693. Numbers of letters cited hereafter in this chapter refer to the total database of 8,014 records in order to include the period from 1660 to 1691 unless otherwise noted.

30. J. Broad, 'Gentry Finances and the Civil War', *EcHR*, 2nd series, 32 (1979), 183–200; E. Gay, 'The Temples of Stowe and their Debts', *HLQ* 2 (1939), 399–438, and 'Sir Richard Temple, the Debt Settlement, and Estate Litigation, 1653–1675', *HLQ* 6 (1943),

255–91; 47-179, rv/jv, Nov. 14 1692; HL ST 175, Sir Richard Temple's day book, July–August 1681, Nov. 17 1683, Aug. 18 1684.

31. 51-499, jv/pl, Oct. 5 1701.

32. 46-246, rv/jv, Dec. 11 1692; 51-122, W. Mason/wc, Nov. 3 1699; 52-751, mc/jv, May 4 1705; 36-27, jv/rv, Dec. 8 1681; 49-21, cst/rv, Jan. 19 1696; 51-112, lg/rv, Nov. 2 1699; 51-128, ea/jv, Nov. 14 1699.

33. 49-644, eli/jv, Apr. 28 1697; 46-523, mk/jv, June 16 1693; 16-26, ea/rv, Nov. 26 1659; 48-382, jv/rv, July 3 1695; [S. Vincent], *The Young Gallant's Academy* (1674), 61; 48-387, eli/rv, Jan. 19 1695.

34. 29-21, jv/rv, Mar. 2 1676; 39-57, jv/rv, March 25 1685; 54-406, Rev. Widdowes/jv, Apr. 12 1711; 32-74, ea/rv, Jan. 18 1679.

35. 48-479, jv/rv, [Aug. 1695?]; 53-519, cc/jv, Nov. 2 1707; 48-619, eli/rv, Dec. 15 1695.

36. 27-8, rv/jv, Mar. 16 1674; 29-21, jv/rv, Mar. 2 1676; 31-59, jv/lshe, June 27 1678; J. Woodhead, *The Rulers of London 1660–89* (1965), 68. See Ch. 5.

37. 27-2, rv/jv, Aug. 31 1674; 33-98, rv/jv, Nov. 17 1698; 33-114, rv/jv, Dec. 4 1680; 33-116, jv/rv, Dec. 8 1679; 33-110, jchu/rv, n.d.; 27-4, mun/jv, Sept 7 1674. 33-98, rv/jv, Nov. 17 1679; 33-124, lg/rv, Dec. 18 1679; 34-11, jv/epv, Dec. 26 1680.

38. PRO PROB 11/550, fo. 35; 33-93, jv/rv, Nov. 7 1679; J. Barry and C. Brooks (eds.), *The Middling Sort of People* (Basingstoke, 1994); N. Rogers, 'Introduction', *Journal of British Studies*, 32 (1993), 299–304; 35-86, jv/rv, June 20 1681; 37-29, rp1/jv, Feb. 6 1683; 33-113, jv/rv, Dec. 4 1680; 33-110, jchu/rv, n.d.

39. 34-160, jv/rv, Oct. 21 1680; 35-3, jv/rv, Dec. 2 1680; 34-65, rv/jv, [May 1680?]; 34-80 nn/jv, [May 1680?]; 34-154, jv/rv, Sept. 30 1680; 34-167, jv/rv, Nov. 1 1680.

40. 33-182, jv/rv, Nov. 20 1680; 34-160, jv/rv, Oct. 21 1680; 34-163, jv/rv, Oct. 28 1680; 34-167, jv/rv, Nov. 1 1680.

41. 53-193, jv/cl, Mar. 17 1706.

42. S. Mullaney, *The Place of the Stage* (Chicago, 1988).

43. GH MS 4251; Strype, *A Survey*, i, book 3, 255–6; Miege, *The Present State of Great Britain* (1707), 135; C. Barron, *The Parish of St. Andrew Holborn* (1979); P. Hunting, 'The Survey of Hatton Garden in 1694 by Abraham Arlidge', *London Topographical Record*, 25 (1985), 91, 107. The Arlidge survey shows 372 leasehold properties and 110 individual leaseholders. Ogilby and Morgan's Map of 1676 shows Hatton Street built up to Little Kirby Steet. It was not completed till the late 1680s.

44. J. Pudney, *Hatton Garden* (1956); Hunting, *Survey of Hatton Garden*, 93–4; CLRO MSS 83, fo. 7 and 42, fo. 3; GH MS 4256.

45. Hunting, *Survey of Hatton Garden*, 91, 96–8, 105; BL Add. MS 29565, fo. 21; 47-369, jv/rv, Apr. 19 1694.

46. 35-36, Jane Nicholas/jv, Apr. 11 1681; 46-228, jv/rv, Nov. 30 1692; Hunting, *Survey of Hatton Garden*, 106; 49-128, jv, Mar. 13 1696; 49-130, jv, Mar. 16 1696; 50-330, J. Yeates/jv, Mar. 31 1698; 41-70, jv/rv, May 18 1687; 41-74, wgro/jv, May 22 1687. In 1693 the average rent was £40 and the average real property assessment was £6. 8s. John paid £8 tax in 1694. Only 14 occupants of 362 in Hatton Garden paid £1 or less, and in 1696 Hatton Garden paid over $\frac{1}{3}$ of the total parish tax. By 1698 John paid an additional 3s. 6d. every quarter for 'watching'.

47. 35-23, jv/rv, Mar. 14 1681; 35-25, jv/rv, Mar. 17 1681; 35-29, jv/rv, Mar. 30 1681; 35-31, jv/rv, Apr. 4 1681; 35-33, jv/rv, Apr. 6 1681; 35-40, jv/rv, Apr. 11 1681; 35-39, jv/rv, Apr. 11 1681; 37-28, epv/jv, Feb. [1682?]; 41-8, jv, Inventory, n.d.; 46-217, jv/rv, Nov. 23 1692.

48. 35-65, munv/jv, May 23 1681; 35-112, jv/rv, Aug. 25 1681; 34-159, rv/jv, Oct. 21 1680.

49. CH 7/53, London Household Account in John's hand, 1682/3 reads: 'House expenses with beer, coal wine etc. at £3 per week or £156; house rent, £53. 5*s*.; water, £3. 5*s*.; chimney, £1; watch, £1. 10*s*.; repairs, £3; E[lizabeth] V[erney], £55; J[ohn] V[erney], £45; coach and horses, farrier, coachmaker, coachman's wages and livery, £80; lying-in £20; children's clothes £20; nurse, £20', for a total of £480 per year. Other 'extraordinaries, as putting boys to apprentice, law (as now Jack Harris puts me to), sickness (as small pox amongst servants), journeys etc.' brought the sum to over £500. HL ST 152, Sir Richard Temple's account book, 1677–1688; R. Grassby, *The English Gentleman in Trade* (Oxford, 1994), 183; J. Rosenheim, *The Townshends of Raynham*, (Middletown, Conn., 1989), 77.

50. 43-1, jv/rv, Aug. 22 1688; WM H468-495; Smuts, 'The Court and its Neighbourhood'; V. Pearl, 'Change and Stability', *London Journal*, 5 (1979), 3–34; D. George, *London Life in the Eighteenth Century* (New York, 1965), 94–6; L. Schwartz, 'Social Class and Social Geography', *Social History*, 7 (1982), 167–85.

51. J. Boulton, *Neighbourhood and Society* (Cambridge, 1987), 230; 35-29, jv/rv, Mar. 24 1681; 35-76, jv/rv, June 2 1681; 40-57, jv/rv, Mar. 30 1686; BL Add. MS 29565, fos. 254, 260, Mar. 1693; 43-48, jv/rv, Dec. 13 1688; 38-12, jv/rv, Sept. 3 1683.

52. J. Habermas, *The Structural Transformation of the Public Sphere* (Cambridge, Mass., 1989); Miege, *The Present State*, 142; Wrigley, 'A Simple Model'; G. Simmel, 'The Metropolis and Mental Life', in *On Individuality and Social Forms* (Chicago, 1971), 324–39; L. Mumford, *The City in History* (1987); O. Handlin and J. Burchard (eds.), *The Historian and the City* (Cambridge, Mass., 1963); C. Freiderichs, *The Early Modern City* (1995); J. Boulton, 'Residential Mobility in Seventeenth–Century Southwark', *Urban History Yearbook* (1986), 11.

53. 33-32, jv/rv, July 31 1679; 45-12, po/jv, n.d.; 45-18, jv/rv, Aug. 4 1691; 51-443, ctor/jv, May 23 1701; 51-478, Advertisement, Sept. 1 1701; HL ST 175; 46-156, po/jv, Oct. 19 1692; 33-93, jv/rv, Nov. 7 1679; 46-448, lg/Mr. Clifton, May 1 1693; 46-505, aden/rv, May 29 1693; 48-83, jv/rv, Dec. 5 1694; 50-512, nn/jv, Oct. 4 1698; 51-266, ebv/jv, May 18 1700; 54-47, flut/jv, Jan. 31 1709; 54-253, rp2/rv2, June 20 1710; C. Jones, 'The London Life of a Peer in the Reign of Anne', *London Journal*, 16 (1991), 140–55.

54. 29-21, jv/rv, Mar. 2 1676; 33-8, jv/rv, July 11 1679; CH 7/91 Bond, John Clifford of London, silkweaver, and his brother, Samuel Clifford of Clerkenwell, Middlesex, brazier, to John Verney to perform covenants; CH 14/4 Agreement between John Clifford . . . with John Verney of London, merchant, to make no further charge . . . concerning John Smith aged four, Oct. 30 1684.

55. 32-153, jv/rv, June 30 1678; 40-36, jv/rv, July 30 1685; 38-66, jv/rv, June 5 1684; 37-1, rv/jv, Aug. 7 1682; 37-13, jv/rv, Nov. 2 1682; 38-64, jv/rv, June 2 1684; 40-36, jv/rv, July 30 1685.

56. J. Albers, 'Papist Traitors and Presbyterian Rogues', in J. Walsh *et al.* (eds.), *The Church of England c.1689–c.1833* (Cambridge, 1993), 317–33; J. Spurr and M. Goldie, 'Politics and the Restoration Parish', *English Historical Review*, 109 (1994), 572–95.

57. D. Bahlman, *The Moral Revolution of 1688* (New Haven, 1957); 36-1, rv/jv, Sept. 26 1681; 36-18, rv/wd, Nov. 19 1681; 37-16, rv/jv, July 31 1687; CH 15/13, notes; 21-1, rv/mons. pappin, May 29 1667.

58. J. Taylor, *The Rule and Exercises of Holy Living* (1658) and *The Rule and Exercises of Holy Dying* (1663); 33-5, rv/jv, Sept. 26 1681; 42-22, rv/jv, July 31 1687; 31-13, munv/rv, Jan. 24 1678; 31-18, munv/rv, Feb. 11 1679; 32-50, rv/munv, Dec. 23 1678; 42-60, rv/jv,

June 3 1688; B. Henning, *The House of Commons 1660–1690* (1983), iii. 635; 39-40, rv/ wc, Feb. 27 1685.

59. 28-18, jv/rv, Mar. 15 1675; 28-22, jv/rv, Mar. 1 1675;T. Liu, *Puritan London* (Newark, Del., 1986), 100; M. Watts, *The Dissenters* (Oxford, 1978), 152, 217, 250; 29-21, jv/rv, Mar. 2 1676; 29-32, rv/jv, Apr. 10 1676; Woodhead, *The Rulers of London*, 139; *A True and Impartial Account of the Poll of the Inhabitants of Broad Street . . .* (1711).

60. 34-109, jv/rv, June 14 1680; 34-112, rv/jv, June 1680; 32-33, jv/rv, Nov. 28, 1678; 32-34, jv/ rv, Dec. 5 1678; CH 14/19, fo. 12, notes; 32-34, jv/rv, Dec. 5 1678; R. Carroll, *The Common-Sense Philosophy of Religion of Bishop Edward Stilllingfleet 1635–1699* (The Hague, 1975).

61. Studies confirming religious centrality in this period include: J. Champion, *The Pillars of Priestcraft Shaken 1660–1730* (Cambridge, 1992); T. Harris *et al.* (eds.), *The Politics of Religion in Restoration England* (Oxford, 1990); M. Griffin, Jr., *Latitudinarianism in the Seventeenth-Century Church of England*, ed. L. Freedman (Leiden, 1992); I. Rivers, *Reason, Grace, and Sentiment* (Cambridge, 1991); J. Scott, *Algernon Sydney and the Restoration Crisis 1677–83* (Cambridge, 1991); W. Spellman, *The Latitudinarians and the Church of England 1660–1700* (Athens, Ga., 1993); J. Spurr, *The Restoration Church of England 1646–1689* (New Haven, 1991).

62. 33-102, jv/rv, Nov. 20 1679; 34-166, jv/rv, Nov. 1 1680; 43-1, jv/rv, Aug. 22 1688; 32-34, jv/ rv, Dec. 5 1678. See Cambridge University Library, Sel 2. 114–126 for a huge pamphlet collection bought and indexed by John Verney with his notes.

63. J. Spurr, 'Latitudinarianism and the Restoration Church', *Historical Journal*, 31 (1988), 62–82; 33-8, jv/rv, July 11 1679; 33-35, jv/rv, Aug. 4 1679; 33-69, jv/rv, Sept. 29 1679; 37-51, jv/rv, May 10 1683.

64. 35-44, jv/rv, Apr. 28 1681; 37-23, jv/rv, Dec. 18 1682; 41-65, jv/rv, May 4 1681.

65. LCC, *Survey of London*, xxxvi. 74–97, 178–9; Summerson, *Georgian London*; 43-108, lg/rv, Oct. 2 1689; 38-36, rv/jv, [1684?]; 38-30, rv/jv, Dec. 26 1683. For maps and views, see GH, Prints, Drawings, and Maps, W2 Cov.

66. See Westminster Library's (WM) long series of Covent Garden rate books. Overseers Accounts WM H468–H495, 1688–1716 were analysed while Collectors' Books were sampled. See also WM H802–3, St Paul's, Covent Garden, Vestry Minutes, 1681–1723; CLRO MS 38, fo. 7, 1693/4; CH 2/1966, Deed, Nov. 1 1634; LCC, *Survey of London*, xxxvi. 97, 303–7; 37-28, epv/jv, [Feb. 1682?].

67. 35-127, jv/rv, May 22 1681; 40-71, jv/rv, June 1686; 32-8, rv/munv, Sept. 27 1678; 16-6, jv/ rv, Dec. 18 1658; 47-643, nn/jv, Oct. 4 1694; Woodhead, *The Rulers of London*, 155.

68. WM H461-472; WM H802, fo. 6ᵛ; LCC, *Survey of London*, xxxvi. 96; HL STTP 10/11, Papers about the case of Sir Richard Temple's right to a pew; 37-63, jv/rv, July 7 1683; 35-132, jv/rv, May 22 1681; 40-4, jv/rv, Apr. 24 1685.

69. 45-69, jv/rv, May 19 1692; CH 14/68, John Verney's lists of offices, n.d.; 46-222, nn/rv, Nov. 29 1692; 48-459, jv/rv, Aug. 21 1695.

70. Henning, *House of Commons*, iii. 154–6; F. Korsten, *Roger North (1651–1734)* (Amsterdam, 1981); 48-271, jcar/rv, May 27 1695; 48-541, jcar/rv, Oct. 9 1695; 53-542, rh/jv, Jan. 16 1708.

71. Gibbons carved the North's monument with Sir Peter Lely as adviser, while Mason worked for Sir Ralph. 33-111, rv, Dec. 3 1679. Lely's name is spelled Lilly in this letter. Sir Ralph's housekeeper Elizabeth Lillie may have been Lely's relative. The maiden name of Sir Ralph's landlady in Lincoln's Inn Fields was Gibbons. She was a copyist

and went to and from country houses copying portraits. She may have been related
to Grinling.

72. 48-290, pa/rv, June 18 1695; 48-286, pa/rv, June 11 1695; 46-250, jv/rv, Dec. 14 1692;
Grassby, *The Englishman in Trade*, 183, 199, 231.

73. W. Hunt, *The Registers of St. Paul's Church, Covent Garden* (1908), iv, no. xxxvi, 134,
296; LCC, *Survey of London*, xxxvi. 178; 40-56, jv/munv, Mar. 24 1685; 48-564, ea/jv,
Oct. 29 1695; WM H5, May 25 1706; WM H468–495. In the eighteenth century, John
would lodge in James Street with a Dutchman, Thomas Cheret, then with a grocer,
Mr Smith. PRO PROB 11/558.

74. 48-42, rv/jv, Oct. 30 1694; 48-44, rv/jv, Oct. 16 1694.

75. The house was insured for £500 in 1708. GH MS 8674/6, Hand-in-Hand Fire and Life
Insurance Society, Fire policy register F, 1707-8, fo. 116, no. 15773; LCC, *Survey of
London*, xli. 162–94; H. Sturgess, *Register of Admissions to the Honourable Society of
the Middle Temple* (1949), i. 218, 308; CH 2/1950–1954, Palmer deeds, 1659–1716;
M. Verney, *Verney Letters of the Eighteenth Century* (1930), 107–8; Bodl MS Eng. Lett.,
c. 438, d. 409, Ralph Palmer's letters and box with Verney bookplate.

76. 34-111, jv/rv, June 16 1680; 36-31, rv/jv, Dec. 15 1681; 37-49, rv/jv, May 3 1683; 40-46, rv/
jv, Dec. 26 1685; 42-42, rp1/jv, Dec. 7 1687; 37-52, jv/jv, May 17 1683; 38-2, jv/rv, Oct. 13
1683; 38-8, jv/rv, Aug. 23 1683; 45-70, jv/A. White, May 25 1692.

77. 38-70, munv/jv, June 19 1684; 40-63, munv/jv, Apr. 24 1686; M. Goldie, 'The Earliest
Notice of Purcell's Dido and Aeneas', *Early Music*, 20 (1992), 392–400. Scholars
disagree if the first performance was at Mr Priest's. In 1689 a factor in Aleppo
inquired if 'Harry [Purcell] has set to the harpsichord the symph[ony] of the . . .
masque he made for Priest's ball'. Along with requests for the score, he sent 'salutes
. . . to Mr. Purcell and all the rest of our bro[ther]s of the string'. PRO SP 110/16, fos.
36, 50, Feb. 15 1689, Aug. 10 1689; J. Keates, *Purcell, a Biography* (1995), 174–87.

78. 38-22, rp1/jv, Oct. 14 1683; 38-49, epv/rv, Apr. 2 1684; 46-198, po/rv, Nov. 15 1692;
46-332, rv/jv, Feb. 8 1693.

79. 33-86, rv/jv, Nov. 3 1679.

80. 33-93, jv/rv, Nov. 7 1679; 33-95, jv/rv, Nov. 10 1679; 36-33, jv/rv, Dec. 16 1681; 37-6, jv/rv,
Oct. 12 1682; 37-4, jv/rv, Oct. 5 1682; 33-74, rv/jv, Oct. 6 1679; 46-146, jv/rv, Oct. 14
1692; 35-54, rv/jv, May 5 1681; 37-8, wc/rp1, Oct. 15 1682. The Palmer family intermarried with the families of John's second and third wives: 51-33, tlaw/jv, Nov. 23
1699; 54-577, Hester Palmer/jv, Sept. 19 1711; 54-605, rp2/rv2, May 29 1712.

81. 35-72, jv/rv, June 2 1681; Strype, *A Survey*, ii, appendix, i, 72. Monuments to the
Palmers and the Cheynes are in Chelsea Old Church.

82. P. Corfield, 'The Rivals', in N. Harte and R. Quinault (eds.), *Land and Society*
(Manchester, 1996); 51-196, lg/jv, Feb. 29 1700; J. Hoppit, *Risk and Failure in Business
1700–1800* (Cambridge, 1987), 96; J. Alexander, 'The Economic Structure of the City
of London at the End of the Seventeenth Century', *Urban History Yearbook* (1989),
47-62; P. Lindert and J. Williamson, 'Revising England's Social Tables 1688–1812',
Explorations in Economic History, 19 (1982), 385–408. The Verneys called merchants
with £10,000 'rich'. M. Verney, *Memoirs*, iv. 161.

83. Strype, *A Survey*, ii, book 5, 256; appendix, ch. 1, 5; D. Defoe, *The Complete English
Tradesman* (Gloucester, 1987), 7; E. Chamberlayne, *Angliae Notitia*, 10th edn. (1677),
287.

84. *The Oxford English Dictionary*, 2nd edn. (Oxford, 1989), ix. 619; R. Grassby, 'The Rate
of Profit in Seventeenth-Century England', *English Historical Review*, 84 (1969), 733.

Grassby suggests that normal profits of an experienced merchant before 1650 were 10% to 15%, dropping to 6% to 12% later in the century.

85. R. Brenner, *Merchants and Revolution* (Princeton, 1993); D. W. Jones, 'London Overseas Merchant Groups at the End of the Seventeenth Century and the Moves Against the East India Company', D. Phil. thesis (Oxford, 1970); G. De Krey, 'Trade, Religion, and Politics in London in the Reign of William III', Ph.D. thesis (Princeton, 1978); H. Horwitz, 'The East India Trade, the Politicians and the Constitution', *Journal of British Studies*, Spring (1978), 1–18; R. Lang, 'London's Aldermen in Business 1600–26', *Guildhall Miscellany*, 3 (1971), 242–65; 28-9, wblu/jv, Jan. 12 1675.

86. John was admitted by servitude with a £20 fine. PRO SP 105/153, fo. 343; A. Beaven, *The Aldermen of the City of London* (1913), i. 77; ii. 111.

87. 'Mr. John Verney, Turkey Merchant was this day admitted into the freedom by redemption'. GH MS 15201/5, fo. 241, Vintners' Company Court Minutes, 1669–1682, Dec. 21 1674. 'Livery fine of £31 13s. 4d. received of Mr. John Verney for admission into the livery'. GH MS 15333/5-6, Vintners' Wardens Account Books, 1658–1712. In 1674 William Roberts gave £50 for building the hall. On June 29 1696, £25 was 'received of Sir John Verney for his fine . . . of the younger wardens of the . . . Company'. Yet Verney does not appear in GH MS 15212/1 A Book of Names of all the Persons admitted into the Freedom of the Worshipful Company of Vintners . . . beginning in April 1658. Nor is he in GH MS 15208, Vintners' Company, Chronological Roll of Liverymen, 1683–1939.

88. 48-575, jv/rv, Nov. 7 1695; 50-334, jv/rv, Apr. 4 1698.

89. Strype, *A Survey*, i, book 1, 176; book 3, 264; *The Charge which is to be Given to every Governor of the Hospital at Bridewell and Bedlam . . .* (17--)); F. Atterbury, *The Power of Charity to Cover Sin: A Sermon Preached before the Governors of the Hospital of Bridewell and Bedlam . . . 1694* (1708); J. White, *A Short History of the Royal Hospitals of Bridewell and Bethlem* (1899); W. Fuller, *Mr. William Fuller's Trip to Bridewell . . .* (1703); 48-423, jv/rv, Aug. 8 1695; 49-124, C. Todd/jv, Mar. 26 1696; 49-216, jv/rv, July 30 1696; 50-590, jv/rv, Jan. 16 1699.

90. W. Scott, *The Constitution and Finance of English, Scottish, and Irish Joint-Stock Companies to 1720* (Cambridge, 1910), i. 1–12; C. Hickman, *A Sermon Preached before . . . the Company of Merchants Trading into the Levant Seas* (1682); 49-11, Tim Betton/ jv, Jan. 30 1696; S. Anderson, *An English Consul in Turkey; Paul Rycaut at Smyrna, 1667–78* (Oxford, 1989); H. Horwitz, 'Testamentary Practice, Family Strategies, and the Last Phases of the Custom of London 1660–1725', *Law and History Review*, 2 (1984), 223–39; J. Ward, *Metropolitan Communities* (Stanford, Calif., 1997).

91. De Krey, 'Trade, Religion, and Politics', iii, appendices and *A Fractured Society* (New York, 1985), 101–2; PRO T70/83; PRO PROB 11/337, fo. 133; Woodhead, *The Rulers of London*, 84–5; 48-332, jv/rv, July 11 1695. Angel's uncle was James Harrington, the political theorist.

92. Soon after Roberts became an officer of the Royal Africa Company, John was made an Assistant. Woodhead, *The Rulers of London*, 139; GH MS 11593/1, fo. 153; CLRO MS 92, fo. 293; PRO PROB 11/545, fo. 57. 51-34, pl/jv, Aug. 21 1699; 53-23, Mary Lupart/jv, July 7 1705; 34-2, jv/epv, Jan. 1680; 48-332, jv/rv, July 11 1695.

93. 34-20, jv/rv, Mar. 12 1680; 51-664, pl/jv, Feb. 3 1702; 33-20, jv/munv, July 21 1679; 45-631, Royal Africa Company Assistants, 1695. After John inherited, Roberts' son-in-law John Deale paid John's debts and sent news about ships. Roberts' other sons-in-law wrote to John from the Levant. 50-119, J. Deale/jv, Aug. 24 1697; 50-97, J. Deale/jv,

Sept. 23 1697; Woodhead, *The Rulers of London*, 83–4, 139; De Krey, 'Trade, Religion, and Politics', iii, appendices; CLRO Inventory No. 1416, 22 July 1678.

94. A. Jessop (ed.), *The Lives of the Norths* (1890), ii. 3, 194–7, 226, 250–1; Grassby, *The English Gentleman in Trade*.

95. Woodhead, *The Rulers of London*, 102–3; De Krey, 'Trade, Religion, and Politics', iii, appendices; CLRO BR/C 1. 9/4 and 15; CLRO BR/R1, fo. 58; CLRO BR/BI/2; CLRO, BR/B/4034, 4035; PRO PROB 11/519, fo. 30; GH MS 15208; G. Lipscomb, *The History and Antiquities of the County of Buckingham* (1847), iv. 231; 54-307, jv/jkna, Sept. 25 1710.

96. G. Torriano, *Of Italian Proverbs* (1666). In 1660 he donated his 'dictionary of the Italian tongue very useful to merchants' to the Levant Company library in Aleppo. 50-383, ctor/jv, June 1 1698; 51-443, ctor/jv, May 23 1701; Woodhead, *The Rulers of London*, 163–4; M. Priestley, 'London Merchants and Opposition Politics in Charles II's Reign', *Historical Research*, 29 (1956), 207, 210, 215; G. Ambrose, 'The Levant Company', B.Litt. thesis (Oxford, 1932), 47; H. Roseveare (ed.), *Markets and Merchants of the Late Seventeenth Century* (Oxford, 1987), 583; CLRO BR/C 1.9, no. 4; CLRO BR/R1, fo. 99; CLRO BR/BI/2; CLRO, BR/B/7069; De Krey, 'Trade, Religion, and Politics', iii, appendices; GH MS 2480/1, fo. 180. A. Jewers, *Monumental Inscriptions of London*, i. *1910–1913*; PRO SP 105/154, fos. 327–9, 338; PRO E401/ 2593, fos. 13, 40, 41; PRO SP110/73, fo. 83; PRO PROB 11/381, fo. 157.

97. CLRO MS 33, fo. 9; T. Dale, Index to the liverymen of London 1700 and 1710, fo. 16, 1933; *The London Directory of 1677*, reprint, 1878; PRO E401/2593, fo. 17; Berks CRO, D/EZ 5 B1, Henry Hunter's Journal, fos. 5–6, Aug. 31 1660; 50-625, sbax/jv, Apr. 19 1699; 51-17, pbax/jv, July 26 1699; 53-152, jv/pbax, Jan. 14 1706; 51-106, sbax/jv, Oct. 24 1699; 51-162, Royal Africa Company Assistants, 1701.

98. 28-25, jv/rv, Mar. 16 1675; 41-10, jv/rv, July 28 1686; 42-17, jv/rv, July 20 1687; Wood, *A History of the Levant Company* (Oxford, 1935), 208. 30-2, Royal Africa Company/jv, Nov. 8 1676.

99. V. Dearing, 'A Walk through London with John Gay and a Run with Daniel Defoe', in J. Plumb and V. Dearing (eds.), *Some Aspects of Eighteenth-Century England* (Los Angeles, 1971), 35; 28-27, jv/rv, Apr. 15 1675; *Great Britain's Glory: Or a Brief Description of the . . . Royal Exchange* (1672); *A Trip from St James's to the Royal-Exchange* (1744); A. Saunders (ed.), *The Royal Exchange* (1997).

100. The walking tour is based upon letters, maps, and Strype, *A Survey*.

101. CH 7/51, 52, 55, 56, Business papers, 1675–88. Thomas Green and Joseph Andrews cut and pressed John's broadcloths. 23-19, munv/jv, June 26 1670; 28-40, jv/munv Aug. 19 1675; 30-22 jv, rv, Mar. 22 1677; 30-48, jv/rv, Oct. 8 1677.

102. For example PRO SP 105/163, fo. 3.

103. Verney is not included in a 1688 list of active merchants trading to Smyrna found in BL Trumbull Add. MS 95. In June 1685 Verney was the 54th subscriber for £100 in the Morea currants joint stock. In May 1687 he was still selling off proceeds of an earlier trade, and in November 1690 he told Ralph: 'I have goods which I would willingly sell before Christmas'. In 1691 he noted his £147 loss in two Russian ships taken by the French. As late as November 1692, John wrote of his £170 concern in Captain Humphreys' ship that had been attacked on the high seas after it left Aleppo. 41-75, B. Saltonstall/jv Mar. 24 1687; 44-49, jv/rv, Nov. 26 1690; 45-17, jv/rv, Aug. 3 1691; 46-190, jv/rv, Nov. 9 1692, SP 110/154.

104. CH 7/51/1-7, 9-14 and 7/52/1-14 include lists of merchants, ships, regulations, and

investments. Values of John's exports varied, but one shipment was worth 4,232 lion dollars in 1677. Another sent in 1678 on the *Asia* and *Barnardiston* comprised 170 cloths valued at £1,506. 17*s*. 6*d*. They ranged from a low of £7. 10*s*. 7*d*. to a high of £10. 5*s*. 10*d*. and an average of about £9. John's imports also varied in value with one shipment of Burma silk on the *Mary and Martha* worth over 3,713 lion dollars in April of 1678. Another in 1682 was valued at over 3, 000 lion dollars. Sonia Anderson estimates that a lion dollar equalled 4*s*. 6*d*. in 1681, while *An Arithmologia . . .* (1693), 115, published in 1693 gives the value of a Lyon dollar at 3*s*. 4p.

See also PRO Levant Company records: Port books, imposition books, Treasurer's ledger books and court minutes. PRO SP 105/167 has records of Verney's exports from 1672 to 1681 (for example, fos. 50, 54, 57, 63, 77, 80, 82, and unnumbered folios from May 1677 to July 1680) sent by the *Thomas and William, Turkey Merchant, Mary and Martha, Levant Merchant, Scipio, Prosperous, Asia, Barnardiston, Anne,* and the *Loyalty.* He also used two private ships, the *Provident* and the *Palestine* in the 1670s. His imports returned on these ships and the *Smyrna Factor, New African, Blossom,* and the *Mediterranean*. PRO SP 105/163, fo. 3 cites a £30 fine paid as an adventurer in 1683 and £120. 10*s*. 1*d*. paid for cloth, fo. 65 cites a £25 fine paid as an adventurer in 1685. A gap in the sources exists until 1694 (PRO SP 105/168) when Verney is no longer listed. PRO SP 105/166 shows imports from 1669 to 1673 when Verney was in Aleppo. William Roberts (fo. 27), Gabriel Roberts (fo. 228), and William Paulden (fo. 5) were regular receivers. PRO SP 105/168 lists outbound duties, 1694–1701. Verney is not on this list.

Citations to specific trades include *Imports*: 28-33, jv/ Mr. Hammond, June 5 1675; 28-49 jv/rv, Sept. 2 1675; 29-32, Capt. P. Hayes/jv, Sept. 20 1676; 29-43, wblu/jv, May 30 1676; 29-44, Capt. Pemberton/jv, Sept. 19 [1676?]; 29-50, Capt. P. Hayes/jv, Oct. 1676; 29-52, N. Orton/jv, Oct. 27 1652; 30-25, wblu, jv, Apr. 25 1677; 30-31, wblu/jv, June 2 1677; 30-35, jv/rv, n.d.; 30-36, wblu/jv, June 5 1677; 30-46, wblu/jv, Aug. 7 1677; 31-11, jshe/jv, Jan. 20 1678; 31-14 jshe/jv Jan. 28 1678; 31-29, wblu/jv, Mar. 22 1678; 31-37, jshe/jv, Apr. 27 1678; CH7/90, Affirmation of Bill of Lading, Dec. 14 1678; 34-15, jshe/jv, Feb. 2 1680; 34-16, jshe/jv, Feb. 8 1680; 34-110, jshe/jv, June 15 1680; 35-14, jv/Mr. Gotham, Apr. 2 1681; 38-23, nn/jv, Oct. 24 1683; 38-60, J. Hanger/jv, May 7 1684; CH 4/5/37/68, Cloth to Smyrna, 1684–5; CH 4/5/37/69, Nov. 7 1684; 39-39, J. Hanger/jv, Mar. 1685; 43-7, J. Hanger/jv, Mar. 30 1685. *Export* citations: 31-16, jshe/jv, Jan. 28 1678; 33-105, jv/rv, Nov. 27 1679; 34-56, jv/rv, May 6 1680.

105. K. Davies, *The Royal African Company* (1957), 60.
106. PRO T70/100–101, General Court minutes, 1671–1720; PRO T70/76–88, Court of Assistants minutes, 1664–1713; PRO T70/107–111, Committee on Accounts, 1680–90; PRO T70/125, 128–30, Committee on Goods, 1680–2, 1692–1720. Stock ledgers and journals examined for references to Verney, Sir Gabriel Roberts, and others: T70/178–9; T70/185–191, 195, 197; T70/1613. PRO T70/78, 81–88 show that John attended the following number of Court of Assistants' meetings (with General Court meetings in parentheses): 1679, 74 (3); 1680, 79 (3); 1681 52 (3); 1686 53 (1); 1687 36 (2); 1688 49 (3); 1691 34 (5); 1692 42 (4); 1696 25 (2); 1697 22 (2). The total was 466 (28) meetings.
107. 41-10, jv/rv, July 28 1686; 42-17, jv/rv, July 20 1687.
108. PRO T70/107, fos. 24–5; PRO T70/78, fo. 205; 42-39, jv/rv, Dec. 6 1687; Davies, *The Royal African Company,* 158; 33-13, jv/rv, July 17 1679; 32-136, jv/rv, May 15 1679; 32-146, jv/rv, June 5 1679; 33-88, jv/rv, Oct. 30 1679.

109. From Jan. 20 1679 to Jan. 11 1680, he received £30. 1s. 8d. for attending 76 of 86 meetings of the Committee of Accounts, on which he served every year of his Assistantship. PRO T70/107, Feb. 3 1681. Gratuities ranged from a low of £24. 8s. in 1692 to £32. 5s. 2d. in 1686. PRO T70/81; PRO T70/83.

110. 46-355, rv/jv, Mar. 12 1693; 48-282, jv/rv, June 6 1695; 29-6, jv/munv, Dec. 22 1675; 43-8, rv/jv, Sept. 2 1688; 44-340, rv/jv, Nov. 11 1693; 46-12, rv/jv, Dec. 14 1692.

111. M. Davies, 'Country Gentry and Payments to London 1650–1714', *EcHR*, 2nd series, 24 (1971), 15–36; Broad, 'Sir Ralph Verney and His Estates, 1630–1696', D. Phil. thesis (Oxford, 1973), 293; 32-16, jv/rv, Oct. 24 1678; *Corporation-Credit, or a Bank of Credit made Current by Common Consent in London* (1682), 3; *Bank-Credit: or the . . . Bank of Credit Examined* (1683), 9–15.

112. 31-81, jv/rv, Aug. 29 1678; 31-82, rv/jv, Sept. 2 1678; 32-2, jv/rv, Sept. 5 1678; 33-62, jv/rv, Sept. 22 1679; 33-72, jv/rv, Oct. 2 1679.

113. John invested in bottomry loans which could gross as much as 36%. Roseveare (ed.), *Markets and Merchants*; V. Barbour, 'Marine Risks and Insurance in the Seventeenth Century', *Journal of Economic and Business History*, 1 (1929), 561–96; W. Winter, *A Short Sketch of the History and Principles of Marine Insurance*, 2nd edn. (New York, 1935); Grassby, *Rate of Profit*, 741; 32-143, Capt. J. Andrews/jv, June 2 1679; CH 7/54, Grant, E. Clapp, mariner, to John Verney, $\frac{1}{32}$ part of ship called the 'Asia', June 29 1681.

114. 5 guineas earned 30 guineas if the *Nathaniel* arrived after June 9 1686, while 10 pieces of gold earned 25 guineas if a Constantinople vessel arrived safely in 1687. 41-40, Assurance upon life of T. Draper, Dec. 6 1686; 41-51, Assurance on the *Rose*, Mar. 12 1687; 40-59, E. Bulwer/jv, Apr. 9 1687; 41-46, W. Sweeting/jv, Jan. 19 1687; 41-34, W. Broughton/jv, Nov. 25 1686; 41-43, J. Flavell/jv, Dec. 8 1686.

115. Broad, 'Sir Ralph Verney and his Estates', 138–9; 40-59, E. Bulwer/jv, Apr. 9 1687; 43-85, jv/wc, May 15 1689; 45-21, jv, 'Wasing Rent Rolls', [June 1691?]; 43-53, jv, [1689?]; 43-110, rv/jv, 1689; 44-61, Particulars of Capt. H. Ferriman's estate, n.d. 39-55, jv/rv, Mar. 25 1685. Grassby in *Rate of Profit* estimates return on London real estate at 8%.

116. North was a more successful trader and received income from corporate office and a wealthy wife. From 1680 to 1691 his total net income from trade totalled only £3,701 in comparison with £8,197 from finance, and 6,254 from office. Grassby, *The English Gentleman in Trade*, 77–8, 86, 182. The Dashwood papers cite a similar turn from trade. Bodl D. D. Dashwood MS A. 1/6, c. 1, May 7 1690.

117. P. Dickson, *The Financial Revolution in England* (1967), 12; L. Neal, *The Rise of Financial Capitalism* (Cambridge, 1990); C. Nicolson, *Writing and the Rise of Finance* (Cambridge, 1994).

118. Dickson, *The Financial Revolution;* D. W. Jones, 'London Overseas Merchant Groups'; Davies, *The Royal African Company;* C. Jones, '"A Fresh Division Lately Grown Up Amongst Us"', *Historical Research*, 68 (1995), 302–17.

119. PRO E401/2594, Subscription book . . . Bank of England; PRO C114/16, Million Bank subscriber list; PRO E401/2593, Subscriptions to a loan at 8% . . . July 14 1698; India Office, IO HM 1–3, List of adventurers and accounts, 1675, 1691, 1693, 1694, 1696, 1699, 1701–1703, 1707; IO L/AG/1/1/5, fo. 445; IO L/AG/1/1/9, fos. 109, 344, and L/AG/1/1/10, fo. 381; Bank of England ledgers A (1) fo. 29. C (3) fo. 1010. (5), fo. 218. (9), fo. 4406. BL Egerton MS 3359, fos. 58–61, List of those proprietors of the Bank of England who are qualified to Vote . . . 1710. Verney is listed in fo. 59.

120. 45-49, rp1/jv, Apr. 14 1692; 55-390, hh/jv, Oct. 7 1714; Broad, 'Sir Ralph Verney and His Estates', 8; H. Bowen, *Elites, Enterprise, and the Making of the British Overseas Empire 1688–1775* (1996), 63; 31-72, jv/rv, Aug. 8 1678.

121. 31-72, jv/rv, Aug. 8 1678; 35-105, jv/rv, Bond for £200, Aug. 1681; 42-6, rv/rpau, June 12 1687; 45-49, rp1/jv, Apr. 14 1692; 52-279, cst/jv, Oct. 12 1703; 55-390, hh/jv, Oct. 7 1714; CH 8/49, Will of Mary Gape, Aug. 14 1680.

122. John invested £500 in 1690 (PRO E401/1986, fo. 236), £900 in 1691/2 (1988, fos. 182, 340), £500 in 1692/3 (1991, fo. 433), £300 in 1696, £600 in 1697/8 (2000, fo. 288), £1,000 in 1698/9 (2002, fos. 536, 573), £1,000 in 1700/1 (2006, fos. 298, 319, 327), £500 in 1701/2 (2008, fo. 413), and £2,000 in 1702 (2009, fos. 94, 113, 120 and 2010, fo. 209). The 1696 amount does not appear in the PRO records but is found in 49-379, T. Cuddon/jv, Dec. 16 1696.

123. 44-51, Numbered orders for annuities, June 16 1693; 49-640, List of numbered orders for annuities, May 5 1694; CH 7/61, 'Order to Pay £15 p.a. to John Verney out of the Exchequer as Interest on £150 Lent by JV for War against France', May 5 1694 lists yearly payments through 1774 when Margaret Cave, the surviving nominee, died.

124. 49-640, Compilation of numbered orders for . . . annuities, May 22 1695; PRO E401/2275, fo. 76. Despite references which affirm ownership, John and his beneficiaries do not appear in other lists of annuity subscribers such as *A Particular Accompt of the . . . Late Million Act . . .* (1694); *A List of Reversionary Annuities . . . Million Bank . . . 1695*; *A List of Surviving Nominees . . . for the Year 1693 and the Sums . . . Paid . . .* (1730); PRO E401/2593; PRO C114/16, Million Bank subscriber list 1695–1700; BL Harley MS 7497-8, *South Sea Subscribers*, 1711; *A List of the Names of Such Proprietors of South Sea Capital Stock . . .* (1823).

125. 44-28, lg/rv, Apr. 1 1690; 46-388, lg/jv, Mar. 24 1693; 46-401, lg/jv, Apr. 5 [misdated, 1693?]; 46-488, pst/rv, May 24 1693; 46-522, pst/rv, June 12 1693; 47-374, cst/rv, Apr. 29 1694; 47-392, cst/rv, May 8 1694; 49-381, eli/jv, Mar. 1 [1696?]; 53-648, ist/jv, Aug. 31 1708; CH 4/6/47/2, Aug. 24 1700, Annuity no. 2204 dated July 7 1693 for £14 per year for Pen Stewkeley Viccars.

126. 47-157, jv/rv, Nov. 2 1693; 47-169, jv/rv, Nov. 11 1693; 47-374, cst/rv, Apr. 29 1694; 47-375, lg/rv, Apr. 24 1694; 47-640, jv/pl, Oct. 14 1694; 48-3, nn/jv, Oct. 11 1694; 48-10, lg/rv, Oct. 16 1694; *Advice to the Women and Maidens of London . . .* (1678); Blackstone, *Commentaries on the Laws of England*, i. (New York, 1827), 343.

127. 47-169, jv/rv, Nov. 11 1693; 48-321, lg/rv, July 17 1695; 50-23, jv/nn, May 22 1697; 49-508, wbus/jv, Jan. 16 1697; CH 1/125; CH 1/141d.

128. John missed only one year when there was 'not at present public fund to let at'. 50-322, Exchequer/jv, Mar. 24 1698; 50-342, Exchequer/jv, Apr. 18 1698; 51-418, jv/T. Bethell, Mar. 20 1701; 51-566, jv/ttip, Nov. 14 1700; 51-649, jv, [1702?]; 53-183, pl/jv, Feb. 3 1700; PRO E401/1985–2040.

129. 50-245, East India Company/jv, Dec. 22 1697. IO, HM 2, fos. 44, 90, 140, 1694 and HM 3, fos. 45, 93, 143, 163, 1701–1707 in the India Office library itemize John's holdings up to £147. 2s. of stock. Letters show that John had more at various times. 51-15, jv, Sept. 1 1699; 51-43, jv/nm, Aug. 27 1699.

130. Broad, 'Sir Ralph Verney and his Estates', 138–42, and 'Gentry Finances', 183–200; 51-129, sbax/jv, Nov. 16 1699; 51-399, jv/pl, Feb. 1 1702; 51-410, J. Warner/jv, Mar. 12 1701; 51-411, rh/jv, Mar. 21 1701; 51-443, ctor/jv, May 23 1701; 51-566, jv/ttip, Nov. 14 1700; 52-84, jv/pl, Aug. 22 1702; 53-15, pl/jv, July 16 1705.

131. 52-215, rp1/jv, Apr. 22 1703; 52-492, jn/jv, June 15 1704; CH 2/433a, b, Deed, June 29/30 1704; CH 1/228, Mortgage, July 1 1704

132. The £800 was from Royal Africa and East India Companies, Million Bank, lottery tickets, annuities, and loans. 52-433, Account with Peter Lupart, July 1703–April 1705; Broad, 'Gentry Finances', 198. CH 4/6/9, *British Merlin*, 1689–1711 records John's rent receipts *c*.1704–9. John never stopped investing in the city and continued to have interests in shipping.

133. PRO T70/100, fo. 99; T70/185, fos. 6, 7, 21, 30, 37, 40, 46, 49, 53, 58, 62, 69, 81; PRO T70/187, Mar. 10 1688; PRO T70/188, fo. 5, July 16 1691, fo. 20, July 30 1691, fos. 116, 118, 120, April 20 1693; PRO T70/83, Aug. 4 1691 and Jan. 21 1692 notes two of John's bonds of £558. 8*s*. and £1,421. In 1693 John was credited with £1,600, Sir Gabriel Roberts with £2,800, George Nicholas with £800.

134. 45-40, jv/rv, Apr. 30 1692; 47-7, nn/jv, Aug. 8 1693; 47-29, nn/jv, Aug. 22 1693; 47-97, jv/rv, Oct. 4 1693; PRO T70/85, Jan. 4, 1698, Feb. 8 1698, June 21, 1698; PRO T70/189, fos. 50, 58; PRO T70/190, fo. 79; PRO T70/191, fo. 91. John was constantly asked for more money. Sir Gabriel Roberts was credited with £5,200 in December 1697 but sold in March 1699.

135. 52-23, jv/pl, Aug. 1 1702; 52-36, pl/jv, Dec. 12 1702; 53-707, hh/jv, Dec. 4 1708; 51-701, pl/jv, Mar. 31 1702; 54-527, J. Eavens/jv, Jan. 3 1712. Peter Lupart 'with a great deal of trouble' sold John's bonds at high discounts. 51-485, pl/jv, Aug. 19 1701; 51-499, jv/pl, Oct. 5 1701. In March 1702 John bought 10 shares at £12 each from Mr. Baxter. PRO T70/197, fo. 147. By 1709 the company was insolvent.

136. 51-205, ea/jv, Mar. 5 1700; 52-716, jv/ist, Mar. 4 1705.

137. *The Mystery of the New Fashioned Goldsmiths or Bankers* (1676); J. Clapham, *The Bank of England* (Cambridge, 1945), 9; 29-28, jv/rv, Mar. 16 1676; 37-30, rp1/jv, Feb. 22 1683; 37-47, rv/jv, Apr. 26 1683; D. Mitchell (ed.), *Goldsmiths, Silversmiths, and Bankers* (1995).

138. 35-136, rv/jv, Sept. 15 1681; D. Coleman, 'London Scriveners and the Estate Market in the Late Seventeenth Century', *EcHR*, 2nd series, 4 (1951), 221–30; F. Melton, 'Deposit Banking in London 1700–1900', in Davenport-Hines *et al.* (eds.), *Business in the Age of Reason* (1987).

139. 29-28, jv/rv, Mar. 16 1676; 37-30, rp1/jv, Feb. 22 1683; 37-47, rv/jv, Apr. 26 1683; Sir A. Heal, *The London Goldsmiths 1200–1800* (1972).

140. Cogges later bought land in Buckinghamshire. Lipscomb, *History and Antiquities*, iv. 457; Woodhead, *The Rulers of London*, 72–3; Beaven, *The Aldermen of the City of London*, ii. 111; De Krey, 'Trade, Religion, and Politics', iii, appendices; 47-179, rv/jv, Nov. 14 1692; HL ST 175, July 1681, Aug. 1684; Jessop, *The Lives of the Norths*, ii. 174–5; F. Price, *A Handbook of London Bankers* (1876), 39, 40, 55, 61. Both men appear in *A List of Goldsmiths Keeping Running Cashes . . .* (1677) in Price, 158, and in Heal, *The London Goldsmiths*, 127, 154. Clapham, *The Bank of England*, 5–6; 46-156, po/jv, Oct. 19 1692.

141. CLRO, *Research Guide* 2: Sworn Brokers' Archives, Draft Report (1995); 8 & 9 William III, C 32, *An Act to Restrain the Number and Ill-Practice of Brokers and Stock-jobbers*, [1697]; CLRO MS 96, fos. 203-8.

142. *An Act for the Regulation of Brokers upon the Royal Exchange* (1673); *Reasons . . . for Continuing the Late Brokers Act* ([1700]); Corporation of London, *Order against Exchange Brokers Obstructing the Thoroughfare* (1700); *A Letter from a Merchant in*

London to a Member of Parliament ([1708?]); *Reasons for Passing the Bill . . . to Restrain the Number and Ill Practices of Brokers and Stock-jobbers* ([1711]).

143. Dickson, *The Financial Revolution*, 487; J. Francis, *Chronicles and Characters of the Stock Exchange* (Boston, 1850), 9–10; J. Houghton, *A Collection for the Improvement of Husbandry and Trade*, 4 vols. (Mar. 30 1692–Sept. 2 1703), i–iv.

144. 50-458, pl/jv, Aug. 9 1698.

145. 42-23, rh/jv, Aug. 6 1687; 45-43, pl/jv, Mar. 4 1692. For Peter Lupart, see: GH MS 5587/1, Fishmongers' Company, May 8 1689; GH MS 5576/2, Feb. 3 1681; GH MS 4049/2, fos. 49, 85; GH MS 2480/1, fo. 49; J. Malcolm, *London Redivivum* (1803), i. 55; GH IGI Index: CLRO MS 6, fo. 19; CLRO MS CF 28/1; PRO C114/16; Heal, *London Goldsmiths*, 197. For the Hoares: see Beaven, *The Aldermen of the City of London*, i. 53; ii, 120; 'Sir Richard Hoare's Vindication, March 16, 1708', *Tracts Relating to Trade . . . #11*; PRO PROB, 11/567, fo. 9; H. Hoare, *Hoare's Bank* (1955); Dale, *Index*, fo. 116; GH Index to Middlesex Polls, 1705, 1714, 1768; GH Middlesex Poll Book, 1714; C. Clay, 'Henry Hoare, Banker, his Family, and the Stourhead Estate', in F. Thompson (ed.), *Landowners, Capitalists, and Entrepreneurs* (Oxford, 1994), 113–38. John opened an account in 1680 at Hoare's Bank as noted in HB Miscellaneous Record Book, 161. HB Ledgers Nos. 2–5 note running balances for John from 1698 to 1705 and active accounts.

146. 54-324, hh/jv, Oct. 21 1710; I. Christie, *British 'Non Elite' MPs 1715–1820* (New York and Oxford, 1995); *The Poll of the Livery-Men of the City of London . . .* (1710); *Advice to the Livery-Men of London Showing that it is for their Interest and Honour, to Choose the Merchants in Trade for their Representatives in Parliament* (1713).

147. See Ch. 1 and the work of Natalie Davis.

148. 46-195, rv/jv, Nov. 13 1692; 46-565, nn/jv, June 30 1693. During this period, Andrew Archer invested in London joint stock companies and married into the Dashwood family. His younger brother was an architect who appeared to be 'a London rather than a county figure'. A. Mimardiere, 'The Finances of a Warwickshire Gentry Family, 1693–1726', *University of Birmingham Historical Journal*, 9 (1963–4), 130–145; Bowen, *Elites, Enterprise* 47–78; J. Cliffe, *The Puritan Gentry Besieged 1650–1700* (1993), 166.

149. 48-517, jv/rv, Sept. 12 1695; 48-476, lg/rv, Aug. 29 [misdated, 1693?]; 47-123, rv/jv, Oct. 15 1693; 20-2, rv/jv, Dec. 19 1664.

150. *Remarques upon Remarques*, 117–18; Miege, *The Present State*, 63; J. Raven, *Judging New Wealth* (Oxford, 1992), 84, 90–1, 96-8; J. McVeagh, *Tradeful Merchants* (1981); N. McKendrick, '"Gentleman and Players" Revisited', in N. McKendrick and R. Outhwaite (eds.), *Business Life and Public Policy* (Cambridge, 1986), 21–37; *The Spectator* (1930), May 19 1711, i. 262–3.

151. M. Hunt, 'English Urban Families in Trade 1660–1800', Ph. D. thesis (New York, 1986), and N. Rogers, 'Money, Land and Lineage', *Social History*, 4 (1979), 437–54, but see Bowen, *Elites, Enterprise Empire*, 68–9.

152. Broad 'Sir Ralph Verney and his Estates', 225–7; P. Cain and A. Hopkins, *British Imperialism: Innovation and Expansion 1688–1914* and *British Imperialism: Crisis and Deconstruction 1914–1990* (1993); Sylvia Thrupp, *The Merchant Class of Medieval London 1300–1500* (Chicago, 1948), 247; Larry Stewart, *The Rise of Public Science* (Cambridge, 1992), 162–9.

153. J. Chown, *A History of Money from A.D. 800* (1994), 60–6. J. Agnew, *Worlds Apart* (Cambridge, 1986), 50, 53; J. Eatwell (ed.), *The New Palgrave* (1987), iii. 519–25.

154. 31-7, rv/jv, Dec. 17 1677; 32-130, rv/jv, Apr. 4 1679; 48-426, jv/rv, Aug. 10 1695.

155. W. Darrell, *The Gentleman Instructed*, 4th edn. (1709), 29; 47-43, po/rv, Sept. 4 1693; J. Beckett, *Coal and Tobacco* (Cambridge, 1981), 17.

156. 47-61, jv/rv, Sept. 13 1693; 48-638, List of proverbs, [1695?]; 51-361, lg/jv, Dec. 25 1700.

157. 'The Anatomy of Exchange Alley', in Francis, *Chronicle and Characters of the Stock Exchange*, 148–9.; J. Pocock, *The Machiavellian Moment* (Princeton, 1975), 447, and *Virtue, Commerce, and History* (Cambridge, 1985); G. Holmes, *British Politics in the Reign of Queen Anne* (1987), 148–52; Bowen, *Elites, Enterprise*, 61.

158. 53-687, jv/ttip, Nov. 11 1708; Bucks CRO DX 1069/2/146 and 150, jv/J. Baker, Sept. 25 1715 and Feb. 19 1717.

159. J. Sekoura, *Luxury* (Baltimore, 1977), 23–6; C. Berry, *The Idea of Luxury* (New York and Cambridge, 1994).

160. T. Aston and C. Philpin (eds.), *The Brenner Debate* (Cambridge, 1985); Cain and Hopkins, *British Imperialism*; Beckett, *Coal and Tobacco*; J. Habakkuk, 'The Rise and Fall of English Landed Families 1600–1800', *Transactions of the Royal Historical Society*, 29–31 (1979–81), 187–207, 199–221, 195–217. For an alternative view, see P. O'Brien and D. Heath, 'English and French Landowners 1688–1789', in F. Thompson (ed.), *Landowners*, 23–62.

161. R. Park, 'Human Migration and the Marginal Man', *American Journal of Sociology*, 33 (1928), 893; G. Germani, *Marginality* (New Brunswick, 1980), 27–8; R. Syme, *Colonial Elites* (1958), 17–21; N. Davis, *Women on the Margins* (Cambridge, Mass, 1995), 210; S. Herbst, *Politics at the Margin* (Cambridge, 1994), 15, 176; E. Mizruchi, *Regulating Society* (1983).

162. L. and J. Stone, *An Open Elite?* (Oxford, 1984); M. Daunton, '"Gentlemanly Capitalism" and British Industry, 1820–1914', *Past and Present*, 122 (1989), 119–58; W. Rubinstein, *Elites and the Wealthy in Modern British History* (Brighton, 1987), and 'Debate: "Gentlemanly Capitalism" and British Industry, 1820–1914', *Past and Present*, 132 (1991), 150–70, and 'Reply' by M. J. Daunton, 170–87; H. Perkin, *The Origins of Modern English Society 1780–1880* (1969); F. Thompson, 'Life After Death', *EcHR*, 2nd series, 43 (1990), 40–61, and 'Business and Landed Elites in the 19th Century', in *Landowners*, 139–170; M. Wiener, *English Culture and the Decline of the Industrial Spirit 1850–1980* (Cambridge, 1981). J. Habakkuk in *Marriage, Debt and the Estates System* (Oxford, 1994), 404–76, includes 72 pages listing non-landed purchasers of country estates.

Notes to Chapter 4

1. 47-240, lg/rv, Jan. 2 1694.

2. H. Davis (ed.), *The Prose Works of Jonathan Swift* (Oxford, 1957), iv. 12; C. Geertz, *The Interpretation of Cultures* (New York, 1973); 23-17, rv/munv, Dec. 30 1669; 48-582, jv/jk, Nov. 12 1695; 48-20, ea/rv, Oct. 23 1694.

3. W. Darrell, *The Gentleman Instructed*, 4th edn. (1709), 13–14; [W. Ramesey], *The Gentleman's Companion* (1676), 1–6; O. Walker, *Of Education* (Oxford, 1687), 55–8; J. Dare, *Counsellor Manners* (1673), 8; W. Harrison, *Elizabethan England*, ed. L. Withington (1890), 7–8; T. Smith, *De Republica Anglorum*, ed. L. Alston (Cambridge, 1906), 39–40; P. Coss, 'The Formation of the English Gentry', *Past and Present*, 147 (1985), 38–64; J. Cooper, 'Ideas of Gentility in Early Modern England', in G. Aylmer and J. Morrill (eds.), *Land, Men, and Beliefs* (1983), 43–77; J. Mason,

Gentlefolk in the Making (New York, 1971); P. Corfield, 'The Rivals: Landed and Other Gentleman', in N. Harte and R. Quinault (eds.), *Land and Society in Britain 1700–1914* (Manchester, 1996).

4. G. Miege, *The Present State of Great Britain* (1707), 263–4; C. de Saussure, *A Foreign View of England*, ed. Mme. Van Muyden (1902), 212; A. Bryson, 'Concepts of Civility in England 1560–1685', D.Phil. thesis (Oxford, 1984), 294; P. Berger and T. Luckman, *The Social Construction of Reality* (Harmondsworth, 1987); *Advice to a Son . . .* (Oxford, 1656); *Art of Complaisance* (1673); Galateo, *Of Manners . . .* (1703); W. Nicholls, *The Duty of Inferiors towards their Superior . . .* (1701).

5. M. Agulhon, *Le Cercle dans la France Bourgeoise 1810–1848* (Paris, 1977); *Penitents et Francs-Macons de l'Ancienne Provence* (Paris, 1968); D. Gordon, *Citizens Without Sovereignty* (Princeton, 1994); D. Goodman, *The Republic of Letters* (Ithaca, New York, 1994); D. Shields, *Civil Tongues & Polite Letters* (Williamsburg, Va., 1997); L. Klein, *Shaftesbury and the Culture of Politeness* (New York, 1994); P. Langford, *A Polite and Commercial People* (Oxford, 1989), 'Polite Manners from Sir Robert Walpole to Sir Robert Peel', *Proceedings of the British Academy*, 94 (1996), 103–25, and 'British Politeness and the Progess of Western Manners', *Transactions of the Royal Historical Society*, 7 (1997).

6. Walker, *Of Education*, 57; Cicero, *De Officiis* (Indianapolis, 1974), xxiv. 9, 28; M. Rostvig, *The Happy Man*, ii (New York, 1971); F. Childs, 'Prescriptions for Manners in English Courtesy Literature and their Social Implications, 1690-1760', D.Phil. thesis (Oxford, 1984), 49–60; D. Erasmus, *De Civilitate Morum Puerilium*, trans. R. Whittington (1540); [Allestree], *Gentleman's Calling* (1679).

7. J. Revel, 'The Uses of Civility', in R. Chartier (ed.), *A History of Private Life*, iii. *Passions of the Renaissance* (1989), 202; Bryson, 'Concepts of Civility', iv–v, 5, 58–63, 113–37, 377–81; P. France, *Politeness and its Discontents* (Cambridge, 1992), 57–9; N. Elias, *The Civilizing Process*, i (New York, 1978); M. Becker, *Civility and Society in Western Europe, 1300–1600* (Bloomington, Ind., 1988); M. James, 'English Politics and the Concept of Honour, 1485–1642', *Past and Present*, Supplement no. 3 (1978).

8. J. Barrell, *The Birth of Pandora and the Division of Knowledge* (1992), xiv; J. Pocock, *Virtue, Commerce, and History* (Cambridge, 1985), 48–9; Gordon, *Citizens Without Sovereignty*, 5–6, 33–42, 52–64; Becker, *Civility and Society*, p. xviii.

9. M. Ketcham, *Transparent Designs* (Athens, Ga., 1985), 1–2; J. Loftis, *Comedy and Society from Congreve to Fielding* (Stanford, Calif., 1959).

10. L. Klein, 'Gender and the Public/Private Distinction in the Eighteenth Century', *Eighteenth-Century Studies*, 29 (1995), 104; N. McKendrick *et al.* (eds.), *The Birth of a Consumer Society* (1983); R. Sennett, *The Fall of Public Man* (New York, 1978).

11. Klein, *Shaftesbury*, 10; P. Borsay, *The English Urban Renaissance* (Oxford, 1989), 279; D. Bahlman, *The Moral Revolution of 1688* (New Haven, 1957); *A Letter from a Minister in the Country to a Gentleman in London with a Project of Promoting the Reformation of Manners* (1701); J. Innes, 'Politics and Morals', in E. Hellmuth (ed.), *The Transformation of Political Culture* (Oxford, 1990), 55–118.

12. T. Woodman, *Politeness and Poetry in the Age of Pope* (1989), 14–15; D. Bond (ed.), *The Spectator*, i (Oxford, 1965), introduction; R. Bond, *The Tatler* (Cambridge, Mass., 1971); A. Humphreys, *Steele, Addison, and their Essays* (1959); E. and L. Bloom, *Joseph Addison's Sociable Animal* (Providence, RI, 1971); N. Phillipson, 'Politics and Politeness in the Reigns of Anne and the Early Hanoverians', in J. Pocock (ed.), *The Varieties of British Political Thought 1500–1800* (Cambridge, 1993), 211–45.

13. D. Hume, *Selected Essays* (Oxford, 1993); J. Rendall, *The Origins of the Scottish Enlightenment* (New York, 1978); I. Hont and M. Ignatieff (eds.), *Wealth and Virtue* (Cambridge, 1983); J. Schneider (ed.), *The Scottish Moralists* (Chicago, 1967); G. Davie, *The Scottish Enlightenment* (1981); Klein, 'Property and Politeness in the Early Eighteenth Century Whig Moralists', in J. Brewer and S. Staves (eds.), *Early Modern Conceptions of Property* (1995), 221–33; Pocock, *Virtue, Commerce, and History*, 48–9; J. Brewer, *The Pleasures of the Imagination* (1998).

14. B. Mandeville, *The Fable of the Bees*, i, ed. F. Kaye (Oxford, 1924); T. Horne, 'Bernard Mandeville's Ironic History of Politeness', in G. Schochet (ed.), *Politics, Politeness and Patriotism* (Washington, DC, 1993), 229–44.

15. J. Holmes, *Women, Men, and Politeness* (New York, 1995), 22–4. Psychologists stress the element of 'face' and presentaton of self: E. Goffman, 'The Nature of Deference and Demeanor', *American Anthropologist*, 58 (1956), 497; M. Sifianiou, *Politeness Phenomena in England and Greece* (Oxford, 1992), 39–40, 86. Anthropologists and sociolinguists show that politeness differs cross–culturally, but there are common factors like social distance and forms of address.

16. Klein, *Shaftesbury*, 3–8 and 'The Political Significance of "Politeness" in Early Eighteenth-Century Britain', in G. Schochet (ed.), *Politics, Politeness and Patriotism*, 75–8; *Oxford English Dictionary*, 2nd edn. (Oxford, 1989), xii. 31.

17. P. France, *Politeness and its Discontents*, 56; L. Klein, 'Gender, Conversation, and the Public Sphere in Early Eighteenth-Century England', in J. Still and M. Worton (eds.), *Textuality and Sexuality* (Manchester, 1993), 107–8.

18. M. Cohen, *Fashioning Masculinity* (1996), 42–53; P. Carter, '"Mollies", "Fops", and Men of Feeling', D.Phil. thesis (Oxford, 1995); T. Woodman, *Politeness and Poetry in the Age of Pope* (1989), 11–16.

19. 37-18, rv/jv, Nov. 20 1682; HL ST 175, Sir Richard Temple's day book, Aug. 30 1680; PROB 11/390, fo. 43; 54-461, bwil/jv, Sept. 9 1711. PRO PROB 11/390, fo. 43; C. 8/444/23; James, 'English Politics and the Concept of Honour'; F. Heal, *Hospitality in Early Modern England* (Oxford, 1990).

20. 35-112, srt/rv, Aug. 1681; 47-479, D. Bridgeman/rv, July 6 1694; 47-69, M. Whitmore/rv, Sept. 21 1693; 28-39, munv/rv, Aug. 19 1675; 35-67, rv/jv, May 23 1681.

21. 23-17, rv/munv, Dec. 30 1669; 26-5, rv/munv, May 22 1673; 38-28, rv/eli, Dec. 13 1683; 38-29, rv/jv, Dec. 25 1683. Ralph paid 7 servants board wages: the steward, house-keeper, two maids, gardener, keeper and boy. Elizabeth Baker gave James and Will board wages of 4s. /week to provide 'only for themselves'. 54-387, ebv/jv, Jan. 8 1711; 35-108, rv/jv, Aug. 7 1681.

22. 35-71, rv/jv, [May 1681?]; 35-103, rv/jv, July 23 1681; 36-31, rv/jv, Dec. 15 1681; 35-46, jv/rv, Apr. 25 1681.

23. 35-132, jv/rv, May 22 1681; 51-38, nn/jv, Aug. 24 1699; 35-70, jv/rv, May 26 1681. C. Levi-Strauss in *The Elementary Structure of Kinship* (Boston, 1967), 56, discusses food exchange. Rich foods like venison were selected for shared consumption.

24. 50-251, jn/jv, 1697; 55-473, wv/jv, Jan. 6 1715; 47-58, lg/rv, Sept. 12 1693; 55-472, wv/jv, Jan. 4 1715.

25. J. Wildeblood, *The Polite World* (1973), 116–23, 142–51; 46-18, po/rv, July 12 1692; 46-558, lg/rv, June 27 1693.

26. Dare, *Counsellor Manners*, 7, 18–19; Childs, 'Prescription for Manners', 146–227; *The Gentleman's Library* (1715), 72, 77; Walker, *Of Education*, 225, 258; PRO T70/107, fo. 11;

The Lady's Preceptor (1743), 49; [N.H.], *The Ladies Dictionary* (1694), 315–16; [A. de Courtin], *The Rules of Civility* (1671), 114–19.

27. 53-172, ea/jv, Feb. 22 1706; 32-52, munv/rv, May 5 1681; 51-213, lg/rv, Mar. 19 1699; 51-587, lg/jv, Dec. 3 1700; 54-359, ebv/jv, Dec. 2 [1710?].

28. 47-77, lg/rv, Sept. 19 1693; 47-314, lg/rv, Mar. 1 1694; 55-639, ml/jv, Dec. 27 1715; 56-172, pv/jv, Feb. 8 1717.

29. 50-200, ea/jv, Oct. 24 1697; 54-419, llit/jv, Feb. 8 1711; 54-149, mc/jv, Dec. 6 1709.

30. J. Cartwright (ed.), *The Wentworth Papers* (1883), 61; *Scheme for a New Lottery: Or a Husband and Coach and Six for 40s.* (1732).

31. 46-31, jv/rv, July 20 1692; L. Gowing, *Domestic Dangers* (Oxford, 1996), 265; 33-117, munv/jv, Dec. 10 1679; 37-60, epv/jv, June 25 1683; 33-14, M. Newman/rv, Aug. 15 1679; D. Garrioch, *Neighbourhood and Community in Paris 1740–90* (Cambridge, 1986), 169-70.

32. 54-418, ebv/jv, Feb. 3 1711; C. Morris (ed.), *The Journeys of Celia Fiennes* (1947).

33. 35-65, munv/jv, May 23 1681.

34. 50-206, nn/jv, Nov. 2 1697; 34-47, nn/rv, Apr. 28 1680; *Wentworth Papers*, 39; 55-480, ml/jv, Jan. 20 1716; De Saussure, *A Foreign View of England*, 221.

35. 53-381, ebv/jv, Apr. 9 1706; N. Harte, 'State Control of Dress and Social Change in Pre-Industrial England', in D. Coleman and A. John (eds.), *Trade, Government and Economy* (1976), 132–65; 46-180, lg/rv, Oct. 31 1692.

36. 55-330, pv/jv, May 18 1714; 50-213, lg/jv, Nov. 11 1697; 53-253, jv/ttip, Sept. 21 1706; 54-461, bwil/jv, Sept. 7 1711; A. Gregory, 'Witchcraft, Politics and Good Neighborhood', *Past and Present*, 133 (1991), 31–66; 53-663, cl/jv, Oct. 13 1708; 49-247, nn/jv, Sept. 1 1696; 46-623, mlv/jv, July 12 1693; 53-33, cst/ebv, Aug. 13 1705.

37. 54-169, ea/jv, Aug. 22 1709; 37-42, jv/rv, Apr. 12 1683; 47-148, jv/eli, Nov. 1 1693; 52-621, cst/jv, Jan. 13 1705; 52-662, cst/jv, Jan. 13 1705; 54-85, tc/jv, May 28 1709.

38. 52-194, rp2/jv, Mar. 9 1703; 48-449, rv/jv, Aug. 18 1695; 47-564, jv/rv, Aug. 25 1694; 47-569, jv/rv, Aug. 30 1694.

39. De Courtin, *Rules of Civility*, 114, 118. See Ch. 6.

40. 51-549, lg/jv, Sept. 4 1701; 50-336, wbus/jv, Apr. 12 1698.

41. 40-51, rv/lg, Mar. 10 1686; Bryson, 'Concepts of Civility', 175; H. P[eacham], *The Art of Living in London* (1642) in T. Park (ed.), *Harleian Miscellany* (1808-13), ix. 84–9; J. Evelyn, *A Character of England* (1659), 198; [C. Burnaby], *The Ladies Visiting Day* (1708), 62; *Humours and Conversations of the Town* (1693), 134.

42. 37-60, epv/jv, June 25 1683.

43. M. Slater, *Family Life in the Seventeenth Century* (1984); Broad, 'Sir Ralph Verney and his Estates'.

44. N. Cott, *The Bonds of Womanhood* (New Haven, 1977) and the work of Natalie Davis.

45. 34-38, po/rv, Apr. 21 1680.

46. 34-49, jv/rv, Apr. 29 1680; 34-70, jv/rv, May 17 1680; 34-45, jv/rv, Apr. 26 1680; M. Tebbutt, *Women's Talk* (Aldershot, 1995), 1–18; P. Spacks, *Gossip* (New York, 1985).

47. 34-78, jv/rv, May 26 1680; 34-82, lg/rv, May 28 1680; 34-81, ebv and jv/rv, May 28 1680; 34-85, nn/rv, May 31, 1680; 34-88, nn/jv, May 31 1680; 34-90, lg/rv, May 31 1680.

48. 34-93, lg/rv, June 3 1680; 34-95, jv/rv, June 6 1680.

49. 34-99, rv/jv, June 7 1680; 34-102, jv/rv, June 9 1680; 34-103, lg/rv, June 9 1680.

50. 34-104, jv/rv, June 10 1680; 34-108, rv/jv, June 14 1680.

51. 34-114, jv/rv, June 21 1680.

52. 34-137, nn/jv, July 22 1680; 26-8, rv/nhob, Oct. 9 1676.

53. 36-21, jv/rv, Nov. 26 1681; 37-60, epv/jv, June 25 1683; 46-466, jv/lg, Nov. 3 1695.

54. See the play *Rashomon* and L. Hunt (ed.), *The New Cultural History* (Berkeley, 1982); H. White, *The Content of Form* (Baltimore, 1987); J. Clifford, *The Predicament of Culture* (Cambridge, 1990); *American Historical Review*, 93 (1988).

55. 46-222, nn/rv, Nov. 29 1692; 48-159, jv/rv, Aug. 21 1695; 45-69, jv/rv, May 19 1692; J. Brewer, '"The Most Polite Age and the Most Vicious"', in A. Bermingham and J. Brewer (eds.), *The Consumption of Culture, 1600–1800: Image, Object and Text* (1993), 341.

56. S. Berkowitz, *An Introduction to Structural Analysis* (Toronto, 1982); 35-71, rv/jv, [May 1681?]; 35-103, rv/jv, July 23 1681; 54-145, rp2/rv2, Nov. 24 1709.

57. 34-105, nn/jv, June 12, 1680.

58. De Courtin, *Rules of Civility*, 130.

59. 54-343, jv/rv, Dec. 5 1719; 46-12, jv/rv, July 9 1692; 47-270, J. Sanders/jv, Jan. 17 1694; 50-367, 'Fringemaker's bill to John Verney', May 13 1698.

60. Coach owners described as merchants were often categorized as gentlemen or esquires in the database's later set of figures. I thank Perry Gauci for this insight and Derek Keene and Olwen Myhill for the data.

61. 50-221, lg/jv, Nov. 17, 1697; 55-374, wv/jv, Sept. 2 1714; G. McCracken, *Culture and Consumption* (Bloomington, Ind., 1988).

62. 53-181, jv/Jane Abdy, Mar. 7 1706; 31-23, jv/munv, n.d. (1678?); 52-629, jv/ml, Dec. 6 1704; 54-387, jv/ebv, Jan. 8 1711; 54-81, ebv/jv, Feb. 3 1711; 54-81, jv/rv2, May 22 1709.

63. *The Complete Works of Montaigne*, trans. D. Frame (Stanford, Calif., 1943), 685–99; C. Singer (ed.), *A History of Technology* (Oxford, 1951), ii. 494–547; R. Straus, *Carriages and Coaches* (1912), 34.

64. [H. Peacham], *Coach and Sedan* (1636), repr. 1925, D^v, F^r; J. Crofts, *Packhorse, Wagon and Post* (1967), 110; Straus, *Carriages and Coaches*, 75; J. Parkes, *Travel in England in the Seventeenth Century* (1925), 67–70; [J. Taylor], *The World Runs on Wheels* (1635) and *The Coaches Overthrown* (1636).

65. Sir Edmund Verney was involved in the licensing of hackney coaches. CH 7/2, Letters patent grant, July 14 1637, to the Marquess of Hamilton, and CH 7/3, Grant, May 18 1639, Charles I to Sir Edmund Verney; *Rules, Directions . . . for Regulation of Hackney Coachmen* (London, 1654); Charles II, *A Proclamation to Restrain the Abuses of Hackney Coaches . . .* (1660); *A List of the 400 Hackney-Coaches Licensed in July and Aug. 1662* (1664); Corporation of London, *Order that Constables should Apprehend all Persons Throwing Squibs and Crackers into Coaches* (1684); James II, *A Proclamation for Restraining the Number and Abuses of Hackney Coaches* (1687); *The Case of the Four-Hundred Coach-men . . .* (1687); *The Case of the Commissioners for Hackney Coaches* [1695?]; Straus, *Carriages and Coaches*, 58, 60; H. Nockolds (ed.), *Coachmakers . . . 1677–1977* (1977), 21; Crofts, *Packhorse, Wagon and Post*, 113. A proclamation in 1601 restricting coach use under the rank of knight was followed by similar edicts.

66. *The Constitution Articles of the . . . Coach and Coach-Harness-Makers* (1702); G. Laverick, *Proposals . . . to Prevent the Stop of Coaches in the Street* [1710?]; *The Case of the Seven Hundred Licensed Hackney Coachmen and Widows . . .* [1711?]; *A Bill for the Relief of the 800 Licensed Hackney-Coach-Men* (1716); *The Case of Thomas Blunt . . . and the 800 Licens'd Hackney Coachmen* [1716]; J. Rowe, *All Sorts of Wheel-Carriage Improv'd* (1734); J. Ashton, *Social Life in the Reign of Queen Anne* (New York,

1929), 376; De Saussure, *A Foreign View of England*, 167; *The Tatler*, No. 144, Mar. 11 1709; 53-553, mc/jv, Feb. 29 1708.

67. J. Taylor, *The Carrier's Cosmographie* (1637); *The New Guide to London*, 2nd edn. (1726); *An Account of the Days of the Going Out of all the Carriers, Waggoners, and Stage-Coaches that come to London* [169?]; Parkes, *Travel in England*, 67, 84; 46-140, jv/mlv, Oct. 11 1682. [R. Burridge], *A New Review of London* (1722), 35–40, adds 148 new stages between 1701 and 1721.

68. Crofts, *Packhorse, Wagon and Post*, 1–21; Ashton, *Social Life*, 374; S. Margetson, *Journey by Stages* (1967). For example, when Sir Walter Calverley fell out of his calesh at night, he hurt his ankles and was lame for three weeks. BL Add. MS 27418, fo. 72^r.

69. Singer, *A History of Technology*, ii. 47, 182; Parkes, *Travel in England*, 71; Straus, *Carriages and Coaches*, 109–46; F. Rogers, *A Manual of Coaching* (Philadelphia, 1901); E. Stratton, *The World on Wheels* (New York, 1972).

70. HL EL MS 10152, Nov. 7 1713–April 20 1714; HL STT 432–3, wchap/srt, Apr. 23 and 28 1689; HL STT 420, wchap/srt, Mar. 3 1689.

71. W. Felton, *A Treatise on Carriages Comprehending Coaches, Chariots, Phaetons, Curricles, Whiskeys etc.* (1796); *Oxford English Dictionary*, ii. 544; Rogers, *A Manual of Coaching* (Philadelphia, 1701); De Saussure, *A Foreign View of England*, 167; 53-38, jv/mc, Aug. 17 1704; H. Wheatley (ed.), *The Diary of Samuel Pepys* (New York, 1942), ix. 214, 290, 325; V. Pearl, 'Change and Stability in Seventeenth-Century London', *London Journal*, 5 (1979), 3–34.

72. Straus, *Carriages and Coaches*, 84, 122; Taylor, *The World Runs on Wheels*; Parkes, *Travel in England*, 77.

73. Nockolds, *The Coachmakers*, 68–9; R. Grassby, *The English Gentleman in Trade* (Oxford, 1994), 187; 54-387, ebv/jv, Jan. 8 1711; CH 7/53, Household account, 1682/3. For coach costs, see HL STT 351, wchap/srt, Jan. 30 1687; HL ST 175 and HL STT 432, wchap/srt, April 23 1689; Rosenheim, *The Townshends of Raynham*, 77; 34-178, rv/jv, Nov. 15 1680; 44-50, jv/rv, Aug. 20 1690; 50-367, 'Fringe makers bill to John Verney', May 13 1698.

74. HL STT 434–5, wchap/srt, April 28 and May 5 1689; HL STTF 59/1; HL ST 155; HL EL 11063, Nov. 8, Nov. 23, Dec. 19, Dec. 21 1706, Dec. 2 1707, Jan. 8 1708; HL EL 8650, 10152, 10206, [late 17th and 18th cent.]; PRO PROB 4/21162, 1683, PROB 4/2571, 1698; PROB 4/7324, 1662, Coachmen's inventories. The Bakers of Penn paid their coachman an annual salary of £6. Bucks CRO D/X 1351/67, 68.

75. 35-87, rv/jv, June 16 1681; 40-72, rv/jv, June 18, 1686; 48-275, ea/rv, June 4 1695; 49-73, rv/wc, May 29 1696.

76. 51-688, lg/jv, Mar. 19, 1702; 31-63, jv/munv, June 4 1678; 49-106, jv/wc, April 29 1696; 53-507, jv/ml, Jan. 29 1708.

77. 34-182, jv/rv, Nov. 20 1680; 34-60, jv/rv, Oct. 21 1680; 33-37, jv/munv, Aug. 7 1679; M. Sorbiere, *A Journey to London in the Year 1698* (1699), 3–4; *The Tatler*, No. 144, Mar. 11 1709.

78. 34-159, rv/jv, Oct. 21 1680; 34-173, jv/rv, Nov. 8 1680; 34-178, rv/jv, Nov. 15 1680; 48-511, jv/rv, Sept. 16 1695; 48-321, jv/rv, July 17 1695; 47-270, J. Sanders/jv, Jan. 17 1694; 49-103, rv/jv, April 15 1696.

79. 48-364, nden/jv, June 30 1695; 48-341, nden/jv, July 7 1695; 48-409, jv/rv, Aug. 1 1695; 48-287, nden/jv, June 11 1695; 46-12, jv/rv, July 9 1692; 48-287, nden/jv, June 11 1695.

80. 53-9, jv/wbus, June 19 1705. CH 1/147 and CH 1/163, second version dated February 16, 1723. John's son Ralph left his wife Catherine 'my coach machine and chariot and

best pair of houses and their harness'. In HL STTP 14/11, Sir Richard Temple left his wife all of his coaches and coach horses.

81. 46-576, lg/rv, July 4 1693; 47-84, lg/rv, Sept. 27 1693; 48-289, June 13 1695; 50-331, lg/jv, Apr. 3 1698; 35-96, lg/rv, July 14 1681; 31-33, jv/rv, April 18 1678.
82. 50-595, ebv/wc, Mar. 4 1699; 48-465, jv/rv, Aug. 24 1695; 50-56, jv/wc, June 16 1697.
83. 43-16, lg/rv, Sept. 12 1688; L. Davidoff, *The Best Circles* (1973), 16; 47-562 through 47-600, Aug/Sept. 1694; 47-565, rv/jv, Aug. 25 1694; 48-20, ea/rv, Oct. 23 1694.
84. 51-542, jv/Mr. Wotton, Aug. 27 1700.
85. 51-542, jv/Mr. Wotton, Aug. 27 1700; 49-282, cst/jv, Oct. 12 1696; Rostvig, *The Happy Man*, 26. Lady Mary Wortley Montagu wrote to Mr Pope: 'I won't trouble you . . . with farewell compliments, which I think generally as impertinent as curtseys at leaving the room, when the visit has been too long already.' *Letters*, Sept. 14 1716, quoted in Wildeblood, *The Polite World*, 145.
86. *The Gentleman's Library*, 205; 38-75, wd/rv, Oct. 18 1683; H. Morley (ed.), *The Spectator*, no. 103, June 28 1711, (1891), 372–4. For a similar comment in the Wentworth Papers, see BL Add. MS 22221, fos. 150–1, Lady Bathurst to Thomas Wentworth, June 8 1707: 'I am afraid your Lordship will think it a compliment to tell you the pleasure I receive by the honour of your letters'. 49-211, nn/rv, July 28 1696.
87. 34-3, munv/rv, [Jan. 1680?]; R. Perry, *Women, Letters, and the Novel* (New York, 1980), 75; T. Sprat, *History of the Royal Society* (1667), repr. 1958.
88. For two bibliographies of English letter-writing manuals, see K. Hornbeak, 'The Complete Letter-Writer in English 1568–1800', *Smith College Studies in Modern Languages*, 15 (1934), 128–45; J. Robertson, *The Art of Letter Writing* (1942), 67–80. For later more informal manuals see T. Goodman, Esq., *The Experienced Secretary* (1707); [John Constable], *The Conversation of Gentlemen Considered* (1738); *The Complete Letter Writer Containing Familiar Letters . . .* (Edinburgh, 1768); J. Hill, *The Young Secretary's Guide* (1696); *The Lady's Preceptor* (1743); S. Richardson, *Familiar Letters on Important Occasions* (1928).
89. 21-1, rv/nhob, [Apr. 1666?]; Cohen, *Fashioning Masculinity*, 9–10, 46–53; M. Kimmel, 'The Contemporary "Crisis" of Masculinity in Historical Perspective', in H. Brod (ed.), *The Making of Masculinities* (Boston, 1987), 121–53.
90. 51-542, jv/Mr. Wotton, Aug. 27 1700; 49-282, cst/jv, Oct. 12 1696.
91. W. Matthews (ed.), *The Diary of Dudley Ryder 1715–1716* (1939), i. 38, 46, 98, 104, 114, 117, 120, June 18, July 2, Sept. 16, Sept. 24, Oct. 11–12, Oct. 16, Oct. 18, 1715; Barker-Benfield, *The Birth of Pandora*, 97–8.
92. 54-387, ebv/jv, Jan. 8 1711.
93. L. Stewart, *The Rise of Public Science* (Cambridge, 1992). For a different view, see S. Pincus, '"Coffee Politicians Does Create"', *Journal of Modern History*, 67 (1995), 807-34.
94. H. Barker and E. Chalus (eds.), *Gender in the Eighteenth Century* (1997), introduction, 1–28; Klein, 'Gender and the Public/Private Distinction', 104–5; A. Vickery, 'Golden Age to Separate Spheres? A Review of the Categories and Chronology of English Women's History', *Historical Journal*, 36 (1993), 383–414; D. Goodman, 'Public Sphere and Private Life', *History and Theory*, 31 (1992), 1–20; D. Gobetti, *Private and Public* (1992).
95. 51-72, lg/jv, Sept. 27 1699; 51-91, lg/jv, Oct. 3 1699; E. Kowaleski-Wallace, *Women, Shopping, and Business in the Eighteenth Century* (New York, 1996), 21.
96. Klein, 'Gender and the Public/Private Distinction', 104.

Notes to Chapter 5

1. D. Defoe, *A Treatise Concerning the Use and Abuse of the Marriage Bed* (1727), 33.
2. 49-84, jv/wc, May 6 1696.
3. For the strict settlement, see below.
4. For example, S. Amussen, *An Ordered Society* (Oxford, 1988); N. Davis, 'Women's History in Transition', *Feminist Studies*, (1976), 83–103; P. Jalland, *Women and Politics* (Oxford Press, 1986); J. Landes, *Women in the Public Sphere in the Age of the French Revolution* (Ithaca, New York 1988); M. Prior (ed.), *Women in English Society* (1985); J. Eales, *Women in Early Modern England 1500–1700* (1998).
5. A. Clark, *Working Life of Women in the Seventeenth Century* (1919); I. Pinchbeck, *Women Workers and the Industrial Revolution 1750–1850* (1930); B. Hill, *Women, Work, and Sexual Politics in Eighteenth-Century England* (Oxford, 1989); S. Cahn, *Industry of Devotion 1550–1660* (New York, 1987)
6. L. Davidoff and C. Hall, *Family Fortunes* (1987); R. Perry, *Women, Letters, and the Novel* (New York, 1980); A. Fletcher, *Gender, Sex, and Subordination in England 1500–1800* (1995); J. Elshtain, *Public Man, Private Woman* (Princeton, 1981).
7. A. Vickery 'Golden Age to Separate Spheres?', *Historical Journal*, 36 (1993), 383–414, and *The Gentleman's Daughter* (New Haven, 1998); L. Klein, 'Gender, Conversation, and the Public Sphere in Early Eighteenth-Century England', in J. Still and M. Worton (eds.), *Textuality and Sexuality* (Manchester and New York, 1993), 100–15; R. Shoemaker, *Gender in English Society 1650–1850* (1998); J. Tosh, 'From Keighley to St. Denis', *History Workshop Journal*, 40 (1995), 193-206.
8. L. Stone, *The Family, Sex, and Marriage in England* (1979); R. Trumbach, *The Rise of the Egalitarian Family* (New York, 1978); A. Macfarlane, 'Review', *History and Theory*, 18 (1979), 103–26; J. Flandrin, *Families in Former Times* (Cambridge, 1979); R. Outhwaite (ed.), *Marriage and Society* (New York, 1981); J. Gillis, *For Better or For Worse* (New York, 1985); S. Okin, 'Patriarchy and Married Women's Property in England', *Eighteenth-Century Studies*, 17 (1983–4), 121–38; G. Schochet, *The Authoritarian Family and Political Attitudes in Seventeenth-Century England* (New Brunswick, 1988).
9. M. Slater, *Family Life in the Seventeeth Century* (1984) and 'The Weightiest Business', *Past & Present*, 72 (1976), 29–54; S. Mendelson, 'The Weightiest Business', *Past & Present*, 85 (1979), 126–35. Patriarchal families are defined as those in which men govern family members and women are considered inferior. In these households women obey male heads, who control and distribute family resources. J. Kelly, *Women, History and Theory* (Chicago, 1986), 11–12.
10. J. Scott, *Gender and the Politics of History* (New York, 1988); N. Chodorow, 'Mothering, Male Dominance, and Capitalism', in Z. Eisenstein (ed.), *Capitalist Patriarchy and the Case for Socialist Feminism* (New York, 1979), 83–106; H. Hartmann, 'The Family as the Locus of Gender, Class, and Political Struggle', in A. Jaggar and P. Rothenberg (eds.), *Feminist Frameworks* (New York, 1984), 341–57; S. Ortner, 'Is Female to Male as Nature to Culture?', *Feminist Studies*, 1 (1972), 5–31; S. Ortner and H. Whitehead, *Sexual Meanings* (Cambridge, 1981); G. Rubin, 'The Traffic in Women', in R. Reiter (ed.), *Toward an Anthropology of Women* (New York, 1975), 157–210; A. Shapiro (ed.), 'History and Feminist Theory', *Feminists Revision History* (New Brunswick, 1994), 1–23. Lydal Roper in *Oepidus and the Devil* (1994), 1–34, has called for a more essentialist interpretation.

11. T. Hitchcock, *English Sexualities 1700–1800* (Basingstoke, 1997); M. Cohen and T. Hitchcock (eds.), *English Masculinities 1600–1800*, (1999); R. Trumbach, 'Sex, Gender, and Sexual Identity in Modern Culture', *Journal of the History of Sexuality*, 2 (1991); T. Laquer, *Making Sex* (Cambridge, Mass., 1990).

12. This was implied in the term 'feme covert'. W. Blackstone, *Commentaries on the Laws of England* (New York, 1827), i. 343; *Baron and Feme* (1719), 7–8; C. Robertson, 'Relative Choices', D. Phil. thesis (Oxford, 1994), 3.

13. W. Gouge, *Of Domestical Duties* (1622); [T.E.], *The Lawes Resolutions of Womens Rights* (1632); [N.H.], *The Ladies Dictionary* (1694), 314–19, 324, 326; [D.B.], *The Honourable State of Matrimony made Comfortable* (1685); J. Turner, *A Discourse on Fornication* (1698); N. Keeble (ed.), *The Cultural Identity of Seventeenth-Century Women* (1994); R. Houlbrooke, *English Family Life 1576–1716* (Oxford, 1988).

14. Robertson, 'Relative Choices', 10, 31; J. Essex, *The Young Ladies Conduct* (1722), 65–6; E. Creffield, *A Good Wife a Great Blessing* (1717), 37. L. Pollock, '"Teach Her to Live under Obedience"', *Continuity and Change*, 4 (1989), 231–58, uses examples from the Verney letters.

15. Bodl Rawl MS D. 78, fos. 278, 311–12, Lady Elizabeth Delaval, *Meditations and Prayers*, *c.*1662–71. Similar tensions are found in G. Savile, *The Lady's New-Years Gift . . .* , 6th edn. (Dublin and Drogheda, 1699), 25.

16. Stone, *Family, Sex, and Marriage*, 127–36, 183; M. Astell, *Reflections Upon Marriage*, 3rd edn. (1706), 22. Letters between daughter and father in S. Richardson, *Familiar Letters on Important Occasions* (1928), 114–20, show the same coercion concerning choice.

17. O. Hufton, *The Prospect Before Her* (1995), 119; A. Laurence, *Women in England 1500–1760* (New York, 1994), 274; R. Adair, *Courtship, Illegitimacy, and Marriage in Early Modern England* (Manchester and New York, 1996).

18. Bodl Rawl MS D. 78, fo. 88. Essex (*Young Ladies Conduct*, 97–8) called for 'suitable agreement and harmony in age, honour, education, and religion: nay even families and fortunes'. Even Mary Astell (*Reflections Upon Marriage*, 40) called for 'as much equality as may be'.

19. In Bodl Rawl Letters MS 51, fo. 25, Lewis Yate wrote to Philip Wharton on Sept. 30 1673 about a young lady who is '18, handsome, well-bred, she is witty and ingenious . . . of a good temper as far as I can see'. Bodl Rawl Letters MS 50, fo. 135, F. Hart/ P. Wharton, Jan. 29 1672, describes a lady 'of a sweet lovely nature and few amongst the mean ones of a more humble carriage . . . . As for her natural parts, they are very good and managed with much sobrietie . . . as for her person, not the least deformable nor yet beautiful, but of a brownish complexion.'

20. Lady Lowther is quoted in D. Hainsworth, 'Fathers and Daughters', in L. Frappell (ed.), *Principalities, Powers, and Estates* (Adelaide, 1979), 18; Robertson, 'Relative Choices', 24–6; M. Wiesner, *Women and Gender in Early Modern Europe* (Cambridge, 1993), 57–8; 33-121, jv/rv, Dec. 1679. [W. Ramesey], *The Gentleman's Companion* (1676), 211, called love 'the product of folly; nay 'tis impossible to love and be wise'.

21. 51-81, ea/jv, Oct. 4 1699; 16-4, rv/M. Eure, July 22 1658; 53-451, rp2/rv2, Aug. 9 1707; 52-329, jv/ml, Feb. 8 1704.

22. Two different points of view about Sir Ralph's forced marriage to Mary Blacknall are found in Slater, *Family Life*, 13, 63–73, and Fletcher, *Gender, Sex, and Subordination*, 160–2.

23. 52-584, tc/jv, Oct. 15 1704; 52-644, tc/rv2, Jan. 9 1705; R. Steele, *The Ladies Library* (1714).

24. 53-353, tc/jv, Mar. 18 1707; 53-425, wtre/jv, July 13 1706; Hitchcock, *English Sexualities*, 42–57.

25. 52-584, tc/jv, Oct. 15 1704; 46-15, rp1/jv, July 12 1692; 52-540, jv/tche, Oct. 22 1704; 49-632, J. Keeling/jv, Apr. 20 1697; 44-27, lg/rv Mar. 12 1690; 54-627, tc/rv2, July 28 1712; *Ladies Dictionary*, 262; Bodl Eng. Letts. MS E29, fos. 36–7, Sarah Henry/Matthew Henry, Mar. 1687.

26. 33-117, munv/jv, Dec. 10 1679.

27. For works in favour of marriage, see [T.H.], *A Treatise of Marriage . . .* (1673); *Marriage Promoted* (1690); *The Delights of Marriage* [1725]; *The Bachelor's Directory*, 2nd edn. (1696). For works against marriage, see *A Satyr Against Marriage* (1700); [W. Ramesey], *The Gentleman's Companion (1676)*, 216–17; [William Seymar], *Marriage Asserted . . .* (1674).

28. Failed negotiations between Angel Harrington and John are analysed below. A similar study of John's rival Thomas Wharton (1648–1715) and a Miss Cabell, daughter of Richard Cabell of Buckfastleigh, Devonshire in 1672–4 is found in Bodl MS. Rawl 50–51. For the Cabells, see F. Colby (ed.), *The Visitation of the County of Devon . . . 1620* (1872), 43. See also R. Grassby, 'Love, Property and Kinship', *English Historical Review*, 113 (1998), 335–50.

29. K. Thomas, 'The Double Standard', *Journal of the History of Ideas*, 20 (1959), 195–216; Essex, *Young Ladies Conduct*, 99, 105; 32-56, rv/munv, Dec. 30 1678; 32-72, munv/rv, Jan. 16 1679; CH 14/4 Agreement of John, Elizabeth, and Samuel Clifford with John Verney of London, merchant, Oct. 30 1684.

30. 53-614, 'Copy of my letter to———'. A love letter from John to an unknown recipient was copied and docketed in his handwriting with a blank where the recipient's name was usually written. See letter to Lord Fermanagh found in correspondence of 1708 marked July 14 and to John from 'deadman, alias S. Smith', 48-110, n.d. and 48-170, Mar. 2 1695.

31. 35-36, jv/munv, Apr. 6 1681; 50-253, jv/wc, Dec. 29 1697;Bodl Rawl Letters MS 50, fo. 245, S. Hieron/P. Wharton, Mar. 18 1673.

32. Blackstone, *Commentaries*, 343; M. Finn, 'Women, Consumption, and Coverture in England, c.1760–1860', *Historical Journal*, 39 (Sept. 1996), 703–22; L. Gowing, *Domestic Dangers* (Oxford, 1996); A. Erickson, *Women and Property in Early Modern England* (1993); J. Greenberg, 'Women in Early Eighteenth Century Common Law and Equity', *Studies in Eighteenth-Century Culture*, 4 (1975), 171–81; M. Salmon, *Women and the Law of Property in Early America* (Chapel Hill, NC, 1986); R. O'Day, *The Family and Family Relationships 1500–1900* (1994), 101.

33. *Baron and Feme* (1719), 85; D. Walker (ed.), *The Oxford Companion to Law* (Oxford, 1980), 376.

34. In the 17th century, the ratio was far below the 10 to 1 standard of the early 18th century. Essex (*Young Ladies Conduct*, 114) cites a 10 to 1 ratio in 1722. L. Stone, *The Crisis of the Aristocracy 1558–1641* (Oxford, 1967), 291; C. Clay, 'Henry Hoare, Banker, his Family, and the Stourhead Estate', in F. Thompson (ed.), *Landowners, Capitalists, and Entrepreneurs* (Oxford, 1994), 122–3; J. Habakkuk, 'Marriage Settlements in the Eighteenth Century', *Transactions of the Royal Historical Society*, 4th series, 32 (1950), 21.

35. 33-119, jv/rv, Dec. 12 1679. BL Add. MS 27418, fos. 96^r–99^r show six months of

complex negotiations in Sir Walter Calverley's Diary and Memorandum Book, 1663–1749. A list of stages is also found in Bodl Rawl Letters MS 50, fo. 149.

36. HL STTP 16/2, Settlement deeds, May 2 1717. William Congreve was a trustee in Viscount Cobham and Anne Halsey's settlement. 34-32, rv/jv, April 14 1680; 46-10, jv/rv, July 6 1692; 53-98, atre/ebv, Dec. 29 1705; 53-236, atre/jv, June 20 1706.

37. Samuel Pepys acted as marriage broker for his patron Lord Sandwich and counselled Lord Carteret's son: 'I taught him what to do; to take the lady away by the hand . . .' Later, he was troubled because of the bride's apparent sadness. R. Latham and W. Matthews (eds.), *Diary of Samuel Pepys* (1972), vi. 159, July 16 1665; vi. 175–6, July 31 1665; O'Day, *The Family and Family Relationships*, 82.

38. CH 1/73, Will, Sir Edmund Verney, PCC Dec. 23 1642; Slater, *Family Life*, 5–11; Broad, 'Sir Ralph Verney and his Estates', 'Gentry Finances'.

39. CH 1/38, Marriage settlement, Apr. 30 1629; Slater, *Family Life*, 13; F. Verney, *Memoirs of the Verney Family* (1970), i. 115-19.

40. Broad, 'Gentry Finances', 189, 194–5, 200; Slater, *Family Life*, 19, 78–107; 39-31, rv/Vere Gawdy, Jan. 12 1685. In Ralph Verney's hand, 'My answer to Lady Gawdy about———'.

41. 16-2, M. Eure/Mrs. Sherrard, May 8 1658; 16-4, rv/M. Eure, July 22 1658; 15-1, rv/munv, Jan. 25 1658; 18-32, rv/ebut, Nov. 15 1661; Broad, 'Gentry Finances', 195; A. Beaven, *The Aldermen of the City of London* (1913), ii. 63. Mary's father, William Abel was sheriff of Bucks, 1661. The scandal concerned the Vintner's Company.

42. 16-5, mun/Dr. Hyde, July 25 1658; 17-14, mun/Dr. Hyde, Aug. 26 1661; 42-74, munv/'E. Phelps, his wench', [1688?]; 18-32, rv/ebut, Nov. 15 1661; 18-33, ebut/rv, Nov. 18 1661.

43. 18-31, 'This shows my Offer to Mun', Nov. 5 1661; 18-1, rv/mun, [Dec. 13 1661]; Broad, 'Sir Ralph Verney and his Estates', 112–15; 18-2, mun/[Dr Hyde?], Nov. 27 1661; 18-10, mav/G. Gale, Feb. 3 1662; 15-1, rv/munv, Jan. 25 1658; 17-14, mun/T. Hyde, Aug. 26 1661; Bucks CRO D/X 337, East Claydon Account Book; Broad, 'Sir Ralph Verney and his Estates', 113, 214–17.

44. Sir Orlando Bridg[e]man, *Conveyances*, 2nd edn. (1689). Bridgeman was one of the first to use the strict settlement. CH 2/60, Marriage settlement, July 1 1662; CH 2/61 Limitation by Mary Verney, Jan. 1 1663; CH 1/111a, b Marriage settlement, June 30, July 1 1662; Broad, 'Gentry Finances', 195; 22-12, rv/M. Elmes, Apr. 6 1688. Ralph thought the agreement was 'very fair, honest, honourable, and in no way injurious to her or any child'.

45. 32-72, mun/rv, Jan. 16 1679; 40-48, munv/E. Phelps, Feb. 11 1686; 38–44, A. R. /rv, Mar. 19 1684; CH 14/19, fo. 9. John recorded that Mun had 'several bastard children, of which three were living at his death'. One was apprenticed to a salesman and one died in India.

46. 30-28, Munv, 'His Last Will and Testament, a Copy', May 9 1677; 23-3, munv/rv, May 24 1669. One version gives £4,000 to his son Edmund, up to £5,000 if more than one son, and £1,000 for a daughter. Thus, cash portions were left to some Verney younger sons in the mid-17th century.

47. Mun died in 1688 and his children died as follows: Ralph 1686; Edmund 1690; Mary 1692. CH 1/127, Agreement, July 25 1694; jv/rv, July 21 1696. William Abel forced his son Richard to pay his sister £9,000 in three years after William's death (CH 2/63 Will of William Abel, PCC March 3 1721). If not, East Claydon would be hers to sell. Richard sold the land for £19,200 to a London goldsmith, who reassigned it to an apothecary and a lawyer. The latter sold it back to John Verney's son Ralph for £25,800. CH 2/64, Assignment of mortgage Jan. 23 1722, reassigned to Paltock

& Snow, memo, Aug. 23 1722; Broad, 'Sir Ralph Verney and his Estates', 146; G. Lipscomb, *The History and Antiquities of the County of Buckingham* (1831). i. 164–5.

48. For other offers, see 28-18, jv/rv, Mar. 15 1675; 29-11, jshep/jv, Jan. 10 1676; 30-35, jv/rv, [June 1677]. One father Sir Robert Knightly was a former trader, later Surrey sheriff. Levant merchant John Sheppard proposed John for his niece, a member of the Dormer family. Sheppard promised to ask for Berkshire land if the marriage was with consent. 31-33, jv/rv, April 18 1678; 31-48, mpal/rv, May 19 1678; 33-15, jv/rv, July 17 1679.

49. 30-35, jv/rv, [June 1677]; 33-74, rv/hv, Oct. 6 1679; 33-70, rv/jv, Sept. 29 1679; 33-118, jv/rv, Dec. 11 1679; 33-71, jv/rv, Oct. 2 1679. See Ch. 3 for the Palmers and their kin.

50. 33-77, jv/rv, [Oct] 1679; 33-108, rv/jv, Dec. 1 1679; 33-74, rv/jv, Oct. 6 1679; 33-86, rv/jv, Nov. 3, 1679; 46-150, lg/rv, Oct. 17 1692. Dr Hamey left Elizabeth £1,000 for a marriage portion. J. Keevil, *Hamey the Stranger* (1952), 153.

51. Pollock, '"Teacher Her to live under Obedience"'; 33-116, jv/rv, Dec. 8 1679; 34-10, rv/jv, Jan. 24 1680; 33-94, rv/jv, Nov. 10 1679; 34-2, jv/epv, Jan. 1680.

52. 33-86, rv/jv, Nov. 3 1679; 33-113, jv/rv, Dec. 4 1679; 33-115, rv/jv, Dec. 8 1680. In fact she was 16, or 24 years younger than John.

53. 45-2, Wasing settlement, n.d.; 33-114, rv/jv, Dec. 4 1679; 33-116, jv/rv, Dec. 8 1679; 34-11, jv/epv, Jan. 26 1680; 33-124, lg/rv, Dec. 18 1679. The sum of £6,000 may have been inflated.

54. 34-2, jv/epv, [Jan. 1680?]; 34-40, jv/rv, Apr. 20 1680; CH 1/119 a, b, Marriage settlement, May 1 1680 (incomplete); Deed, July 8 1692, 'To secure £2,000 to Elizabeth Palmer Verney if she survive John Verney'; CH 1/120, Lease, May 4 1680; Berks CRO D/EMt/T1/9–10, Marriage settlement, May 4–5 1680; CH 1/121, Bond, May 5 1680; 34-22, legal document, [March 20 1680?]; 34-11, jv/epv, Jan. 26 1680; 34-55, Copy of bond, May 5 1680; Broad, 'Sir Ralph Verney and his Estates', 152; 34-58, rv/jv, May 9 1680.

55. 34-69, rv/jv, May 17 1680; 34-67, rv/jv, May 13 1680; 34-101, jv/munv, June 9 1680; 34-141, jv/rv, June 27 1680; 34-121, rv/jv, [June?]1680.

56. 51-6, nn/jv, July 12 1699; 39-36, jv/epv, Feb. 14 1685; L. Stone, *Family, Sex, and Marriage*, 194.

57. 35-142, epv/jv, Sept. 24 1681; 40-14, jv/rv, May 6 1685.

58. 38-65, rv/jv, June 5 1684; 35-140, epv/jv, Sept. 25 1681.

59. 45-1, Sir J. Bridgeman/rv, Feb. 21, 25 1691; 48-33, rv, 'Proposals of Marriage between Mr Verney and Mrs Judith Bridgeman', [Dec. 1691?].

60. 45-26, jv/po, Oct. 4 1691; 45-79, 'Marriage License between John Verney and Mary Lawley', June 11 1692; PRO PROB 11/433, fo. 131, Will of Sir Frances Lawley, Oct. 1696; Strype, *A Survey*, i, book 1, 115; [G.E.C.], *Complete Baronetage* (Exeter, 1902), ii. 140–2; Sir G. Younghusband, *The Jewel House* (1921), 122; G. Armytage (ed.), *Allegations for Marriage Licenses Issued by the Vicar-General of the Archbishop of Canterbury* (Harleian Society, 31; 1890), 223; GH MS 15212/1, fo. 1., Vintner's List. Sir Francis met John at the Rainbow coffee-house which was used as security in the settlement. 45-29, jv/rv, Dec. 10 1691.

61. 46-18, po/rv, July 12 1692; 46-366, rv/jv, [1693?]; 34-39, M. Whitmore/mlv, n.d. [April 1680?].

62. 45-42, rv/jv, Feb. 23 1691; 45-85, jv/rv, June 30 1692; 45-50, jv/rv, Apr. 30 1692.

63. CH 1/125, Marriage settlement, July 5 1692; 45-50, jv/rv, April 30 1692; 45-55, rv/jv, April 18 1692; 46-1, rv/jv, July 2 1692; 47-561, jv/tv, Aug. 24 1694.

64. 45-68, jv/rv, May 18 1692; 51-133, tlaw/jv, Nov. 23 1699; 53-320, jv/llaw, Jan. 29 1707; 54-553, flaw/jv, Mar. 10 1712; 54-477, H. Palmer/jv, Sept. 19 1711.

65. 46-140, jv/mlv, Oct. 11 1692; 48-223, Easter Le Gay/jv, Apr. 8 1695; PRO PROB 11/337, fo. 133; J. Woodhead, *The Rulers of London, 1660–1689* (1965), 84–85; 48-332, jv/rv, July 11 1695; 48-296, jv/rv, [June 1695?]; 48-297, jv/lg, June 12 1695. Angel's uncle was James Harrington, the political theorist, who proposed limits on women's portions.

66. 48-296, jv/rv [June 1695?]. The text says mother-in-law but implies the present term for stepmother. 48-332, jv/rv, July 11 1695. £12,000 in land might have yielded £600 per year if we assume the rate was 5%. If Angel had given £6,000, the ratio of portion to jointure would have been 10 to 1.

67. 48-363, jv/rv, June 29 1695. For a debate on this topic, see B. Todd, 'The Remarrying Widow', in M. Prior (ed.), *Women in English Society* (1985), 54–92, and 'Demographic Determinism and Female Agency', *Continuity and Change*, 9 (1994), 421–50; J. Boulton, 'London Widowhood Revisited', *Continuity and Change*, 5 (1990), 323–55.

68. My emphases. 48-370, rv/jv, July 14 1695; 48-348, rv/jv, July 21 1695; 48-371, rv/jv, July 1 1695; 48-402, jv/rv, July 31, 1695.

69. Bucks CRO D/X 761–900, 1069, 1351, Baker family papers, 1680–1776; PRO PROB 11/461, fo. 91, Will of Daniel Baker, May 24 1693; CLRO Orphan Deed No. 7, Daniel Baker, Bond of Thomas Richardson, June 20 1639; J. Jenkins, *A History of the Parish of Penn* (1938), 136, 146; Phillips Auctioneers Catalogue, July 2 1981, Sale No. 23, 406, Item 250, Manuscripts from Sheffield Park, Sussex. Lord Sheffield has annotated the volume: 'Particulars of Estates and Property of Great Grandfather Baker'. Child's handwriting specimen of 'Daniel Baker of Christ's Hospital, 1671, his piece' is in BL Sloane 994, fo. 21b. Baker papers include several deposits. Catalogue numbers are as of Nov. 1997. AR 56/96 has been converted to D/X 1351.

70. CLRO MSS 83, fo. 7, and 42, fo. 3; 49-124, C. Todd/jv, Mar. 26 1696. Baker is not listed as Alderman in A. Beaven, *The Aldermen of the City of London* (1908–1913) and other CLRO records.

71. Bucks CRO D/X 1351/30, 67–8; 49-333, jv/db2, Dec. 1 1696. For Daniel Baker II's diary, 1690–1705, see DX 1069/1/1. For his wills, see Bucks CRO D/X 1351/75–81. He and his son Daniel are cited in H. Sturgess (comp.), *Register of Admissions to the Honourable Society of the Middle Temple* (1949), i. 205, Feb. 6 1682, and i. 262, July 11 1707.

72. PRO PROB 11/461, fo. 91; PRO PROB 11/516, fo. 175, Will of Barbara Baker, July 31 1701; Bucks CRO D/X 1069/2/130; Bucks CRO D/X 1351/68–9, 71–74, 85, 89, 102. Baker's larger properties were in Holborn, Bloomsbury, Cheapside, and near St Paul's. In Bucks CRO D/X 1351/68, his son Daniel estimated a total gross estate of £6,276 with £5,605 remaining after charges, while in Bucks CRO D/X 1351/69 he estimated £8,459 with £7,692 after charges. Bucks CRO D/X 1069/2/130 gives a third estimate of £6,097 with £5,327 after charges.

73. 49-403, pa/jv, Sept. 17 1696; 49-308, Lady Keeling/jv, Nov. 12 1696; J. Keates, *Purcell, a Biography* (1995), 178 notes that a Miss Baker, a Dutch young gentlewoman, sang the role of Venus in Venus and Adonis produced at Mr Priests's school in 1689.

74. 49-447, ebv/jv, Oct. 18 1696; 49-470, ebv/jv, Dec. 29 1696; G. Savile, *The Lady's New-Years Gift*, 60. *The Ladies Dictionary*, 473 called a good wife one who 'never crosses her husband in the spring tide of his anger, but stays till it is ebbing-water, and then she mildly argues the matter, not so much to condemn him, as by that means . . . to . . . let him by degrees see his error'.

75. Berks CRO D/EMt/T1/15–17, Settlement deeds, Mar. 18–19, 1697; CH l/141a–c, Leases,

Mar. 18 1697; CH 1/141d, Marriage settlement, Mar. 19 1697. Although no jointure is specifically noted, a rent charge for £200 to Elizabeth is found in CH 1/141d and CH 1/146, Lease, Oct. 17 1707.

76. 49-542, Feb. 10 1697. M. Verney (ed.), *Verney Letters of the Eighteenth Century* . . . , 2 vols. (1930), i. 18–19; 50-78, jv/wc, July 3 1697; Bucks CRO D/X 1069/2/152, ebv/ J. Baker, n.d.; Bucks CRO D/X 1069/2/54, R. Tighe/J. Baker, July 4 1717; Bucks CRO D/X 1351/69, 72–3.

77. CH 1/147, Will of John Verney, Viscount Fermanagh, June 23 1713, John gave his wife her ring, earrings, dressing plate, silver, £50 for mourning, a coach and horses, and defined her Wasing rights. Berks CRO D/EMt/T1/16; CH 1/148, Lease of Wasing estate for 59 years, Feb. 12, 1718. For Elizabeth's property, see Bucks CRO D/X 1351/71, 85–6, 89 and D/X 1069 3/3–4 for her funeral expenses and furniture. She died intestate. Bucks CRO D/X 1351/87 is the administration of her estate, Jan. 7 173[7].

78. J. Cooper, 'Patterns of Inheritance and Settlement by Great Landowners from the Fifteenth to the Eighteenth Centuries', and J. Thirsk, 'The Debate on Inheritance', in J. Goody *et al.* (eds.), *Family and Inheritance* (Cambridge, 1976), 177–327; L. Carr, 'Inheritance in the Colonial Chesapeake', in R. Hoffman and P. Albert, *Women in the Age of the American Revolution* (Charlottesville, Va., 1989), 155–208.

79. E. Spring, *Law, Land and Family* (1993), 9–10; N. Davis, 'Ghosts, Kin and Progeny', *Daedalus*, 106 (1977), 87–114. Habakkuk, *Marriage, Debt, and the Estates System*, 211–12.

80. Habakkuk, 'Marriage Settlements', 16, 216. C. Clay in 'Property Settlements, Financial Provision for the Family, and Sale of Land by the Greater Landowners 1660–1790', *Journal of British Studies*, 21 (1981), 22, notes that landowners might not understand or remember items in their marriage settlements. But the Verneys carefully studied and kept legal documents. If they did not understand something they drew up lists of questions for their lawyers.

81. Broad, 'Gentry Finances', 197.

82. Berks CRO D/EMt/T1/1–7, Wasing Deeds.

83. M. Butler, 'Early Liberal Roots of Feminism', in M. Shanley and C. Pateman (eds.), *Feminist Interpretations and Political Theory* (Cambridge, 1991), 74–94; M. McKeon, 'Historicizing Patriarchy', *Eighteenth-Century Studies*, 28 (1995), 295–322.

84. For women's writing, see S. Mendelson, 'Stuart Women's Diaries and Occasional Memoirs', and P. Crawford, 'Women's Published Writings', in M. Prior (ed.), *Women in English Society* (1985), 181–212, 232–64, and appendix; L. Schwoerer, 'Seventeenth-Century English Women Engraved in Stone?', *Albion*, 16 (1984), 389–403.

85. M. Astell, *Reflections upon Marriage*, 3rd edn. (1706), preface, [10]; R. Perry, 'Mary Astell and the Feminist Critique of Possessive Individualism', *Eighteenth-Century Studies*, 23 (1990), 444–57; S. Staves, *Players' Sceptres* (Lincoln, Nebr., 1979), 113.

86. J. Locke, *The Second Treatise of Government* (1952), para. 82, 46; C. Pateman, *The Sexual Contract* (Cambridge, 1988), 82–94; R. Weil, 'Sexual Ideology and Political Propaganda in England, 1680–1714', Ph.D. thesis (Princeton, 1991). For more rosy views of women's position see M. Ezell, *The Patriarch's Wife* (Chapel Hill, NC, 1987), 36–49; M. Shanley, 'Marriage Contract and Social Contract in Seventeenth-Century English Political Thought', *Western Political Quarterly*, 32 (1979), 79–91.

87. 46-349, eli/rv, Mar. 11 1693; 48-278, jv/rv, June 5 1695; 53-739, jv/rv2, Jan. 30 1709; HL STT 406, wchap/srt, Jan. 20 1689. L. Stone, *Road to Divorce* (Oxford, 1990), 96–120; R. Outhwaite, *Clandestine Marriage in England 1500–1800* (1995); R. Brown, 'The

Rise and Fall of Fleet Marriages' in Outhwaite, *Marriage and Society*, 117–36; D. Lemmings, 'Marriage and the Law in the Eighteenth Century', *Historical Journal*, 39 (1996), 339–60.

88. 46-490, lg/rv, May 25 1693; 51-584, lg/jv, Nov. 24 1701; 51-121, lg/jv, Nov. 14 1699.

89. PRO PROB 11/461, fo. 91; PRO PROB 11: 433 fo. 131; 47-52, A. Woodward/rv, Sept. 7 1693; 51-424, lg/jv, April 3 1701.

90. For Hester, see 42-54, nden/rv, March 30 1688; 42-56, rv/nden, Apr. 2 1688; 45-24, lg/rv, Sept. 9 1691. For Molly, see 46-523, mk/jv, June 16 1693; 47-219, jk/rv, Dec. 16 1693; 48-155, lg/rv, Feb. 12 1695. For Pen, see 48-411, jv/rv, Aug. 3 1695; 48-412, lg/rv, Aug. 3 1695.

91. 48-447, pv/jv, Aug, 1695; 48-463, jv/hst, [Aug, 1695?]; 48-478, lg/rv, Aug. 29 1695; 48-459, jv/rv, Aug. 21 1695. John Evelyn altered his will after his daughter eloped to make her feel her 'undutifulness'. E. De Beer (ed.), *Diary of John Evelyn* (Oxford, 1955), iv. 461–2, July 27, Aug. 2 1685.

92. J. Habakkuk, 'The Rise and Fall of English Landed Families 1600–1800', *Transactions of the Royal Historical Society*, 29 (1979), 194; *Marriage, Debt, and the Estates System*, 215; Hainsworth, 'Fathers and Daughters', 17; [J. Swift], *An Essay on the Mischief of Giving Fortunes with Women in Marriage* (1727), 44, 48–9.

93. Flandrin, *Families in Former Times*, 168; 52-195, lg/jv, Mar. 1 1703; Bodl Add. MS D.40; B. Henning, *The House of Commons 1660–1690* (1983), iii. 697–700; BL Egerton 4162, fo. 232, A. Wharton/T. Wharton, Apr. 1 1681; PRO C.104/110, part 1, Lee of Ditchley Papers.

94. 49-67, nn/jv, June 1 1696; J. Cartwright (ed.), *The Wentworth Papers 1705–39* (1883), 40; 'The Levelers', *Harleian Miscellany* (1811), xii, 195–6; *Scheme for a New Lottery* (1732); L. de Gaya, *Marriage Ceremonies as Now used in All Parts of the World*, 3rd edn. (1704), 9; V. Brodsky, 'Single Women in the London Marriage Market', *Newberry Papers in Family and Community History*, No. 80-2 (Chicago, 1980), my emphases).

95. 52-212, lg/jv, Apr. 17 1703; 49-395, lg/jv, Nov. 19 1696; Bucks CRO D/X 1069/2/141, jv/ J. Baker, June 22 1714; 51-639, pv/jv, Dec. 14 1701; ; 49-182, cst/rv, June 14 1696; 51-196, lg/jv, Feb. 29 1700.

96. 48-621, lg/rv, Dec. 21 1695; 48-290, pa/rv, June 18 1695; 49-24, cst/rv, Jan. 16 1696.

97. Slater, *Family Life*, 78–104; 52-552, ist/jv, Sept. 2 1704; 52-642, jv/cst, Dec. 24 1704.

98. 52-658, cst/jv, Jan. 3 1704; 53-312, ea/jv, Jan. 9 1707; 50-200, ea/jv, [Sept. 1697?].

99. 47-124, pa/rv, Oct. 16 1693; 48-84, rv/jv, Dec. 9 1694; *Ladies Dictionary*, 466–7; 34-19, pv/jv, [Mar. 1680?]; 47-428, cst/rv, June 24 1694; 47-434, June 3 1694; 49-87, cst/rv, May 3 1696; 49-511, lg/wc, Jan. 14 1697.

100. 46-70, lg/M. Lloyd, Aug. 24 1692; 54-93, mc/jv, June 9 1709; 48-621, lg/rv, Dec. 21 1695; 46-4, rv/nn, July 3 1692.

101. 52-554, C. Dunk/jv, Sept. 11 1704. Stone, *Family, Sex, and Marriage*, 215–16 and D. Thomas, 'The Social Origins of Marriage Partners of the British Peerage', *Population Studies*, 26 (1972), 99–111, see a decline in peers' marriages to heiresses, but Habakkuk, 'Rise and Fall', 29 (1979), 191, and *Marriage, Debt, and the Estates System*, 217, cites the importance of gentry heiresses, noting that there were more of them than those in the peerage.

102. 51-326, kst/pv, Dec. 12 1700; Clay, 'Property Settlements', 28, and 'Henry Hoare, Banker', 122–3, 131.

103. For the Verneys' portions, see R. Sedgwick, *The House of Commons 1715–54* (1970),

ii. 496; L. Namier and J. Brooke (eds.), *The House of Commons 1754–90* (1964), iii. 580–2; [G.E.C.] *The Complete Peerage* (1926), v. 295–6; BL Stowe MS 4; BL Egerton MS 2353, Settlement of lands of Ralph, 2nd Earl Verney, 1767, fos. 124–5; Lipscomb, *History and Antiquities*, i. (1831), 183–4. Mary Nicholson's jointure was only £1,600. For the Halsey settlement, see HL STTP 15/17, Sept. 17 1715.

104. R. Outhwaite, 'Marriage as Business', in N. McKendrick and R. Outhwaite (eds.), *Business Life and Public Policy* (Cambridge, 1986), 21–37; Laurence, *Women in England*, 232; Broad, 'Gentry Finances', 196–7.

105. Boulton, 'London Widowhood', 342–3; Lemings, 'Marriage and the Law', 357–8; L. and J. Stone, *An Open Elite* (Oxford, 1984), 118–26, and *Family, Sex, and Marriage*, 37–50; Outhwaite, 'Marriage as Business', 30–7.

106. T. Hollingsworth, 'Demography of the British Peerage', *Population Studies*, 18 (1964), supplement, 1–108; 52–91, ea/jv, Nov. 28 1702; A. Malcolmson, *The Pursuit of the Heiress* (Belfast, 1982).

107. W. Betham, *The Baronetage of England* (1804), iv. 87–100; J. Burke, *Extinct and Dormant Baronetcies of England, Ireland and Scotland* (1844), 323–6; Lipscomb, *History and Antiquities*, iii. 454–63; 51-431, ea/jv, Apr. 8 1701.

108. Verney (ed.), *Verney Letters of the Eighteenth Century*, i. 122; 51-698, ebv/jv, Mar. 28 1702; 52-9, lg/jv, July 16 1702.

109. 52-10, 'Copy of Colonel Lovett's Papers', July 1702; 52-138, Mr. Sol Broderick/jv, Jan. 8 1703.

110. 52-200, jv/cl, Mar. 29 1703; 52-8, cl/jv, July 18, 1702; Historical Manuscripts Commission, 10th Report, appendix, part VI, Braye MSS (1887), xxxii. 104–252; Leics CRO, Braye MS 23D57/232; 55-618, jv/ml, Dec. 4 1715; 55-625, ml/jv, [Dec. 1715?].

111. S. Staves, *Married Women's Separate Property* (Cambridge, Mass., 1990), 95–130. Staves points out the benefits of $\frac{1}{3}$ dower guaranteed by law in contrast to jointures at the groom's discretion might be less than $\frac{1}{3}$ of the estate. But Habakkuk in *Marriage, Debt and the Estates System*, 81–2, 86–9, notes that jointures bypassed dower rules and might be received despite conditions like adultery.

112. 52-171, tche/jv, Jan. 28 1703. Cheret's family were probably weavers who emigrated to England from Holland in the 1660s and placed memorials in St Paul's Church, Covent Garden. GH MS 4657A/2, fo. 100; Strype, *Survey*, ii, book 6, 92; IGI Index; W. Hunt (ed.), *Registers of St. Paul's Church, Covent Garden* (Harleian Society; 1906–8), i, no. xxxiii, 51, 55, 62, 75, 96; iii, no. xxxxv, 77; iv, no. xxxvi, 210, 213, 247; GH Index to Middlesex Polls, 1705, shows that Cheret voted Tory.

113. Leics CRO, Braye MS 23D57/232. The Caves' marriage portions were generally higher than the Verneys'. Younger sons received handsome sums.

114. Verney (ed.), *Verney Letters of the Eighteenth Century*, i. 256; Betham, *Baronetage of England*, i. 375–86; [G.E.C.], *The Complete Baronetage* (Exeter, 1902), ii. 93–5; J. Nichols, *The History and Antiquities of the County of Leicester* (1807), iv, part 1, 350–9; B. Henning, *House of Commons*, ii. 33; J. Bridges, *The History and Antiquities of Northamptonshire* (Oxford, 1791), i. 578–83.

115. G. Holmes, *British Politics in the Age of Anne* (1967), 40; H. Broughton, *Family and Estate Records in the Leicestershire Record Office* (Leicester, 1991), 7–8; Leics CRO Braye MS 23D57/2, 3, 6, 17, 18, Marriage settlements; 52-172, jv/tche, Jan. 31 1703.

116. Holmes, *British Politics*, 250–1; 52-464, tc/jv, May 17 1705; Sedgwick, *House of Commons*, i. 536.

117. 52-185, tc/jv, Feb. 24 1703; 52-155, ebv/jv, Feb. 16 1703; 52-182, ebv/jv, Feb. 18 1703; 52-169, ebv/jv, Feb. 20 170; 352-154, 'List of Wedding Expenses', Feb. 16 1703.

118. 52-192, ea/jv, Feb. 27 1703; 52-190, lg/jv, Feb. 25 1703; 52-212, lg/jv, Apr. 17 1703; 52-197, lg/jv, Mar. 9 1703; Habakkuk, 'Rise and Fall', 30 (1980), 203.

119. 52-276, tche/jv, Oct. 14 1703; 52-277, rp2/rv2, Oct. 11, 1703; Leics CRO Braye MS 23D57/35, *Cave v. Cave*; 52-481, jv/mc, June 3 1704.

120. 52-397, jv/tche, Mar. 2 1704; 52-409, jv/Mr. Martyn, Feb. 17 1704; 52-406, Mr. Martyn/ jv, Feb. 22 1704; Leics CRO Braye MS 23D57/22, May 3 1704. John paid £3,000. Portions for daughters were £4,000 if one, £5,000 if two. Income from certain lands were reserved for Margaret's son if Cave remarried. Safeguards for securing her jointure were also inserted.

121. Leics CRO Braye MS 23D57/22; Leics CRO 23D57/35; Leics CRO 23D57/39; *Journals of the House of Commons 1705–1708*, vols. 15, 71, 74, 84, 120, 148, 151, 156; J. Nichols, *History . . . of Leicester*, iv. 352–3; Leics CRO Braye MS 23D57/41, 4 Anne 1705, 'An act to enable Sir Thomas Cave, Bart. to sell certain lands . . .' Leics CRO 23D57/45–46. Sir Richard Hoare, banker to both Caves and Verneys, was involved.

122. PRO PROB 11/569, fo. 125. Two daughters received £4,000 each, a younger son would have £1,000, and £6,000 went to one daughter if no son.

123. 52-240, jchu/jv, July 10 1703; 53-109, jv/tc, Dec. 28 1705.

124. 52-212, lg/jv, Apr. 17 1703; L. Glassey, *Politics and the Appointment of Justices of the Peace* (Oxford, 1979), 211–12.

125. 52-241, llaw/jv, July 12 1703; 52-247, tche/jv, Aug. 11 1703; 52-296, tche/jv, Nov. 9 1703; 52-298, tche/jv, Nov. 13 1703; 52-299, jv/tche, Nov. 16 1703.

126. 52-297, jv/tche, Nov. 11 1703; E. Viney, 'The Buckinghamshire Lieutenancy', *Records of Buckinghamshire*, 19, part 2 (1972), 124; [G.E.C.], *Complete Peerage* (1912), ii. 313– 14; J. Sainty (comp.), *List of Lieutenants . . .* (1979), 52–3; 52-518, H. Egerton/jv, July 4 1704; CH 1/228, CH 2/433a, b, CH 2/469a, b, CH 2/470 a, b, CH2/471, Deeds, June, July 1704; 53-98, atre/ebv, Dec. 29 1705; 53-238, atre/jv, June 6 1706; 53-291, wtre/jv, Nov. 1 1706.

127. 53-100, atre/ebv, Nov. 29 1705; 53-201, ebv/jv, Mar. 13 1706; 53-223, Countess of Mon. and Peterborough/Mr. Tregea, Apr. 1706; 53-100, atre/ebv, Jan. 6 1706 (answer).

128. S. Staves, 'Separate Maintenance Contracts', *Eighteenth Century Life*, 11 (1987), 78– 101; 53-238, atre/ebv, June 6 1706.

129. 53-427, jv/atre, June 18 1706; 53-426, jv/atre, June 23 1706.

130. 53-426, jv/atre, June 23 1706.

131. 53-261, rp2/jv, Oct. 22 1706.

132. H. Andrews, 'The Pasc[h]all Family of Great Baddow and Springfield, Essex', *Essex Archaeological Society Transactions*, New Series 23 (1958), 54–65; W. Metcalfe (ed.), *The Visitations of Essex* (Harleian Publication Society, 13; 1878), 11–12, 88–9, 260–2; P. Morant, *The History and Antiquities of the County of Essex* (1768), ii. 17–18.

133. 50-97, ea/jv, July 24 1697; 52-50, jv/ea, Sept. 29 1702; 53-340, jv/ea, Feb. 16 1707; 52-339, ea/jv, Feb. 12 1707;; 53-345, jv/rv2, Feb. 16 1707.

134. 53-346, atre/ebv, Feb. 20 1707; 53-352, atre/jv, Mar. 12 1707; S. Staves, 'Pin Money', *Studies in Eighteenth Century Culture*, 14 (1985), 47–97; 53-360, rp2/rv2, Mar. 10 1707; 53-369, pa/jv Mar. 11 1707; 53-347, ea/jv, Feb. 28 1707; 53-451, rp2/rv2, Aug. 9 1707; 53- 354, rp2/rv2, Mar. 10 1707.

135. 53-366, jv/rv2, Mar. 31 1707; 53-480, I. Comyns/jv, Sept. 20, 1707; 53-388, jv/rv2, Apr. 10 1707; 53-345, jv/rv2, Feb. 16 1707; CH 2/1587, Marriage settlement, Oct. 16 1707.

136. CH 1/143, CH 1/144a, b, CH 1/145, CH 1/146, CH 2/1587, Settlement deeds, Oct. 1707; CH 2/1588, Division of Paschall estate between two co-heiresses, Feb. 19 1708. £4,000 purchase of land near London was required. For Ralph Verney's wills, see CH 1/162–168, 1721–1737.

137. 53-388, jv/rv2, Apr. 10 1707; 53-412, rp2/jv, May 20 1707.

138. 53-644, rp2/jv, Aug. 23 1708.

139. CH 1/147; 53-475, jv/J. Gardiner, Sept. 16 1707, 55-421, nm/jv, Nov. 16 1714; Sedgwick, *House of Commons*, ii. 495–6; Namier and Brooke, *House of Commons*, iii. 580–2; BL Egerton MS 2353, fos. 6, 18–19, 124–5; [G.E.C.] *Complete Peerage* (1926), v. 295–6; W. Musgrave, *Musgrave's Obituary Prior to 1800* (1900), iv. 292 and iii. 201.

140. 52-298, jv/tche, Nov. 16 1703.

141. J. Beckett, 'English Landownership in the Later 17th and 18th Centuries', *EcHR*, 2nd series, 30 (1977), 567–81, and 'Family Matters', *Historical Journal*, 39 (1996), 249–56; L. Bonfield, 'Affective Families, Open Elites, and Strict Family Settlements . . .', *EcHR*, 2nd series, 36 (1986), 341–54, 'Marriage, Property, and the "Affective Family"', *Law and History Review*, 1 (1983), 297–312, and *Marriage Settlements 1601–1740* (Cambridge, 1983); M. Chesterman, 'Family Settlements in Trust', in G. Rubin and D. Sugarman (eds.), *Law, Economy, and Society 1750–1914* (Abingdon, 1984), 124–67; C. Clay, 'Marriage, Inheritance, and the Rise of Large Estates . . .', *EcHR*, 2nd series, 21 (1968), 503–18; A. Erickson, *Women and Property in Early Modern England* (1993); B. English and J. Saville, 'Family Settlements . . .', *EcHR*, 2nd series, 33 (1980), 556–8; J. Habakkuk, 'English Landownership 1680–1740', *EcHR*, 2nd series, 10 (1940), 2–17, *Marriage, Debt, and the Estate System*, and earlier articles; B. Holderness, 'The English Land Market in the 18th Century', *EcHR*, 2nd series, 27 (1974), 557–76; E. Spring, 'The Family Strict Settlement and Historians', *Canadian Journal of History*, 18 (1983), 379–98.

142. 49-217, jv/rv, July 30 1696. As Elizabeth Delaval noted of a friend in Bodl Rawl. MS D. 78, fo. 317: 'He is now an eldest brother, and yet for all that he is not very easy in his fortune.'

143. Staves, *Married Women's Separate Property*; CH 1/147; PRO PROB 11/569, fo. 125; HL STTP 14/11, Sir Richard Temple's will and codicials, 1683–1697. Temple gave Mary Knapp £300 to be paid within a year after his death and an extra £100 p.a. over and above her jointure, but he revoked the latter in a codicil in another copy of his will, BL Stowe, 840, fo. 15^r.

144. Bridg[e]man, *Conveyances*, 226; Hainsworth, 'Fathers and Daughters', 16; F. Sulloway, *Born to Rebel* (New York, 1996), p. xiv; Bodl Rawl MS D. 78, fo. 129; [J. Swift], *An Essay on the Mischief of Giving Fortunes*, 61.

145. BL Stowe 840, fos. 14^r, 15^v; HL STTP 14/11, 1683–1697. L. Bonfield ('Affective Families', 341–54) argues that fathers lost control over younger sons by providing for them in settlements. The Verneys and Caves also left children money in wills.

146. 48-560, ea/rv, Oct. 29 1695; 51-175, ea/jv, Jan. 13 1700.

147. Laurence, *Women in England*, 272; O'Day, *The Family and Family Relationship*, 77; Vickery, 'Golden Age', 411.

148. 46-135, cst/rv, Dec. 8 1692; 46-524, jk/rv, May 16 1693; 48-155, lg/rv, Feb. 12 1695.

149. The story of Lettice Porter will be told in another paper.

150. 52-554, cdun/jv, Sept. 11 1704; 52-581, rp2/jv, Oct. 17 1704.

151. V. Larminie, *Wealth, Kinship, and Culture* (Woodbridge, Suffolk, 1995), F. Harris, *A

Passion for Government (Oxford, 1991), J. Eales, *Puritans and Roundheads* (Cambridge, 1990). Mary Blacknall helped save Claydon from sequestration.

152. 35-89, rv/jv, June 20 1681; 47-447, nn/jv, June 15 1694; R. Houlbrooke, 'Women's Social Life and Common Action . . . to the Eve of the Civil War', *Continuity and Change*, 1 (1986), 171.

153. 28-39, munv/rv, Aug. 19 1675; 28-48, jst/rv, Sept. 2 1675; 52-654, jv/mc, Jan. 28, 1705; 53-17, tc/jv, June 30 1705.

154. Ezell, *The Patriarch's Wife*; C. Clinton, *The Plantation Mistress* (New York, 1982).

155. 53-696, etv/ebv, Dec. 28 1708; 53-34, etv/ebv, Aug. 4 1705; 55-108, ebv/jv, Apr. 28 1713.

156. 31-51, rv/mpal, May 31 1678; M. Tebbutt, *Women's Talk?* (Aldershot, 1995), 1–18; P. Spacks, *Gossip* (New York, 1985).

157. *Ladies Dictionary*, 480–1, notes different types of widows' behaviour. 55-412, jv/rv2, Nov. 1 1714; 32-130, rv/jv, [1679?]; 30-3, jv/rv, [1676?]; 50-165, nn/jv, Sept. 25 1697.

158. BL Add. MS 71573; BL Stowe MS 840; HL STTP 14/11; HL STTP 14/3, Abstract of marriage settlement, 1677–1715 and various deeds; HL STTP 15/19, Agreement, Feb. 16 1716; HL STTP 16/1, Draft of indenture, Mar. 5 1717. The Temples limited jointures to a percentage of portion, as did the Caves.

159. 53-573, mc/jv, Apr. 19 1708; 53-567, ml/jv, Mar. 25 1708; 51-196, lg/jv, Feb. 29 1700; 51-231, ea/jv, Apr. 8 1700; BL Evelyn Papers L4, Susan Draper/Mary Evelyn, Aug. 26 1689.

160. V. Brodsky, 'Widows in Late Elizabethan London', in L. Bonfield *et. al.* (eds.), *The World We have Gained* (Oxford, 1986), 122–54; BL Add. MS 4454, fo. 68ᵛ; Todd, 'The Remarrying Widow', but see Boulton, 'London Widowhood', 344; CH 1/147; BL Stowe MS 840; HL STTP 14/11 states that Mary Knapp Temple is to have an extra £100 per year only if she 'remains unmarried'.

161. 49-67, nn/jv, June 1 1696; E. Wrigley and R. Schofield, *The Population History of England 1541–1871* (Cambridge, Mass., 1986), 176, 257–65; E. Wrigley, 'Marriage, Fertility, and Population Growth in Eighteenth-Century England', in Outhwaite (ed.), *Marriage and Society*, 149–52, 176–8; Stone, *Family, Sex, and Marriage*, 40–1; Boulton, 'London Widowhood', 345; Hufton, *Prospect Before Her*, 252.

162. 47-637, ea/rv, Oct. 2 1694; 55-4, ml/jv, Nov. 23 1712; 51-484, lg/rv, Aug. 16 1701; 23-21, Peg Elmes's inventory, June 2 1670; 35-6, L. Sheppard's will, Dec. 4 1680; 36-19, lg/rv, Nov. 21 1681; Bodl Rawl MS D. 78, fo. 87.; 50-167, cst/jv, Sept. 29 1697; 48-461, jv/rv, Aug. 25 1695; 49-473, Legacies, n.d.; 30-29, jv/rv, May 28 1677; 48-386, po/rv, July 23 1695.

163. Slater, *Family Life*.

164. Writing on this topic is bound to become plentiful. At present, see the work of Tim Hitchcock and Rudolph Trumbach.

165. J. Habakkuk, 'The Rise and Fall of English Landed Families, 1600–1800', *Transactions of the Royal Historical Society*, 29–31 (1979–81), 187–207, 199–221, 195–217.

166. Habakkuk, 'Rise and Fall', 29 (1979), 194; L. Bonfield, 'Marriage Settlements and the Rise of the Great Estates', *EcHR*, 32 (1979), 483–93.

167. Stone, *Family, Sex and Marriage*, 40–1; M. Kimmel, 'The Contemporary "Crisis" of Masculinity in Historical Perspective', in H. Brod (ed.), *The Making of Masculinities* (Boston, 1987), 126; Wrigley and Schofield, *Population History*, 176, 257–65; *Female Grievances Debated in Six Dialogues . . . with Proposals for . . . Taxing such Bachelors as Refuse to Marry*, 4th edn. (1727), 159–64; *Marriage Promoted*, 30–1.

168. P. Carter, '"Mollies", "Fops", and Men of Feeling', D.Phil. thesis, (Oxford, 1995); Hitchcock, *English Sexualities*, 58–65.

169. G. Mosse, *The Image of Man* (Oxford and New York, 1996), 8; R. Nye, *Masculinity and the Male Codes of Honour in Modern France* (New York and Oxford, 1993); J. Barrell, *The Birth of Pandora and the Division of Knowledge* (1992); M. Breitenberg, *Anxious Masculinity in Early Modern England* (Cambridge, 1996); C. Murphy, Jr., *Beyond Feminism* (Washington, DC, 1995); M. Cohen, *Fashioning Masculinity* (1996); Kimmel, 'The Contemporary 'Crisis' of Masculinity', 121–53; M. Roper and J. Tosh, *Manful Assertions* (1991).

170. 51-486, lg/jv, Aug. 28 1701; 50-70, Bill, June 24 1697; 50-249, List, [1697]; 53-173, rp2/jv, Feb. 11 1706; Sedgwick, *House of Commons*, ii. 496.

171. Sedgwick, *House of Commons*, ii. 496; [G.E.C.], *The Complete Peerage* (1926), v. 295–6; Lipscomb, *History and Antiquities*, i (1831), 183–4; BL Egerton MS 2353; Habakkuk, *Marriage, Debt, and the Estates System*, 55.

172. J. Rosenheim, *The Townshends of Raynham* (Middletown, Conn., 1989); HL STT 235, wchap/srt, Oct. 1673; Henning, *House of Commons*, iii. 536; 28-38, jst/rv, Aug. 19 1675; 28-39, mun/rv, Aug. 19 1675; HL STTP 13/29, Release of Hester Knapp's Dower, Oct. 14 1678; HL STTP 13/30, Hester Knapp's will, Dec. 23 1678; HL STTP 13/31 About Mary Knapp's title to her father's estate, Jan. 4 1679; HL STTP 14/3; HL STTP 15/19. Mary received an extra £400 p.a. in pin money.

173. *Musgrave's Obituary Prior to 1800*, iii. 125; Sedgwick, *House of Commons*, ii. 98; I. Christie, *British 'Non-Elite' MPs 1715–1820* (New York and Oxford, 1995), 44; HL STTP 15/17. In this copy portions for younger sons were blank. HL STT 1483, J. Miller/Viscount Cobham, About difficulty in paying jointures, July 5 1718. Cobham had nothing left unsettled except Lady Temple's jointure. HL STTP 16/2. Edmund Halsey retained part of Anne's portions to pay Cobham's debts. HL STTP 16/3, Anne Halsey's jointure, [1717?].

174. P. Roebuck, *Yorkshire Baronets 1640–1760* (Oxford, 1980), 263; Beckett, *The Rise and Fall of the Grenvilles*, 32, 41; Habakkuk, *Marriage, Debt, and the Estates System*, 196; W. Smith (ed.), *Grenville Papers* (1852), i. 423; Henning, *House of Commons*, iii, 536; [G.E.C.], *Complete Peerage* (1953), xii. 657–61; W. Gibson, '"Withered Branches and Weighty Symbols": Surname Substitution in England 1660–1880', *British Journal of Eighteenth Century Studies*, 15 (1992), 17–33.

Notes to Chapter 6

1. 44-62, rv/nden, Jan. 2 1691.

2. F. O'Gorman, 'Campaign Rituals and Ceremonies', *Past and Present*, 135 (1992), 79–115.

3. J. Rosenheim, *The Townshends of Raynham* (Middletown, Conn., 1989) and *The Emergence of a Ruling Order: English Landed Society 1650–1750* (1998); J. Brewer, *The Sinews of Power* (1988); N. Landau, *The Justices of the Peace 1679–1760* (Berkeley, 1984).

4. M. Kishlansky, *Parliamentary Selection* (Cambridge, 1986); D. Hirst, *The Representative of the People* (Cambridge, 1975); J. Gruenfelder, *Influence in Early Stuart Elections 1604–1640* (Columbus, Oh., 1981); F. O'Gorman, *Voters, Patrons, and Parties* (Oxford, 1989).

5. P. Jenkins notes a similar break accompanied by the rise of party in *The Making of a Ruling Class* (Cambridge, 1983), pp. xxi–xxv, 283–4.

6. Kishlansky, *Parliamentary Selection;* J. Broad, 'Sir John Verney and Buckinghamshire Elections, 1696–1715', *Historical Research,* 56 (1983), 195–204; G. Holmes, 'The Influence of the Peerage in English Parliamentary Elections 1702–13', B.Litt. thesis (Oxford, 1952).

7. For the Temples, see G. Clarke, 'The History of Stowe II, The Rise of the Temple Family', *Stoic,* 22 (1967), 261–265 and 'The History of Stowe V, The Early Life of Richard Temple, Viscount Cobham', *Stoic,* 23 (1968), 116–120; G. Davies, 'The Political Career of Sir Richard Temple (1634–97) and Buckingham Politics', *HLQ* 4 (1940), 47–83; E. Gay, 'The Rise of an English Country Family', *HLQ* 1 (1938), 376–90; 'The Temples of Stowe and their Debts', *HLQ* 2 (1939), 399–438; and 'Sir Richard Temple, the Debt Settlement, and Estate Litigation', *HLQ,* 6 (1943), 255–91; B. Henning, *The House of Commons 1660–1690* (1983), iii. 536–44; G. Lipscomb, *The History and Antiquities of the County of Buckingham* (1847), i. 601 and iii. 84–110; Betham, *Baronetage of England,* v. 136–8; W. Page (ed.) *Victoria History of Buckinghamshire* (1927), iv. 229–38.

8. 34-14, nden/rv, Jan. 1680; 39-35, nden/rv, Feb. 9 1685; 48-494, nden/rv, Sept. 28 1695; 29-20, rv/munv, Feb. 17 1676.

9. For Denton, see Lipscomb, *History and Antiquities,* iii. 16–22; M. Verney, *Bucks Biographies* (Oxford, 1912), 115; 'Hillesden Account Book, 1661–67', *Records of Buckinghamshire,* 11 (1919), 135–44, 186–98, 244–55; G. Scott, *All Saints Church, Hillesden, Buckinghamshire,* n.d.

10. C. Brooks, *Pettifoggers and Vipers of the Commonwealth* (Cambridge, 1986); W. Prest, *The Rise of the Barristers* (Oxford, 1986); Bodl Carte MS 79, fo. 171.

11. B. Snell (ed.), *The Minute Book of the Monthly Meeting of the Society of Friends from the Upperside of Buckinghamshire, 1669–90* (Buckinghamshire Archaeological Society, 1; 1937), p. iii; PRO, 'List of Non-Parochial Registers', *Lists and Indexes* (General Register Office, 42; 1969), 7, 112.

12. 31-9, rv/munv, Jan. 10 1678; 40-32, S. Clarke/rv, June 27 1685; 29-32, rv/jv, Apr. 10 1676; 42-35, jv/rv, Nov. 30 1687.

13. HL STT 1640, R. Price/srt, Jan. 9 1692; 29-12, munv/rv, Jan. 27 1676; 30-43, munv/rv, July 23 1677; 33-78, K. Dormer/rv, Oct. 1679; 32-133, rv/munv, Apr. 1679. The Dormers and Lees were cited 103 and 208 times, respectively.

14. 31-69, munv/rv, July 29 1678; 33-99, munv/jv, Oct. 30 1679.

15. CH 4/5/43-66, Estate correspondence 1690–1716; 30-26, srt/rv, May 2 1677; HL STT 254, wchap/srt, May 7 1682; HL STT 282 wchap/srt, Apr. 18 1683.

16. HL STT 340, wchap/srt, Nov. 26 1686; HL STT 343, wchap/srt, Dec. 12 1686; 45-65, rv/jv, May 9 1692; Broad, 'Sir Ralph Verney and his Estates', 247–57.

17. B. Willis, *The History and Antiquities of the Town . . . of Buckingham* (1755), 42–3, and *Notitia Parliamentaria* (1715), 90, 112; Henning, *House of Commons,* iii. 536–44; Clarke, 'The Rise of the Temple Family', 261; BL Stowe MSS 180 and 304; HL STTCLI 2/19, Inventory, May 19 1697.

18. For examples of Temple's changing positions, see BL Add. MS 32094, fo. 26; BL Add. MS 35865, fos. 212–13; BL Add. MS 47131, fos. 2–4; BL Stowe MS 163, fos. 174–6; BL Stowe MS 304, fos. 184–5; BL Stowe MS 223, fos. 453–4; BL Harl MS 7020, fo. 33; Henning, *House of Commons,* 541–2.

19. Henning, *House of Commons*, iii. 542–3; HL RB 89602, no. 46, [T.W.], *The Matter of Fact of Sir Richard Temple's Case Truly Stated* ([169?]); Bodl Carte MS 32, fos. 597–8.
20. 39-40, rv/wc, Feb. 27 1685; Henning, *House of Commons*, iii. 634–5.
21. 32-23, wd/rv, Nov. 3 1678; 33-10, mun/jv, July 14 1679; 32-113, mun/rv, Mar. 10 1679.
22. Henning, *House of Commons*, iii. 542–3, 635; Davies, 'The Political Career of Sir Richard Temple', 73, 75.
23. E. de Beer, 'Members of the Court Party in the House of Commons 1670–78', *Historical Research*, 11 (1933–4), 19; L. Glassey, *Politics and the Appointment of Justices of the Peace 1675–1720* (Oxford, 1979), 64–5.
24. The Verney letters confirm the early development of party described in T. Harris, *Politics under the Later Stuarts* (1993), 1–25 cf J. Scott, *Algernon Sidney and the Restoration Crisis 1677–1683* (Cambridge, 1991), 4–22; 30-37, jv/munv, June 28 1677; 30-40, rv/munv, July 2 1677; 31-27, munv/rv, Mar. 28 1678; Bodl Carte MS 79, fo. 176. My emphases.
25. 35-80, lg/rv, June 9 1681; 35-44, munv/rv, Apr. 21 1681; 35-95, nden/rv, July 11 1681.
26. 37-14, wd/rv, Nov. 4 1682; HL STT 269, wchap/srt, Nov. 19 1682; 44-10, lg/rv, Feb. 19 1690; Harris, *Politics under the Later Stuarts*, 1–25; Jenkins, *The Making of a Ruling Class*, p. xxiii.
27. Broad (ed.), *Buckinghamshire Dissent*, 77. This figure is for 1706 and includes three hamlets. D. Elliot in *Buckingham* (1975), 239, estimates 1, 525 people in the parish in 1725. Willis, *History . . . of Buckingham*, 29, 270.
28. HL STTM, 6/13, [1674< >1682]; Henning, *House of Commons*, i. 139–40; A. Jenkinson, 'Buckingham Borough', in W. Page (ed.), *Victoria History of Buckinghamshire* (1925), iii. 472.
29. Eliott, *Buckingham*, 208; M. Reed (ed.), *Buckinghamshire Probate Inventories* (Buckinghamshire Record Society, 24; 1988), esp. no. 150; 37-50, munv/jv, May 7 1683; Willis, *History . . . of Buckingham*, 50; Jenkinson, 'Buckingham Borough', 472.
30. HL RB 372059, [T. Carew], *An Historical Account of the Rights of Electors . . .* (1755), 96–101; T. Oldfield, *The Representative History of Great Britain and Ireland* (1816), iii. 52–7; F. Ragg, 'Political History', in Page (ed.), *Victoria History of Buckinghamshire*, iv. 541–8; Kishlansky, *Parliamentary Selection*, 205–6. In this chapter, 'burgesses' describes Corporation members and 'populace' describes freeholders who had voting rights. 'Populace' was a restrictive term and did not include the general public.
31. Henning, *House of Commons*, i. 139, iii. 542; 32-78, rv/munv, Jan. 24 1679; 33-44, *A Letter from a Freeholder*, (Aug. 23 1679); 32-67, munv/rv, 1679; 32-92, nden/rv, Feb. 6 1679; 32-94, munv/jv, Feb. 13 1679; 32-110, munv/jv, 1679.
32. 33-15, jv/rv, July 17 1679; 32-108, munv/rv, Feb. 1679. For Wharton's wealth, see BL Egerton MS 3519, fos. 238–9. Wharton's spending was rumoured at up to £1,700, not £200 as Mun anticipated. There were 860 dinners reported at one inn, 800 bottles of sack at another, and 15,000 men entertained.
33. 33-42, wgro/rv, Aug. 21 1679; *A True Account of What Passed at the Election of Knight of the Shire . . .* (Aug. 30 1679); *A Letter from a Freeholder of Buckinghamshire . . .* (Aug. 23 1679); *The Answer of the Burgesses . . . to . . . Sir Timber Temple* (Sept. 16 1679); *New News of a Strange Monster found in Stowe Wood* (1679); 33-67, munv/jv, Sept. 25 1679; *A Rare Shew of the Monster of Stowe Woods . . .* (n.d.); *A Mild but Searching Expostulatory Letter from the Plain-dealing Farmers of . . . Buckingham* (n.d.).
34. *A Letter from a Freeholder . . .* (Aug. 23, 1679); 33-48, jv/rv, Aug. 28 1679; 33-54, jv/rv, Sept. 1679; 33-42, wgro/rv, Aug. 21 1679; 33-67, munv/jv, Sept. 25 1679.

35. HL STTL, Case 226, 'The King vs Robinson . . .' [1679?]; BL Stowe MS 180, fos. 98–100; J. Ebsworth (ed.), 'The Sale of Esau's Birth-right or the New Buckingham Ballad', *Bagford Ballads* (Hertford, 1878), part 4, Nos. 16–17, 764–8; 'A Political Ballad of the Seventeenth Century', *Records of Buckinghamshire*, 11 (1919), 233–41; HL STT 246, wchap/srt, May 2 1680. Browne Willis attributed the Buckingham Ballad to Charles Blount.

36. 35-22, rv/srt, Feb. 12 1681; HL STT 2450, rv/srt, Feb. 7 1681; HL STTE 1/11, Petition to the Parliament, [1681].

37. HL STT 313, wchap/srt, Dec. 16 1683; HL STT 314, wchap/srt, Dec. 18 1683; HL STT 319, wchap/srt, Apr. 6 1684.

38. HL STTM 6/32, 'Letters Patent . . . Constituting the Town a Free Borough . . .', [July 23 1684]; HL STTM 6/34, 'Buckingham Bailiff and Burgesses, Heads of Alternatives of . . . the New Charter', [1684]; HL STT 327, wchap/srt, July 20 1684.

39. Kishlansky, *Parliamentary Selection*, 201–23; 39-39, rv/wc, Feb. 25 1685; 39-61, srt/rv, Apr. 1 1685; 39-42, rv/wc, March 2 1685; 39-55, srt/munv, March 24 1685; 39-56, wbus/rv, Mar. 24 1685.

40. J. Barry, 'Provincial Town Culture, 1640–1780: Urbane or Civic?', in J. Pittock and A. Wear (eds.), *Interpretation and Cultural History* (1991), 198–234; 39-55, srt/munv, Mar. 24 1685.

41. 39-57, jv/rv, March 25 1685; 39-63, jv/rv, Apr. 8 1685; 40-3. jv/rv, Apr. 23 1685; 40-2, jv/rv, Apr. 22 1685.

42. 32-87, rv/munv, Jan. 30 1679; 39-40, rv/wc, Feb. 27 1685; 39-43, rv/wc, Mar. 5 1685; 39-44, H. Hyde/rv, Mar. 7 1685; 40-26, rv/jv, May 15 1685; Davies, 'The Political Career of Sir Richard Temple', 72–6; 41-37, jv/rv, Dec. 1 1686; 41-67, jv/munv, May 4 1687; 42-49, 'Mandamus from the king . . .', Feb. 25 1688; 42-51, srt/rv, Mar. 1688; HL STT 69, W. Barton/Baron Jeffreys, Dec. 12 1687.

43. 43-58, rv/srt, Jan. 8 1689; 43-72, rv/wc, Jan. 26 1689.

44. 43-61, wc/rv, Jan. 13 1689; HL STT 219, wchap/wc, Jan. 15 1689. Tyrrell received 110 votes and Temple had 109. Verney spent more than the £1. 18s. 6d., cited in 43-57, wc/rv, 'Some Election Expenses', Jan. 3 1689 and Henning, *House of Commons*, i. 139, 142. He spent at least £11. 16s. on the day of the election for the crier, poll clerks, ringer, and music.

45. HL STT 413, wchap/srt, Feb. 17 1689; 44-4, wc/rv, Feb. 10 1690; 44-1, nden/rv, Nov. 4 1689; HL STT 478, wchap/srt, Feb. 11 1690; 44-5, lg/rv, Feb. 14 1690; 44-7, rv/jv, Feb. 16 1690; K. Feiling, *The History of the Tory Party 1640–1714* (Oxford, 1924), appendix 2, 496.

46. 44-12, rv/jv, Feb. 21 1690; 44-8, munv/rv, Feb. 18 1690.

47. 44-10, lg/rv, Feb. 19 1690; 44-13, lg/rv, Feb. 22 1690. Nancy's father was Dr William Denton, one of Sir Ralph's closest friends.

48. 44-30, rv/nden, Mar. 30 1690; 44-32, jv/rv, Apr. 6 1690; 44-62, rv/nden, Jan. 2 1690/91; 44-10, lg/rv, Feb. 19 1690.

49. Bucks CRO D/X 1069/2/50, R. Tighe/J. Baker, May 15 1715.

50. See Henning, *House of Commons 1660–90*; Sedgwick, *House of Commons 1715–54*; and Lipscomb, *History and Antiquities*, for all Buckinghamshire leaders. For Sir Edmund Denton, see R. Gardiner (ed.), *Registers of Wadham College Oxford*, Part 1. *1613–1719* (1889), Feb. 21 1695; BL Stowe MS 750, fo. 13, Mar. 10 1709.

51. 30-27, P. Wharton/rv, May 5 1677; Bodl Add. MS D. 40, Marriage Settlement; BL Egerton 4162, fo. 232, A. Wharton/T. Wharton, Mar. 22 1681; PRO C104/110, Part l., Wharton papers.

52. Bodl Carte MS 79-81; Bodl Rawl Letters MS 49-51; J. Carswell, *The Old Cause* (1954), 27–127; Henning, *House of Commons*, iii. 697–700; 49-326, srt/nn, Nov. 30, 1696; 49-339, db2/jv, Dec. 5 1696; G. Holmes, 'The Influence of the Peerage', appendix A, 175; BL Egerton MS 3519, fos. 238–9; BL Add. MS 70014, fo. 355.

53. HL, Cheyne papers in the Ellesmere Collection; Bodl Top Bucks MS C1, fos. 102, 105; Bodl Willis MS 20, fo. 69; Henning, *House of Commons*, ii. 51–3; Lipscomb, *History and Antiquities*, iii, 331–2; W. Gaunt, *Kensington and Chelsea* (1975), 17, 24; PRO PROB 11/622, fo. 174; BL Add. MS 40774, fos. 104–5. BL Add. MS 61628, fo. 153 illustrates Cheyne's power.

54. M. Wiesner, *Women and Gender in Early Modern Europe* (Cambridge, 1993), 239. For an early view, see L. Namier, *The Structure of Politics at the Accession of George III* (1929).

55. CH 4/5/49/103, A. Dover/jv, Nov. 30 1696; 49-516, jv/wc, Jan. 20 1697; 49-582jv/wc, Mar. 10 1697; CH 4/5/50/88, jv/jchu, Mar. 9 1697/8; 50-305, jv/wc, Mar. 3 1698; 49-544, jv/wc, Feb. 10 1697; 50-559, jv/wc, Feb. 24 1697; 50-571, ebv/wc Dec. 27 1698. Broad notes that Sir Ralph's harsh policy of rack-renting changed at the end of the 17th century when arrears rose to as much as 59% in 'Sir Ralph Verney and his Estates', 247–57.

56. CH 4/5/54/6, jv/wc, May 21 1701; CH 4/5/53/10, jv/wc, June 12 1700; CH 4/5/56/26, jv/wc, June 30 1703 (endorsed June 13); CH 4/5/53/6, wc/jv, June 2 1700; 50-277, jv/wc, Jan. 23 1698. J. Beckett makes similar points about Sir James Lowther in *Coal and Tobacco* (Cambridge, 1981), 30–31, but see G. Mingay, 'Thrumpton: A Nottinghamshire Estate in the Eighteenth Century', *Thoroton Society Transactions*, 61 (1958), 50–6 for a benevolent landlord.

57. CH 4/5/54/19, wc/jv, June 15 1701.

58. 50-272, jv/wc, Jan. 19 1698; 50-281, jv/wc, Jan. 26 1698; 50-349, jv/wc, Apr. 27 1698; 50-565, ebv/wc, Dec. 13 1698; 50-40, eli/jv, June 6 1697; CH 4/5/50/49, wc/jv, Jan. 9 1698; 49-173, rv/wc, June 17 1696; 47-91, rv/jv, Oct. 1 1693; 46-384, wc/rv, Mar. 20 1693.

59. 49-536, jv/wc, Feb. 4 1697; 55-325, jv/rv2, [1714?]; 53-362, jv/N. Wright, Mar. 14 1707; 55-620, jv/rv2, Nov. 29 1715; 49-610, jv/wc, Mar. 25 1697.

60. 48-479, jv/rv, Aug. 29 1695; 48-619, eli/rv, Dec. 15 1695; 49-317, eli/jv, Nov. 22 1696; 53-519, cc/jv, Nov. 2 1707; CH 4/5/63/19, cc/jv, Mar. 9 1712; CH 4/5/63/15, cc/jv, Mar. 2 1712; 52-544. R. Stapp, jv, Aug. 11 1704; 48-140, wc/rv, Feb. 3 1695; 48-212, eli/rv, Apr. 14 1695; CH 4/5/50/37, wc/jv, Dec. 26 1697; CH 4/5/50/49, wc/jv, Jan. 9 1698.

61. 54-411, wbus/jv, Mar. 2 1712; 48-533, rv/jv, Sept. 15 1695; E. Thompson, 'Eighteenth-Century English Society', *Social History*, 3 (1978), 133–65; 'Patrician Society, Plebeian Culture?', *Journal of Social History*, 7 (1974), 382–405.

62. G. Holmes, *British Politics*; J. Plumb, *The Growth of Political Stability* (1967); W. Speck, *Tory and Whig* (1970); C. Jones (ed.), *Britain in the First Age of Party 1680–1750* (1982); Brewer, *The Sinews of Power*; W. Speck, 'The House of Commons 1702–14: A Study in Political Organization', D. Phil. thesis (Oxford, 1965).

63. V. Stater, *Noble Government* (Athens, Ga., 1994); J. Sainty, *Lieutenants of Counties 1585–1642* (1970); L. Glassey, *Politics and the Appointment of Justices of the Peace 1675–1720* (Oxford, 1979). John bought R. Kilburne's *Choice Presidents upon All Acts of Parliament Relating to [the] Office and Duty of a Justice of the Peace*, 3rd edn. (1685) for Sir Ralph.

64. Holmes, 'The Influence of the Peerage', 140, 146–8; J. Grego, *A History of Parliamentary Elections and Electioneering in the Old Days* (1886), 69.

65. 51-617, lg/jv, Dec. 9 1700; 51-626, lg/jv, Dec. 13 1700; 51-114, lg/jv, Nov. 7 1699; 51-71, lg/jv, Sept. 26 1699; 56-139, nm/jv, Nov. 14 1716.

66. Cheyne entered the House of Lords after the Union with Scotland. For a computer-based analysis of Buckinghamshire voting patterns, see W. Speck and W. Grey, 'Computer Analysis of Poll Books, An Initial Report', and W. Speck *et al.*, 'A Further Report', in *Historical Research*, 43 (1970), 105–12 and 48 (1975), 64–90. GH Poll Book, 1705; Bucks CRO Poll Books, 1700/1, 1702, 1710, 1713.

67. Holmes, *British Politics*; G. Holmes and W. Speck, *The Divided Society* (1967); W. Speck, *Tory and Whig* (1970); J. Plumb, 'The Growth of the Electorate in England from 1600–1715', *Past and Present*, 45 (1969), 90–116.

68. Holmes, 'The Influence of the Peerage'; Broad, 'Sir John Verney and Buckinghamshire Elections'.

69. 49-324, nn/jv, Nov. 29 1696; 49-332, jv/tpig, Dec. 1 1696.

70. 43-66, jchu/wc, n.d.; 49-409, jv/wc, Dec. 19 1696; 49-346, wbus/jv, Dec. 6 1696; 49-351, wbus/jv, Dec. 12 1696; 49-364, wbus/jv, Dec. 19 1696.

71. 49-410, jv/wc, Dec. 17 1696; 49-344, jchu/jv, Dec. 6 1696; Walpole MSS, Horatio Walpole, Jr. to Robert Walpole, Sept. 9 1710, quoted in J. Plumb, *Sir Robert Walpole: The Making of a Statesman* (1972), i. 163–4.

72. 49-334, jv/ttyr, ebat, srt, Dec. 26 1696.

73. 49-557, eli/jv, Feb. 21 1697; 50-451, R. Hill/jv, July 22, 1698; J. Clark, *Goodwin Wharton* (New York, 1984); Bodl Gough Bucks MS 5, fos. 101, 103; Lipscomb, *History and Antiquities*, iv. 444–5, 455–6; BL Sloane MS 4039, fo. 302; BL Add. MS 70264; 48-636, jv/lc, n.d. For Hill see Bucks CRO D/W/76; Bucks CRO D/W/97/8.

74. 50-453, jv/Dr. Woodhouse, July 23 1698; 50-538, lg/rv, Nov. 2 1698; 51-39, jv/Capt. Cross, Aug. 26 1699; 51-565, jv/ttip, Nov. 14 1700; 50-448, jv/llit, July 21 1698.

75. 50-464, lc/jv, July 30 1698; 50-500, lc/jv, Sept. 14 1698; 50-484, rhil/jv, Aug. 17 1698.

76. 50-535, jv/ed, Oct. 28 1698; 50-540, Bez Knight/jv, Nov. 3 1698; Bodl Willis MS 8, fo. 155, cf. R. Walcott, *English Politics in the Early Eighteenth Century* (Oxford, 1956) who stressed the importance of kinship to faction.

77. 50-526, List of Buckinghamshire burgesses, Oct. 25 1698; 50-531, nn/jv, Oct. 27 1698; 50-551, H. Seaton/jv, Nov. 20 1698; 50-552, lc/jv, Nov. 19 1698; 50-557, 'Sir Edmund King's certificate of Sir John Verney's health', Dec. 6 1698; 51-99, lg/jv, Oct. 17 1699; 50-568, jv/wc, [Dec. 1698?]; 50-565, ebv/wc, Dec. 13 1698. It is not clear whether John actually stood at a poll in this election.

78. 51-16, lg/jv, July 25 1699; 51-61, lg/jv, Sept. 12 1699; 51-111, lg/jv, Oct. 31 1699; 51-31, lg/jv, Aug. 15 1699; 51-46, lg/jv, Aug. 29 1699; 55-306, jv/rv2, May 13 1714.

79. 51-107, lg/jv, Oct. 24 1699; 51-631, lg/jv, Dec. 16 1701; 53-94, rp2/jv, Dec. 9 1705; *Postboy*, no. 2401, Sept. 30–Oct. 3 1710; 55-370, jv/wv, Sept. 5 1714.

80. *The Principles and Designs of the High Church Party . . .* (1710); 55-150, ebv/jv, June 30 1713; 51-617, lg/jv, Dec. 9 1700; 55-270, [wv, 1714].

81. 51-557, lc/jv, Nov. 5 1700; 51-558, jv/lc, Nov. 10 1700; Lipscomb, *History and Antiquities*, i. 415, 428; Henning, *House of Commons*, ii. 221–2; Bodl Willis MS 8, fo. 151; 51-587, lg/jv, Dec. 3 1700; 51-617, lg/jv, Dec. 9 1700; 51-357, jv/lc, Dec. 19 1700. Dormer wrote the Verneys 16 letters.

82. 51-630, F. Knollys/jv, Dec. 16 1700; 51-361, lg/jv, Dec. 25 1700; 51-357, jv/lc, Dec. 19 1700.

83. Poll books or abstracts for 1698, 1700/1, and 1701 are found in Bucks CRO D/X 933; Bodl Willis MS 8, fos. 151, 154; HL EL 35C20 (formerly 8629A). Handwritten abstracts

vary from official returns and show why polls were checked for fraud and unintended mistakes. For county totals, see History of Parliament Trust data. 1701 totals for Cheyne vary from 1353 to 1853 in abstracts. 51-379, lc/jv, Jan. 2 1701; 52-358, jv/lc, Jan. 21 1705.

84. 51-721, jchu/jv, May 10 1702; 51-722, jv/jchu, May 13 1702; 51-724, jchu/jv, May 19 1702; 11-8, jv/jchu, [n.d.]; J. Locke, *Of Civil Government, Second Treatise on Government* (South Bend, Ind., 1955), 68, 146.

85. 51-519, jv/lc, Nov. 18 1701; Bucks CRO D/X 933, *1702 Poll Book.* Cheyne later blamed John for his loss in 51-703, lc/jv, Apr. 2 1702.

86. 51-548, T. Smith/jv, Sept. 2 1700; HL EL 10751, fo. 4, Account of the Buckinghamshire sessions, 1702; 52-231, lc/jv, June 14 1703; Bodl Carte MS 79, fo. 694, [n.d.]; CH 14/2, Letters Patent, Grant to John Verney, June 16 1703. John's title was not as prestigious as that of an English Viscount and was probably arranged by Lord Cheyne, who was the first to congratulate him.

87. 52-521, mc/jv, July 5 1704; 52-524, W. Bartlet/jv, July 10 1704; 52-590, F. Duncombe/jv, Oct. 28 1704; HL STT 2658, J. Wittewronge/H. Andrewes, Nov. 3 1704; 52-357, lc/jv, Jan. 16 1705; GH, *Buckinghamshire Poll Book,* 1705; Bodl Gough Bucks 1/3; 53-114, bwil/jv, Dec. 15 1705; 53-191, jv/nm, Mar. 22 1706; 52-682, jv/tc, Feb. 4 1705; Bodl Ballard MS 38, fo. 137; Holmes, *British Politics,* 128.

88. BL Add. MS 33225, fo. 17; 53-631, ea/jv, Aug. 3 1708; 54-53, llit/jv, Apr. 17 1709; Bodl Ballard MS 21, fo. 123.

89. Bucks CRO D/X 1069/2/35; BL Add. MS 70217; 54-305, bb/jv, Sept. 23 1710; 54-306, jv/bb, Sept. 26 1710; 55-172, L. Thomson/jv, Aug. 12 1713.

90. Bucks CRO D/MH/40/1; Bodl Gough Bucks 1/4; Speck and Grey, 'Computer Analysis of Poll books, An Initial Report'; Broad, 'Sir John Verney and Buckinghamshire Elections', 200; 54-318, jv, 'Charges in Procuring Freeholders', 1710; 54-303, Capt. Chapman/jv, Sept. 14 1710; 54-304, D. Seaton/jv, Sept. 22 1710.

91. Bucks CRO D/MH/40/1; Bodl Gough Bucks 1/4; 54-313, db2/jv, Oct. 7 1710; 54-309, db2/jv, Sept. 27 1710; 54-356, vlld/rv2, Dec. 24 1710; *The Principles and Designs of the High Church Party . . .* (1710).

92. 54-343, jv/rv2, Dec. 5 1710; Clarke, 'The Early Life of Richard Temple, Viscount Cobham', 119; 54-333, jv/rv2, Nov. 30 1710; 54-549, jv/rv2, Feb. 28 1712; BL Stowe MS 223, fos. 453–4, 1710; BL Add. MS 70331-3, fo. 206, [1712]; History of Parliament Trust data.

93. Feiling, *The History of the Tory Party,* 442; J. Ashton, *Social Life in the Reign of Queen Anne* (New York, 1929), 130; Holmes, *British Politics,* 21–3; 53-573, mc/jv, Apr. 19 1708; 53-39, tc/rv2, Aug. 13 1705; 55-81, rp2/jv, Mar. 24 1714.

94. Bucks CRO DX/1069/2/144; 56-146, tc/jv, Dec. 5 1716; *Spectator,* no. 181, June 2 1711. For the same social divisions in 18th-century Philadelphia, see E. Rasmussen, 'Democratic Environment—Aristocratic Aspiration', *Pennsylvania Magazine of History and Biography,* 90 (1966), 155–82.

95. 37-45, jv/munv, Apr. 2 1683; 52-33, ebv/jv, Sept. 5 1702; 52-102, lg/jv, Dec. 12 1702; Jenkins, *The Making of a Ruling Class,* 267; 54-667, tc/jv, Oct. 10 1712; 56-85, tc/jv, Aug. 6 1716; 56-127, jv/rv2, Oct. 7 1716.

96. 54-439, ml/jv, June 22 1711; 55-9, wv/jv, Nov. 29 1712; 54-463, tc/jv, Oct. 15 1711; W. Speck, *Whig and Tory,* 31; 55-97, jv/rv2, Apr. 5 1713; 54-490, jv/wv, Oct. 11 1711.

97. 54-537, T. Newman/jv, Jan. 19 1712; 54-593, ebv/jv, May 1 1712; 55-31, jv/rp2, Dec. 30 1712.

98. 54-365, lc/jv, Dec. 6 1710; BL Add. MS 70217, W. Cheyne/R. Harley, Aug. 12 1710, Aug. 20 1713, Nov. 12 1711; BL Add. MS 4291, fo. 241; HL EL 10456, Account Book of Lord Cheyne, Clerk of the Pipe, 1712–20; 54-515, lc/jv, Dec. 18 1711.
99. 50-259, nlut/jv, Dec. 1697; 54-619, jv/E. Lane, Aug. 2 1712; 54-562, ebv/jv, Mar. 22 1712.
100. 54-394, jv/rv2, Jan. 18 1711; HL STT 25, E. Andrewes/H. Andrewes, Sept. 1705; Clarke, 'The Early Life of Richard Temple, Viscount Cobham', 116–20; T. Prime, *Some Account of the Temple Family* (New York, 1887); Lipscomb, *History and Antiquities*, iii. 84–109; BL Add. MS 17677 FFF, fo. 147; BL Add. MS 31143, fos. 445-7; BL Add. MS 61307, fo. 173; BL Add. MS 61312, fos. 134-5.
101. 55-157, nm/jv, July 25 1713; HL STTM 7/63, Dec. 24 1716; Bucks CRO D104/69, Mar. 3 1711.
102. 55-110, nm/jv, May 3 1713; 55-113, ebv/jv, May 5 1713.
103. 55-99, jv/rv2, Apr. 14 1713; 55-117, ebv/jv, May 11 1713.
104. For the Chaloners, see Bucks CRO AR 3/38, Dr Chaloner's Grammar School, 1596–1896, and D/A/T/54, Steeple Claydon Parish Register, Sept. 5 1713; Lipscomb, *History and Antiquities*, iii. 80, 336; M. Verney, *Bucks Biographies*, 90. After John bought land from William Chaloner of Steeple Claydon in 1704, his son Charles became John's steward. Another son, a clergyman, received a living with John's aid.
105. 55-117, ebv/jv, May 11 1713; 55-173, T. Prior/jv, Aug. 11 1713; CH 4/5/64/8, cc/jv, May 17 1713; CH 4/5/64/11, cc/jv, May 24 1713; CH 4/5/64/22, cc/jv, June 25 1713.
106. 50-571, ebv/wc Dec. 27 1698; 56-64, ebv/jv, May 25, 1716.
107. 54-597, ebv/jv, May 6 1712; 55-139, ebv/jv, May 28 1713; 56-63, ebv/jv, May 26 1716; 55-35, jv/rp2, Jan. 8 1713; 55-149, ebv/jv, June 26 1713; 55-144, ebv/jv, June 20 1713; 55-150, ebv/jv, June 30.
108. HL STT 2450, rv/srt, Feb. 7 [1681]; 53-587, wbut/jv, Apr. 20 1708; 56-161, cpv/rv2, Jan. 7 1717.
109. *Postboy*, no. 2838, July 16–18, 1713; Bodl Ballard MS 38, fo. 162; Bucks CRO PB/17/1, D/FR/128/11.
110. 55-165, jv/rv2, Aug. 6 1713; 55-281, jv/rv, Mar. 9 1714; HL EL 10729, Abstract of election account, 1713; HL EL 10734, Election bills, 1713; HL EL 10728, 'Expenses in Procuring Freeholders . . .' 1713; 55-185, T. Wisdome/jv, Sept. 8 1713; HL EL 10737, 1713; HL EL 10740, W. Theed/Mr. Roberts, [1710? 1719?]; Broad, 'Sir John Verney and Buckinghamshire Elections', 202–3. John spent almost £500.
111. HL EL 10730, J. Robarts/lc, Nov. 18 1713.
112. 55-202, jv/wv, Oct. 4 1714; 55-200, jv/rv2, Oct. 4 1713; 55-215, tc, jv, Nov. 2 1713; 55-230, ebv/jv, [1713]; F. O'Gorman, 'Campaign Rituals and Ceremonies', *Past and Present*, 135 (1992), 79–115.
113. 55-182, tc/jv, Sept. 5 1713; 51-617, lg/jv, Dec. 9 1700; 50-367, jv/wc, May 17 1698; 49-325, nn/jv, Nov. 30 1696.
114. 29-9, munv/rv, Jan. 3 1676; 51-99, lg/jv, Oct. 17 1699; 50-560, ebv/wc, Dec. 1 1698; Bucks CRO D/X 1069/2/140.
115. L. Klein, 'Gender and the Public/Private Distinction', *Eighteenth-Century Studies*, 29 (1995), 102; E. Chalus in 'Women in English Political Life 1754–1790', D.Phil. thesis (Oxford, 1997).
116. 22-1, jv/lc, received 20 Nov. 1667; HL EL 10705, ebv/lc, Sept. 21 1714; 55-132, jv/rv2, June 4 1713; 55-281, jv/rv2, Mar. 9 1714; Sedgwick, ii. 129; HL EL 10705, ebv/lc, Sept. 21 1714; 55-313, S. Harcourt. jv, June 3 1714; 55-311, wv/jv, May 27 1714; Bucks CRO D/X 1069/2/139.

117. Bodl Ballard MS 25, fos. 111–12; BL Add. MS 70292, 'Notes and dates as to the Elec: [tion] Bucks from Aug. 4 1714', Sept. 6, 7, 9, 13, 14, 16, 21, 30 and Oct. 8, 9, 1714. (BL notes Lord Wharton's handwriting); BL Add. MS. 70266, R. Hampden/T. Wharton, Sept. 16 1714; For Wharton's motivations, see HL EL 10731, T. Wharton, 'A True Copy Examined by J. Robarts, Nov. 24 1714'; Sedgwick, ii. 39.

118. C. Russell, *The Fall of the British Monarchies 1637–42* (Oxford, 1991); J. Morrill, *Revolt of the Provinces* (1976); J. Clark, *English Society 1688–1832* (Cambridge, 1985).

119. T. Harris *et al.* (eds.), *The Politics of Religion in Restoration England* (Oxford, 1990) and *Popular Culture in England 1500–1850* (1995); S. Pincus, *Protestantism and Patriotism* (1995); N. Rogers, *Whigs and Cities* (New York, 1990); J. Black and J. Gregory (eds.), *Culture, Politics, and Society in Britain 1660–1800* (Manchester, 1991); T. Claydon, *William III and the Godly Revolution* (Cambridge, 1996); L. Glassey (ed.), *The Reigns of Charles II and James VII and II* (1997); M. Knights, *Politics and Opinion in Crisis 1678–1681* (Cambridge, 1994).

120. Three copies of the announcement of the pact are HL EL 10721 with 15 signatures, 55-396 with 17, and 55-394 with 21. The following narrative is based on Verney and Temple correspondence, Wharton's notes found in BL Add. MS 70292, Cheyne/ Harley letters in the HL Ellesmere Collection, Bodl Ballard MSS 10 and 38, and BL Add. MS 20217.

121. BL Add. MS. 70266, R. Hampden, Oct. 19 1714; 55-412, jv/rv2, Nov. 1 1714; 55-429, ml/ jv, Nov. 29 1714; 55-399, jv/lc, Oct. 17 1714; Nottingham University, Portland Harley MSS, Pw2Hy 944, R. Hampden, Dec. 16 1714; East Sussex RO, Glynde MS, GLY 795, T. Wharton/R. Hampden, Oct. 9 and Nov. 29 1714.

122. HL EL 10700, J. Robarts/lc, Nov. 7 1714; HL EL 10695, J. Robarts/lc, Nov. 18 1714.

123. HL EL 10768, lc/bwil [1714]; 55-425, jv/lc, Nov. 28 1714; 55-427, lc/jv, Nov. 25 1714; 55-439, lc/jv, Dec. 2 1714; 55-442, jv/lc, Dec. 5 1714.

124. HL EL 10715/16, Nov. 30 1714; HL EL 10722, twha/lc, Dec. 7 1714; 55-458, jv/rv2, Dec. 26 1714; HL EL 10714, J. Fleetwood/lc, Dec. 25 1714; Bodl Ballard MS 31, fo. 32.

125. 55-451, R. Hampden, printed circular letter, Dec. 18 1714.

126. Colley, *In Defiance of Oligarchy* (Cambridge, 1982), 12; R. Rosaldo, *Ilongot Head Hunting 1883–1974* (Stanford, Calif., 1980). J. Black–Michaud defines the feud as a relationship or 'form of communicative behaviour uniting parts of society in alliance and locking opposed groups in hostile competition over shared values which are exchanged and intensified through such interaction' in *Cohesive Force: Feud in the Mediterranean and the Middle East* (Oxford, 1975) 208.

127. 55-601, tc/jv, Oct. 26 1715; 56-126, tc/rv2, Oct. 5 1716; 55-640, rp2/rv2, Dec. 27 1715; 55-401, tc/jv, Oct. 18 1714.

128. Bucks CRO D/X 1069/2/51; P. Monod, *Jacobitism and The English People 1688–1788* (Cambridge, 1989); Bucks CRO D/X 1069/2/146.

129. 55-635, db2/jv, Dec. 24 1715; R. Sedgwick, *House of Commons*, ii. 495; Bucks CRO D/ X 1069/2/150.

130. *Stow: The Gardens of the Right Honourable Richard Lord Viscount Cobham, Addres'd to Mr. Pope* (1732); Page, *Victoria History of Buckinghamshire*, iii. 307; W. Musgrave, *Musgrave's Obituary Prior to 1800*, ed. G. Armytage (1900), iii. 125; Sedgwick, *House of Commons*, ii. 98; 55-405, jv/pv, Oct. 12 1714; 55-415, pa/jv, Nov. 6 1714; 55-500, jv/rv2 Mar. 6 1715.

131. J. Beckett, *The Rise and Fall of the Grenvilles* (Manchester and New York, 1994); W. Smith (ed.), *The Grenville Papers*, i (1852).

132. Sedgwick, *House of Commons*, ii. 496; L. Namier and J. Brooke (eds), *House of Commons, 1754–90* (1964). iii., 580–2; [G.E.C.], *The Complete Peerage* (1926), v. 295–6; BL Stowe MS 4; BL Egerton MS 2353, Settlement of Lands of Ralph, 2nd Earl Verney, 1767; Lipscomb, *History and Antiquities* (1831), i. 183–4.

SELECT BIBLIOGRAPHY

Manuscript Sources

Bank of England
Ledgers A (1), fo. 29. C (3), fo. 1010. (5), fo. 218.

Berkshire County Record Office
D/EMt/T1/1–17. Deeds and settlements, 1639–1730.
D/EZ 5 B1. Henry Hunter's journal, 1660–78.

Bodleian Library
Add. D.40. Wharton marriage settlement, 1673.
Ballard 10, 21, 31, 33, 38. Dr Charlet's letters.
Bankes 14 and 62. JP returns, 1632–5.
Carte 25, 32, 79–81. Political papers.
D.D. Dashwood A.1/6, c.1. Dashwood papers.
Eng. Hist. c.482. Herrick papers.
Eng. Letts. c.438, d.409. Ralph Palmer's letters and Verney bookplate.
Eng. Letts. e.29. Henry letters.
Eng. Misc. c.2, fo. 3. Browne Willis, library catalogue, 1710–20.
Gough Bucks 3, 4, 5. Bucks material.
Pigott B4. Pigott family papers.
Rawl D.78. Elizabeth Delaval, Meditations and Prayers, c.1662–71.
Rawl Letters 50, 51. Wharton papers.
Top Bucks C1, C4. Bucks material.
Willis 1, 7, 8, 9, 19, 20, 30, 32. Bucks material.
Pollbooks. London, Middlesex, Bucks.

British Library
Add. 4291. Harley letters.
Add. 17677 FFF. State Papers.
Add. 19143, 32500, 32504. North papers.
Add. 22185, fo. 13. East India Company subscribers.
Add. 22221, 22226. Wentworth papers.
Add. 27418. Sir Walter Calverley's diary, 1663–1749.
Add. 28087. Papers concerning Buckinghamshire, c.1637–1700.
Add. 29565, 29572. Hatton–Finch papers.
Add. 31143. Wentworth papers.
Add. 32094, 35865. Parliamentary papers.
Add. 32703. Newcastle papers.
Add. 33225. Hare letters.
Add. 61307, 61312, 61628. Blenheim papers.
Add. 40774, fos. 104–5. Vernon papers, 1699.
Add. 70014. Portland papers.

Add. 70217, 70264. Harley papers.

Add. 70266. Hampden/Wharton letters.

Add. 70292. Election notes from 1714. [T. Wharton].

Add. 70331. Canvassing list, 1712.

Add. 72516. Trumbull letters.

Burney newspaper collection.

Egerton 2353. Settlement of Ralph, 2nd Earl Verney, 1767.

Egerton 3359, fos. 58–61. Bank of England proprietors, 1710.

Egerton 3519, 4162. Wharton papers.

Evelyn Papers L4. Mary Evelyn's letters, 1689.

Harley 7020, fo. 33. List of officers.

Harley 7497–8. South Sea Company subscribers, 1711.

Sloane 994, fo. 21b. Daniel Baker's signature, 1671.

Sloane 4038–9. Sloane letters.

Stowe 4. Verney bookplate.

Stowe 163, 180, 191, 304, 750. Political papers.

Stowe 223, fos. 453–4. Canvassing list, 1710.

Stowe 802. Richard Grenville's assessments, c.1637–40.

Stowe 840, fos. 12–16. Sir Richard Temple's will, 1697.

Trumbull Add. 95. Merchant list, 1688.

Buckinghamshire County Record Office

AR 3/38. Dr Chaloner's grammar school.

BAS 340/22/4. Court baron, 1701.

D104/69. Perkins v Temple, 1706–12.

D/A/T/54. Steeple Claydon parish register.

D/A/We/34/122. John Churchill's will, 1640.

DA/We/49/193. William White's will, 1705.

D/C/3/61, D/X 933, D/MH/40/1, PB/17/1, D/FR/128/11. County poll books, 1685, 1700/1, 1702, 1710, 1713, 1722.

D/DR. Drake Papers.

D/W/76. Sir Roger Hill's letters, 1677–93.

D/W/97/8. Sir Roger Hill's diary, 1690s and early 18th century.

D/X/171/50. Assignment, 1684.

D/X 337. East Claydon account book.

D/X 761–900. Records of the Baker family, 1680–1769.

D/X 1069. Additional records of the Baker family, 1657–1778.

DX 1351 (formerly AR 56/96). Baker papers deposited 1996, 1668–1769.

PR 51/1/2. East Claydon parish register, 1690–1720.

PR 52/12/1. Middle Claydon overseers' accounts, 1680–1730.

PR/143/1/15–16. Marsh Gibbon index to christening and burials.

W557. William Coleman's will, 1703.

Glebe terriers and parish registers

Buckinghamshire County Reference Library

Local History Division files.

Cambridge University Library

Sel 2.114–126. Verney collection of Popish Plot Pamphlets.

Claydon House, Buckinghamshire

(For a complete list of Verney papers, see NRA 21959, S. Ranson, *The Verney Papers Catalogued for the Claydon House Trust*, 1994).

CH 1/1–169, 205–229, 467–74. Settlements, wills, and mortgages.

CH2. Deeds of Verney and other families.

CH 4/5/34/48. Letter, Dec 1 1681.

CH 4/5/37/68–9. Cloth to Smyrna 1684–5.

CH 4/5/43–66. Estate correspondence: Ralph and John Verney with stewards William Coleman, Charles Chaloner, and others. *c*.1690–1716.

CH 4/6/4. John Verney's financial accounts for Sir Ralph, London, 1679–95.

CH 4/6/9. Leather book, *British Merlin*, 1689 with rent receipts, *c*.1704–9.

CH 4/6/47/2. Annuity, 1693.

CH 7/2–3, 37, 50–62, 90, 91, 96; 14/4, 20, 49, 68. Business and finance papers, *c*.1675–82.

CH 7/53. John Verney's London household account, 1682–3.

CH 8/2–7, 14–18, 33–42, 49, 52–3, 74–84, 95–7, 101. Trustee papers, 17th–18th centuries.

CH 10/8–12. Miscellaneous correspondence.

CH 11/24. Answers to inquiries about the Church. *c*.1640.

CH 11/22/1–2. Middle Claydon parish register, 1657–1722.

CH 12/1–17. Maps of the Claydons, 17th-19th centuries.

CH 14/1–75. Grants of titles and genealogical papers.

CH 15/1–57. Miscellaneous papers including 'Faults in the Book of Mr Verney's Descents of Baronets', *c*. 1690.

Verney Papers on microfilm. 1642–1720. See Appendix VI: The Verney Papers: Citations and Abbreviations

Corporation of London Record Office

BR/B/1–8039. Brokers' bonds, 1697–1870.

BR/BI/1,2. Index to brokers' bonds.

BR/C 1.9, BR/R1. Lists of brokers, 1697, 1707–8.

CF 28/1. Alphabet of freedoms, 1681–1700.

6, fo. 19 and 7, fos. 15, 39. All Hallows Lombard St. assessments, 1695.

38, fo. 7. St Paul's, Covent Garden assessments, 1693/4.

56, fo. 1. St Martin Outwich assessments, 1696

74, fo. 5. Cornhill assessments, 1695.

83, fo.7 and 42, fo. 3. Hatton Garden assessments, 1692/3, 1693/4.

92, fo. 293 and 96, fos. 203–8. Repertories of aldermen, 1686/7, 1691/2.

Inventory no. 1416, 22 July 1678.

London inhabitants within the walls. Index, 1695.

Mayor's Court Decrees. Box 255E, Oct 1661.

Mayor's Court Interrogatories. 6/120A&B, *T. Wilson* v. *E. Harris*, 1661.

Guildhall Library

2480/1. Jewers, A. Monumental inscriptions of London, i., 1910–13.

4049/2. All Hallows Lombard Street vestry minutes, 1667–1702.

4251. St Andrew Holborn vestry minutes, 1624–1714.

4256. St Andrew Holborn account book, 1683–97.

4657A/2. Weavers' Company indices to lists, 1661–94.

5587/1. Fishmongers' Company index to freedom admissions, 1592–1752.

5576/2. Fishmongers' Company register of freedom admissions, 1650–98.

8674/6. Hand-in-Hand Fire and Life Insurance Society, fire policy register F, 1707–8, fo. 116, #15773.

9054/2. Archdeaconry of London index of wills.

10823/1. Boddington memoranda book, *c.*1640–1766.

11593/1. Grocers' Company register of apprentices, 1629–1665.

15201/5. Vintners' Company court minutes, 1669–82.

15208. Vintners' Company chronological roll of liverymen, 1683–1939.

15212/1. 'A Book of Names of all the Persons Admitted into the Freedom of the Worshipful Company of Vintners', 1658–1768.

15333/5–6. Vintners' company wardens' account books, 1658–1712.

Buckinghamshire poll books, 1705, 1713, 1722.

Dale, T. Index to the Liverymen of London: 1700 and 1710, 1933.

Folio 1035. A list of the names of subscribers of land and money towards the National Land Bank.

IGI Index. London, Buckinghamshire.

Index to Middlesex Polls, 1705, 1714, 1768. Middlesex poll book, 1714.

London poll book, 1710, 1713, 1722.

Hoare's Bank
HB Miscellaneous Record Book, 161; HB Ledgers #2–5, 1698–1705.

Huntington Library, San Marino, California
Stowe Collection: Temple Papers
1660–1740: STT Accounts. STT Catalogues, Lists, and Inventories. STT Correspondence, 1653–1757. STT Customs. STT Deeds. STT Elections. STT Genealogy. STT Legal. STT Literature. STT Manorial. STT Maps. STT Parliament. STT Personal (including wills and settlements). STT Religion.

Individual Volumes: ST 50, 53–4, 152–3, 155–8, 175. Account books of Sir Richard and Viscount Cobham for London and Stowe, 1654–1719. ST 365. Catalogue of Books at Stowe, [>1697].

Ellesmere Collection
1660–1740: EL 8518–8535. Militia papers, 1670s-1715. EL 8598–8947, 9440–9570. Bridgewater Papers, household accounts, 1650–1693. EL 9414–9439. Recusants papers, 1695–1696. EL 10081–10096, 10110. Political papers, early 18th century. EL 10111–10259. Miscellaneous papers. EL 10440–11146. Cheyne papers, 16th-18th centuries.

Individual volumes: EL 34/C/3. Patrick Bamford, *The Complete Keeper* [1693]; EL 8631–2, 8639, 8641, 8645, 8656. Bridgewater family accounts, 1689–90.

India Office Library
HM 1–3. List of adventurers and accounts, 1675, 1691, 1693, 1694, 1696, 1699, 1701–1703, 1707.

Ledgers, L/AG/1/1/5, L/AG/1/1/9, L/AG/1/1/10. Index, 1664–1779.

Leicestershire County Record Office
23D57. *Braye Papers.*
Cave family and estate records (1–59 and generally).
Political papers (2875–3023), especially 1711 and 1714/15 election.
5D67, DE2399. Uncatalogued deposits.

Public Record Office

C104/109/2, C104/110/1. Lee of Ditchley papers.

C114/16. Million Bank subscriber list, 1695–1700. Dividend book, 1701–6.

C231/9. Crown Office docket book, 1700–21.

E179/80/354, E179/324. Hearth tax, 1662.

E190/62/1. Port book, 1674–5.

E401/1985–2040. Exchequer receipt books, 1690–1717.

E401/2275. Subscribers to annuities, 1695–6.

E401/2593–2595. Subscription books, 1698, 1708–10.

E401/2599–2600. Lottery, 1710.

PROB 4/21162, 1683; 4/2571, 1698; 4/7324, 1662, Coachmen's inventories.

PROB 11. Wills of gentry and merchants

Levant Company Records

SP 105/152–156. Court of Assistants' minutes, London, 1660–1706.

SP 105/161–164. Financial accounts, 1658–1772.

SP 105/166–69. Imposition books, 1669–81, 1694–1710.

SP 110/55–6 Court of Assistants' minutes, Aleppo, 1650–65.

SP 110/12–14, 16 and SP 110/73. Letters from Aleppo factors, 1668–90.

SP 110–154. Morea joint stock.

SP 35/33/54, Broadsheet.

SP 44/274/172, Warrants of venison, 1696.

Royal Africa Company Records

T70/76–88. Court of Assistants' minutes, 1664–1713.

T70/100–101. General Court minutes, 1671–8, 1678–1720.

T70/107–111. Committee on Accounts, 1680–90.

T70/125, 128–30. Committee on Goods, 1680–2, 1692–1720.

T70–178. Stock subscription book, 1713.

T70–179. Receipts for money advanced, 1716.

T70/185–191, 195, 197. Stock ledgers, 1674–1719.

T70/1613. Index, 1696–1699.

Westminster Library

H5, H8. St Paul's, Covent Garden collectors' books, 1706, 1708.

H468–495. St Paul's, Covent Garden overseers accounts, 1689–1716.

H802–803. St Paul's, Covent Garden vestry minutes, 1681–1723.

Primary Sources

An Account of the Days of the Going Out of all the Carriers, Waggoners, and Stage-Coaches that come to London (169[?]).

ADDISON, J., *The Sir Roger de Coverley Papers from The Spectator 1711–1712* (New York, 1945).

Advice to a Son or Directions for your Better Conduct (Oxford, 1656).

Advice to the Livery-Men of London showing that it is for their Interest and Honour, to Choose the Merchants in Trade for their Representatives in Parliament (1713).

Advice to the Women and Maidens of London (1678).

[ALLESTREE], *The Gentleman's Calling* (1679).

[ANDREWES, L.], *Holy Devotions* (1655).

The Answer of the Burgesses . . . to . . . Sir Timber Temple (Buckingham, 1679).

An Arithmologia, Being a Mirror, Breviate, Treasure, Mate, for Merchants, Bankers, Tradesmen, Mechanicks . . . (1693).

The Art of Complaisance (1673).

ASTELL, M., *Reflections upon Marriage*, 3rd edn. (1706).

ATTERBURY, F., *The Power of Charity to Cover Sin: A Sermon Preached before the Governors of the Hospital of Bridewell . . .* 1694 (1708).

The Bachelor's Directory, 2nd edn. (1696).

Bank-Credit: or the . . . Bank of Credit Examined (1683).

[BARNARD, J.], *A Present for an Apprentice* (1740).

BARNETT, G. (ed.), 'Scheme of the Income and Expense of the Several Families of England, Calculated for the year 1688', *Two Tracts by Gregory King* (Baltimore, 1936), 31.

Baron and Feme (1719).

BAXTER, R., *Compassionate Counsel to All Young Men* (1691).

The Beau Defeated: Or the Lucky Younger Brother, A Comedy ([1700]).

BECKFORD, P., *Thoughts on Hunting* (Sarum, 1782).

BLACKSTONE, W., *Commentaries of the Laws of England*, 2 vols. (New York, 1827).

BLOME, R., *The Gentleman's Recreation* (1686).

BRIDG[E]MAN, O., *Conveyances*, 2nd edn. (1689).

BRINKWORTH, E. (ed.), *Episcopal Visitation Book for the Archdeaconry of Buckingham* 1662 (Buckinghamshire Record Society, 7; 1947).

BRUCE, J. (ed.), *Notes of Proceedings of the Long Parliament* (Camden Society, 31; 1845).

—— *Letters and Papers of the Verney Family down to . . .* 1639 (Camden Society, 56; 1853).

[BRYDALL, J.], *Jus Primogeniti . . .* (1699).

[BURNABY, C.], *The Ladies Visiting Day* (1708).

BURRIDGE, R., *A New Review of London* (1722).

CARTWRIGHT, J. (ed.), *The Wentworth Papers 1705–1739* (1883).

CAVENDISH, M., *CCXI. Sociable Letters . . .* (1664).

CHAMBERLAYNE, E., *Angliae Notitia*, 10th edn. (1677).

Character of a Town Gallant (1675).

The Charge which is to be Given to every Governor of the Hospital at Bridewell . . . [17––].

La Chasse de Gaston Phoebus, Compte de Foix (Paris, 1854).

CICERO, *De Officiis* (Indianapolis, 1974).

The Cities Great Concern (1674).

A Compleat Guide to All Persons Who have any Trade . . . with the City of London (1740).

[CONSTABLE, J.], *The Conversation of Gentlemen Considered* (1738).

Corporation-Credit, or a Bank of Credit made Current by Common Consent in London (1682).

Corporation of London, *Order against Exchange Brokers Obstructing the Thoroughfare* (1700).

The Country Gentleman's Vade Mecum (1699).

[COURTIN, A. DE], *The Rules of Civility* (1671).

COX, N., *The Gentleman's Recreation* (1697).

CREFFIELD, E., *A Good Wife a Great Blessing* (1717).

CROSS, A., *Eighteenth-Century Documents Relating to the Royal Forests, the Sheriffs, and Smuggling* (New York, 1928).

Cynegetica or Essays on Sporting (1733).

DARE, J., *Counsellor Manners* (1673).

DARRELL, W., *The Gentleman Instructed*, 4th edn. (1709).

[D.B.], *The Honourable State of Matrimony made Comfortable* (1685).

DEFOE, D., *A Treatise Concerning the Use and Abuse of the Marriage Bed* (1727).

—— *The Complete English Tradesman* (Gloucester, 1987).

DUMONT, J., *A New Voyage to the Levant* (1696).

EDWARD OF NORWICH, *The Master of the Game*, ed. W. and F. Baille-Grohman (1904).

ELAND, G., *Shardeloes Papers of the Seventeenth and Eighteenth Centuries* (1947).

ESSEX, J., *The Young Ladies Conduct* (1722).

EVELYN, J., *A Character of England* (1659).

Familiar and Courtly Letters to Persons of Honour and Quality by Monsieur Voiture . . . (1701).

[FELTON, H.], *A Dissertation on Reading the Classics and Forming a Just Style* (1713).

FELTON, W., *A Treatise on Carriages Comprehending Coaches, Chariots, Phaetons, Curricles, Whiskeys, etc . . . .* (1796).

Female Grievances Debated in Six Dialogues . . . with Proposals for . . . Taxing such Bachelors as Refuse to Marry, 4th edn. (1727).

The Freemen of London's Necessary and Useful Companion . . . (1706).

FULLER, W., *Mr. William Fuller's Trip to Bridewell . . .* (1703).

GALATEO, *Of Manners, or Instructions to a Young Gentleman* (1703).

GAYA, L. DE, *Marriage Ceremonies as Now used in All Parts of the World* (1704).

The Gentleman's Library (1715).

GILDON, C., *The Post-Boy Robb'd of his Mail*, 2nd edn. (1706).

GILES, J., *Lex Mercatoria: or the Merchants' Companion . . .* (1718).

GOODMAN, T., *The Experienced Secretary* (1707).

GOUGE, W., *Of Domestical Duties* (1622).

GOUGH, W., *Londinium Triumphans* (1682).

GRATIUS THE FALISCAN, *Cynegeticon or a Poem of Hunting*, trans. Christopher Wase (1654).

Great Britain's Glory: Or a Brief Description of the . . . Royal Exchange (1672).

A Guide for Malt-Worms [1715?].

HACKNEY COACHES, Guildhall Library proclamations and pamphlets.

HAINSWORTH, D., and WALKER, C. (eds), *The Correspondence of Lord Fitzwilliam of Milton and Frances Guybon, his Steward 1697–1709* (Northampton, 1990).

Hell upon Earth or the Town in An Uproar (1985).

HICKMAN, C., *A Sermon Preached Before . . . the Company of Merchants Trading into the Levant Seas* (1682).

HILL, A., *A Full and Just Account of the Present State of the Ottoman Empire* (1733).

HILL, J., *The Young Secretary's Guide* (1696).

'Hillesden Account Book, 1661–67', *Records of Buckinghamshire*, 11 (1919), 135–44, 186–98, 244–55.

HORWOOD, A. (ed.), *The MSS of Sir Harry Verney, Bart. at Claydon House, Co. Bucks* (Historical Manuscript Commission, 7; 1879), 433–509.

HOUGHTON, J., *A Collection for Improvement of Husbandry and Trade*, 4 vols. (Mar 30 1692–Sept 2 1703).

Humours and Conversations of the Town (1693).

JAMES, W., and MALCOLM, J., *General View of the Agriculture of the County of Buckingham . . .* (1794).

JESSOP, A., (ed.), *The Lives of the Norths*, 3 vols. (1890).

JONES, E., *A Trip through London*, 5th edn. (1718).

KILBURNE, R., *Choice Presidents upon All Acts of Parliament Relating to the Office and Duty of a Justice of the Peace*, 3rd edn. (1685).

LAURENCE, E., *The Duty of a Steward to his Lord* (1727).

LE HARDY, W., and RICKETT, G. (eds), *Calendar to the Sessions Records, County of Buckingham, 1678–1718*, 4 vols. (Aylesbury, 1933–51).

A Letter from a Freeholder of Buckinghamshire . . . (Aylesbury, 1679).

A Letter from a Merchant in London to a Member of Parliament [1708?].

A Letter from a Minister in the Country to a Gentleman in London with A Project of Promoting the Reformation of Manners (1701).

A List of Goldsmiths Keeping Running Cashes (1677).

A List of Proprietors of South Sea Capital Stock . . . (1823).

A List of Reversionary Annuities . . . Million Bank . . . 1695.

A List of Surviving Nominees . . . for the Year 1693 *and the Sums . . . Paid . . .* (1730)

The London Directory of 1677 (1677).

McCULLOCH, J. (ed.), *Early English Tracts on Commerce* (Cambridge, 1952).

MALCOLM, J., *London Redivivum* (1803).

MANWOOD, J., *A Treatise of the Laws of the Forest*, 3rd edn. (1665).

MARIUS, J., *Advice Concerning Bills of Exchange* (1700).

M[ARKHAM], G., *Country Contentments or the Husbandman's Recreation*, 6th edn. (1649).

Marriage Promoted (1690).

MATTHEWS, W. (ed.), *The Diary of Dudley Ryder 1715–1716*, 2 vols. (1939).

MAUGER, C., *Mauger's Letters Written Upon Several Subjects* (1671).

MAUNDRELL, H., *A Journal from Aleppo to Jerusalem . . . 1697*, 5th edn. (Oxford, 1732).

The Merchant's Daily Companion (1684).

A Mild but Searching Expostulatory Letter from the Plain-dealing Farmers of the Neighbouring Villages to the Men of Buckingham (n.d.).

MURET, P., *Rites of Funeral, Ancient and Modern . . .* (1683).

The Mystery of the New Fashioned Goldsmiths or Bankers (1676).

[NELSON, W.], *The Laws of England Concerning the Game . . .* (1727).

The New Guide to London, or Directions to Strangers, 2nd edn. (1726).

New News of a Strange Monster found in Stowe Wood (1679).

A New View of London (1708).

[N.H.], *The Ladies Dictionary* (1694).

NICHOLLS, W., *The Duty of Inferiors towards their Superior . . .* (1701).

The Noble Art or Venerie of Hunting (1575).

NORTHTONUS, C., *The Younger Brother's Advocate: Or a Line or Two for Younger Brothers with their Petition to the Parliament* (1654/5).

[PARKE, J.], *A Warning to London in Particular* (1679).

A Particular Accompt of the . . . Late Million Act . . . (1694).

P[EACHAM], H., *The Art of Living in London* (1642), in T. Park (ed.), *Harleian Miscellany* (1808–13), ix. 84–9.

—— *Coach and Sedan* (1636), repr. 1925.

PENTON, S., *The Gentleman Instructed* (1688).

The Poll of the Livery-Men of the City of London . . . (1710).

POTE, [J.], *The Foreigners' Guide*, 2nd edn. (1729).

POWELL, T., *Tom of All Trades* (1631).

The Principles and Designs of the High Church Party . . . (1710).

[Ramesey, W.]., *The Gentleman's Companion* (1676).

Reasons . . . for Continuing the Late Brokers Act ([1700]).

Reasons for Passing the Bill . . . to Restrain the Number and Ill Practices of Brokers and Stock-jobbers [1711].

Reed, M. (ed.), *Buckinghamshire Probate Inventories* (Buckinghamshire Record Society, 24; 1988).

Remarques upon the Humours and Conversations of the Town (1673).

Remarques upon Remarques (1673).

[Roberts, J. Ap], *An Apology for a Younger Brother or a Discourse Providing that Parents May Dispose of their Estates to which of their Children they Please* (Oxford, 1641).

Roseveare, H. (ed.), *Markets and Merchants of the Late Seventeenth Century* (Oxford, 1987).

Rowe, J., *All Sorts of Wheel-Carriage Improv'd* (1734).

Rules, Directions, By-laws Devised and Made by the Court of Aldermen . . . for Regulation of Hackney Coachmen (1654).

Rycaut, P., *The Present State of the Ottoman Empire*, 3rd edn. (1670).

Sandford, F., *The Order and Ceremonies Used for the Solemn Interment of . . . George, Duke of Albemarle* (1670).

A Satyr Against Marriage (1700).

Savile, G., *The Lady's New-Years Gift: Or Advice to a Daughter*, 6th edn. (Dublin and Drogheda, 1699).

Scheme for a New Lottery: Or a Husband and Coach and Six for 40s. (1732).

[Seymar, W.], *Marriage Asserted . . .* (1674).

Shirley, E., *Some Account of English Deer Parks* (1867).

Smith, W. (ed.), *The Grenville Papers*, i (1852).

Snell, B. (ed.), *The Minute Book of the Monthly Meeting of the Society of Friends from the Upperside of Buckinghamshire 1669–1690* (Buckinghamshire Archaelogical Society, 1; 1937).

Somerville, W., *The Chace, a Poem* (1735).

Sorbiere, M., *A Journey to London in the Year 1698* (1699).

The Statutes at Large Made for the Preservation of the Game (1726).

Steele, R., *The Ladies Library, written by a Lady [G. Berkeley]* (1714).

Stow, W., *Remarks on London* (1722).

Strype, J., *A Survey of the Cities of London and Westminster*, 2 vols. (1720).

[Swift, J.], *An Essay on the Mischief of Giving Fortunes with Women in Marriage* (1727).

[T.E.], *The Lawes Resolutions of Womens Rights* (1632).

[T.H.], *A Treatise of Marriage . . .* (1673).

[T.W.], *The Matter of Fact of Sir Richard Temple's Case Truly Stated* [169?].

[Taylor, J.], *The World Runs on Wheels* (1635).

—— *The Coaches Overthrown* (1636).

—— *The Carrier's Cosmographie* (1637).

Teonge, H., *The Diary of Henry Teonge* (1927).

Thévenot, J. de, *The Travels of Monsieur de Thévenot* (1687).

Torriano, G., *Of Italian Proverbs* (1666).

A Trip from St James's to the Royal-Exchange (1744).

A True Account of What Passed at the Election of Knight of the Shire . . . (1679).

A True and Impartial Account of the Poll of the Inhabitants of Broad Street . . . (1711).

Turner, G. (ed.), *Select Pleas of the Forest* (Selden Society, 13; 1901).

Twici, W., *The Art of Hunting*, ed. H. Dryden (Northampton, 1908).

Verney, F. (ed.), *Memoirs of the Verney Family during the Civil War*, Vols. 1–2 (1892).

Verney M. (ed.), *Memoirs of the Verney Family during The Commonwealth 1650 to 1660*, Vol. 3 (1894).

—— *Memoirs of the Verney Family during the Restoration to the Revolution 1660 to 1696*, Vol. 4 (1899).

—— (ed.), *The Verney Letters of the Eighteenth Century from the MSS. at Claydon House*, 2 vols. (1930).

[Vincent, S.], *The Young Gallant's Academy* (1674).

Walker, O., *Of Education* (Oxford, 1687).

Watts, I., *The Art of Reading and Writing English* (1721).

Watts, T., *An Essay on the Proper Method for Forming the Man of Business . . .* (1716).

The Way to Promotion, or the Young Man's Guide to Preferment (1682).

White, J., *A Short History of the Royal Hospitals of Bridewell and Bethlem* (1899).

Whiteman, A. (ed.), *The Compton Census of 1676* (Records of Social and Economic History, New Series, 8; 1986).

Willis, B., *The History and Antiquities of the Town . . . of Buckingham* (1755).

—— *Notitia Parliamentaria* (1715).

Secondary Sources

Adair, R., *Courtship, Illegitimacy, and Marriage in Early Modern England* (Manchester and New York, 1996).

Agnew, J., *Worlds Apart* (Cambridge, 1986).

Agulhon, M., *Penitents et Franc-Macons de l'Ancienne Provence* (Paris, 1968).

—— *Le Cercle dans la France Bourgeoise 1810–1848* (Paris, 1977).

Anderson, S., *An English Consul in Turkey: Paul Rycaut 1667–78* (Oxford, 1989).

Andrews, H., 'The Pasc[h]all Family of Great Baddow and Springfield, Essex', *Essex Archaelogical Society Transactions*, New Series 23 (1958), 54–65.

Appleby, J., *Economic Thought and Ideology in Seventeenth-Century England* (Princeton, 1978).

Ashton, J., *Social Life in the Reign of Queen Anne* (New York, 1929).

Barbour, V., 'Marine Risks and Insurance in the Seventeenth Century', *Journal of Economic and Business History*, 1 (1929), 561–96.

Barker, H., and Chalus, E. (eds), *Gender in the Eighteenth Century* (1997).

Barron, C., *The Parish of St. Andrew Holborn* (1979).

Barry, J., 'Provincial Town Culture 1640–1780: Urbane or Civic?', in J. Pittock and A. Wear (eds), *Interpretation and Cultural History* (1991), 198–234.

—— and Brooks, C. (eds), *The Middling Sort of People* (Basingstoke, 1994).

Beaven, A., *The Aldermen of the City of London*, 2 vols. (1908–13).

Becker, M., *Civility and Society in Western Europe, 1300–1600* (Bloomington, Ind., 1988).

Beckett, J., *Coal and Tobacco* (Cambridge, 1981).

—— 'Absentee Landownership in the Later Seventeenth and Early Eighteenth Centuries', *Northern History*, 19 (1983), 87–107.

—— *The Rise and Fall of the Grenvilles* (Manchester and New York, 1994).

Beier, A., and Finlay, R. (eds), *London 1500–1700: The Making of the Metropolis* (1986).

Ben-Amos, I., *Adolescence and Youth in Early Modern England* (New Haven, 1995).

BERKOWITZ, S., *An Introduction to Structural Analysis: The Network Approach* (Toronto, 1982).

BERMINGHAM, A., and BREWER, J. (eds), *The Consumption of Culture 1600–1800* (1993).

BERRY, C., *The Idea of Luxury* (New York and Cambridge, 1994).

BIRLEY, D., *Sport and the Making of Britain* (Manchester, 1993).

BLACK, J., and GREGORY, J. (eds), *Culture, Politics, and Society in Britain 1660–1800* (Manchester, 1991).

BLACK-MICHAUD, JACOB, *Cohesive Force: Feud in the Mediterranean and the Middle East* (Oxford, 1975).

BLOOM, E., and BLOOM, L., *Joseph Addison's Sociable Animal* (Providence, RI, 1971).

BOISSEVAIN, J., *Friends of Friends* (Oxford, 1974).

BOND, D. (ed.), *The Spectator*, 5 vols. (Oxford, 1965).

BOND, R., *The Tatler* (Cambridge, Mass., 1971).

BONFIELD, L., *Marriage Settlements 1601–1740* (Cambridge, 1983).

—— 'Affective Families, Open Elites, and Strict Family Settlements . . . ', *EcHR*, 2nd series, 36 (1986), 341–54.

BORSAY, P., 'The English Urban Renaissance', *Social History*, 2 (1977), 581–601.

—— 'The London Connection', *London Journal*, 19 (1994), 21–35.

BOTT, E., *Family and Social Network* (1957).

BOULTON, J., *Neighborhood and Society* (Cambridge, 1987).

—— 'London Widowhood Revisited', *Continuity and Change*, 5 (1990), 323–55.

BOWEN, H., *Elites, Enterprise, and the Making of the British Overseas Empire 1688–1775* (1996).

BRAILSFORD, D., *Sport, Time, and Society* (New York, 1991).

BREITENBERG, M., *Anxious Masculinity in Early Modern England* (Cambridge, 1996).

BRENNER, R., *Merchants and Revolution* (Princeton, 1993).

BRETT-JAMES, N., *The Growth of Stuart London* (1935).

BREWER, J., and PORTER, R. (eds), *The World of Goods* (1993).

BROAD, J., 'Gentry Finances and the Civil War: The Case of the Buckinghamshire Verneys', *EcHR*, 2nd series, 32 (1979), 183–200.

—— 'Sir John Verney and Buckinghamshire Elections', *Historical Research*, 56 (1983), 195–204.

—— 'Whigs and Deer Stealers in Other Guises', *Past and Present*, 119 (1988), 56–72.

—— 'The Verneys and the Sequestrators in the Civil Wars, 1642–1656', *Records of Buckinghamshire*, 27 (1985), 1–9.

—— 'The Verneys as Enclosing Landlords 1600–1800', in J. Chartres and D. Hey (eds), *English Rural Society 1500–1800* (Cambridge, 1990), 27–53.

—— (ed.), *Buckinghamshire Dissent and Parish Life 1669–1712* (Buckinghamshire Record Society, 28; 1993).

BROD, H. (ed.), *The Making of Masculinities* (Boston, 1987).

BRODSKY, V., 'Single Women in the London Marriage Market', *Newberry Papers in Family and Community History*, No. 80–2 (Chicago, 1980).

CAIN, P., and HOPKINS, A., *British Imperialism: Innovation and Expansion 1688–1914* and *British Imperialism: Crisis and Deconstruction 1914–1990* (1993).

CARRUTHERS, B., *City of Capital* (Princeton, 1996).

CHRISTIE, I., *British 'Non Elite' MPs 1715–1820* (New York and Oxford, 1995).

CLARK, P. (ed.), *The Early Modern Town: A Reader* (New York, 1976).

CLARKE, G., 'The History of Stowe II, The Rise of the Temple Family', *Stoic*, 22 (1967), 261–5.

—— 'The History of Stowe V, The Early Life of Richard Temple, Viscount Cobham', *Stoic*, 23 (1968), 116–20.

CLAY, C., 'Property Settlements, Financial Provision for the Family, and the Sale of Land by the Greater Landowners 1660–1790', *Journal of British Studies*, 21 (1981), 18–38.

—— 'Henry Hoare, Banker, his Family, and the Stourhead Estate', in F. Thompson (ed.), *Landowners, Capitalists, and Entrepreneurs* (Oxford, 1994), 113–38.

CLAYDON, T., *William III and the Godly Revolution* (Cambridge, 1996).

CLIFFE, J., *The Puritan Gentry Beseiged 1650–1700* (1993).

COHEN, M., *Fashioning Masculinity* (1996).

Continuity and Change, 7 (1992). Issue devoted to birth-order.

COPLEY, S., 'Commerce, Conversation, and Politeness in the Early Eighteenth-Century Periodical', *British Journal for Eighteenth-Century Studies*, 18 (1995), 63–77.

CORFIELD, P., 'Walking the City Streets', *Journal of Urban History*, 16 (1990), 132–74.

—— 'The Rivals: Landed and Other Gentlemen', in N. Harte and R. Quinault (eds), *Land and Society* (Manchester, 1996), 1–33.

—— *Power and the Professions in Britain 1700–1850* (New York, 1995).

CRESSY, D., *Birth, Marriage, and Death* (Oxford and New York, 1997).

CROFTS, J., *Packhorse, Wagon, and Post* (1967).

DAUNTON, M., '"Gentlemanly Capitalism" and British Industry, 1820–1914', *Past and Present*, 122 (1989), 119–58 and 132 (1991), 170–87.

DAVIDOFF, L., *The Best Circles* (1973).

DAVIES, G., 'The Political Career of Sir Richard Temple (1634–97) and Buckingham Politics', *HLQ* 4 (1940), 47–83.

DAVIES, K., *The Royal African Company* (1957).

DAVIES, M., 'Country Gentry and Payments to London 1650–1714', *EcHR*, 2nd series, 24 (1971), 15–36.

DAVIS, N., 'Ghosts, Kin and Progeny', *Daedalus*, 106 (1977), 87–114.

—— 'Beyond the Market: Books as Gifts in Sixteenth-Century France', *Transactions of the Royal Historical Society*, 5th series, 33 (1983), 69–87.

—— 'Art and Society in the Gifts of Montaigne', *Representations*, 12 (1985), 24–32.

—— 'The Shapes of Social History', *Storia Della Storiografia*, 17 (1990), 228–34.

DAVIS, R., *Aleppo and Devonshire Square* (1967).

DE KREY, G., *A Fractured Society* (New York, 1985).

DENING, G.,, *Islands and Beaches* (Honolulu, 1980).

De Roover, R. 'Scholastic Attitude Toward Trade and Entrepreneurship', in J. Kirshner (ed.), *Business, Banking, and Economic Thought* (Chicago, 1974), 336–45.

DICKSON, P., *The Financial Revolution in England* (1967).

DIX, W., 'The Hunting Library of Laurence Roberts Carton '07', *Princeton University Library Chronicle*, 15 (1953), 43–5.

EALES, J., *Women in Early Modern England 1500–1700* (1998).

ELIAS, N., *The Civilizing Process*, i (New York, 1978).

ELLIOTT, D., *Buckingham: The Loyal and Ancient Borough* (1975).

ERICKSON, A., *Women and Property in Early Modern England* (1993).

EZELL, MARGARET, *The Patriarch's Wife* (Chapel Hill, NC, 1987).

FISHER, F., 'The Development of London as a Centre of Conspicuous Consumption', in E. Carus-Wilson (ed.), *Essays in Economic History* (1962), ii. 197–207.

FLANDRIN, J., *Families in Former Times* (Cambridge, 1979).

FLETCHER, A., *Gender, Sex, and Subordination in England 1500–1800* (1995).

FRANCE, P., *Politeness and its Discontents* (Cambridge, 1992).

FRANCIS, J., *Chronicles and Characters of the Stock Exchange* (Boston, 1850).

FREIDERICHS, C., *The Early Modern City* (1995).

GARRIOCH, D., *Neighbourhood and Community in Paris 1740–90* (Cambridge, 1986).

GAY, E., 'The Rise of an English Country Family: Peter and John Temple to 1603', *HLQ* 1 (1938), 376–90.

—— 'The Temples of Stowe and their Debts', *HLQ* 2 (1939), 399–438.

—— 'Sir Richard Temple, the Debt Settlement, and Estate Litigation', *HLQ* 6 (1943), 255–91.

GEERTZ, C., *The Interpretation of Cultures* (New York, 1973).

GITTINGS, C., *Death, Burial, and the Individual in Early Modern Europe* (1984).

GOLDIE, M., 'The Earliest Notice of Purcell's Dido and Aeneas', *Early Music*, 20 (1992), 392–400.

GOODMAN, D., *The Republic of Letters* (Ithaca, New York, 1994).

GOODMAN, J., *Stories of Scottsboro* (New York, 1994).

GOODY, J., *et al.* (eds), *Family and Inheritance* (Cambridge, 1976).

GORDON, D., *Citizens Without Sovereignty* (Princeton, 1994).

GOWING, L., *Domestic Dangers* (Oxford, 1996).

GRANT, J., 'The Gentry in London in the Reign of Charles I', *University of Birmingham History Journal*, 8 (1962), 197–202.

GRASSBY, R., 'The Rate of Profit in Seventeenth-Century England', *English Historical Review*, 84 (1969), 721–51.

—— 'English Merchant Capitalism in the Late Seventeenth Century', *Past and Present*, 46 (1970), 87–107.

—— 'The Personal Wealth of the Business Community in Seventeenth-Century England', *EcHR*, 2nd series, 23 (1970), 220–34.

—— 'Social Mobility and Business Enterprise in Seventeenth-Century England', in D. Pennington and K. Thomas (eds), *Puritans and Revolutionaries* (Oxford, 1978), 354–81.

—— *The English Gentleman in Trade* (Oxford, 1994).

—— *The Business Community of Seventeenth-Century England* (Cambridge, 1995).

GREEN, E., *Birth Order, Parental Interest, and Academic Achievement* (San Francisco, 1978).

GREENSPAHN, F., *When Brothers Dwell Together* (New York, 1994).

GREGO, J., *A History of Parliamentary Elections and Electioneering in the Old Days* (1886).

HABERMAS, J., *The Structural Transformation of the Public Sphere* (Cambridge, Mass., 1989).

HABAKKUK, J., 'English Landownership 1680–1740', *EcHR*, 2nd series, 10 (1940), 2–17.

—— 'Marriage Settlements in the Eighteenth Century', *Transactions of the Royal Historical Society*, 4th series, 32 (1950), 15–30.

—— 'The Rise and Fall of English Landed Families, 1600–1800', *Transactions of the Royal Historical Society*, 29–31 (1979–81), 187–207; 199–221; 195–217.

—— *Marriage, Debt, and the Estates System* (Oxford, 1994).

HAINSWORTH, D., 'Manor House to Counting House', in F. McGregor and N. Wright (eds), *European History and its Historians* (Adelaide, 1977), 66–74.

—— 'Fathers and Daughters', in L. Frappell (ed.), *Principalities, Powers, and Estates* (Adelaide, 1979), 15–21.

HARMAN, L., *The Modern Stranger: On Language and Membership* (Berlin, 1988).

HARRIS, TIM, *Politics under the Later Stuarts: Party Conflict in a Divided Society 1660–1715* (1993).

HASKELL, T., and TEICHGRAEBER, R. (eds), *The Culture of the Market* (Cambridge, 1993).

HEAL, A., *The London Goldsmiths 1200–1800* (1972).

HEAL, F., 'The Crown, the Gentry, and London', in C. Cross *et al.* (eds), *Law and Government under the Tudors* (Cambridge, 1988), 211–26.

—— *Hospitality in Early Modern England* (Oxford, 1990).

—— and HOLMES, C., *The Gentry in England and Wales 1500–1700* (Stanford, Calif., 1994).

HENNING, B., *The House of Commons 1660–1690*, 3 vols. (1983).

HILL, B., *Women, Work, and Sexual Politics in Eighteenth-Century England* (Oxford, 1989).

HIRSCHMAN, A., *The Passions and the Interests* (Princeton, 1977).

HITCHCOCK, T., *English Sexualities 1700–1800* (Basingstoke, 1997).

HOARE, H., *Hoare's Bank* (1955).

HOLLINGSWORTH, T., 'Demography of the British Peerage', *Population Studies*, 18 (1964), supplement, i–108.

HOLMES, G., *Augustan England: Professions, State, and Society 1680–1730* (1982).

—— *British Politics in the Reign of Queen Anne* (1967).

HOLMES, J., *Women, Men, and Politeness* (New York, 1995).

HOPKINS, P., 'The Verney Collection of Popish Plot Pamphlets', *Bulletin of the Friends of the Cambridge University Library*, 9 (1988), 5–15.

HOPPIT, J., *Risk and Failure in Business 1700–1800* (Cambridge, 1987).

HORNBEAK, K., 'The Complete Letter-Writer in English 1568–1800', *Smith College Studies in Modern Languages*, 15 (1934), 128–45.

HORWITZ, H., 'The Mess of the Middle Class Revisited', *Continuity and Change*, 2 (1987), 263–96.

HOULBROOKE, R., *Death, Religion, and the Family in England 1480–1750* (New York, 1998).

HUFTON, O., *The Prospect Before Her* (1995).

HUMPHREYS, A., *Steele, Addison, and their Essays* (1959).

HUNT, L. (ed.), *The New Cultural History* (Berkeley, 1982).

HUNT, M., *The Middling Sort* (Berkeley, 1996).

HUNTING, P., 'The Survey of Hatton Garden in 1694 by Abraham Arlidge', *London Topographical Record*, 25 (1985), 83–110.

ISAAC, R., *The Transformation of Virginia, 1740–1790* (Chapel Hill, NC, 1982).

JENKINS, P., *The Making of a Ruling Class: The Glamorgan Gentry 1640–1790* (Cambridge, 1983).

JONES, C., 'The London Life of a Peer in the Reign of Anne', *London Journal*, 16 (1991), 140–55.

JONES, D., 'London Merchants and the Crisis of the 1690s', in P. Clark and P. Slack (eds), *Crisis and Order in English Towns 1500–1700* (1972).

KEEBLE, N. (ed.), *The Cultural Identity of Seventeenth-Century Women* (1994).

KELLY, J., *Women, History, and Theory* (Chicago, 1986).

KETCHAM, M., *Transparent Design: Reading, Performance and Form in the Spectator Papers* (Athens, Ga., 1985).

KETTERING, S., 'Gift Giving and Patronage in Early Modern France', *French History*, 2 (1988), 131–51.

KEY, N., 'The Political Culture and Political Rhetoric of County Feasts and Feast Sermons 1654–1714', *Journal of British Studies*, 33 (1994), 223–56.

KISHLANSKY, M., *Parliamentary Selection: Social and Political Choice in Early Modern England* (Cambridge, 1986).

KLEIN, L., 'Gender, Conversation, and the Public Sphere in Early Eighteenth-Century England', in J. Still and M. Worton (eds), *Textuality and Sexuality* (Manchester and New York, 1993) 100–15.

—— *Shaftesbury and the Culture of Politeness* (New York, 1994).

—— 'Property and Politeness in the Early Eighteenth Century Whig Moralists', in J. Brewer and S. Staves (eds), *Early Modern Conceptions of Property* (1995), 221–33.

—— 'Gender and the Public/Private Distinction in the Eighteenth Century', *Eighteenth-Century Studies*, 29 (1995), 97–109.

KNIGHTS, M., *Politics and Opinion in Crisis 1678–1681* (Cambridge, 1994).

KNOKE, D., and KUKLINSKI, J., *Network Analysis* (Beverly Hills, Calif., 1982).

KOWALESKI-WALLACE, E., *Women, Shopping, and Business in the Eighteenth Century* (New York, 1996).

LADURIE, E., *Montaillou: The Promised Land of Error* (New York, 1978).

—— *The Mind and Method of the Historian* (Chicago, 1981).

LANG, R., 'London's Aldermen in Business: 1600–25', *Guildhall Miscellany*, 3 (1971), 242–65.

LANGFORD, P., *Public Life and the Propertied Englishman 1689–1798* (Oxford, 1991).

—— 'Polite Manners from Sir Robert Walpole to Sir Robert Peel', *Proceedings of the British Academy*, 94 (1996), 103–25.

LARMINIE, V., *Wealth, Kinship, and Culture* (Woodbridge, Suffolk, 1995).

LAURENCE, A., *Women in England 1500–1760* (New York, 1994).

LE GOFF, J., 'Merchant's Time and Church's Time in the Middle Ages', in *Time, Work and Culture in the Middle Ages* (Chicago, 1980).

LEVI-STRAUSS, C., *The Elementary Structure of Kinship* (Boston, 1967).

LEVINE, D. (ed.), *Georg Simmel: On Individuality and Social Forms, Selected Writings* (Chicago, 1971).

LIPSCOMB, G., *The History and Antiquities of the County of Buckingham*, 4 vols. (1831–47).

McCRACKEN, G., 'The Exchange of Children in Tudor England', *Journal of Family History*, 8 (1983), 303–13.

MACFARLANE, A., *The Family Life of Ralph Josselin* (Cambridge, 1970).

McKENDRICK, N., *et al.* (eds), *The Birth of a Consumer Society* (1983).

—— and OUTHWAITE, R. (eds), *Business Life and Public Policy* (Cambridge, 1986).

MALCOLMSON, A., *The Pursuit of the Heiress* (Belfast, 1982).

MANNING, R., *Hunters and Poachers* (Oxford, 1993).

MAUSS, M., *The Gift: Forms and Functions of Exchange in Archaic Societies*, trans. I. Cunnison (New York, 1967).

MENDELSON, S., 'The Weightiest Business: Marriages in an Upper Gentry Family', *Past & Present*, 85 (1979), 126–35.

MILARDO, R., *Families and Social Networks* (1988).

MIMARDIERE, A., 'The Finances of a Warwickshire Gentry Family, 1693–1726', *University of Birmingham Historical Journal*, 9 (1963–4), 130–45.

MINGAY, G., *The Gentry* (1976).

MITCHELL, D. (ed.), *Goldsmiths, Silversmiths, and Bankers* (1995).

MITCHELL, J. (ed.), *Social Networks in Urban Situations* (Manchester, 1969).

Mosse, G., *The Image of Man* (Oxford and New York, 1996).

Motley, M., 'Educating the English Gentleman Abroad: The Verney Family in Seventeenth-Century France and Holland', *History of Education*, 23 (1994), 243–56.

Nockolds, H. (ed.), *Coachmakers: A History of the Worshipful Company of Coachmakers and Coach Harness Makers 1677–1977* (1977).

Nye, R., *Masculinity and the Male Codes of Honour in Modern France* (New York and Oxford, 1993).

O'Gorman, F., 'Campaign Rituals and Ceremonies: The Social Meaning of Elections in England, 1780–1860', *Past and Present*, 135 (1992), 79–115.

Okin, S., 'Patriarchy and Married Women's Property in England', *Eighteenth-Century Studies*, 17 (1983–4), 121–38.

Ortner, S., and Whitehead, H., *Sexual Meanings* (Cambridge, 1981).

Outhwaite, R., *Clandestine Marriage in England 1500–1800* (1995).

Page, W. (ed.), *Victoria History of Buckinghamshire*, 4 vols. (1905–27).

Parkes, J., *Travel in England in the Seventeenth Century* (1925).

Pateman, C., *The Sexual Contract* (Cambridge, 1988).

Peck, L., *Court Patronage and Corruption in Early Stuart England* (Boston, 1990).

Perkin, H., *The Origins of Modern English Society 1780–1880* (1969).

Perry, R., 'Mary Astell and the Feminist Critique of Possesive Individualism', *Eighteenth-Century Studies*, 23 (1990), 444–57.

Phillips Auction Catalogue, July 2 1981. Sale No. 23,406, Item 250, Manuscripts from Sheffield Park, Sussex.

Phillipson, N., 'Politics and Politeness in the Reigns of Anne and the Early Hanoverians', in J. Pocock (ed.), *The Varieties of British Political Thought 1500–1800* (Cambridge, 1993), 211–45.

Pincus, S., '"Coffee Politicians Does Create"', *Journal of Modern History*, 67 (1995), 807–34.

Plumb, J., 'The Walpoles, Father and Son', in *Studies in Social History*, (New York, 1955), 179–207.

Pocock, J., *Virtue, Commerce, and History* (Cambridge, 1985).

Pollock, L., 'Younger Sons in Tudor and Stuart England', *History Today*, 34 (1989), 23–9.

—— '"Teach Her to Live under Obedience"', *Continuity and Change*, 4 (1989), 231–58.

Porter, R., *London: A Social History* (Cambridge, Mass., 1994).

Power, M., 'The East and West in Early-Modern London', in E. Ives *et al.* (eds), *Wealth and Power in Tudor England* (1978), 167–85.

Price, F., *A Handbook of London Bankers* (1876).

Priestley, M., 'London Merchants and Opposition Politics in Charles II's Reign', *Historical Research*, 29 (1956), 205–14.

Quitt, M., 'Immigrant Origins of the Virginia Gentry', *William and Mary Quarterly*, 45 (1988), 629–55.

Rasmussen, E., 'Democratic Environment–Aristocratic Aspiration', *Pennsylvania Magazine of History and Biography*, 90 (1966), 155–82.

Raven, J., *Judging New Wealth* (Oxford, 1992).

Reed, M., *A History of Buckinghamshire* (Chichester, 1993).

Robertson, J., *The Art of Letter Writing* (1942).

Roebuck, P., 'Absentee Landownership in the Late Seventeenth and Early Eighteenth Centuries', *Agricultural History Review*, 21 (1973), 1–17.

—— *Yorkshire Baronets 1640–1760* (Oxford, 1980).

ROGERS, F., *A Manual of Coaching* (Philadelphia, 1901).

ROGERS, J., *The Early History of the Law of Bills and Notes* (Cambridge, 1995).

ROGERS, N., 'Money, Land and Lineage', *Social History*, 4 (1979), 437–54.

—— *Whigs and Cities* (New York, 1990).

ROPER, M., and TOSH, J., *Manful Assertions* (1991).

ROSENHEIM, J., *The Townshends of Raynham* (Middletown, Conn., 1989).

—— *The Emergence of a Ruling Order: English Landed Society 1650–1750* (1998).

ROSTVIG, M., *The Happy Man: Studies in the Metamorphoses of a Classical Ideal*, 2 vols. (New York, 1971).

RUBIN, G., 'The Traffic in Women: Notes on the Political Economy of Sex', in R. Reiter (ed.), *Toward an Anthropology of Women* (N.Y, 1975), 157–210.

RUBINSTEIN, W., 'Debate: 'Gentlemanly Capitalism' and British Industry, 1820–1914', *Past and Present*, 132 (1991), 150–70.

SAHLINS, M., 'The Spirit of the Gift', *Stone Age Economics* (Chicago, 1981).

SANDFORD, M., 'The Squire and his Relations', *Origins* (1987), 87–93.

SANDMAIER, M., *Original Kin* (New York, 1994).

SAUNDERS, A. (ed.), *The Royal Exchange* (1997).

SCHOCHET, G., *Politics, Politeness and Patriotism* (Washington, 1993), 229–44.

SCHWARTZ, L., 'Social Class and Social Geography', *Social History*, 7 (1982), 167–85.

SCOTT, J., *Gender and the Politics of History* (New York, 1988).

—— *Algernon Sidney and the Restoration Crisis 1677–1683* (Cambridge, 1991).

SEDGWICK, R., *The House of Commons 1714–1754*, 2 vols. (New York, 1970).

SENNETT, R. (ed.), *Classic Essays on the Culture of Cities* (Englewood Cliffs, NJ, 1969).

SHANLEY, M., 'Marriage Contract and Social Contract in Seventeenth-Century English Political Thought', *Western Political Quarterly*, 32 (1979), 79–91.

SHIELDS, D., *Civil Tongues & Polite Letters* (Williamsburg, 1997).

SHOEMAKER, R., *Gender in English Society 1650–1850* (1998).

SIFIANIOU, M., *Politeness Phenomena in England and Greece* (Oxford, 1992).

SIU, P., 'The Sojourner', *American Journal of Sociology*, 58 (1952), 34–44.

SLATER, M., *Family Life in the Seventeenth Century: The Verneys of Claydon House* (1984).

—— 'The Weightiest Business', *Past & Present*, 72 (1976), 29–54.

SMUTS, J., 'The Court and its Neighbourhood', *Journal of British Studies*, 30 (1991), 117–49.

SPECK, W., and GREY, W., 'Computer Analysis of Poll Books, an Initial Report', *Historical Research*, 43 (1970), 105–12.

—— *et al.*, 'A Further Report', *Historical Research*, 48 (1975), 64–90.

SPRING, E., *Law, Land and Family* (1993).

STAVES, S., 'Pin Money', *Studies in Eighteenth Century Culture*, 14 (1985), 47–97.

—— 'Separate Maintenance Contracts', *Eighteenth Century Life*, 11 (1987), 78–101.

—— *Married Women's Separate Property in England* (Cambridge, Mass., 1990).

STONE, L., *The Family, Sex, and Marriage in England* (1979).

—— 'The Residential Development of the West End of London in the Seventeenth Century', in B. Malament (ed.), *After the Reformation* (Philadelphia, 1980), 167–212.

—— 'The Revival of Narrative', *Past and Present*, 85 (1979), 3–24.

—— *Road to Divorce: England 1530–1987* (Oxford, 1990).

—— 'Social Mobility in England 1500–1700', *Past and Present*, 33 (1966), 16–55.

—— 'The Verney Tomb at Middle Claydon', *Records of Buckinghamshire*, 16 (1955–6), 66–82.

—— and STONE, J., *An Open Elite? England 1540–1880* (Oxford, 1984).

STONEQUIST, E., *The Marginal Man* (New York, 1937).

STRAUS, R., *Carriages and Coaches* (1912).

SULLOWAY, F., *Born to Rebel* (New York, 1996).

TEBBUTT, M., *Women's Talk* (Aldershot, 1995).

THIRSK, J., 'Younger Sons in the Seventeenth Century', *History*, 54 (1969), 358–77.

THOMAS, D., 'The Social Origins of Marriage Partners of the British Peerage', *Population Studies*, 26 (1972), 99–111.

THOMAS, K., 'The Double Standard', *Journal of the History of Ideas*, 20 (1959), 195–216.

—— *Man and the Natural World* (New York, 1983).

—— 'Numeracy in Early Modern England', *Transactions of the Royal Historical Society*, 37 (1987), 103–32.

THOMPSON, E., *Whigs and Hunters* (Harmondsworth, 1977).

—— 'Eighteenth Century English Society: Class Struggle without Class?', *Social History*, 3 (1978), 133–65.

THOMPSON, F. (ed.), *Landowners, Capitalists, and Entrepreneurs* (Oxford, 1994), 113–38.

THRUPP, S., *The Merchant Class of Medieval London 1300–1500* (Chicago, 1948).

TODD, B., 'The Remarrying Widow', in M. Prior (ed.), *Women in English Society* (1985), 54–92.

—— 'Demographic Determinism and Female Agency', *Continuity and Change*, 9 (1994), 421–50.

TRUMBACH, R., *The Rise of the Egalitarian Family* (New York, 1978).

—— 'Sex, Gender, and Sexual Identity in Modern Culture', *Journal of the History of Sexuality*, 2 (1991), 186–203.

TURNER, V., *Dramas, Field and Metaphors* (Ithaca, New York, 1974).

VAN DER WOUDE, A., *et al.* (eds), *Urbanization in History* (Oxford, 1990).

VAN GENNEP, A., *The Rites of Passage* (Chicago, 1964).

VERNEY, H. (ed.), *The Verneys of Claydon: A Seventeenth-Century English Family* (1968).

VERNEY, M., 'Claydon House', *Records of Buckinghamshire*, 5 (1878), 419–20.

—— *Bucks Biographies* (Oxford, 1912).

—— *In Memory of Margaret Maria Lady Verney* (1930).

VERNEY, P., *The Standard Bearer: The Story of Sir Edmund Verney Knight-Marshal to King Charles I* (1963).

VICKERY, A., 'Golden Age to Separate Spheres?', *Historical Journal*, 36 (1993), 383–414.

—— *The Gentleman's Daughter* (New Haven, 1998).

WALSH, J., *et al.* (eds), *The Church of England c.1689–c.1833* (Cambridge, 1993).

WARD, J., *Metropolitan Communities* (Stanford, Calif., 1997).

WEITZMAN, A., 'Eighteenth-Century London: Urban Paradise or Fallen City?', *Journal of the History of Ideas*, 36 (1975), 469–80.

WETHERELL, C., 'Network Analysis Comes of Age', *Journal of Interdisciplinary History*, 19 (1989), 645–51.

WHYMAN, S., 'Land and Trade Revisited: The Case of John Verney, London Merchant and Baronet 1660–1720', *London Journal*, 22 (1997), 16–32.

—— '"Paper Visits": The Post-Restoration Letter as Seen through the Verney Archive', *Epistolary Selves* (Aldershot, 1998).

WIESNER, M., *Women and Gender in Early Modern Europe* (Cambridge, 1993).

WILLIAMS, R., *The Country and the City* (1973).

WOOD, A., *A History of the Levant Company* (Oxford, 1935).

WOODHEAD, J., *The Rulers of London 1660–1689* (1965).

Wordie, J., *Estate Management in Eighteenth-Century England: The Building of the Leveson–Gower Fortune* (1982).

Wrigley, E., 'A Simple Model of London's Importance 1650–1750', *Past and Present*, 37 (1967), 44–70.

—— 'Urban Growth and Agricultural Change', *Journal of Interdisciplinary History*, 15 (1985), 683–728.

—— and Schofield, R., *The Population History of England 1541–1871* (Cambridge, Mass.,1986).

Unpublished Dissertations

Ambrose, G., 'The Levant Company: Mainly from 1640–1753', B.Litt. thesis, (Oxford, 1932).

Bearman, P., 'Relations into Rhetorics', Ph.D. thesis (Harvard, 1985).

Brant, C., 'Eighteenth-Century Letters', D.Phil. thesis (Oxford, 1988).

Broad, J., 'Sir Ralph Verney and his Estates 1630–1696', D.Phil. thesis (Oxford, 1973).

Bryson, A., 'Concepts of Civility in England 1580–1685', D.Phil. thesis (Oxford, 1984).

Carter, P., '"Mollies", "Fops", and Men of Feeling', D.Phil. thesis (Oxford, 1995).

Chalus, E., 'Women in English Political Life 1754–1790', D.Phil. thesis (Oxford, 1997).

Childs, F., 'Prescriptions for Manners in English Courtesy Literature, 1690–1760', D.Phil. thesis (Oxford, 1984).

De Krey, G., 'Trade, Religion, and Politics in London in the Reign of William III', Ph.D. thesis (Princeton, 1978).

Holmes, G., 'The Influence of the Peerage in English Parliamentary Elections 1702–13', B.Litt. thesis (Oxford, 1952).

Johnson, A., 'Buckinghamshire, 1640–60: A Study in County Politics', MA thesis (Swansea, 1963).

Jones, D. W., 'London Overseas Merchant Groups at the End of the Seventeenth Century and the Moves Against the East India Company', D.Phil. thesis (Oxford, 1970).

Speck, W., 'The House of Commons 1702–14: A Study in Political Organization', D.Phil. thesis (Oxford, 1965).

Weil, R., 'Sexual Ideology and Political Propaganda in England 1680–1714', Ph.D. thesis (Princeton, 1991).

INDEX

Abel, Mary (Molly), *see* Keeling, Mary
Abel, Mary, *see* Verney, Mary
Abel, William 159
Abel family 18, 20, 92, 116–18, 120, 123, 140
Adams, Rev Charles 60
Adams, Elizabeth (1633–1721), aunt of John
    Verney 8, 25–6, 32, 42, 58, 60, 67, 78,
    91–2, 94, 112, 127, 129, 135–6, 142
Adams, Margaret (Peg) 3–4, 16, 23, 35, 127–8
adultery 126, 140
agriculture 18–20
Aleppo 17, 39–40, 47–55, 60, 66–7, 73
almshouse 19
Amersham (Bucks.) 162, 172–6
Anne, Queen (1665–1714) 27, 133, 148, 161, 166,
    168–70, 173
annuities 15, 24, 26–7, 37, 42, 69, 76, 78, 98,
    114–16, 120, 122, 125, 130, 142
apothecaries 5–6, 21–2, 59, 76, 125
apprentices 41–8, 52–3, 63, 68, 70
artisans and craftsmen 5–6, 17, 19–20, 62, 68, 71
assizes 22, 153, 155, 170
Atkins family 21, 60
Aylesbury (Bucks.) 15, 18, 141, 148–9, 153, 160,
    167

bachelors 6, 113, 128, 134, 144
Baker, Barbara 121–2
Baker, Daniel (1628–1700) 25–6, 71, 121–2
Baker, Daniel (1659–1727) 121, 176
Baker, Elizabeth, *see* Verney, Elizabeth
Baker, Samuel 167
Baker family 122, 140
Bank of England 46, 76, 82, 136, 176
bankruptcy 52, 77–9, 103, 160, 177
Basinghall Street (London) 61
bastards 16, 42, 69, 113, 156
Bath (Somerset) 9, 57, 59, 94, 101, 133–4, 137
Baxter, Peter 72
Baxter, Simon 72, 77, 79
beer 18, 19, 63
Berkshire 15–16, 22, 48, 72, 124, 144
Bertie, Robert, 3rd Earl Lindsey 69
biographical guides 188–96
bills of exchange 73, 78
birth order 12, 110, 112, 124, 127, 138, 144, 178
Bishops 41, 48, 62, 65–7, 125, 165
Blackmore, Dr Richard 25–6
Blacknall, Mary, *see* Verney, Mary
blessings 33, 137
Blois (France) 38–9, 41

Bludworth, Sir Thomas 52
books 14, 23, 39–42, 48, 55–6, 63, 65, 81, 100, 136
booksellers 40, 59, 73
Bottle Claydon (Bucks.) 171
bribery 32, 53, 148, 151, 154, 167
Bridewell (London) 71, 121
Bridgeman, Dorothy 90
Bridgeman, Judith 119
Bridgeman, Sir Orlando 116, 139
Bridgewater, *see* Egerton
brokers 17, 25, 28, 32, 161, 170, 172–3; *see also*
    financiers and financial brokers, marriage–
    brokers
Bromley, William 131, 133
Browne, John 131
Buckingham borough (Bucks.) 21, 141, 148, 151,
    153–7; *see also* elections
Buckinghamshire 14–37, 57, 69, 72, 75, 101, 107,
    121, 129, 133; *see also* elections, gentry, politics
Burgoyne, Sir Roger 42, 66
burials, *see* funerals
Busby, Sir John 10, 46, 150
Busby, William 20, 95, 155, 162
Busby family 18, 21, 46, 92, 125, 150
Butterfield, Rev William 19, 27

Calvert, Catherine, *see* Catherine Wright
Calvert, Harry (1801–94), *see* Verney, Sir Harry
Calvert, Richard 145
Carlisle, *see* Howard, Edward
Cary, John 24, 33
catholics 21, 39, 60; *see also* popery
Cave, Margaret née Verney (1685–1774),
    daughter of John Verney 58–9, 94, 103, 130–3,
    141
Cave, Sir Roger 130–3
Cave, Sir Thomas (1682–1719) 58–9, 112–13, 120,
    130–3, 141, 148, 161, 168–9, 171–3, 175–6
Cave family 131–3, 137–8, 140, 145, 169
Chaloner, Charles 171, 176
Chaloner, William 20, 70
Chaloner family 70
Chambers, Anna, *see* Temple, Anna
Chambers, Thomas 146
Chaplyn, William 102, 105, 145, 150, 152
charity 16, 23, 25, 27, 78, 127, 129
Charles I (1600–1649) 15, 56
Charles II (1630–1685) 24, 67, 74, 104, 155, 160
Chelsea, *see* Little Chelsea
Cheret, Thomas 130, 133
Chesham (Bucks.) 169

politics (*cont.*)
156–7, 164, 168–9; and women 7, 170–3, 179;
see also elections, Whigs, Tories
Pollard, Ralph 16
poll books 20, 149, 161, 165, 167, 171
Porter, Lettice 22
portraits 4, 25, 36, 48, 59, 63, 68, 136
popery 14, 21, 39, 154, 168; *see also* catholics
Popish Plot 66, 151
prayers 34, 50, 65
pregnancy 63, 106, 112, 119, 140–1
Price family 46
primogeniture 14, 43–6, 123, 143–4
privacy 11, 16, 20, 25, 34–6, 60, 69, 93, 102
public and private spheres 4, 108, 110, 140–2, 173
Purcell, Henry 69, 224 n., 77

Quainton (Bucks.) 22, 166, 168
quakers 21, 63, 149, 164, 166–7
Queen's evil 161, 169

races 22, 92, 148, 168–9,
Rainbow coffee-house 64, 119
relationships, *see* social relationships
religion 14–15, 34, 39, 65–7, 164–5
Roades, Thomas 16
roads 15, 68, 101–2
Roberts, Sir Gabriel (1635–1715) 42, 51–2, 60, 63,
66–7, 71–2, 78
Roberts, Gabriel 2: 72
Roberts, Lewes 44
Roberts, William 48, 51–2, 72
Roberts family 72
Royal Africa Company 17, 66–7, 72–74, 78,
119–20
Royal Exchange, *see* Exchange
Royal Society 102

St Amand, James 68
St Andrew Holborn (London) 62, 66, 122
St Paul's (London) 66, 68, 73
Scanderoon 49
servants 6–7, 16, 19, 26–7, 34, 36, 60, 64, 90, 105,
113, 117, 128, 160, 170
sex and sexuality 64, 102, 111, 113, 116, 119, 122,
140–1, 144
Seymour, Sir Henry 165, 167
Sheppard, John 48, 51–2
Sherrier, Edward 159
ships 49, 73, 75, 79, 80
shops and shopkeepers 6, 58, 60–4, 67, 70–1, 73
smallpox 70, 126
Smithfield (London) 20, 126
sociability, generally and 4, 50, 87–109, 181–2,
185
social code 10, 28, 87–99, 103–9, 156–7; *see also*
women
social life, *see* country, London

social mobility 4, 11, 46, 48, 58, 60, 70, 100–1,
107–9, 120
social networks: in the country 17–23, 27–33;
in London 67–73, 78–80, 91–6, 99, 120
social relationships 6, 10, 87–89, 99, 107–9,
178–9; father/daughter 112, 129–33; father/
son 16–17, 38–40, 53, 115–17, 132–8, 141–5;
husband/wife 110–14, 117–22, 141; landlord/
tenant 53, 140–51, 157–61; patron/client 23–33;
siblings 40, 44–5, 49, 52, 138–9; women/
women 96–9, 141–3
social status 6, 18, 27–30, 46–8, 100–1,
103–5, 107–9, 183–4
social structure 18, 27–33, 83–4
spectacles 64–6, 93
spinsters 113, 127–8, 136, 143
Spring Garden 95
Stallwood, Benjamin 62
Stanford Hall (Leics.) 131–2
Steeple Claydon (Bucks.) 20, 70, 74, 77, 117,
160–1, 166
Stewkeley, Cary 21–2, 36–7, 77, 106, 127–8, 140
Stewkeley, Isabella 77
Stewkeley, Hugh 127
Stewkeley, John 7, 113
Stewkeley, Katherine (Kitty) 143
Stewkeley, Penelope (Pen), *see* Viccars, Penelope
Stillingfleet, Dr Edward 66
stocks and bonds 42, 59, 72, 74–5, 78–9, 82, 161,
130, 166 176
Stony Stratford (Bucks.) 167
Stowe 21, 31, 90, 150, 153–4, 163, 172, 176–7
Stuart, James Francis Edward, the
'Pretender' 165, 168, 175–6

Temple, Anna née Chambers 129, 146
Temple, Anne née Halsey 129, 146
Temple, Hester, Countess 146
Temple, John 151
Temple, Mary née Knapp 90, 94, 138, 141–2, 146
Temple, Sir Richard (1634–1697) 31, 33, 36, 56,
63–4, 68, 79, 90, 103, 105, 139, 141–2, 145–57
Temple, Richard, (1675–1749), Viscount
Cobham 146, 150–77
Temple family 21, 46, 59, 80, 129, 131, 145–77
tenants, *see* social relationships-landlord/tenant
Tenison, Archbishop of Canterbury 65
theatre 40, 42, 59, 64, 67, 72, 90
Tipping, Sir Thomas 94, 166
tips 24, 26, 29, 114
titles 6, 22, 88, 100, 134, 137–8, 166
Tories 152–3, 164–76
Torriano, Charles 72, 77, 79
Torriano, George 72
trade and trading 38–54; activities 70–4;
attitudes to 38, 43–5, 80–5; gentry sons in
46–8; language of 117, 120–1, 126–7; trading of
John Verney 226–7 n., 104; *see also* merchants

Whig/Tory conflict 148, 164–73
Whig/Tory compromise 173–5
White, Captain 70
White, Frank 74
White, Mrs 70
Whitmore, Anne, *see* Lawley, Anne
Whitmore, Mary Aunt 119
widows 82, 105, 117, 127, 142–3, 160
William III (1650–1702) 17, 101
Willis, Browne 40, 90, 161, 166
wills 36–7, 71, 102, 125, 135–6, 138, 143, 145
Winchendon (Bucks.) 158, 164
Windsor (Berks.) 65, 74, 131, 141, 170, 172

Winwood, Richard 90
women: and coaches 105–9; dependency of 113,
   127–9, 141; and gifts 143; and investments
   75–7, 125; power of 10, 93–9, 105–9, 140–3,
   170–3, 179; and the social code 4, 87–109, 179;
   and visiting 93–99; *see also* gentlewomen
   companions, politics, spinsters, widows
workmen 19, 159–60
Wright, Catherine née Calvert (d. 1827),
   assumed name of Verney 145
Wright, Rev. Robert 145

younger sons 11, 38–54, 83–4, 138–9, 145, 178–9